FASCISM IN EUROPE

FASCISM IN EUROPE

◆

edited by
S. J. Woolf

METHUEN
LONDON & NEW YORK

First published as European Fascism in 1968
by Weidenfeld & Nicolson
This edition published in 1981 by
Methuen & Co. Ltd
11 New Fetter Lane, London EC4P 4EE
Published in the USA by
Methuen & Co.
in association with Methuen, Inc.
733 Third Avenue, New York, NY 10017
© 1968, 1981 S.J. Woolf
Printed in Great Britain
Richard Clay (The Chaucer Press) Ltd,
Bungay, Suffolk

British Library Cataloguing in Publication Data

Fascism in Europe.
1. Fascism — Europe — History
I. Woolf, S.J.
335.6'094
ISBN 0-416-30230-0
ISBN 0-416-30240-8 Pbk

CONTENTS

—•—

CONTRIBUTORS

S. Andreski, M.Sc.(Econ.), Ph.D.(Lond.), Professor of Sociology, University of Reading.

Z. Barbu, Ph.D.(Glasgow), D.Phil.(Cluj), Professor of Sociology, University of Brasilia, Brazil.

G. Carpinelli, Ricercatore, Faculty of Political Science, University of Turin, Italy.

T. K. Derry, M.A., D.Phil.(Oxon.), author of *A History of Modern Norway* (1973).

Malene Djursaa, B.A., Ph.D.(Essex), Cand. Mag. (Aarhus).

J. Erös, D.Phil.(Heidel.), Ph.D.(Manch.), formerly Senior Lecturer in Political Institutions, University of Keele.

A. J. Nicholls, M.A., B.Phil.(Oxon.), Fellow of St Antony's College, Oxford.

Paul Preston, M.A., D.Phil.(Oxon.), Reader in Modern History, Queen Mary College, University of London.

C. I. W. Seton-Watson, M.C., M.A., Tutor and Fellow in Politics, Oriel College, Oxford.

R. Skidelsky, M.A., D.Phil.(Oxon.), Professor of International Studies, University of Warwick.

K. R. Stadler, B.A.(Bristol), M.A.(Lond.), Ph.D.(Nott.), Professor of Modern and Contemporary History, Linz University, Austria.

H. R. Trevor-Roper, M.A. (Oxon. and Cantab.), Master of Peterhouse, Cambridge.

A. F. Upton, M.A.(Oxon.), A.M.(Duke), Reader in Modern History, St Andrew's University.

G. Warner, M.A. (Cantab.) Professor of Modern History, University of Leicester.

S. J. Woolf, M.A., D.Phil.(Oxon.), Professor of History, University of Essex.

PREFACE

The present volume consists of a collection of essays, partly new, partly revised, originally published under the title *European Fascism* in 1968. The origins of that earlier volume were a series of lectures and seminars held by the Graduate School of Contemporary European Studies of the University of Reading; and I am grateful to the chairman and members of the Graduate School for permitting some of the essays to be reprinted.

This volume includes six new essays on Italy, Denmark, Great Britain, Belgium, France and Spain, and substantially revised essays on Poland and postwar fascism, as well as my introductory essay. In addition the bibliographies have been revised and brought up to date. Fascism has been the subject of considerable research since the original symposium appeared. I believe that the present volume has taken serious account of this research, and will serve (as did its predecessor) as a helpful comparative study and a stimulus to further research.

Stuart Woolf

1
INTRODUCTION

❧

S. J. Woolf

Perhaps the word fascism should be banned, at least temporarily, from our political vocabulary. For like other large words — democracy, reactionary, radical, anarchy — it has been so misused that it has lost its original meaning; or, at least, it has been so overlaid with newer and broader connotations that the narrower, historical sense almost seems to require apologetic inverted commas.

Probably no single historical example could meet the exacting requirements of a carefully constructed sociological model of fascism (or indeed of democracy). But this does not mean that neither really existed. Historically speaking, fascism was originally understood to describe both an ideology and a particular political — and, to some extent, cultural, economic and social — system of a specific geographical area in a delimited period of time — Europe between the wars. It is open to discussion whether the Japanese regime of the 1930s or Argentina in the 1940s or certain more recent developments in the Third World can, strictly speaking, be described as fascist. The word, unfortunately, has certain commode-like tendencies — the more you stuff into it, the more it takes. But there can be no doubt about the correctness of its usage for the interwar period in Europe.

Indeed, one of the conclusions which emerges most clearly from research in recent years is the difference between fascism and the authoritarian movements which increasingly dominated central and eastern Europe after the first world war. At politically opportune moments, approval might be expressed of fascism as a system of government by Horthy, Dollfuss, Pilsudski or Svinhufvud. But the regimes they controlled, or were trying to create, were not fascist. Any 'real' fascist from Hungary, Austria, Poland or Finland would have told you so. For these fascists claimed they were trying to create something different, to break with the existing structure of power and forge a new, wholly disciplined state which would revive real or mythical glories of a past age or achieve a new pre-eminence for their race. Admittedly, their claims should be examined with a degree of scepticism. For such fascists were, at best, disingenuous in their refusal to recognize how much of fascism actually existed in the authoritarian regimes they were attacking and trying to infiltrate.

In fact, the contrast between ambitions and practice, so evident in Italy and Germany, held true in the central European fascisms as well. Fascist aims everywhere were ambitious, ambiguous, contradictory or simply nebulous. Fascist practice — which only triumphed unquestionably in Italy and Germany — was to be found to some degree in all the right-wing regimes of central Europe, although in no instance was any regime peaceably transformed into a full-blown fascism. It needed Hitler's aggression to achieve such a transformation. Until then — the later 1930s — the native fascists continued to grumble bitterly about the inadequacies of their respective regimes. In a sense, this is understandable. For in Italy and Germany fascist regimes emerged *subsequently* to their period of opposition and striving, so allowing their members time to forget or rationalize (and historians facility to point out) the contradictions between the two separate phases. In Austria, Hungary, Rumania or Poland the two phases were as if partially superimposed: given the existence of certain fascist elements in right-wing authoritarian regimes, it was difficult to be so totally hostile and revolutionary as in western-type parliamentary democracies. These regimes obliged the fascist leaders to be more precise in their ambitions, and by placing these ambitions side by side with certain existing practices may well have rendered the contrast more immediate and frustrating.

Some historians of fascism lay great stress on its 'revolutionary' character. Their arguments rest essentially on fascist ideology. But the ideology can be defined as revolutionary in a different, even contradictory, manner: as a revolutionary reaction against modern society, with its connotations of industrialism, individualism and bourgeois values; or, alternatively, as a technocratic, modernizing credo. In terms of the hybrid social composition of the early fascist movements (primarily nationalist and anarcho-syndicalist), perhaps these contradictory elements are not so surprising. But any discussion of fascist ideology also needs to bear in mind its function; in this sense, more revolutionary than the ideology itself was its role in gaining for fascism a mass base among social groups which, by any definition, were dissatisfied with and reacting against existing society. Moreover, the more revolutionary the ideology, the greater the 'betrayal' by fascist leaders as, scenting the vicinity of power, they opened negotiations with the élites of this society.

Such general remarks touch upon some of the complexities of the fascist phenomenon in Europe. Fascism was strongly nationalist and firmly rooted in the historical development of each country. Yet increasingly it laid claims to its importance as an international system capable of replacing democracy or communism. Fascism developed as a counterpoise to the socialist threat in industrialized countries. Yet fascist movements sprang up like mushrooms in some of the most backward and unlikely countries of Europe. Fascism vaunted the *Führerprinzip*, but in many countries — such as Hungary, Poland, Finland — it failed to produce an outstanding leader. Fascist ideology proclaimed revolutionary changes in a modern society, but its rituals exuded a deep nostalgia for a return to a mythical medieval past. Fascist strength was based on the urban or rural petty bourgeoisie, but once in power fascism turned for support to the industrialists and big landowners. These complexities and contradictions cannot be explained in any simple, or single, manner. They can only be studied in their individual manifestations, in terms of their national peculiarities.

But three general distinctions can be made which seem to me to assist one's understanding of European fascism. They are: the difference between fascism in western Europe and fascism in central and eastern Europe; the contrast between early fascist claims and later fascist actions; and the changing character of fascism in the 1920s, 1930s and during the second world war.

The first distinction, between the western and the central and eastern European movements, is extremely broad. Opinions vary as to whether racialism was a particular characteristic of central European fascism, or a trait intrinsic to all fascisms (except Italian, until its later phases), tactically played down in countries where public opinion was most hostile. Apart from anti-semitism, it is of course possible to find certain general conditions common to both western and central Europe (as it is also possible to find an exception to almost every such condition). Strong nationalist feeling is the most obvious example, common to Europe from Spain to Finland, with the exception of Austria, where the collapse of the empire led to confusion between nationalism and pan-Germanism. Anti-socialism is another trait, as even in countries where marxism was not a real threat, the menace of bolshevik Russia offered a convenient whipping-boy. Weak and inefficient parliamentary government was yet another characteristic to be found, to a greater or lesser degree, throughout Europe between the wars. The effects of the first world war, both immediate and long-term, cannot be underestimated as a necessary condition without which it is difficult to imagine the rise of fascist movements and their success. For the war not only brought in its aftermath economic and political disruption to almost all the countries of Europe. It also 'politicized' the peoples of the different countries to a hitherto unknown degree, so encouraging the growth of mass parties. At the same time it allowed the right to exploit patriotism, it dulled reactions towards violence, and it created vast masses of ex-combatants who were to form the most fertile seedbeds of nascent nationalism and fascist movements. The future fascist parties in almost all the countries of Europe traced their origins back to the numerous groupings of patriotic associations which emerged or re-emerged in strength after the war.

Yet, if certain 'pre-conditions' of fascism seem common to all the countries, there can be no doubt that central and eastern European fascism remained distinct from that of the west. It is easy, and in certain respects necessary, to make further distinctions, as Lackó does, when he proposes a triple typology of the advanced capitalist countries of the west, economically backward Balkan states and fascisms in central and eastern European states with more advanced levels of capitalist development (from Austria and Czechoslovakia to Poland, Hungary and Rumania). The difficulty with this subdivision of central and eastern Europe is that one can continue to find relatively important differences within Lackó's large but heterogeneous third grouping of fascisms; whereas the distinction between the Balkan and the other fascisms of central and eastern Europe pale in significance when compared to those of western Europe. Neither the simple east-west dichotomy nor the tripartite division adequately account for the connections between the particular forms of Iberian fascisms and the colonial traditions and presence of a strong commercial class in Spain and Portugal. Nevertheless, the basic distinction remains that between the core of industrialized countries and most other states of Europe economically dependent on the west and with relatively 'traditional' social structures.

This can be seen in terms of the 'pre-conditions' for fascism, as well as of the fascist movements themselves. In western societies, with established traditions of parliamentary democracy, literacy and political education − as in England, Scandinavia, Belgium and Holland − fascist movements were only likely to obtain support among groups which felt particular dissatisfaction or grievances against their society − in ethnic frontier areas, among rural voters, technocratically minded civil servants, conservatives experiencing difficulties in adapting successfully to the challenges of 'modern' society. Even among these groups the flow-through of membership pointed to the casual nature of a fascist party's growth, usually at a moment of economic crisis. The high level of integration of these societies, as seen in the 'thickness' of their organizations and informal associations (religious, economic, political and cultural) worked against any sustained growth of fascist parties, particularly in the 1930s, when the awareness of the dangers of fascism could lead to its deliberate isolation by political, religious and cultural leaders — as in the case of Degrelle's Rexism. In this sense, Germany offers the counter-proof, where the prolonged nature of the crisis and the shallowness of democratic traditions led to the disintegration of such defensive networks. In most of central and eastern Europe parliamentary democracy, set up by the victors of the world war, was often little more than a parody.

But fascism was not just the product of industrialized societies. It emerged as a significant force in a large number of agrarian societies. For it is not inaccurate to include among agrarian societies countries such as Spain, Austria or Finland, where the existence of modern industry and a large working class in a clearly delimited geographical area had as yet made little impact on the mores and traditional pattern of rural society. In industrialized countries, such as Germany, northern Italy or France, the emergence of fascism as an organized, articulated party is relatively easy to understand in terms of a political, economic, social and psychological crisis. In agrarian societies, without a large or significant middle class, it is far less easy to understand. It would perhaps be possible to describe the Finnish peasant smallholders as offering a mass base similar to that of the petty bourgeoisie and so explain the support for the Lapua movement. But it is not possible to equate similar social categories with the support given to the Rumanian Iron Guard. The 'middle class' interpretation of fascism — while perfectly valid for industrialized countries — is, in fact, inadequate as a general explanation, because it fails to account for the significant fascist movements in backward or agrarian societies (of which, after all, there were a considerable number in Europe between the wars). It needs, at least, to be supplemented by other interpretations, some perhaps sociological in character, others far more political.

It would evidently be crude to regard all the agrarian societies as basically the same. There were clearly important political and social differences which help to explain why fascist movements should have been particularly important at specific moments in some agrarian societies, but not in others. For example, only in Spain did feeling about the monarchy run so deep that the existence of a republic was regarded (by the monarchists naturally) as a national shame to be washed out, if necessary in blood; for in Austria and Hungary the issue was too recent and lacked the historical roots to engender such deep feelings. Similarly, there is a difference between agrarian societies with a relatively advanced degree of political education or respect for law and those with an extremely traditional pattern of society and overwhelming illiteracy. In the former, with a large educated class (not necessarily middle class), such as Finland, specific factors — like the very real threat of bolshevism, weak governments and the world economic crisis — offered an opening for a fascist movement with a strongly defined structure.

Elsewhere in central and eastern Europe — with the curious exception of the self-destructive Rumanian Iron Guard — fascism as an organized and articulated party would not seem to be a characteristic. Why was this so? Political life in such agrarian, sometimes even semi-feudal societies was dominated by conservative or reactionary circles. The left never represented a threat, as political authority was exercised by the traditional sources of power — the land-owners, the Church, perhaps the bankers. In Hungary and Poland, as in Rumania and Yugoslavia, almost the entire political spectrum was composed of the right. In such political systems, fascism could make little headway as it lacked the necessary freedom to manoeuvre. This was particularly true where a military *coup d'état* had formally consecrated the predominance of the right. Where no 'bolshevik' threat existed, it was difficult for a fascist movement to act as a rallying-point of reaction — for the space had already been occupied by the politically powerful and socially respectable forces of the right.

Under authoritarian regimes, in fact, fascism's main hope was to permeate the entire system, and in particular the army. In this — as can be seen in the cases of Hungary or Poland — it was successful, especially after the triumph of nazism. But unless the army was prepared to carry out a specifically fascist coup, fascism could only hope to set the tone for the whole regime, not to gain control. A fascist-minded army, which lacked a fascist leader, spelled doom for a fascist takeover — for the Church, for all its sympathy, could hardly (or was reluctant to) provide a leader.

It is this state of frustration that explains the conspiratorial nature of fascism in central Europe. No doubt an old tradition of conspiracies, a deep and widespread network of freemasonry, lay behind this trait. But in so authoritarian a setting conspiracy offered the main chance of influencing those in control of the army GHQ. In western Europe, fascism and nazism possessed their private armies — the squads, the SA. In central and eastern Europe, the fascist paramilitary organizations could not hope to rival the army. For fascism in these countries was a movement from above, an attempt to transform an already existing authoritarian regime into a fascist dictatorship from within. It only developed as a spontaneous movement from below if the repercussions of an economic or international crisis were such as to upset the economic-social equilibrium to a degree where enfranchised but apathetic groups of the population blamed the conservative government for being insufficiently radical. By the late 1930s, such repercussions began to be felt under the impact of nazi expansion. It was, for instance, at this time that racialism began to develop as a prominent feature in Hungary.

Two other features distinguishing western from central European fascism can be noted: the 'socialist' claims of western fascism; and the extreme romanticism of the central European movements.

The socialist or corporativist claims of fascism have often been noted. The Italian revolutionary syndicalists and cor-porativists, the very name of the German National Socialist Party, the Spanish vertical syndicates, the Portuguese national syndicalists, Mosley's driving concern with the problem of unemployment left contemporaries bewildered and have sometimes made historians uncertain about where to locate fascism in the political spectrum. It is worth remembering that such combinations of socialist ideals and nationalistic feeling predated fascism: in Italy, Germany and Austria nationalistic movements of workers existed at the turn of the century. But one also needs to note the particular categories of workers attracted to fascism, such as artisans, skilled workers, low-ranking employees, tenant farmers. Fascist 'socialism', in fact, would be more accurately defined as syndicalism or populism. It was a special type of socialism — a socialism of class collaboration, not of class conflict. The German worker was to enjoy a respected but subordinate place within the strong nation. For the élitist, hierarchical concept of fascism could not conceive of a privileged position for the worker. If any class was to enjoy a privileged place, it was to be the 'small men', the businessmen or farmers, the 'healthy' German middle class, the Italian 'productive bourgeoisie'. It was a socialism without the economic claims of expropriation or the political claims of the dictatorship of the proletariat.

It was, in any case, a socialism of western fascisms, not of those of central or eastern Europe. This is not surprising, given the industrialized character of many western European countries and the presence of large urban masses. If social reform meant anything in central and eastern Europe, it meant agrarian reform; such were the claims of the Hungarian fascists of the 1930s. But, in fact, social reform — whether urban or rural — did not loom large in the fascist programmes of these areas. Its absence offers a more clear-cut version of fascism. Whatever the ambiguity or confusion of western fascism, there can be no doubt about the reactionary character of the central and eastern European examples.

To compensate, however, the romanticism of central European fascism appears far more prominently. The ritualistic preoccupations of fascism are, of course, to be found in all countries, from the French Cagoulards to the Hungarian Arrow Cross, from the Rumanian Iron Guard to the Norwegian Nordisk Folkereisning. The very hostility of fascism towards freemasonry would, ironically, seem to have encouraged it to cultivate archaic ceremonies. Rites were the exemplification of history. For almost all fascisms — precisely because they were so nationalistic — looked back to the past and desired both to revive some bygone age of glory and to prove their movements to be the culmination of their country's history. The Teutonic master-race, the new Roman empire, the Turanian Hunters, the Nordic tribes were all motifs on the same theme, as was the search for 'precursors' of fascism. In western Europe, this desire for a return to a pre-industrial and pre-French Revolution society, where hierarchy was respected and social stability assured, offers yet one more contradiction in movements which claimed to embody the true future, the transcendence of liberal capitalism and marxist expropriation.

In western fascisms the contrast is striking because of the modern nature of fascism as an articulated and often mass movement of reaction. In central European fascisms, as the modernity diminished, the romanticism grew stronger. For it acquired apocalyptic, millenarian overtones. It was not merely a question of a man of destiny. It was a faith so deep that it could even become self-destructive, as in Rumania. It was a belief that fascist success would bring salvation, that all problems would be solved miraculously in the new kingdom of heaven. This messianic feeling was far stronger in central and eastern European fascism than in the west. 'National character' is the unenlightening phrase often employed to explain away such differences. But perhaps it was more a consequence of fascism's need in these regions to work within the system, a consequence of its relatively subordinate position, its greater influence as an opposition movement than in the west, but its lesser likelihood of achieving power. Excited by the symbolic use of sword and oath, central European fascists went forth to indulge in the chivalric shedding of blood. If fate proved hostile they yielded to death as true and gallant knights.

The second, and perhaps most obvious, distinction in a discussion of European fascism is that between fascism out of power and fascism in power, between ambitions and practice, between the origins of fascism and the regimes. It is not easy to compare fascist regimes as — fortunately for the modern world — so few movements ever achieved full power. There are far more instances of fascisms *manqués*. It is commonplace to point to the contradictions between the revolution-

ary claims of fascism in opposition and the conservative practices of fascist regimes. In abstract terms, it might be argued
that parliamentary leaders who fail to carry out their
promises once in power behave in a similar manner. But the
fundamental difference is that parliamentary leaders work
within the system, whereas fascist leaders were determined
to change the system itself (Sir Oswald Mosley is perhaps the
sole partial exception).

But the contrast between fascist promises and practice
needs to be examined more closely, unless its sole purpose is
to serve as a contemptuous expression of dismissal of fascism
and hence of its study. For there is some continuity between
fascism in opposition and fascism in power, in terms of both
personalities and policies. Who were the early leaders who
managed to retain positions of influence in the regimes? For
Spain the question is perhaps inappropriate, as the leaders
were in good part killed in the civil war. But in Italy and
Germany the left-wing fascist leaders desirous of genuine
social change were those who failed to assert themselves, who
disappeared or were placed in positions where they were
unable to further the causes for which they had once fought.
The 'intellectuals' of fascism in opposition, usually closely
identified with the movement's most revolutionary claims,
proved the victims of the regimes. Strasser or Rosenberg,
Massimo Rocca or Panunzio were but typical instances.

Conversely, the policies that were continued were those
most concerned with either the permanent conservation of
power or the development of the economic and military
strength of the state. That such policies should have aroused
less opposition from the traditional centres of power than
would have attempts totally to subvert the existing structure
of society is evident. But it would be inaccurate to conclude
that fascist regimes inevitably compromised and abandoned
their revolutionary ambitions. Hitler's control over Germany,
his transformation of its economic system – and indeed its
'intellectual' climate – are clear evidence to the contrary.
Fascist regimes selected from the various aims they had expressed in their years of opposition. Indeed, given the eclectic
and catholic character of Italian fascist aims before 1922, it
would have proved impossible not to select. The important

questions are what was selected and why? And to what
degree did the regimes prove able to implement their selec-
tions? The test of the strength of a fascist regime must surely
lie in its capacity to direct inevitable compromises in its own
favour, to follow through its aims, even if such aims needed
to be partially or temporarily modified by the force of
external circumstances. Nazism emerges successfully from
such a test, Francoism and Italian fascism fail.

Naturally the whole problem of fascist regimes cannot be
summed up in so simplified a manner. It would distort,
because of its exclusive concentration on the 'internal' lines
of communication of a single regime. The impact on fascist
policies of international trends, such as the economic crisis of
the early 1930s or the breakdown of the League of Nations,
cannot be ignored. The new tensions created by the pursuit
of such policies and their effect on the claim to permanency
of the regime need to be assessed. But the point of departure
– in practical more than ideological terms – remains the link
between fascism in opposition and fascism in power. Fascist
regimes were conditioned, to a greater or lesser extent, by
what they proclaimed and what they represented in their
early days.

Perhaps the two most significant aspects of fascist regimes
are their method of utilizing the existing machinery of power
and their intervention in the economy. No fascist regime
seized power with a ready-made blueprint of aims. The structure of the state administration was rapidly changed to
ensure the supreme position of the leader and the permanency of the regime. There can be no doubt about the crucial
importance of the leader to a fascist movement: no movement without a leader succeeded in establishing itself as a
regime. Less important – at least to judge by the examples of
Salazar and Franco – were the charismatic qualities of the
leader. But the greater part of the old machinery of state
continued to be used. Fascist regimes superimposed the party
on the existing structure of the state. The party was to serve
as the channel of communication between the leader and the
masses. Hence the creation of a network of party organs
parallel to those of the old state. The result was undoubtedly
to create a new political system. The old economic and even

cultural centres of power and influence might remain, but a
new political class was emerging. The unusually rapid growth
in the size of the bureaucracies was an external symptom of
this transformation.

But the final result was to create new strains, new tensions.
Within the regimes ambiguous dualities of power resulted
from this fusion of the new order with the old. In Italy the
king remained alongside the Duce; in Portugal the head of
state continued to be chosen from among the army leaders.
At lower levels, in Germany and Spain as much as in Italy or
Portugal, the militia or SA maintained an equivocal relationship with the army; the Church and its organizations were
never absorbed by the regime.

The party inevitably changed in nature from its years of
opposition. In Spain and Portugal the small fascist parties
which had existed before the military seizure of power
drowned within the newly created official parties. But even
in Italy and Germany — where the fascists and not the
military seized power — the party changed in character.
Indeed, one of the most striking results of recent research
into the social composition of fascism is the extremely high
mobility of party membership, shown definitively in the
study of Danish fascists, but equally valid for the Italian and
German cases. Of course, it does not follow that those who
dropped out or were expelled from the party were necessarily
the most 'revolutionary' members. But it is reasonable to
assume that many had initially been attracted by the very
extremism of the 'total' solutions proposed by fascist ideology, and withdrew (not always voluntarily) because of the
failure of the regimes to live up to their expectations. No
longer was to be found that dedication so typical of fascist
movements in opposition, particularly marked in countries
where fascists were in a small minority and rationalized their
existence by the cult of the élite, of the 'chosen'. No longer
were to be found those characteristically youthful party
members and especially young intellectuals, typical of backward societies like Rumania where university students enjoyed particular prestige but risked unemployment because
of lack of vocational training. The change was inevitable not
only because the original members grew old, not only because

the 'new waves' of carpet-baggers swelled party numbers, but because the functions of the party changed with the assumption of power. Exclusiveness and dedication were bound to disappear as the party tried to identify itself, sometimes in an almost literal sense, with the nation. Youth could not but suffer as the party crystallized into a bureaucratic instrument.

In its new role, the party remained a relatively loose organization, despite the appearance of monolithic unity. Its very looseness served the purposes of the leader as it enabled him to conserve control by fostering rivalry among his immediate subordinates and their organizations. This undoubtedly worked against the formation of a body of party members adequately unified and professional to solve the problem of the succession, to ensure the permanency of the regime after the leader's death. But, in practical and immediate terms, this was hardly the leader's preoccupation. Ultimately, however, this system of departmental and local autonomy led to confusion. Competing agencies created unclear lines of communication, contradictory sources of authority beneath the leader. At its least efficient, chaos and *sottogoverno* resulted — as in Italy and Spain. At its most efficient — in Germany — separate and conflicting policies were pursued by nazi leaders in rivalry with each other.

Fascist intervention in the economy was an inevitable result of the exaltation of the state. Autarky, however, whether of the Italian or German variety, needs to be judged against the world trend towards protectionism which rapidly gathered force during the years of the depression. Autarky was not just a political measure designed to mobilize the economic resources of the country for war. It was also a response to the protectionist policies of non-fascist countries. As a policy, it was more successful in the industrial than in the agricultural sector. For it was easier to persuade the big industrialists of the advantages of a cartel than to force the absentee landowners into capital investment when reasonable profits were already generated by protection. Moreover, ruralism, an ideological constant of the regimes through its identification with stability and the small man, worked against increases in productivity. This explains, at least in

part, the failure of the Italian and Spanish regimes to transform the agricultural sector and the structure of landowner-
ship.

Intervention in industry proved more effective. It is true
that the nazi development of the chemical industry was a
conscious choice, whereas the Italian creation of a state
holding company, IRI, was an accidental and traditional
result of the state's policy of salvaging sick industries. But
in both instances the fascist regime did gain substantial
control over industry — at least to the extent that the regimes
dragged the industrialists down in their *Götterdämmerung*.
Fascist economics may have been improvised, short-sighted,
inequitable and erroneous. But they existed.

The final distinction I would make is in the periods of
fascism. It is enough to look at the chronological tables in
this volume to realize the changes in fascism as a European
phenomenon from the 1920s to the 1930s and 1940s.

In the 1920s fascism remained a national characteristic
with virtually no international implications. Italian fascism,
as the prototype, was clearly a source of interest and admiration for enthusiastic fascists elsewhere (as it was for leading
statesmen in western parliamentary democracies). Mussolini's
desire to extend his sphere of influence in the Danubian basin
also had inevitable repercussions on fascist movements in this
area: the Austrian Heimwehr is the most obvious example.
But fascism as yet did not aspire to a role of universality.
Born of nationalistic movements, concerned to vindicate
nationalistic aspirations, the very obsession of the various
fascisms with their country's past bore witness to their local,
limited preoccupations.

By the later 1920s and 1930s, however, fascist leaders all
over Europe were explicit about the international implications of their cause, and consciously looked towards Italy
or (increasingly) Germany as a model to be imitated once
power had been won. The stillborn 'fascist international' was
merely the outward manifestation of this growing internationalism. Such a development was perhaps inevitable, for
if fascism stood for social stability at home, it signified subversion abroad. There can be no doubt about the immense

importance of the nazi seizure of power in this period: 1933 saw the emergence of a new fascist Mecca which rapidly supplanted the old shrine at Rome. As nazi influence spread, fascism became more extremist and racialist. The year 1936 and the Spanish civil war marked another major development, as international fascism felt called upon to challenge international bolshevism.

Although Hitler and Mussolini, in supporting fascist movements, intended to use them as a means to threaten and control authoritarian governments in particular, rather than to install them in power, infiltration could go too far and topple existing regimes, as occurred in Austria even before the *Anschluss*. But a basic contradiction existed between the deep-rooted nationalistic character of all fascisms and their international aspirations. Even in the 1930s, national fascisms, like the Lapua or Rexist movements, could lose popular support because of their imitation of foreign ideology and practices. When war broke out, this contradiction emerged with force in the frustrations and isolation of the fascist parties and regimes in countries under nazi occupation, as in Denmark and Norway. But it can be seen as clearly in the discussions about the new order, to be established after an Axis victory.

In their varying and discordant statements about the new order the 1940s' vintage of fascist leaders were, logically enough, stating their faith in the new international system which they hoped would prevail. Yet the very contradictions of these statements reflected not merely the ambiguities of the concept of the new order as expressed in nazi Germany, but the effective tensions within, and limitations of, international fascism. The future relationship of the Teutons and the Latins was never overtly faced, at least in concrete terms. The French fascists might hope for a partnership. At the other end of Europe, the Finns — although not Aryan — might calculate on finding a place in the sun at the expense of the Russians. But what hope existed for Polish fascists in the event of a nazi victory? And where would the other Slav fascists find themselves? The Hungarian fascists, by the end, were in good part hostile to the Germans. With reason, for the Austrian fascists, although they had hoped to be the dominant influence in the Balkans and northern Italy, had already paid the price for their internationalism — the end of their national identity. For movements born of exacerbated nationalistic feeling and nurtured on the exaltation of war and the bloody suppression of the weak, fascist internationalism was a contradiction in terms. Even if race hatred could have been attenuated, geographical space did not exist to requite the demands of all. The new order meant the triumph of select fascist movements over the others and the nazis made no attempt to hide this. Its interest lies not only in the concrete proposals it contained, but as a symbol of the illogicality of an internationalized fascist movement as it emerged in its final phase. So long as fascism developed separately in individual countries, related to and concerned with national developments, this illogicality did not appear. But, with the war, as its exponents proclaimed a *Weltanschauung* capable of transforming the world, the implausibility of the claim became apparent. Fascism, a fundamentally nationalistic movement, could not offer a viable alternative to the more genuinely international pretensions of capitalist democracy or communism.

What of fascism since 1945? In Spain and Portugal it survived the shock of the war, more through the isolation of these countries than through the merits of the regimes. In other countries fascist movements have started up once more. Yet it seems unlikely that fascism — in its prewar form — could re-emerge as a major threat in western Europe. The conditions which assisted fascism after 1918 no longer hold true, or exist in attenuated form. The end of the war and transition to peace did not produce the same shock and repercussions throughout society in 1945 as occurred after 1918: the shock was cushioned by American aid. Socialism is no longer a bogey-man in western European countries, while anti-bolshevism has been so internationalized by the cold war that it can hardly be monopolized by any single national movement. Weak parliamentary government has not disappeared, but at the national level there is a greater respect for the law (perhaps due to the extension of the power of the state), possibly reinforced by the growth of international

organisms. Irredentism and the desire for the liberation of
ethnic brothers from foreign rule, while still existing, is no
longer in the forefront of national and international politics,
as the horizon has broadened to an inevitable consideration
of world problems. Despite left-wing criticism since the mid-
1960s, and even if the present economic crisis is as serious as
that of the interwar years, anti-capitalism remains implausible
as a rallying cry for fascism, not least because in the world
context European societies are still cushioned against the
worst´ effects of crisis by capitalism and the welfare state.
'Total' solutions ring hollow in a nuclear age.

Most of the particular elements of fascist strength are no
longer possible or are inappropriate. Its 'catch-all', inter-class
mass base is characteristic of both christian democrat and
social democrat parties, working within the framework of
parliamentary democracy. Imperialism can hardly offer the
basis for a popular appeal, in a decolonized world. In fact,
neo-fascism has only managed to maintain one significant
element of prewar fascism — its violence — to which it has
added an anachronistic defence of 'white European civilization'. Even if neo-fascist terrorism has been shown to
possess unhealthy connections with state security services,
and has presented a superficial attraction to some deprived
and bored adolescents, it has proved unable to threaten
seriously the overthrow of western parliamentary democracies. But if fascism of the old variety does not seem likely
to re-emerge, this does not mean that its place might not be
taken by a new version, a new-style mass movement of
reaction. In marxist terms, endangered capitalism can
generate its own defence. Even in non-marxist terms, the
diminished credibility of both capitalism and western democratic regimes can encourage the search for alternative paths.
Fascism, after all, need not begin from outside the existing
system: it can also work from within.

2

THE PHENOMENON
OF FASCISM

✦

H. R. Trevor-Roper

The public appearance of fascism as a dominant force in
Europe is the phenomenon of a few years only. It can be
precisely dated. It began in 1922-3, with the emergence of
the Italian fascist party which Mussolini led to power in the
famous, or mythical, 'march on Rome' of 1922, which was
followed, next year, by Hitler's abortive Munich *putsch*. It
came of age in the 1930s when 'fascist' parties sprang up
throughout Europe and were brought to power, sometimes
by conspiracy, sometimes by civil war, but always under the
patronage of Hitler and Mussolini, bound together, as a force
in European politics, by the Axis Pact of 1936. It ended in
1945 with the defeat and death of the two dictators, the collapse or scurry of their European clients. Of course there were
'precursors' of fascism before 1922, whom it is easy, and
fashionable, now to discover. But in the public history of that
time they had no place, and a historian writing in 1920 would
probably not even have noticed them: at most, he would
have dismissed them as separate, parochial figures. Equally,
since 1945, there have been movements on which the uncritical dogmatists of the left have been quick to fasten the
name of fascist. But these are but the ghosts of the true fascist
movement which threatened and dominated the Europe of
the 1930s. The great age of fascism, the period when it
seemed an international movement, capable — however
violently — of solving the problems of the world, was a brief

and distinctive period in European history. It is inseparable
from the special experience of one generation: the generation
which flourished — or failed to flourish — between the two
world wars.

Nevertheless, when we have said this, how grossly we have
simplified the phenomenon! Fascism may be limited in time
and place, it may have a clear beginning and a clear end in
public history, it may seem easily defined; but this unity, this
definition, was artificially imposed upon it. Behind the one
name lie a hundred forms. The abstraction, so convenient as a
term of abuse, is singularly unhelpful as a means of definition. By comparison, communism, its ideological antithesis,
though also a term of abuse, is clear and definite. Communism leads us back, past all its heresies and deviations, to a
single intellectual source. It has a doctrine, or a dogma, which
can be stated and whose identity is proclaimed by all its
adherents throughout the world. Fascism has no such intellectual rigour, no agreed prophets. Its origins are plural,
divergent, imprecise. If it acquired, in the 1930s, an apparent
unity, that was simply because Hitler and Mussolini, in their
years of power, imposed a uniform colour upon an ill-
assorted hodge-podge of ideas whose origins, from country to
country, are very diverse.

How diverse those origins are is obvious once we look
at the different 'national' forms of fascism. Behind the
disciplined Germanized movements of the 1930s with
their common features of authoritarianism, nationalism,
militarism, anti-semitism, we discover the ultra-conservative,
secularized Catholic French nationalism of the Action
Française; the pan-German, anti-semitic Catholic socialism
of Karl Lueger in Vienna; the rodomontade of d'Annunzio
and the electoral mechanics of Giolitti in Italy; the century-
old tradition of rural *caciquismo* and military *pronuncia-
mientos* in Spain. And farther back still, to our surprise,
among the prophets of fascism, we can discern those former
liberal heroes of the nineteenth century, Giuseppe Mazzini
with his 'Young Italy', whom time has changed from the
idol of Victorian drawing-rooms into the forerunner of
Mussolini, with his *Giovinezza*, and those 'good Germans' of
the Frankfurt parliament whose slogan of *Einheit, Freiheit*

und Macht would not have been disavowed by Hitler. These men would no doubt have been shocked had they seen the last form of the movement to which they had contributed their ideas, just as Burke and Carlyle would also have been shocked at their contribution; but to these, as to those, the line of descent can nevertheless be traced.

This is not to say that fascism has no distinctive, positive content, that it is merely a congeries of disparate national movements, artificially drawn or forced together by German power in the 1930s. There were some common features even in the early formative years, and afterwards, in the years of power, the various national movements, though independent in origin, borrowed ideas from each other and so helped to build up, retrospectively, a common ideology. But it is important to realize that fascism, by its very nature, being a movement of aggressive nationalism, began in a more disorderly fashion than communism, and preserved that disorderly quality to the end. Communism is an international doctrine which has gradually been adjusted to differing national circumstances. Fascism is the exact opposite: a series of non-intellectual, even anti-intellectual, national reactions artificially united and transformed into an international doctrine by the facts of power. And the history of fascism, as an ideology, is largely the history of this transformation.

Let us consider how this transformation came about. To do so, we must begin by looking back, far beyond the public emergence of fascism, to the mid-nineteenth century, the period of what we may call the liberal breakthrough. For the triumph of free capitalism in the nineteenth century, which provoked, directly, the new movements of socialism and communism, provoked also, indirectly, the other authoritarian movement which was to appear as their antidote. Or at least, to be more precise, it generated some of the intellectual raw material out of which fascism would, long afterwards, be compounded. This raw material consisted of ideas which, at the time, were purely conservative. Only later, in the very different circumstances of the twentieth century, would they become radical.

For the liberal breakthrough of the last century was not

achieved painlessly. In England indeed, thanks to constant economic expansion and an elastic political system, the shock was cushioned. But on the continent of Europe it was not. In France the 'bourgeois' victory was achieved only through a series of revolutions. In Germany and Italy it was inseparable from a struggle for national unity which, at times, was a civil war. In such a civil war there were victims as well as victors, and the victims did not surrender quietly. The old élite of Europe, the aristocracy, the landlords, the established churches, and their theorists, nursed their wounds and meditated revenge on the upstart bourgeoisie which seemed everywhere to have triumphed over them. It was out of these disgruntled meditations in manor houses and vicarages that some of the first fascist fantasies were born.

Of course, many of them were absurd archaisms, the agonized myths of a defeated class. Karl Marx made heavy, Germanic mirth at the antics of the Young England group in Britain: 'feudal' aristocrats presenting themselves as the champions of the working class against the new materialist tyranny. Liberals everywhere poured scorn on the 'Vaticanism' of Pope Pius IX: his wholesale ideological condemnation of the whole philosophy of 'liberal' progress. The anti-semitic myth elaborated by over-heated French clergymen passed unnoticed in the educated world. And who, outside Wilhelmian Germany, could take seriously the rhetorical theories of the faded French aristocrat, the comte de Gobineau, who sought to save the hierarchical principle by associating it with a Teutonic master-race? In the days of liberal triumph, of that 'leaping and bounding prosperity' which Gladstonian England seemed to promise, in perpetuity, to all who would imitate it, such follies were dismissed out of hand. They seemed ridiculous: the last convulsions of a dying *ancien régime*, twilight phantoms, unworthy of serious attention by the complacent masters of the new day.

Indeed, in their own right, as ideas, they were ridiculous. The nineteenth-century prophets of fascism, or those who now seem to be their prophets, were often phantom figures. They were the idiot-fringe of defeated conservatism. Their eyes were turned back to the past. They looked away in disgust from the liberal triumph; they had no understanding of the future, no interest in it; and they took refuge in a world of illusion. But for all that they have their significance. History teaches us that even the most tenuous phantoms can come to life if objective circumstances change. The fantasies of one generation can provide the mental furniture, even the life-blood, of another. Nobody could have predicted that the heraldic archaisms of Young England, the hierarchical clericalism of Pius IX, the anti-semitism of Gougenot des Mousseaux, the racialism of Gobineau would become part of a twentieth-century myth which would nearly conquer the world. And yet this is what would happen. It would happen not because these ideas themselves had any validity, but because objective circumstances would change. The bourgeois triumph would become a bourgeois retreat; and that same European bourgeoisie, which had been liberal in its days of triumph, would, in its days of retreat, borrow and reanimate these phantoms generated by the retreating forces of an older regime.

Some political thinkers did indeed foresee the future, at least in general terms. In England, Lord Acton insisted that the organic structure of society would not tolerate the insult of continuous *laissez-faire*. In Switzerland Jacob Burckhardt — like Acton an aristocrat and a pessimist — was more precise. The liberal, democratic juggernaut, he declared, was heading for disaster, and in the end would be taken over by very illiberal, undemocratic drivers who alone would be able to steer it. And these new masters would not be the old ruling dynasties, tamed by defeat and too 'soft-hearted' for so stern a task. They would be *Gewaltmenschen*, men of power, *'terribles simplificateurs'*, who would 'rule with utter brutality'. By 'a presentiment that may now seem completely mad, but yet will not leave me', Burckhardt suggested that this fearful tyranny of the future would be first established in industrial Germany.

In the 1890s, when it was uttered, Burckhardt's prophecy might indeed seem 'mad'. Europe was still prosperous and liberalism still seemed to offer continuing prosperity. Even the defeated old order found it more profitable, in general, to invest in the new world than to denounce it. The European aristocracy became industrialized, the landed classes *embour-*

geoisées. Even the new industrial working classes hoped to benefit by the liberal system — or at least they saw no practical alternative to it. In the generation before the first world war, the intellectual position of liberalism might be frayed at the periphery but its economic power remained strong. Even where it was weak, as in central Europe, its weakness was ascribed rather to the survival of older patterns of organization than to any inherent defect in the liberal order. Where liberalism did not prosper it was, said the liberals, because there was not enough of it. The remedy was to have more. And this remained the remedy even at the end of the first world war. In 1918, after all, it was the liberal, western powers that were the victors. Did not their very victory prove the claims of the liberal system? Therefore liberalism must be exported everywhere. Parliamentary democracy and economic *laissez-faire* was the gospel which, as preached by President Wilson, was now to save the whole world.

And yet already, by that time, the economic foundations of liberalism had begun to crack. The victory of 1918 did not in fact usher in a new era of general prosperity. The physical damage done by the war was too great. Recovery was difficult and slow. And in the meantime, while the west was preaching the saving virtues of liberalism, voices from the east were offering, to the hungry working classes of central Europe, a new means of salvation. In 1917 the Russian revolution had broken out, and from 1917 to 1923 the Russian communists preached not socialism in one country but world revolution. This was the catalytic force which gathered up the intellectual detritus of the Gobineaus and the Gougenots and rearranged it in a new, dynamic pattern. Faced by the terrible threat of bolshevism, the European middle classes, recently so confident, took fright. And in their fright they found themselves crouching in the same postures and adopting some of the ideas which they had once ridiculed in their own previous victims.

For fascism, as an effective movement, was born of fear. It might have independent intellectual roots; it might owe its form, here and there, to independent national or personal freaks; but its force, its dynamism, sprang from the fear of a new, and this time a 'proletarian', revolution. As long as 'liberal' economics had worked, as long as *laissez-faire* had led to economic expansion, with adequate benefits for the working classes, the middle classes had felt safe. But once the economy began to contract, and liberal economics left the proletariat no cushion between unemployment and starvation, no remedy except the revolution to which they were now summoned by Russia, the nemesis foreseen by the nineteenth-century conservatives seemed to have arrived. So each stage in the rise of European fascism can be related to a moment of middle-class panic caused either by economic crisis or by its consequence, the threat of socialist revolution. It was after the great success of the socialists in the Italian elections of 1919 that Italian fascism became a political force. Hitler's first bid for power in Germany — the Munich *putsch* of 1923 — came in the year of the great inflation, when the communists reckoned on seizing power in Berlin. His rise to power in the state followed the world depression of 1929-32. The Spanish Falange was the response to Spanish anarchism, Franco's coup the response to the electoral victory of the Popular Front.

European fascism, then, is the political response of the European bourgeoisie to the economic recession after 1918 — or rather, more directly, to the political fear caused by that recession. Before all else, it was anti-communist. It lived and throve on anti-communism, and its anti-communist virtue, which made it international, covered a multitude of sins. But apart from its social base and its anti-communist spirit, it had little else to unite it. It was a heterogeneous movement which varied greatly from country to country. For this there were two obvious reasons: one historical, the other structural. Historically, fascism was essentially nationalist. Structurally, it was never simple: it was always something of a coalition.

The nationalism of the various fascist parties was inseparable from history. In the days of its advance, the European bourgeoisie, like the Asiatic and African bourgeoisie of today, had always been nationalist. It had been particularly nationalist in the two countries where national unification had been a condition of its power: Italy and Germany. Now, in the days of its retreat, its nationalism remained constant, easily inflamed. But nationalism, which draws upon and exaggerates the differences of national character, necessarily varies from country to country. Consequently fascism reflected this variety. Italian fascism and German fascism were necessarily more distinct than Italian communism and German communism would be.

Secondly, behind the vague term of 'fascism' there lie, in fact, two distinct social and political systems which the opportunism of politicians and the muddled thinking of journalists have constantly confused. These two systems are both ideologically based. Both are authoritarian, opposed to parliamentary liberalism. But they are different; and the confusion between these essentially different systems is an essential factor in the history of fascism. They can be conveniently described as 'clerical conservatism' and 'dynamic fascism'. Almost every fascist movement has been compounded of both these elements, but in varying proportions; and the variety of the proportions bears some relation to the class structure of the society concerned. It is therefore important to distinguish between these two ingredients in the mixture.

Clerical conservatism is the direct heir of the aristocratic conservatism over which the liberal bourgeoisie triumphed in the second half of the nineteenth century. Driven into postures of absurd reaction in the days of Pius IX, it was modernized in form, and given a more respectable political philosophy, in the reign of his successor Leo XIII, whose encyclical *Rerum Novarum* of 1891 remains its charter. For the next thirty years, while liberal movements rose and fell in Europe, the Catholic Church continued to preach its alternative gospel; and with the crisis of liberalism in the 1920s, it believed that its hour had come. Liberalism, the anti-clerical bourgeois nostrum of the nineteenth century, had failed. Socialism, the anti-clerical workers' doctrine of the twentieth century, which had revealed its true character in Russia, must not be allowed to succeed. So the Church everywhere sought to resist socialism — which, on the continent, was everywhere, at least theoretically, marxist — and those political parties which seemed to compromise with it, even if, like the 'christian democrats', they were not anti-clerical. Instead, it offered the conservative ideal of the 1890s: an ordered, hierarchical, undemocratic, 'corporative' state.

That was all very well in countries in which the social structure had not changed, or had not changed too much, since the 1890s: countries like Spain, Portugal, rural Austria, Hungary. But what of those societies which had been radically transformed by industrialism: societies in which the middle class, in its crisis, was not only frightened and radical — that might be true anywhere — but powerful? In the highly industrialized countries the middle class was not only the effective ruling class: it had also absorbed large sections of the other classes in society. It had transformed the landed classes into its tributaries, so that they no longer represented an independent interest. It had imposed its values upon them. Even more important, it had drawn to it, often out of the working class, a large 'lower-middle class' of artisans, shop-keepers, petty civil servants, skilled workers, who had also accepted 'bourgeois' ideas, and who, as the most exposed members of the middle class, were the most zealous defenders of its status. This 'lower-middle class' provided the social force of 'dynamic fascism'.

It is easy to see how this could happen. In times of economic crisis, landlords, capitalists, professional men, might feel themselves sinking within their class; but less secure members of the middle class might well feel themselves falling out of it. Their social betters might cushion their decline, or sense of it, by reserves of property or education. These had little of either, and they felt themselves betrayed. By practising the 'bourgeois' virtues of industry and thrift they had risen from the proletariat, which they therefore felt entitled to despise. Now, thanks to an impersonal crisis for which they were not responsible, they were in danger of being thrown back into it, or subjected to its mercy. With the fanaticism of the frontiersman, they would fight in defence of their status. They would be the front-fighters, the stormtroopers, even the pace-makers of the 'bourgeois' resistance. Only, in their keeping, the philosophy of the bourgeoisie would no longer be liberal. Liberalism was a luxury which they, of all men, could least afford. They would believe in hierarchy, even in an aristocratic hierarchy — up to a point: for a hierarchy above them, provided it did not betray them, was some guarantee of a hierarchy below. But 'liberalism', to them, was a purely relative concept. It might have served its turn in the past, but now circumstances had changed. Besides, the liberal ideals — indeed, all political ideals — had been devalued. A new cult had arisen, for their benefit: the cult of force.

Once again we are taken back to the 1890s — that incubatory period of fascism. It was then that the old world began to crack, even if the cracks were invisible to the natural eye. It was then also that the new doctrines began to take form. Already Marx had declared that all political ideals were relative, mere rationalizations of the interest of struggling classes. Now Freud carried the same process further, arguing that motives are different, often fundamentally different, from the professions in which the human mind instinctively clothes them. Once such devaluation of ideas was accepted, it was natural to draw certain consequences. If political ideals were merely a smoke-screen, concealing the struggle for power, why should we not cut out the hypocrisy, recognize that the political world is a jungle, and fight openly for power? The socialists had already drawn some of those consequences; why should not their adversaries do so too? So, while conservatives defended the social hierarchy by appeals to religious or political ideals, more radical men, repudiating all such ideals — or using them cynically as mere means of propaganda — defended it by quite different arguments. Georges Sorel wrote of the illusions of progress, the necessity of violence, the utility of the 'myth'; Vilfredo Pareto of the iron law of oligarchy, the perpetuation of the élite; Nietzsche of the superman, who is a law to himself. These writers were largely unnoticed by the established prophets of conservatism — though it was in dialogue with Nietzsche that Burckhardt made his notable prophecy. They were to be the teachers of the new generation of fascists — who also, often grossly, perverted their teaching.

Thus fascism proper, what I have called 'dynamic fascism' — the cult of force, contemptuous of religious and traditional ideas, the self-assertion of an inflamed lower-middle class in a weakened industrial society — is radically different from ideological conservatism, the traditional 'clerical conservatism' of the older regime, modified and brought up to date for the twentieth century. Both were authoritarian. Both defended social hierarchy. But the difference between them is as great as that between the divinely consecrated absolutism of the Stuart kings and the naked, unconsecrated absolutism of Hobbes. Nevertheless these two different political forms are constantly confused. They were confused in fact – for both were brought together by common fear of communist socialism in the 1920s. They were confused by design: in order to attain power, 'fascists', like Hitler, would pose as conservatives, and 'conservatives', like Franco, would pose as fascists. This confusion was sometimes justified by tactical success. But in a cheating match, the tactical success of one party is the tactical defeat of another, and it also led to disappointment and recrimination. The German conservatives were to find that, instead of a docile tool, they had raised up a Frankenstein monster who detested the Church and whose last ambition was to liquidate the European aristocracy. Hitler, in his turn, was to complain that he had poured out blood and treasure to establish Franco in power in Spain, only to find that he had raised up a contemptible creature of dukes and priests. The two forms were also confused in the vocabulary of the left. Socialists, hating both, easily treated them as one, and denounced the rule of Dollfuss in Austria, or Franco in Spain, or Horthy in Hungary, as 'fascist'. This was excusable in the 1930s when the confusion was general and politics required opposition to both. It is less excusable now, when fascism is dead and our need is not to oppose but to understand.

In order to see how this confusion was exploited by the dictators we may look at the rise to power of both Hitler and Mussolini. The pattern of events is remarkably similar. In each case the Catholic Church played a significant and positive role; and it did so because – with the conservative classes generally – it supposed that 'dynamic fascism' could be used as the instrument of 'clerical conservatism'. In each case the calculation proved wrong: the Church, by its opportunism, gave itself not a tool but a master.

First, let us take Mussolini, the founder of political fascism. Mussolini's later history has made him appear a mere windbag, a flatulent demagogue who was allowed to flourish, for a time, by the craven inactivity of the western powers. Certainly this is the character which he wears in that revealing document, the diary of his Foreign Secretary and son-in-law, Count Ciano. And yet Mussolini cannot be entirely deflated. He was, after all, the founder of a formidable political movement, and but for him history would have been very different. Hitler himself, who would be very critical of Mussolini at times, nevertheless paid constant tribute to his achievement. In 1924, in *Mein Kampf*, written when Mussolini's power was still a recent growth, he wrote firmly that Mussolini was 'in the front rank of world statesmen' because he had shown, in a yielding time, that the drift towards communism could be stopped and society be set firmly on another base. Later, in his wartime *Table Talk*, Hitler reiterated his admiration. If it had not been for the example of Mussolini, he said, he doubted whether he would have had the courage, the conviction, to embark on his own quest of power: he would not have believed that any human effort could have turned the tide. And at the very end, when he at last recognized defeat and, seeking the cause of it, blamed 'my fatal friendship with Mussolini', he nevertheless paid tribute to Mussolini himself as indisputably the greatest of his contemporaries, 'almost equal to myself'. There can be no question that Hitler's admiration for Mussolini, though somewhat oppressive, was genuine. He showed it in the truest possible way: by imitation.

Consider how Mussolini came to power. He himself was an ex-socialist demagogue who had transferred his radicalism from the socialist to the nationalist cause. Both as a socialist and as a nationalist he was, in Italian circumstances, anti-clerical: his early writings included works entitled 'There is no God' and 'The Cardinal's mistress'. He was thus, at first sight, an unnatural ally for the old conservative classes who, by definition and in natural opposition to anti-clerical liberalism, were clerical. But the conservative, clerical classes were conscious of their need. They might have social strength. They might have a respectable doctrine: the doctrine of the 'corporative' state. But in an industrial society they lacked mass support. The *Popolari*, or 'christian democrats', seemed too radical. Therefore, when this new lower-middle-class movement presented itself, they did not look too critically at it. Provided it was anti-socialist, they were prepared to overlook its anti-clericalism. On their side, the new 'fascist' ideologues, though themselves essentially atheist, were prepared to use religion as a convenient 'myth'. Thus in France Charles Maurras, the founder of the Action Française, was himself an atheist, but regarded Catholicism as a political necessity, and on this basis had been courted by Pope Pius X, who did not hesitate to condemn a genuine Catholic party, the French christian democrats. On the same basis, Pius XI decided to invest in the atheist Mussolini rather than in the Italian christian democrats or *Popolari*. In 1922, on the eve of Mussolini's 'march on Rome', the Pope ordered all priests to withdraw from politics and thus, at a critical moment, hamstrung the *Popolari*. Next year, he demanded the resignation of Don Luigi Sturzo, their secretary-general. Finally, in 1924, after the murder by the fascists of the socialist leader Matteotti, the Pope condemned the *Popolari* and ordered all priests to resign from their party. By these successive acts the papacy destroyed the only popular movement which might have outbidden Mussolini. It did so — it seems clear — for two reasons. First, it distrusted the whole parliamentary system as incapable of resisting the growth of socialism. Secondly, it believed that the new, authoritarian, 'fascist' movement, in spite of its overt 'atheism', would accept the social necessity of Catholicism and make a satisfactory concordat with the Church; which is precisely what Mussolini then did (1925-9), although the Pope would afterwards complain, in his encyclical *Quadragesimo Anno*, that he did not honour all the terms of the concordat.

Ten years later, exactly the same pattern of events was repeated in Germany. The papacy was obsessed by fear of communism, and saw Italy and Germany as the bastion of the Church, and of society, in Europe. But Pius XI had no more confidence in the Catholic Centre Party, which ruled in republican Germany, than in the Italian christian democrats, who might have ruled in Italy. In the years of economic crisis, the Centre Party seemed unable to check the rise of communism. It also ruled through a parliament, the Reichstag, in which the Protestant and socialist members were always able to prevent a concordat with the Catholic Church. The Pope was therefore ready, at the crucial moment, to switch his support from the Catholic Centre Party to the Nazi Party, on the assumption that the latter, though openly anti-religious — indeed, condemned as such by the German hierarchy — would provide mass support for a conservative regime which, being independent of parliamentary parties, would make a satisfactory concordat with the Church. This, once again, is precisely what happened. Evidently on advice from Rome, Mgr Kaas, the leader of the Centre Party, advised his supporters to vote for the Enabling Act which legalized Hitler's dictatorship. Having done so, Kaas himself appeared in Rome to work out the details of the concordat. Once again, as in Italy, the Pope would afterwards complain, in his encyclical *Mit brennender Sorge*, that the terms of the concordat were not honoured; but he did not denounce either the concordat or the nazi government of Germany.

Thus both in Italy and in Germany the fascist party moved into power through a similar door. That door was held open for it by the Catholic Church. Of course it was not only the Catholic Church which was responsible. The Church, in this, acted as the representative of conservative society. It intervened, at a crucial moment, to give its ideological blessing to the surrender of conservative society: a surrender already made, not only by conservative politicians, but deep in the body of society. And so it was not only the Church which was deceived by the result. Like the Church, the conservative classes in both Italy and Germany supposed that, by patronizing Mussolini and Hitler, they had enlisted support for a conservative programme. These vulgar demagogues, they thought, could be used to destroy 'socialism' at the grass-roots, or rather, in the streets. Then they could be discarded. In fact, the reverse happened. It was the conservative patrons and their ideas that were discarded, the vulgar demagogues that survived.

How did this happen? It happened, I suggest, for two main reasons. First, neither Hitler nor Mussolini was interested in being a 'conservative' ruler: both were revolutionaries who saw and relished the possibility of radical power. Second, in both Germany and Italy they saw a basis for that power: a lower-middle class made radical by social fear. Themselves familiar with this class, its fears and aspirations, they believed that they could mobilize it as a dynamic force in the state and thereby realize ambitions unattainable by mere conservative support.

Clerical conservatives assumed a stable or at least a static society. Hitler and Mussolini saw that so negative a philosophy could have no appeal to their supporters. They undertook to ensure the prosperity and the self-respect of the frightened middle classes. But they also went further. Unlike the conservatives, who represented only the possessing classes, and the socialists, who represented only the working classes, they undertook to defend the interests of the lower-middle classes without disturbing the existing social hierarchy. Repudiating the suicidal doctrine of class war, they emphasized the organic unity of the nation in its natural hierarchy. But that hierarchy was to be preserved at all levels, not merely at the summit of society: indeed, the conservative classes must pay for their privileges by defending those of their inferiors. And if the lower-middle classes were thus to be guaranteed in their status, the working classes must not feel neglected in theirs. They too must be economically secured and made to share in national identity, national glory. Thus, from the basis of the lower-middle class, Hitler and Mussolini preached a doctrine which could attract both conservatives, whose own ideology lacked dynamism, and socialists, whose aims had been discredited and whose policies had failed. They were also able to enlist the idealism of men who were weary of class interests and economic claims.

But how was such dynamism to be realized? Claiming to represent the nation, not a mere class, the dictators could not, like the socialists, advocate an internal redistribution of resources. Some improvements could be made by greater efficiency: by the use of power to eliminate waste and increase production; by more energetic marketing, fiscal devices, currency control. But equally — and the gospels of nationalism, force and racial superiority would naturally encourage this — they could be gained by internal or foreign aggression: the spoliation of a social 'out-group' at home or the conquest of 'inferior' races abroad. An upper class which lacked ideas or ideals of its own, which had already lost the initiative when it accepted nihilist demagogues as its protectors, was not likely to make a solid front in defence of Jews or foreigners, provided its interests were spared. Industrialists were prepared to pay something towards the cost of a dictatorship which controlled their workers, prevented strikes, and might ultimately widen markets and increase profits. So, little by little, the conservative classes who had brought the fascist dictators to power found themselves the prisoners of that power. They were imprisoned because that power, in a highly industrialized society, had another and wider base.

Thus the dynamism of fascism depends directly on the existence of a strong industrial middle class — and on the malaise of that class. Germany was more highly industrialized than Italy, and it was in Germany that the 'fascist' dictatorship was most complete. In 1934 Hitler seemed the tool of the German conservatives. They had brought him to power. They stood by while he murdered the radicals on his left. But by 1936 he was independent of them and could begin to subdue the right. By 1944 German conservatives were in the mood to murder him, and failed. In Italy no such complete dictatorship was possible. Though he often raged at them, Mussolini was never able to destroy either the papacy or the monarchy (Hitler was fortunate in having no such permanent institutions in his way), and ultimately the monarchy was the means of his overthrow. To the end, Italian fascism was unable to dominate Italian society as German nazism dominated German society. In the early years, the years of internal violence, the *fascisti* had beaten up Italian Jews; but in the years of war, when anti-semitism again became the rule in Italy, it could not be enforced. Society was stronger than government, and the Jews were safer in Italy than anywhere else in Axis-dominated Europe.

At the opposite end of the scale from Germany is Spain. In 1936-9, when civil war raged in Spain, the rest of Europe saw the struggle as a war between 'fascism' and 'communism'. This was not entirely untrue. While the struggle lasted,

German and Italian patronage of one side, Russian patronage of the other, did indeed encourage the ascendancy of the 'fascist' Falange as against Franco here, the communists as against the republicans and anarchists there. But it was a temporary truth only. Once the struggle was over, the native Spanish pattern reasserted itself. The explanation is clear enough. In Spain there had been no such industrial development as in Germany or Italy. The bourgeoisie had been too weak to make, far less to maintain, an effective 'liberal' regime; and there was no social basis for 'dynamic fascism'. The attempted *coup d'état* of General Franco, like that of General Carmona in Portugal ten years earlier, was a conservative *pronunciamiento*. Carmona had entrusted political power to a professional economist, Dr Salazar, who established an efficient mercantile dictatorship with nothing specifically 'fascist' in it. Franco ruled in Spain as the regent of a conservative monarchy, like Admiral Horthy in Hungary. Both Franco and Salazar — in differing degrees — were allies of the Catholic Church. Their government was 'corporative': its philosophy that of Leo XIII. The papacy would have its little quarrels with both of them in time to come, but it was never disappointed in their system of government: an unparliamentary, conservative, clerical police state.

It is true, there was in Spain an authentic 'fascist' party. The Falange, founded by José Antonio Primo de Rivera, was a native party, and it had all the marks of true 'dynamic' fascism. It was nationalist, idealist, aggressive, based on the urban lower-middle class. But that class, so formidable in industrial Germany, was feeble in agrarian Spain, and a number of accidents — regional rivalry, the failure to control Madrid and Barcelona during the war — made it feebler still. During the civil war, in order to humour his fascist backers, Franco uttered fascist slogans and played up the Falange. But at best he was half-hearted, as the German ambassador repeatedly complained. Even had he been serious, it is doubtful — given the limited success even of Mussolini — whether he could really have made the Falange an instrument of radical power. And after 1942, when he had broken with Hitler, he ceased even to pretend. The Falange subsided. It dropped its radical gestures. It became a mere freemasonry of job-hunters. And Franco subsided too. He allowed himself to be absorbed into the conservative society of which he was really the champion. He abated his imperialist claims, forgot *Hispanidad*, and became the caretaker of the authoritarian 'kingdom' of Spain. His fascism, always factitious, simply withered away.

Much of the 'fascism' of the interwar years was factitious: an artificial 'fascist' colour temporarily imposed on native conservative movements by the example or domination of Germany and Italy. In the late 1930s almost every 'conservative' movement in continental Europe borrowed a 'fascist' colour and during the second world war many 'fascist' movements were artificially created in conquered countries for which there was no native social base. Rightwing authoritarian rulers, like Marshal Pétain or Admiral Horthy, yielded gradually and reluctantly to the 'fascist' policies which German patronage forced on them. Clerical bosses like the Catholic priests Fr Hlinka and Fr Tiso in Slovakia converted themselves into 'fascist' rulers. Dr Salazar in Portugal, like General Franco in Spain, took on a temporary fascist hue. He accepted the advice of Himmler in order to reorganize the Portuguese police, and set up the Greenshirts to keep up with the Italian Blackshirts and the German Brownshirts; which afterwards, like the Spanish Blueshirts, declined into a mere boy-scout organization. Fascist 'movements', esoteric and ridiculous, were hatched, by the warm sun of Rome and Berlin, out of the most unpromising matter even in stable industrial societies like Britain and Belgium, or were created as mere subsidized instruments of German power, as in Norway. Such movements were almost entirely derivative. Who would have heard of the Iron Guard in Rumania, or the Arrow Cross in Hungary, if it had not been for the sustaining power of Germany? No doubt they had a base in their own countries, just as the Falange had a base in Spain. But in those rural societies, it was a narrow base, and without the German example, and German support, they would have remained impotent pressure-groups on the fringe of politics; just as the Rumanian and Hungarian communist parties would have been impotent without the support of Russian power.

The extent to which 'international fascism' was really a generalization of the German model by means of German power is illustrated by the racialism and anti-semitism which is often regarded as an essential feature of it. The doctrine of race was published by a Frenchman, the comte de Gobineau, and an Englishman, Houston Stewart Chamberlain; but both Gobineau and Chamberlain were repudiated by their own countries and accepted only in Germany. It was the Germans who, having annexed Strasbourg from France in 1870, enriched it with the Gobineau Museum, to advertise the French prophet whom they had also annexed; and Chamberlain, who lived in Germany, was one of Hitler's earliest supporters. Anti-semitism has been endemic in Europe for centuries, but from the 1920s it was only in Germany that it assumed a rabid form, only there that society was willing to tolerate systematic persecution. The independent national conservative movements were, in general, quite untainted by it. Italian society, which tolerated fascism, would not tolerate anti-semitism. General Franco, after the war, openly sought to woo the small Jewish communities of Spain. Marshal Pétain in France, Admiral Horthy in Hungary, resisted and sought to limit the persecution of the Jews which was imposed upon them by Germany. In fact, we may say that, in this respect, 'fascism' was simply the means of generalizing, in a reluctant Europe, the pathological attitudes of German society. Without German power there would no doubt have been occasional pogroms in eastern Europe, but the systematic destruction of the Jews, even by native 'fascist' governments, is unthinkable.

But indeed 'international fascism' itself is unthinkable without Germany. Remove nazism from the Europe of the 1930s, and what would have happened? In every country we can see the rudiments of a national conservatism, sometimes traditional, sometimes radical. In every country this national conservatism was inflamed by the economic crises of the 1920s and the threat of communist revolution — which was real enough: we should not forget the communist regime of Bela Kun in Hungary, overthrown by Admiral Horthy in 1920, or the communist hopes in Germany, culminating in 1923. But in every country which was affected by these fears, the form of resistance was different. Only in industrial countries with a radical, organized working class was there a native base for dynamic 'fascism'; and even here there were notable differences from country to country. Who can tell how Italian fascism would have developed had it not been for the fatal dependence on nazi Germany? Mussolini might even have subsided, like Franco, into a mere Latin dictator, preserved in power (if at all) by electoral manipulation and diversionary rhetoric — 'Nice, Savoy, Tunis, Malta' serving the one as Gibraltar served the other. 'Fascism' would then have a different definition, without racialism, without public atheism, without Nordic nonsense or German *Schadenfreude*. It was German power, and that alone, which gave a hideous similarity to national anti-communist movements, so that the party of Flemish autonomy could be tainted with nazi colours and local tensions in the Balkans could be inflamed by the irrelevant fantasies of Teutonic pedants.

Conversely, with the collapse of German power, the unifying force has dissolved and today it is impossible to speak any longer of 'fascism' in a significant sense. It is not merely that the ideas and the gestures are discredited by defeat. The essential conditions of fascism are absent: the economic crisis, the danger of proletarian revolution, the unifying patronage of a dominant industrial power. Behind these accidental circumstances there are, of course, certain permanent attitudes which were incorporated in fascism, and should those circumstances recur, a 'dynamic fascism' might incorporate them again. But the pattern would be different, and it would be safest not to use the old word: a word which, by now, is either precisely dated or a meaningless term of abuse.

3

ITALY

✦

S. J. Woolf

Italian fascism was the first fascist movement and regime and remained virtually alone for half its life. Hence its seizure and exercise of power tend to be used as the parameter of fascist movements in other countries. But the novelty of the Italian experience needs to be kept in mind, even if it would be inappropriate to press any analogy with the uniqueness of, for example, the 'first' industrial revolution in England (as fascism never conditioned the development of other societies as directly or effectively as industrialism). During the first decade of the regime, when other fascist movements arose with increasing frequency, the Italian example undoubtedly served in many respects as a model. But at the same time the younger fascisms — and particularly German nazism — influenced the development of this original model. In this latter period, there is thus a double perspective constantly to be borne in mind, of the extent to which the development of Italian fascism was conditioned by its emergence from a position of isolation among the 'normal' patterns of government current in Europe to one where it represented the father-figure, but only a single instance of a more general, new type of state structure.

One other methodological problem needs to be noted: interpretations of Italian fascism are conditioned by the particular visual angle adopted, by concentrating on the fascist movement or alternatively on the fullblown regime.

For a long time the dominant interest in the origins of fascism led to extremely superficial interpretations of the regime. The contrast between the ideology, style and actions of the early movement, with the vitality and apparent modernity of its approach, and the bureaucratic, heavy-handed compromises and almost caricatural rhetoric of the regime easily lead to contradictory interpretations either of the abandonment of a right-wing revolutionary potential, or of the irrelevance of the early ideology. This contrast between claims and achievement is greater for Italian fascism than for German nazism, but the continuity between movement and regime (for example, in terms of leadership groups or of goals) makes it impossible simply to separate the former from the latter.

It is hardly surprising that the foreign statesmen and journalists of western European countries did not judge the fascist seizure of power to be a particularly threatening event. If not a Balkan-type military *coup*, it remained remote, a matter concerning Italy, which could not repeat itself even in neighbouring countries, as the official French press congratulated itself. Even more, it was easy to regard fascism as another product of the confusing postwar situation. At worst, Mussolini would prove as weak as his predecessors. At best, it seemed possible that he would finally offer Italy strong government and strengthen the anti-bolshevik forces. If it was difficult to approve of the violence of some of his supporters, one needed to remember that the Italian case was a special one, because of the total breakdown of the authority of the state, and that in any case a 'responsible' Mussolini would soon restrain his blackshirts.

So benevolent an attitude was strongly encouraged by fascist propaganda. Mussolini's acute sensibility to foreign opinion led to the rapid development of a widespread network of propaganda, with carefully chosen representatives sent abroad. The basic success of this policy can be easily judged by the willing acceptance of the fascist viewpoint put forward in England by Luigi Villari, son of a famous historian and an English mother. The authoritative French newspaper *Le Temps* could theorize at the beginning of 1924 that fascist rule would slowly transform the parliamentary system along the lines of the English two-party system, with the fascists as tories and their right-wing liberal supporters as a whig coalition. Even the murder of a leading member of the parliamentary opposition, Matteotti, in June 1924 could hardly shake the optimism of conservative circles. For fascism represented primarily anti-bolshevism and the rule of order and strong government.

The success of fascism's projection abroad of this reassuring self-image could be illustrated by countless examples. It appealed to the national pride of the millions of Italian emigrants across the world, from the United States to Australia, almost everywhere despised and rejected by their host countries. It became part of the chit-chat of such unlikely circles as the story-writers of the *Boys Own Paper* (whose 1924 public-school hero proposed starting 'a company of Fascisti — like that Italian bloke who got fed up with excessive rags and organized a counter-party of orderly creatures'). It even evoked a hymn of praise in the 1923 *Wall Street Journal* to Mussolini, the 'blacksmith's son' who 'cleansed and rescued' Italy:

> Word-froth and demagogues and drones
> Banned; sweat and service praised;
> Desks manned when A.M. intones,
> Langorous Italy dazed!
> (J.P. Diggins, *Mussolini and Fascism*, 1972, p. 158)

In business and conservative circles, not until the invasion of Abyssinia in 1936, and then almost entirely because of the dangerous nature of fascist foreign policy, did a partial revision of this superficial assessment of fascism begin.

At the other end of the political spectrum, judgements of fascism were equally out of focus. Early communist interpretations at least attempted to analyse the social composition of fascism, but were hampered by the rigidity of their overall analysis of its relationship to the crisis of capitalism. Initially dismissing fascism as a 'white terror', the Communist International only slowly moved towards acknowledging and offering explanations for its mass base; not until 1935 did Togliatti at Moscow propose a detailed analysis of the regime's mechanisms of organizing support.

These assessments from right and left contain elements of truth but remain partial and unsatisfactory, not so much because of inadequate information as because of the ideological blinkers through which Italian fascism was viewed. Foreign observers saw in fascism what they wanted to see, judging it according to the relationship they thought it bore to their own more immediate problems and to their *Weltanschauung*. For the same reasons most Italian politicians offered equally partial assessments and did not begin to realize the fundamental break with the past that fascism represented until the murder of Matteotti and the fascist laws of 1925 left them no alternative.

There can be little doubt that it was the inability of the opposition parties to think other than in terms of the old pattern of politics that convinced them for so long that fascism was no more than a parenthesis, a transient interruption of the 'normal' course of politics. In no other way is it possible to explain the persistent adoption of tactics aimed at denouncing before public opinion the illegality of fascist measures and the corruption of its government. The communists alone stood outside this framework, but were restricted for their part by their more or less general acceptance of the analysis of the Communist International.

Given these premises, it is not surprising that the detailed discussions of fascism, which emerged with increasing frequency from 1921, either concentrated on a single element or aspect of the new movement, or else listed its component parts and concluded that fascism was too contradictory to last. On the liberal side, one of the most acute critics, Luigi Salvatorelli, explained fascism in terms of an aggressive nationalist mythology which had contaminated the lower-middle classes in the war; such feeling was exacerbated by petty-bourgeois hatred of the anti-patriotic socialists and by fears of the decline of their own economic and social position, threatened by inflation and the rise of mass parties. The communists regarded the agrarian terrorism of fascism as incompatible with rational bourgeois capitalism. Not only the communists, but the social democrats and even some progressive liberals like Amendola analysed a conflict of interests between lower-middle-class and capitalist support of fascism, and saw in the discontent of the former an element which would bring fascism to a rapid end. The anarchist Luigi Fabbri judged fascism to be a preventive counter-revolution of all the forces of social conservation. The mixed support of left-wing revolutionary syndicalists and ex-combatants, of lower-middle-class and extremely youthful elements, of the landowners of the Po valley and the industrialists of the north were all noted and judged to be as incompatible and contradictory as the sources of fascist ideology or the succession of fascist programmes.

Since these early discussions, the researches of contemporaries (such as Tasca and Salvemini) and historians offer a far fuller and reasonably clear analysis of the origins of fascism and its seizure of power. Their conclusions can be grouped in two separate but convergent sets of problems — the conditions of crisis in Italy which fascism was able to exploit, and the characteristics of the fascist movement itself.

The nature of the crisis is not in dispute, although historians disagree in the weight they assign to the different elements. None would deny that intervention and the over-stretching in the first world war of Italy's resources (human, social and political, as well as economic) were directly responsible for the crisis. Much debate and some confusion has been generated by the closely related question of whether the war represented a sharp break in the course of Italian history, or confirmed the continuity of weaknesses within the unified state, merely swelling and finally lancing abscesses which had long been festering within the body politic. In more specific terms, the willingness of so many representatives of the state to abandon parliamentary democracy in 1920-2 can be linked to the authoritarian proposals of the prewar nationalists, but also to the older conservative desire for strong government personified by Sonnino in the 1890s and rationalized in terms of the élitist theories of Pareto and Mosca. In the economic field, the war can be interpreted as raising to a new level the consequences of a longer-term, unbalanced process of industrialization, in which certain heavy industries (primarily iron and steel and shipbuilding), closely connected to banks and already in fair part reliant on government pro-

tection and orders, now gained an enormous degree of independence in alliance with the bureaucracy, annexing many
of the decisional powers formerly vested in the parliamentary
state.

Such debates about continuity confuse the issue, because
the prewar weaknesses of Italy do not seem so markedly out
of line with the cleavages and tensions characteristic of new
western nation-states (to adopt Linz's terminology). If most
of the ideology of the fascist movement can be found in the
prewar nationalist party and revolutionary syndicalism (anti-
parliamentarianism, anti-democracy, anti-individualism, the
productivist vision of an industrial society), this would still
not account for fascism without the polarizing effects of
intervention and the war. At most, one can point to the relative prominence of nationalist and syndicalist groupings as
indicative of the weakening and possible breakdown of the
consensual system in the years between the Libyan and the
world war. It was in the climate of these years that Mussolini
gained his reputation as a revolutionary socialist.

The war created the Italian crisis in multiple ways. It
polarized the political spectrum, already over intervention in
1915, increasingly during the course of the conflict (especially after the defeat of Caporetto), and definitively after
its end, when d'Annunzio's remarkable arousing of a defiant
Italian nationalism was identified with anti-socialism. Fascism's exploitation of nationalist ideology, its consistent
attack on bolshevik saboteurs, neutralist during the war and
subversive since its end, are of course elements to be found in
other extreme right-wing movements. In Italy they gained
particular strength because of Mussolini's personal break with
the socialists over the issue of intervention in the war in
1914-15, and because of the deep split caused by the war in
the one major state where the socialists had refused to abandon their internationalism for the sake of bourgeois patriotism, a refusal they never failed to proclaim even after the
victory. Nevertheless, the trumpeting of anti-bolshevism and
nationalist myths in the form of the 'mutilated' victory
— whose fruits were to be seen in d'Annunzio's occupation
of Fiume in 1919 — would not have been adequate. After all,
the nationalist party stood for the same ideals — far more

coherently than the fascists — but remained an élite group with little popular support. Fascism was able to achieve more because of the unexpected changes wrought by the war, and because of its own claims and, even more, its style.

It is difficult, in fact, to conceive of fascism achieving mass support without the new sense of political consciousness which existed in Italy after 1918. The war had had the effect of arousing in the nation for the first time an awareness of the state, a sense of belonging to the country shared by the millions who had participated in the exhausting struggle. Although the levels and forms of participation varied between city and countryside, north and south, their overall effects were felt throughout society and the state. The parliamentary system was paralysed, with the triumph of the mass-based antagonistic socialist and Catholic parties. The class struggle reached new levels, culminating in occupations of both factories and landed estates, and the threat of revolution. Demobilization on a massive scale was disruptive, not only because of inadequacy of employment opportunities, but because of the high expectations aroused by the earlier expansion of secondary and higher education and promises made during the war.

To compound the political, institutional and social crisis were the problems of economic readaptation to conditions of peace. Some industrialists (linked to overcommitted bankers) were threatened with collapse and looked to the state. Inflation accelerated the redistribution of income, to the benefit of some categories — large proprietors, new peasant landowners, shopkeepers, organized factory workers and agricultural labourers in the Po valley — but threatened the profits of industrialists and the economic and social status of others, such as employees and similar groups dependent on fixed incomes and pensions. Too little is known about the secondary networks (trading organizations, chambers of commerce, veterans' clubs, teachers' associations) to which these groups belonged, but it seems likely that it was through these networks, rather than as isolated or alienated individuals, that these categories, loosely described as 'petty bourgeoisie', gave support to fascism. The fall in inflation is also linked to fascism in the sense that as the boom profits of such agricultural products as sugar and hemp fell during 1920, the large landowners of the Po valley turned to fascism in order to smash the socialist and Catholic labour organizations.

Fascism claimed to be a revolutionary movement. Its initial programme, of June 1919, certainly reads like a revolutionary manifesto. Nor is this surprising, given that it was based in good part on the syndicalist ideas of De Ambris (who was also to provide the corporativist 'charter' for d'Annunzio at Fiume) and the futurist technologically inspired enthusiasms of Marinetti. Its novelty lay not in the attacks on war profiteers or the assertions of republicanism and anti-clericalism, but in the combination of nationalism and 'productivism', or national syndicalism, which was meant to appeal to both veterans and producers. Ideologically, it was a combination that could be dated back to the hybrid alliance of 1915, but which had acquired more vociferously patriotic overtones with the hardening of nationalism during the war. It is essentially (although not exclusively) on the basis of the attractions exercised by this programme that the historical rehabilitation of the 'revolutionary' character of fascism rests: a revolution based not on class, but on a producer-structured national society, usually coloured by anti-bourgeois, technological, and/or an aesthetically anarchistic vision of the future. This first fascist programme was clearly aimed at winning support away from the left-wing parties. The total failure at the 1919 elections was not merely because fascism was a 'latecomer', which found the political space to the left already occupied (as Linz observes acutely), but also because of suspicion of Mussolini's motives.

Fascism in this 'first wave' was characterized by its urban basis and by its looseness of structure. The very word *fascio* carried emotive overtones acquired in the previous generation: from the revolt of the Sicilian *fasci* of workers in 1892 to the democratic *fascio* organized against an authoritarian *coup* at the end of the century, from the interventionist *fascio* of 1914-15 to the *fascio* of national defence organized after the defeat of Caporetto in 1917. It implied extra-parliamentary activities, through despair of and contempt for the normal constitutional paths. But because of its early use by the left wing it also carried the implication of a revol-

utionary end. Finally, it denied the creation of an organization with a formal and more or less rigid structure, but
implied a looser association outside and above parties, a
grouping of men with frequently differing viewpoints for a
specific end. Renzo de Felice has even suggested that initially
Mussolini conceived of the *fasci* as a purely temporary
electoral bloc.

The *fascio* was merely one of many voluntary ex-servicemen's associations which sprang up immediately after the war
in small towns and cities — although it differed from most
such associations in its virulent nationalism. It was quin-
tessentially a local organization, whose vitality depended
upon the personal leadership qualities of one man, usually an
ex-officer. The *fascio* revived the sense of comradeship, the
cameraderie of the trenches, the temporary bypassing of the
social barriers of peacetime life; and hence, alongside drifters
and students with heroic images of fighting, it attracted precisely those soldiers and NCOs who had identified most completely with the war, sometimes *arditi* or assault troops, who
now found it particularly difficult to adjust to 'normal' life.
But these original *fasci* were not simply veterans' clubs. They
were political associations, which attracted idealistic ex-
combatants and syndicalists, who were hostile equally to
bourgeois capitalism and to the internationalism of the
bolsheviks, who practised direct democracy at the meeting-
hall of the *fascio* and believed in the possibilities of creating
a fairer society through direct action. Precisely because the
fascio was so general in its aims and so new, it was not bound
by the commitments of nationally structured parties (like the
socialists or Catholic *Popolari*) or longstanding clienteles (like
the liberals). It was able to accommodate both syndicalists
and right-wing nationalists, with each *fascio* assuming the
particular hue most suited to the inclinations of its leader (or
ras) and the political divisions of its region.

The strength of fascism derived from the autonomy of
these local leaders and their willingness to compromise with
the landowners. Although Mussolini had created a central
committee of the *fasci*, there was little control over successful *ras*, precisely because without such local leaders the movement would have lost political weight. Fascism's trans-

formation into a mass movement took place from late 1920 and during 1921, as the socialist threat ebbed, after the September occupation of the factories: 80,000 members by March 1921, 218,000 in December, 332,000 in May 1922. All the case studies of regions of the Po valley, central Italy and Apulia in the south explain this sudden success in terms of the change in political direction of the *fasci*, from left to right, moving out of the cities into the countryside, repaying the financial and physical assistance of the landowners by the punitive expeditions of armed squads, destroying socialist and Catholic trade unions and co-operatives. Only in a city like Trieste was the local *ras*, Francesco Giunta, able to construct a mass base on the ethnic divisions of the frontier. Military-style terrorism, with the collusion of the police, regular military and civilian authorities of the state, was the basis of fascism's growth. Each local *fascio* was able to attract support by its syndicalist, anti-bourgeois image and its squadrist defence of the 'small man' (sharecropper, tenant farmer, new smallholder, shopkeeper) against the fear of socialist collectivization. Fascism spread most rapidly where socialism appeared most revolutionary, as at Ferrara and Bologna; in consequence, it only affected a few areas of the south, such as Apulia and Naples. With the destruction of the socialist and Catholic unions, the *fasci* set up their 'autonomous syndicates', which organized intermediate peasant strata in the countryside and non-manual workers (especially in public employment) in the cities.

The contrast between the reactionary violence of agrarian fascism and the moderate populist syndicalism or nationalism of urban fascism was noted by contemporaries, including Gramsci. Many of the original urban fascists protested, and some resigned, at the evident manipulation of fascism by the landowners. The political wing of the movement, particularly the fascist deputies elected in 1921, were concerned lest continuing violence alienate support. But the very success of the *ras* in creating a mass base through intimidation and the takeover of existing secondary networks frustrated the attempts of the political wing, and even of Mussolini, to exercise central control. There could be no more telling contrast to Hitler's assertion of control over the nazi movement in 1926 than the power of Balbo at Ferrara, Grandi at Bologna, Farinacci at Cremona, Turati at Brescia, Starace at Trent and all the lesser *ras*. It was this autonomy of the *fasci* that explains their contradictory ideological positions, able to graft themselves on to local traditions, to exploit local rivalries, to appear republican, syndicalist, nationalist, according to the strength of the local social groupings and political traditions. In the Romagna the fascists could win the support of the republicans because of their traditional hostility to the socialists; in the lower Po valley they could appear as syndicalists and win the peasants after destroying the Catholic trade union organizations; in the Alto Adige they could exploit the reactionary form of irredentism; in the Mezzogiorno, after the 'march on Rome', they could pre-empt the nationalists by allying themselves with the local notables. The conflict over whether fascism was republican or monarchical, the resistance of the *ras* to the pacification agreement with the socialists, the transformation of the movement into a party, even the 'march on Rome', can be seen as episodes of the struggle between the military and political wings of fascism, between rural and urban fascism, between the *ras*, each able to appeal to his own squadrist base, and Mussolini, indispensable as the only leader of national political stature, but unable to impose his authority on the *ras*. More than its negative ideology and theatrical style, it was this unusual and uneasy combination of electoral politics and paramilitary violence that enabled fascism to seize power.

The history of fascism as a regime can be divided into various phases. Of these, the first period — October 1922 to January 1925 — is marked by the continuing struggle between the 'intransigent' and 'revisionist' wings of the party. The revisionists, like the intransigents, were a loose grouping, united primarily by their opposition to continual violence now that the party had become the government. The most moderate of the revisionists, right-wing constitutional ex-liberals, expected the fascist party to 'normalize' itself in the image of conservative liberalism. More radical were the nationalists, with their aggressive philosophy of the modern industrial state. The acceptance of a nationalist ideology by fascism has often been noted. The union of the two parties in 1923 was regarded at the time by Salvatorelli as the conquest of the fascist Goliath by the nationalist David. There can be little doubt that the amorphous character of fascist ideology facilitated the infiltration of the compactly organized nationalist group, which provided fascism with four keepers of the seal and a substantial proportion of the top hierarchy and bureaucracy.

But in these first years, as fascism consolidated its hold on power by changing the electoral law to ensure for itself a two-thirds majority (1923), the leading revisionists were those attracted to fascism because of its identification with managerial efficiency. This technocratic wing has been identified with the ex-syndicalist Massimo Rocca and the so-called 'groups of competence', whose aims were to replace both the deadhand of bureaucracy and class conflict by the enhancement of productive skills. Rocco's expulsion from the party (PNF) through his involvement in Matteotti's murder marked the end of any serious anti-bureaucratic drive. But the belief in fascism as a weapon of efficiency to reform the structures of the state initially and for many years attracted a substantial number of intellectuals and experts outside the party, as well as a minority within — agronomists like Arrigo Serpieri, educationalists like Lombardo Radice, convinced by Giovanni Gentile's reform of the school curriculum.

For Mussolini and the revisionists the major problem was the continued violence and dissidence of the intransigents. A few fascist *ras* were purged, such as Padovani at Naples who opposed the party's policy of penetrating the south through compromises with the local notables. A militia (MVSN) was created to incorporate and discipline the squadrists, at the same time giving institutional recognition to the party's paramilitary force. But the uncontrollable activities of the provincial squadrists discredited Mussolini and the PNF in the country and abroad, and finally, through the atmosphere of generalized violence, generated the deepest crisis of fascism until 1943, with the popular reaction against the murder of Matteotti. Even if the authoritarian solution of the crisis to which an uncertain Mussolini was pushed by the intransigent militia consuls appeared to mark the triumph of the intransigents, with the appointment of Farinacci as party secretary, their defeat lay in the very element that had constituted their strength in earlier years — their individual autonomy as *ras*. The decentralized nature of their power necessarily worked against its perpetuation once fascism as an opposition movement claimed authority as a government. Precisely because the strength of the individual *ras* was based on a local, sharply delimited region, authority within the fascist party was too widely diffused to permit the elaboration of a collective alternative strategy to that of the fascist government. The aims and ideals of the *ras* were too contradictory, their suspicion and jealousy of each other too deep, ever to make it possible for them even to conceive of putting together a common programme in defence of what they might regard as 'genuine' or 'pure' fascism.

The very term 'intransigence' (like so many other fascist terms) was a highly ambiguous concept, which shifted in meaning according to the *ras* and the issue in dispute. Balbo was regarded as an intransigent as much as Farinacci, although his 'normalizing' tactics in the Ferrarese were almost the antithesis of Farinacci's continued incitement of disorder. The Cremona *ras* was seen as an intransigent because of his vociferous eulogies of squadrism, the *ras* of Ferrara because of his association with the militia. In their own very different ways, Turati and Starace were equally intransigents. In the end, 'intransigence' meant little more than identification with the earliest 'heroic' days of fascism, above all of provincial fascism. Even in this sense 'intransigence' often implied particular connotations, the cult of spontaneous action, anti-bureaucratic behaviour, the exercise of rights of almost private property over the 'conquered' province. In this sense, the conflicting and often nebulous elements of what later theorists and propagandists grandiloquently called the ideology of fascism, in its early stages amount to little more than the sharply contrasting political inclinations of the individual *ras* — the republican tendencies of a Balbo, the monarchism of a De Vecchi, the working-class populism of a Turati, the industrialist ties of a Ciano. All that held them together was their determination to defend their provincial bastions, the basis of their standing in the party.

At the same time, the deliberate creation of the myth of Mussolini made it increasingly difficult to challenge his leadership without endangering, perhaps even threatening the collapse of fascism itself. It is significant that the only real threat to depose Mussolini, which led to the resolution of the Matteotti crisis, came not from the *ras* themselves, but — *in extremis* — from the militia consuls. During the course of the crisis *ras* as opposed in their political attitudes as the intransigent Farinacci and the normalizer Bottai publicly agreed in their identification of Mussolini and fascism.

If the *ras* had no alternative to Mussolini to offer at the moment of crisis, they were also singularly ill-equipped to convert the role and function of their squadrist followers within the regime. Because no satisfactory role could be found for the squadrists in the new regime, their leaders, the *ras*, were deprived of the provincial support upon which they based their claim to influence and power. Farinacci, as party secretary, failed — and could not but fail — in his bid to legalize fascist illegality. Indeed, his very attempt to strengthen the party by centralization could only be effected by the destruction of 'rasdom', or at least of rival *ras*. When his job was done, Farinacci was himself dismissed for inciting squadrists against anti-fascists. The policies of his successors, Turati and Giuriati, completed the task of purging the party of squadrists or precipitating their silent defection. If Farinacci survived as the embodiment of squadrist, intransigent fascism, this was probably less because of Mussolini's reluctance to break with comrades of his early years (as Federzoni thought), but rather because he had become the rallying-point of a certain type of 'frondism' within the regime, a counter-balance to the 'frondism' of the most conservatively moderate fascist *gerarchi*.

Farinacci as party secretary (1925-6) attempted to 'fascistize' the state by bypassing normal administrative channels and legalizing even the abuses and improvisations of intransigent fascists as a means of asserting the authority of a purged and purified party over the state. His was only one of various, conflicting approaches towards the problem of transforming the party into a regime during the years 1925 to 1932, but particularly until 1929. In the following decade, from 1932, despite the rhetoric about the identification of the two, party and state assumed very separate identities, policies regulating their roles took divergent directions, until the party-regime was ultimately emptied of most meaningful contact with Italian society.

For Farinacci's successor as party secretary, Turati (1926-30), the role of the party remained central, even if strictly subordinate to the state. Within the regime the party had two functions: it was to form the seedbed for the new generation, which was to be educated in true fascist values, uncontaminated by the liberal or marxist beliefs of the current generation inherited by fascism. But to achieve this end, the party also needed to penetrate Italian society at the most intimate level, in capillary manner, winning support down to the village level by the creation of mass auxiliary structures, such as the fascist youth (Balilla) and the leisure organizations. Squadrism and spontaneous violence were stamped out, the corollary to Mussolini's confirmation of the authority of the state prefect over the fascist federal: 'Good-bye, my valiant comrade Cudgel; now the Law and the Prefects watch over and protect me!', read the bitter-sweet words of an intransigent fascist cartoon. But the methods of achieving this new role, by centralized discipline and purges, removed from the party precisely those with most idealism and enthusiasm, the fascists of the early years. Turati's successor, Giuriati (1930-1), might still conceive of the party as creating an active functional élite, free from corruption, the herald and leader of the new fascist generation. But the hierarchical centralization removed all vitality and dedication, leaving a disgruntled core of unemployed (and unemployable) ex-fascists, whose Saturday-night expressions of discontent were carefully monitored by the police. Under Starace (1931-9), the party became a bloated instrument of propaganda, formal membership of which was a legal or practical necessity.

The problem of the legitimation of the regime remained central to the discussions and legislation of the later 1920s.

Balbo was preoccupied about the dangers of leaving fascism without mediating forces between itself and the monarchy. For the regime's inability to abolish the monarchy and so ensure the total loyalty of the army (and indeed of some of the fascist leaders themselves) left a permanent threat — which finally proved reality — of a confrontation between the two. For Balbo, it was crucial not only to preserve the militia as a trustworthy military force, but to maintain the political prerogatives of parliament so as to avoid a further strengthening of the monarchy.

Far móre important, as a practical attempt to broaden support, was Edmondo Rossoni's development of the fascist syndicates. Given the destruction of working-class institutions, some means were needed to mediate the tensions and disputes arising out of the work-process on the shop floor, particularly given the widespread belief in the need to improve productivity, if not by technical innovation, at least by the so-called 'scientific organization' of labour. For Rossoni, exclusive representation of the working class by the fascist syndicates was only the first stage towards 'integral syndicalism', with employers as well as workers within the syndicates, subject to the superior interests of the 'productive state'. But the Palazzo Vidoni pact of 1925 marked a first defeat, through the power of the industrialists' organization, Confindustria, not only to conserve its independence, but to obtain the suppression of the workshop committees and hence the removal of 'union' representatives from the factory. Although an obligatory labour tribunal was created and significant control over filling job vacancies was given to the syndicates, Rossoni's concern to create a personal power base through the syndicates led to his downfall in 1928 with the breakup and soon the legal downgrading of his unified confederation.

The syndicates potentially offered the possibility of enlarging the base of the regime because of their mediating function in work-processes, which were changing, to the disadvantage of the workers, in these two decades. It was for this reason that Togliatti and communists working underground in Italy argued the importance of infiltrating the syndicates in the later 1930s. The syndical leadership, whether through conviction or to retain credibility, on occasion (as in 1925 and 1929) clamorously identified with the workers' demands and generally endeavoured to resolve industrial conflict, despite the renewed failure to obtain shopfloor representation in 1929. It can be argued that they obtained some support, limited strictly to their presence in the work-process. As the syndicates were subordinated and bureaucratized through party control and the corporative structure in the 1930s, the dichotomy between their industrial and political functions must have become more marked.

For Bottai, the creation of the new fascist state was to be achieved through corporativism. The very ambiguity of this instrument of class collaboration allowed a variety of interpretations. Initially (with the creation of a ministry in 1926) it was seen as regulating labour relations. But during the period of most intense discussions and legislation (between 1928 and 1934, especially at the much publicized 1932 congress of Ferrara), corporativism was assigned a variety of roles. For an anarcho-syndicalist like Lanzillo, it could even be regarded as the institutionalization of class syndicates, which were to take over the running of state economic activities. For the intellectuals Volpicelli and Spirito, the 'owner corporation' implied worker participation, while 'absolute corporativism' was a means of creating a new technically equipped ruling group. For Bottai, the corporations were successively organs of economic self-government (assisted by the mediation of the state) and the mechanism through which to impose state planning. But in practice the corporative structure, which was only created slowly and inconsistently through the 1930s, was sabotaged by the other ministries and big industry, generated bureaucracy rather than economic control, and was ignored as the practical instrument of state control.

Party, syndicates and corporativism were all included, but subordinated, within the ideology of the ex-nationalist Alfredo Rocco, who between 1926 and 1929 was responsible for the construction of an authoritarian regime in place of the old individualist liberal state. There can be little doubt that Rocco and his followers saw themselves as laying the basis for a new 'national' ruling class, not limited to the fascist party. At the cultural level, Gentile's project for the *Enciclopedia Italiana* similarly aimed at drawing together all intellectuals within the framework of a national encyclopaedia, above the factional divisions created by fascism.

Rocco's ideas were rigidly coherent. He, more than the philosopher Gentile, was the true ideologist of the regime. And the structure he tried to create differed in fundamental aspects from that of the nazis, because of its subordination of all elements — including the fascist party — to the state. The basis of this new integralist ideology was to be found in the German legal concept that individual liberties did not exist before the state, but that the state limited its own power in order to strengthen itself by conceding individual liberties.

The consequences which derived from this were clear. All private freedoms, whether of individuals or associations, were only acceptable if approved of by the state. Private property was to be protected in the social interest, as the proprietor was an organ of the state. Class conflict weakened the community, and the private settlement of industrial disputes by the parties concerned could no longer be permitted: hence the creation of an obligatory labour tribunal. At the same time, the existence of mass organizations could not be ignored or denied; but, logically, the corporations were to possess no autonomy, as the syndicalists wanted and even the industrialists supported, but were to be tightly controlled by the state. Analogously, the party was to be subordinated to, and integrated within, the state by its legal recognition as a public organ, exemplified supremely in the creation of the Grand Council of Fascism, and in the utilization of the party's various bodies, developed systematically in order to indoctrinate all branches of society. On the one hand, rule by decree and the virtual elimination of the legislature were justified on the grounds that only a strong executive could avoid weakening disputes and achieve true efficiency. On the other hand, the militia and the security laws were necessary in order to protect the state against internal subversion.

But at the same time this strong state was to be a modern state, accepting the developments of capitalism in both the economic and the social sphere. The tendency of capitalism towards monopolies was to be encouraged, because it increased productivity and so the strength of the state. Thus cartels were to be built up, while the new state was to shape the entire commonweal on the hierarchical model of capitalism. By the subordination of all the élites of modern society — industrial enterprises, trade unions, the party, the bureaucracy — under the authoritarian control of the state, no ruling classes could be formed outside the system. Finally, in this rigidly hierarchical society, mass support was to be ensured, on the one hand by high wages (along the lines of Henry Ford's philosophy), and on the other hand by the creation of 'direct' channels of communication between the masses and the leaders through the party.

Rocco's vision was certainly powerful, and together with Federzoni he succeeded in creating the basic structure of an authoritarian reactionary state. But for many reasons he succeeded only in part. His fascist state failed because of the resistance of forces both within and outside fascism and because of the incapacity of this self-contained national entity to resist the impact of outside forces, both political and economic, beyond its control. The Concordat of 1929 tore an irreparable rent in the fabric Rocco had so laboriously woven because of the concessions it made to the Church in educational matters and over the autonomy of Catholic Action from the authority of the state. The ideology of the Church was established alongside that of the monarchy, despite the contradiction between both and Rocco's fascist ideology. Industry remained more or less independent until the economic crisis, and the armed forces virtually autonomous until 1940.

It was the economic crisis, by destroying the identification of the regime-state with modernizing forces, that effectively defeated Rocco's attempt to integrate all social groups within the structures of a 'totalitarian' state. The support of non-fascist technocrats, whose faith in fascism as the instrument of rationalizing and modernizing change had held out the promise of an innovative future, turned into a prop to maintain a heavy-handed regime. In this sense, the much debated issue of the stabilization of the lira in 1927, when Mussolini imposed on the industrialists a far lower exchange rate ('quota 90') than they judged economically viable, can be seen as having contradictory effects: while it marked the assertion of the party-state over a powerful sectorial interest group and consolidated the support of that segment of the petty bourgeoisie dependent on fixed income, it also closed many paths to extending real and potential support by removing the crucial benefits of an expanding economy. The world economic crisis compounded the deflationary effects of 1927, seriously damaging the credibility of the regime's claims, not only in the eyes of the urban working class and agricultural day-labourers, but also in those of the small working man, the petty proprietor and tenant farmer, the shopkeeper and businessman. Only minute groups of intellectuals, mostly students, periodically revived discussion about fascism's dynamic future role, through corporativism in 1932, as a universal creed in the so-called 'fascist international' of 1934, through its spiritual message in the 'school of fascist mysticism' in 1938-40.

A fundamental consequence of this prolonged crisis was to separate the identity of state and party in the 1930s, each acquiring distinctive roles and policies. The economic depression reduced the vaunting ambitions of the PNF as vanguard and seedbed of the new society to more mundane functions as welfare and recreational agency. These auxiliary structures, above all the Opera Nazionale Dopolavoro, were expanded on a massive scale precisely in the crisis period until 1934. The organization of leisure time appeared to serve multiple functions: it acted as compensation for material hardships; it offered employment to the white-collared faithful; it encouraged collective participation, thus strengthening the image of solidarity, and stimulated local initiative, broadening the consensual base. As Togliatti noted at the time, *dopolavoro* played a central role in the regime's search for mass support. In some respects it was undoubtedly successful: sport, organized holidays and recreational activities, the deliberate fostering of popular culture, reviving local traditions, obtained widespread participation from factories to country towns. But *dopolavoro*'s recreational activities appeared more successful than its educational or social-assistance functions; while in the major factories, where *dopolavoro* structures were most strongly developed, the direct intervention of PNF officials was effectively resisted. Even the nature and limits of consent obtained through such agencies remains unclear: peasant family structures were likely to have remained as impermeable to the fascist message of sponsored village festivities as factory workers' sense of class to *dopolavoro* sports and subsidized holidays. Certainly the explicitly fascist youth organizations felt endangered by competition, when Catholic Action groups expanded after the Concordat — which was an underlying reason for the conflict between Church and state in 1931.

In contrast to its activity in the organization of leisure, the role of the party in economic policy was reduced by the crisis to marginal importance. The major new element — state intervention — occurred outside the framework of the corporative system, and arguably only became 'fascist' during the autarkic phase of the later 1930s, when foreign policy required control over the economy. The economic ministers and experts — De Stefani, Volpi di Misurata, Beneduce, Guarneri — were industrialists and bankers, *commis d'état* more than fascists. The Italian economy was too dependent on the international economy to permit a distinctive fascist 'third way' until the links with this international economy had been snapped by the closure of emigration, American capital loans and export markets. The regulation of credit and the creation of IMI and IRI were initially state responses to the crisis, although subsequently they could be used to increase state intervention in support of an aggressive foreign policy. Within this perspective fascism's ties with capitalism not surprisingly favoured the advanced monopolistic sectors: its productivist ideology combined with practical necessities in turning the regime towards encouragement of the technologically modern branches of industry and the capitalist landowners of the Po valley. Stockpiling, obligatory consortia to hold prices and construct new industrial plant can all be interpreted as merely accentuating, however sharply, pre-existing oligopolistic tendencies. In this sense, economic policy worked against the early anti-capitalist fascist ideology of the 'small man' and even against the consolidation of social stability of Rocco's state. That this policy should have led to a structural change in the economy, a 'mixed economy' with the state as industrial entrepreneur and banker, was due less to the fascist regime than to the world crisis. But it was then possible for the regime again to assert its primacy over economic policy in the final years, from the mid-1930s, when the independence of the big firms was increasingly enmeshed in the controls of the autarkic state. This final development was because of the intimate links between economic policy and foreign policy.

Fascist foreign policy offers the terrain where the identification or confusion of state and party within the regime operated in reverse order to that in other fields: the continuity with the pre-fascist diplomacy of the Italian state was most marked in the 1920s, precisely in the years of fascism's most committed efforts to create an innovative regime; whereas aspects of the ideology of the regime effectively influenced this foreign policy from the mid-1930s, when the party-regime had most visibly failed.

There has been much discussion about the character of fascist imperialism. Pre-fascist precedents can easily be found for the policy of balancing between opposing powers, for the insistence on the Mediterranean as Italy's rightful sphere of influence, for the economic penetration of the Balkan-Danubian area and the military claims in Africa, for the 'revisionism' over the peace treaties. Mussolini's personal responsibility, his unsophisticatedly old-fashioned view of a European domination of a colonial world, his miscalculations over the changes in Europe, are only too evident. But in style and practice, in motivation and consequences, Italian foreign policy, already from 1926-7 but supremely from 1934, was clearly marked and increasingly conditioned by fascist ideology. The aggressive social-Darwinist concept of international relations, the policy of demographic growth employed both as proof of Italy's strength and as justification for her search for living space, the combination of negotiation and intimidation, the insistence on the primacy of the regime over economic reality, were all intimately connected to the ideology of fascism, from its early years. But the Abyssinian invasion can also be viewed as partially successful compensation for fascism's internal failure to win the stability of consensus: for the rhetoric of fascism's 'historic mission' effectively acted as an ideological drumroll to enlist volunteers, particularly from the poorest and most densely populated regions in southern Italy. Intervention in Spain, the growing alignment with nazi Germany, even the racialist policy, were consequences of Mussolini's apparent belief in his own assertions of the decline of the over-mature western democracies and the future of the young totalitarian regimes.

By these final years — possibly from his withdrawal to Palazzo Venezia in 1929, certainly from the much vaunted *decennale* of 1932 — Mussolini had become an increasingly remote dictator, dominated by an uncontrolled and intermittent exercise of personal power. His preoccupation with the emergence of potential rivals, as much as the concentration of power (and ministries) within his own hands, weakened the regime. But the failure of the party as regime cannot be imputed simply to Mussolini. It was embedded within the contradictions of the party-regime itself.

Indoctrination through education and propaganda reached new levels in the 1930s, as fascism strove to identify Italian society with itself. But they were constantly and increasingly belied by the growing isolation of the regime. Education and propaganda had never been ignored by fascism. But the regime was late in developing systematic policies. Gentile's 1923 reform of schools was only superficially fascist; propaganda was limited to press censorship and crude eulogies about the achievements of the Duce and his regime. Between 1933 and 1936, influenced by the nazi example, propaganda in fascist Italy became a major activity of the regime under Ciano, with the attempt to control all cultural activities, from the press and theatre to tourism and the new instruments of cinema and radio. Rhetoric and ceremonies, couched in religious and military terms, pursued the Italian citizen from dawn to dusk, with their incessant repetition of fascism's revival of Roman glories and Mussolini's omniscience. The cult of youth was bureaucratically transformed by Starace into the succession of fascist organizations through which children were expected to pass, according to sex-role, from infancy to adulthood. School texts, especially history books, were filled with propaganda. Hierarchy and obedience became the dominant keynotes.

The wheels of these propaganda efforts rotated to little effect, except to provide employment for the faithful. Catholic orthodoxy, spearheaded by the aggressive and ubiquitous Jesuit, father Gemelli, head of the Catholic university of Milan, filled the void left by the regime, in an attempted *reconquista* of Italian society by the Church. Nazi ideology, apparently so much more efficient and successful, ultimately convinced Mussolini to introduce his own anti-semitic policy, without pressure from Hitler.

Within this dictatorship, power was far more fluid than in nazi Germany. No *Führerprinzip* existed in Italy, in the sense of vesting the second-rank leaders with powers analogous, albeit subordinate, to those of the Führer himself. The relative influence and power of the *gerarchi* depended on their relationship to a notoriously suspicious Duce. The device of avoiding the nomination of a successor by the Gran Consiglio served to underline Mussolini's pre-eminence. Loyalty flowed in a single direction, upwards from the *gerarchi* to the Duce, who for his part had no scruples about abandoning even his most faithful followers, such as De Bono. A consequence of this inability of the *gerarchi* to consolidate their power (in contrast to the *Gauleiter*) was that, through their public behaviour and private life-style, the *gerarchi* became symbolic of the gap between the façade and the reality of fascist Italy, between the verbal rhetoric of heroism and grandeur and the drab monotony and conformism of daily life. Their individual attitudes and aspirations, even their attempts to influence policy, only rarely had a direct impact on Italian society comparable to that of the nazi *Gauleiter*. They stood apart from the people, against a backcloth of rhetorical romanity, the brokers of clientelistic favours in the inflated bureaucratic undergrowth of a regime permeated by corruption. *Gerarchi* as different as De Bono, Farinacci and Bottai could voice their disquiet about the direction fascism had taken. But the responsibility lay as much with them as with the Duce. They had become totally isolated from the life of the Italian people, intriguing against each other at the court of their emperor. By the final years, the air of unreality became ever more pronounced. With the possible exception of Bottai, they had drunk so deeply of their own rhetoric that they seemed unaware that they were acting in a vacuum. The final episode of 25 July 1943, when the Grand Council voted to depose Mussolini, is symbolically appropriate, as well as historically significant, in that the *gerarchi* — ultimately conscious of their own impotence, of their inability to assert an independent role — were only capable of engaging in a palace plot, as court lackeys turning against their leader. The *gerarchi* still seemed unaware of their own total failure, through the destruction of their fascist base and the bankruptcy of the entire regime.

4

GERMANY

◆

A. J. Nicholls

The belief that there is something inherently autocratic, aggressive and militaristic in the German character is one which dies hard and has certainly not died yet. Historical myths built up about the German nation in one world war were reinforced by the experience of a second. Our understanding of the Nazi Party has suffered as a result.

The tendency to over-stress the significance of real or imaginary national characteristics has been aided by the fact that the nazis themselves wished to emphasize these for their own benefit. In this as in other matters, their propaganda has been picked up and exploited by Germany's critics. The interpretations of Germany's past by friends and foes of the Third Reich exhibit remarkable similarities. Both wish to demonstrate that Germany's national history contained the seeds of Hitlerism and that great names in German philosophy, religion and culture were forerunners of the nazi era.

Needless to say, this kind of interpretation — which sees the Third Reich as a logical culmination of Germany's national development — has found many critics. Professor Gerhard Ritter, for example, pointed out that on the continent of Europe between the world wars dictatorship was the rule rather than the exception and that Germany was actually the last state where an important dictatorship was established. 'The Germans themselves', he claimed, 'were more surprised than anyone else by the rapid rise of the

National Socialist Party to a position in which overall power in the state was at its disposal.' [1] Fascism was to be seen as a European rather than a German phenomenon — the product of tendencies common to many countries in which there were urban populations bereft of a ruling class and deprived of the Christian religion. Totalitarian tyranny grew, he wrote, 'where the great socially disorganized, intellectually uniform masses in the modern city awaken to political consciousness, and where the former public authorities with their roots in the dim past (monarchy or parliamentary government) are destroyed or discredited'. [2] This association of national socialism with the newly awakened and the politically uneducated has a good deal to recommend it, but it can lead to misunderstanding. It might be taken to imply that nazism is the product of urbanization and democracy — a belief which has some validity in the purely chronological sense, but which masks the true nature of Hitler's appeal and of the social groups from which he mainly drew his support. In particular it seems to link his party with Soviet communism, and indeed the apparent similarity of these 'totalitarian' movements has sometimes been remarked upon. Yet it would be wrong to seek the explanation for Hitler's success in a proletarian mass eager for social revolution. There was a great deal that was revolutionary about national socialism from a political viewpoint, and its leaders were certainly unknown and politically inexperienced men. But their appeal was not mainly directed at the lowest stratum of society and their most important objectives were not socially revolutionary.

If one looks at the programme of the National Socialist Party, adopted in February 1920 and declared immutable by Hitler six years later, one sees at once that this is the policy of a political group aiming at national self-assertion rather than social revolution. The fact that the nazis called themselves a 'socialist' workers' party has obscured the special meaning given to socialism by Hitler's supporters. This confusion was increased by the nazi tendency to talk of a 'National Revolution' with which they would sweep away the aberrations of the Weimar republic. Their revolution was to be very different from that envisaged by communists or even social democrats. What Hitler understood by socialism was perhaps best explained by his reported exclamation: 'Why need we trouble to socialize banks and factories? We socialize human beings.' The national socialist worker wanted a strong German nation within which he should have an honoured, but subordinate, place. This was the sense in which Anton Drexler first founded his German Workers' Party. It was the defeatism of his working-class colleagues in a Munich railway works which had spurred Drexler into action, not their inferior position within Germany's social structure.

This attitude towards the workers did not change, even after Hitler had taken the party in hand and given it mass appeal. The workers themselves might be flattered by the nazi claims that only they and not the ageing bourgeoisie were capable of asserting Germany's position in the world; they might have their social ambitions stimulated by Goebbels' insistence that the term proletariat was a degrading Jewish invention, and that in national socialist Germany they would receive the recognition due to them as a creative work-force, but status promotion of this kind did not imply a major economic reorganization for the benefit of the indus-trial working class.

In fact, the 25-point nazi programme was quite clear in its references to social policy. Point 16 demanded the creation of a healthy middle class and its protection by the state. The nature of this middle class was made evident by a reference to the immediate communalization of department stores and their rental at low rates to small businessmen. By the same token, point 13 required that all trusts and large-scale com-panies should be nationalized. The purpose here was not to place the means of production in the hands of the working class, but to uphold the principle that the independent businessman, directing his own factory or commercial under-taking, should be preferred to the anonymous corporation, whose shareholders had no function in the direction of the business. Basic to these superficially socialist principles was the belief that a distinction could be drawn between para-sitic capital — the capital of the broker and the stock-exchange dealer — and so-called creative capital invested and administered by the individual farmer or works-proprietor for the benefit of his own concern. This was the principle enun-

ciated by the party's so-called economic expert, Gottfried
Feder. He described it as destroying the thraldom of interest.
It would liberate Germany's constructive middle-class
element from the chains of a legal and financial system
beneficial only to international financiers and Jews. Feder
himself, whose sincerity is not open to doubt, vehemently
denied any intention of interfering with the savings or investments of Germany's struggling middle class. The declared
purpose of nazi economic policy was to defend the property
of the small businessman, the shopkeeper, the farmer and the
craftsman against marxist expropriation on the one hand and
subjection to parasitic capitalists on the other.

This is not to say that there were not many in the national
socialist movement who harboured bitter resentments against
Germany's wealthier classes, and others who genuinely hoped
that nazi domination would lead to a complete social change.
But the resentments found other, more easily destructible
targets, and the social reformers saw their hopes dashed in
practice. The major social changes which have occurred in
twentieth-century Germany were caused not so much by the
Third Reich as by the war which it began and the defeat
which ensued.

The fact was that the whole concept of class was regarded
by the nazis as a Jewish invention designed to set Germans
against one another. The real purpose of the movement was
to evade social friction by denying the validity of class differences and channelling social energy into national expansion.
Most of the national socialist programme was concerned with
this.

First of all came the demand for a greater Germany whose
frontiers should include all German-speaking people. Then
came claims for equality with other powers, and the acquisition of land for food supplies and settlement areas for
excess population. Steps were to be taken to preserve the
racial purity of the German population. Only those of
German blood were to count themselves citizens of the
German state and aliens were to be either expelled or treated
as underprivileged persons. Alien influences were also to be
eliminated from the press, a people's army was to be set up,
public health safeguarded, and religious freedom protected so

long as it did not endanger the interests of the state or the
German race. There was to be a strong central government.
This was not a programme which seemed to have much
relevance to a twentieth-century industrial society. Its most
suitable testing ground might have been the state of Sparta.

The extent to which nationalism of the most extreme and
even biological kind dominated the programme is in contrast
to the official policy of the Fascist Party in Italy, whose
leader had, after all, been a celebrated socialist. How was it
that Hitler's party came to adopt this programme, and how
far did it respond to genuine impulses within Germany in
1920?

There is no easy answer to this question and even an
approximation must contain enormous over-simplifications.
But it is perhaps no coincidence that we can group the
answers under two headings: the first national, the second
social. The national aspect goes back to 1866, when the
Prussian victory over Austria ensured that German unification would be under the aegis of Prussia and would exclude
the German-speaking lands of the Habsburg empire. This
meant that the most ambitious plans of German nationalists
were thwarted. Bismarck's alliances with Vienna – perpetu-
ated by his successors – seemed to deny any hope that all
Germans might one day enjoy a common frontier. In
addition there was a certain feeling of disillusionment abroad
in Germany in the decades before the Great War. Unification
had not brought quite the golden era some enthusiasts had
expected. Romantic urges to purify or perfect the German
nation manifested themselves widely, especially among
'middle-class youth'.

Unification had brought social change with it – or had at
least accelerated changes already in progress. With the introduction of freer trade and careers open to talent many
industrious but inflexible individuals were left behind in the
race for prosperity. Craftsmen found their businesses
threatened by factory production. Shopkeepers and
merchants were faced with large-scale competitors – department stores and the like – which introduced a new element
in their own struggle for profits. Capitalist techniques in
agriculture meant that many small farmers could not face

the competition of more efficient food producers in their own country, while free trade cut food prices by bringing in cheap grain from abroad. There was nothing very unusual in these developments — they were taking place all over western and central Europe — but it does seem that Germany possessed elements capable of reacting more powerfully against the liberal wave than was the case in either Britain or France. For one thing, liberalism had not conquered political power in Germany, despite the empire's apparently advanced constitution. The old ruling groups — the nobility, the land-owners, the higher civil service and the army — had never relinquished their control over the political executive.

When, in the 1880s, the economic boom which followed Germany's unification fell away into a depression, when European agriculture began to face one of the most serious crises in its history, and when political influence was taken from liberal groups and put in the hands of more conservative forces, the opposition to liberal ideas became more pronounced. Many of the beliefs which characterized national socialism were to enter the political vocabulary of Germany and other parts of central Europe in the last two decades of the nineteenth century.

These might be roughly summed up as follows. At the root of the liberal view of society lies the belief that social groups are the sum of a number of individuals each of whom shares the same basic rights as a human being. This atomistic view was deeply resented by those who pictured the community as an organic institution, in which status and its accompanying duties were pre-ordained by God and nature. On a slightly less exalted plane, those who could make a success out of individual rights and freedoms were opposed by others who feared for their security in a genuinely free society. One symptom of this was the widespread hostility towards Roman law to be found among conservative and nationalist groups towards the end of the nineteenth century. Roman law was seen as a foreign importation beneficial only to the rich man and his paid lackey — the lawyer. Traditional or common law — rooted in custom — was the only real safe-guard for honest men. It comes as no surprise to notice that point 19 of the national socialist programme was the abolition of Roman law — which 'served a materialist world order' — and its replacement by 'Germanic law'.

Similarly, constitutions and parliamentary government, and particularly parliamentary parties, were regarded with suspicion or contempt. These were artificial, corrupt constructions, designed to enable clever but unscrupulous individuals to better themselves at the expense of the community. However, the aim was not the destruction of freedom, but the creation of a truly German freedom which would somehow be purer than that of the west.

Fundamental to these views were three major propositions; firstly, that political equality was a bad, unnatural thing, and that man should be content to obey those set apart by nature to rule him; secondly, that urban life was less valuable to a nation than rural life; and thirdly, that the backbone of the nation was to be found in what was called the *Mittelstand*, loosely translated as the middle class, but signifying a very different group from Marx's class of capitalists and entrepreneurs. In the mouths of German nationalists, *Mittelstand* was supposed to mean that hard-working, creative stratum of the community set above the unskilled mob at the bottom and more modest than the parasitic aristocrats at the top of the social scale. These were the farmers, the businessmen, the craftsmen, the officials. The ideas I have been describing amounted to a rejection of the enlightenment of the eighteenth century on the political plane and the industrialization of the nineteenth century on the economic plane.

This did not mean that their proponents believed that they were backward-looking. On the contrary, they were able to pervert some of the scientific developments of the nineteenth century to support their own political beliefs. The Darwinian concept of survival of the fittest was used to give the old arguments against natural equality a new vigour. Racial theories which seemed to be scientific could justify intolerance towards foreigners. Above all, the old Christian suspicion of Jewry was reinforced by this pseudo-scientific approach.

Hostility to urban life and to Jews was associated with a romantic yearning for a mythical past, in which heroic and racially pure Germans lived together without class bitterness or exploitation in what was described as a *Volksgemeinschaft* or folk association. *Völkisch* ideology as it developed in the decades before the first world war was a mixture of mythical history — in which the German race was extolled as the foundation of true culture and civilization — and mythical science — in which biological theories about the survival of the fittest were exploited to demonstrate that the German race was biologically superior to others. This did not exclude a mystical element in *völkisch* thought, and, indeed, the use of reason and experimental method to arrive at truth was scorned as unnatural or even un-German. Many of the sects which propagated such views were wild and woolly in the extreme. Sun-worshippers, nudists and disciples of Wotan probably did not have much impact on German society as a whole. They were the lunatic fringe of an already irrational movement. But *völkisch* ideas did penetrate a wide section of Germany's middle class in the Wilhelmine period. Novels, *völkisch*-minded schoolmasters, and a youth movement in which *völkisch* attitudes — and particularly anti-semitism — were not uncommon, helped to make such concepts familiar to romantically inclined German youth. On the political plane a number of right-wing organizations made some of the general assumptions upon which *völkisch* ideology was based seem respectable to people who would have rejected the cruder anti-semitic political parties which made their appearance in Germany during the 1880s. For example, one organization which attracted many respectable Germans was the Pan-German League. Originally established in 1890 to protest against the surrender of German claims over Zanzibar to the British, it had as its purpose 'the animation of a German-national state of mind, in particular the awakening and cultivation of the awareness of the racial and cultural solidarity of all German peoples'. Although the pan-Germans were not officially anti-semitic, many of their leaders accepted anti-semitic views. By the same token most of the anti-semitic and *völkisch* groups accepted the extreme nationalism current among the pan-Germans. In 1914 it seemed that these political elements, despite their social influence, were waging a losing battle against liberalism and social democracy. Before the outbreak of war they themselves were on the defensive against an expanding and politically organized working class, and a confident belief that parliamentary power would be expanded in Germany to liberalize the empire politically as well as economically.

The right radical element in Germany regarded the outbreak of the first world war as a blessing and a challenge. It created an atmosphere of communal effort overcoming class divisions, and focused national energies on winning glory for the Reich. At the same time it required unwavering resolution from the German people. When reformist elements began to question the policy of the Imperial Government, and to demand political changes which would give the Reich parliament more power, they encountered furious hostility on the right. A lot of public servants and army officers came to associate liberalism in politics with defeatism and even with treachery. Many soldiers who had first begun to think politically as a result of their experiences in the war came to agree with this judgement. Hitler later boasted that the men who died for Germany did so with *Deutschland, Deutschland über Alles* on their lips and not 'universal and secret suffrage'. [3] Like most of his utterances this was a gross oversimplification; many front soldiers were social democrats or progressives and many later welcomed the revolution. But Professor Ernest Nolte is surely right when he refers to the support Hitler was able to find among the politically virgin elements in Germany who were provoked into political activity for the first time by the war and its aftermath.

With German defeat in the war the pessimistic predictions of the anti-semites and pan-Germans about Germany's future if total victory was not attained apparently came true. Germany was completely liberalized, with an undeniably democratic constitution and a government coalition of parties representing the old left-wing reformist opposition in the Wilhelmine empire. At the same time Germany was humbled by her enemies and threatened with economic chaos and political disorder at home. Looked at from the right, the strongest social force in her republic seemed to be a working class addicted to an internationalist marxist ideology. When national shame and political defeat were compounded by financial losses of a truly staggering character — such as those

suffered by many Germans as the result of the disastrous inflation in the early 1920s — it is not surprising that a lot of
people were willing to accept an over-simplified explanation
of Germany's problems. It should also be pointed out that,
whereas under the empire of Wilhelm II most of the nationalist critics of the German government had loudly proclaimed
their loyalty to the dynasty and the state, they felt no such
need to bend the knee before the new republic. Indeed true
patriotism involved complete rejection of all that German
democracy stood for.

This is not to say that most German judges, professors,
teachers, officers, farmers and civil servants became national
socialists or anti-semites with the collapse of the German
empire. But many such people did sincerely doubt whether
the Weimar republic was compatible with German greatness,
and as that republic developed they seemed to see their
suspicions confirmed.

In the early years of the Weimar republic there was
violence on Germany's eastern frontier and civil disturbance
at home. This contributed to the formation of militarized
organizations — most of which had originally been supported
by the state to provide armed forces at a time when the army
was in disintegration. These volunteer formations were overwhelmingly nationalist and anti-republican in character, and
their members, who were often ex-servicemen disillusioned
with the prospect of a return to civilian life, blamed the
republic for Germany's defeat in the war. Politics in Germany
took on a pseudo-military character in that nationalist
elements were fond of parades, marches, uniforms and the
like. Violence was not uncommon. But after the failure of
the Kapp *putsch* in March 1920 the volunteer formations did
not usurp the function of the state. They never made themselves masters of towns or provinces. Instead they looked to
the army or state authorities for approval and even financial
support.

At the same time a number of extreme nationalist and
specifically *völkisch* parties established themselves in various
parts of Germany. Some, like the German Socialist Party,
made a direct appeal to the working classes. Anton Drexler's
German Workers' Party in Munich fitted this category,

although it received discreet support from a socially superior group — the mysterious *Thule Gesellschaft*, a racialist order established in Munich during the war.

Drexler's party did not attract much attention and precious few workers made their way to it. What changed its fortunes was the Munich Soviet Republic in April 1919. The shock which this communist-led enterprise administered to the middle classes of that and other Bavarian cities was severe. Officials and army leaders made up their minds that nothing like it should ever happen again, and they deliberately encouraged political movements which seemed likely to combat bolshevism. As is well known, one of the army's political education lecturers was Adolf Hitler, and as an agent for the Bavarian military he was sent to investigate the German Workers' Party. Hitler's arrival ensured that this insignificant group would not only survive, but grow and prosper.

Little mention has so far been made of Hitler because it was necessary to stress the extent to which national socialist ideas and a *völkisch* state of mind existed in Germany before him. In the realm of general theory Hitler was not very important for the development of German fascism, although it has been claimed that he produced a more compelling amalgam of *völkisch* ideas than any previously available.

When he first joined the Nazi Party — it took its name and programme in 1920 — Hitler had no official position. He was simply a valuable speaker and a link with the Bavarian Army, a man who had brought with him a number of recruits from military circles. Hitler made himself indispensable to the party by exploiting these two personal advantages. Like all such bodies the party was short of money and members; Hitler improved its fortunes by organizing more and better publicized meetings, and by rousing the participants in such meetings with his own oratory. At the same time his connection with the army brought him financial support — some of which, for example, was used to buy the party paper, the *Völkische Beobachter* — and the benevolent neutrality of the police authorities even when his followers were rowdy or violent.

Hitler's technique as a speaker was to play upon antagonisms and fears already present in his audience, to simplify these and take them to their utmost extremity. He did not excel in argument, and very soon strong-arm men at his meetings made any discussion impossible. He pictured the German nation as surrounded by mortal enemies, the victor powers in the war, the bolsheviks and the Jews. He always associated social democracy of any kind with bolshevism under the general umbrella of marxism — a habit which found a ready echo in Bavaria, where the mild coalition government in Berlin was seen by many as an agent of red revolution. By organizing his own paramilitary formation — the SA — Hitler conformed to the increasing militarization of the extreme nationalists in Bavaria at this time, and also made his movement more attractive to frustrated ex-army men. The SA paraded in style, carrying banners and wearing swastika arm-bands. But they never approached the achievements of the Italian fascist squads in preparing the ground for Hitler's march to power. Opposition parties on the left might find themselves involved in an occasional street battle with the SA, but on the whole they had more to fear from the Bavarian government. Even later on in 1932, when the SA had 400,000 members, it was used mainly to overawe, to impress and to frighten the public, and as a useful bargaining lever in political deals. Only after Hitler had come to power did provincial Germany feel the real might of the SA, and even then its reign of violence was cut short within eighteen months.

On the organizational level Hitler established himself as a dictator within his party, and was able to maintain this position even when the party had been eclipsed after the abortive Beer Hall coup in November 1923. This was a very important fact, because, although the *völkisch* opposition to the Weimar republic was disunited, the Nazi Party itself was to be the means to final victory. Without this party base Hitler could not have attained power. Despite their military trappings and their denial of any relationship to the corrupt political parties of the Weimar republic, the nazis were organized as a political party, with membership dues, meetings and a party press. Hitler laboured to build up this party's strength on the ground in Munich and its environs, and here he gained an advantage over all other *völkisch* rivals. They were mostly generals without armies, seeking to create an umbrella movement to cover the whole of the German-speaking continent. Hitler avoided this mistake. His party could boast six thousand members in 1921, and he resisted attempts to subordinate it to other groups. When Drexler and some committee members tried to oppose this policy, Hitler faced them with an ultimatum and was accorded dictatorial powers. The party could not afford to let him go. The movement soon became the most powerful *völkisch* political organization in southern Germany. Many of the men Hitler recruited at that stage were to lead the party until its final collapse in 1945.

Dictatorial organization — and deliberate worship of the *Führerprinzip* — became a feature of the nazi movement. Originally this was not true of the party, some of whose members, such as Rosenberg, spoke of traditional German democracy — by which they referred to tribal elections in a mythical past and not to the type of electoral activity represented by modern liberalism. But within the framework of German nationalist movements as a whole there had always been a tendency to equate obedience to a leader and discipline with German — and therefore desirable — attitudes of mind.　·

This dictatorial power was exercised in a personal way and did not necessarily involve ideological uniformity along the lines made familiar among communists in the Third International. So long as Hitler was sure of the personal loyalty of a local party organizer he was content. If differences over policy threatened to weaken the unity of the party Hitler would often proceed by inserting rival groups to compete against possible dissidents, as he did in the case of the Strasser brothers who, for a long time, ran their own publishing house in Berlin. They were finally undermined by the activities of Goebbels — Hitler's protégé. This system of controlled autonomy and fostered rivalry persisted in nazi practice into the Third Reich.

One other characteristic emerged from the early years of the Nazi Party, and that was the predominantly middle-class nature of its appeal. Despite the word 'workers' in the title its membership never displayed an overwhelmingly working-class character and the percentage of workers among its leading functionaries was small. Its prosperity depended on support from decidedly non-proletarian sources — including respectable families like the Bechsteins, White Russian émigrés, and even some wealthy sympathizers in foreign countries. In disputes on policy which involved class conflict Hitler usually steered his party away from proletarian paths. In 1922 he refused to let his followers participate in a widely supported Munich rail strike. He rejected support for a campaign to expropriate the property of German royal houses. He prevented more openly socialistic elements in the north German sections of his party from changing the party's programme in a sense more frightening to capitalist elements in society. He never missed an opportunity to impress upon the business community the respect his party had for Germany's captains of industry, and when he came to power he made no attempt to remove these men from their role as the backbone of Germany's economic system.

Hitler was never, of course, the tool of heavy industry or of any other capitalist group. Among the seventeen million people who voted for him in 1933 there were many in the working class. But the backbone of his support was the provincial *Mittelstand* in Protestant Germany.

In 1930 came the breakthrough for the Nazi Party. It received nearly six and a half million votes and 107 seats in the German parliament. Two years later this figure had risen to 13.7 million, a total never approached by any other political party in the history of the republic. Hitler himself never regarded the parliamentary activities of his party as anything but a means of exerting pressure on the republican system so that it might eventually be smashed. He did not become a member of the Reichstag until March 1933, by which time he was already Reich Chancellor.

These were the slump years and there is no doubt that the economic depression was an immediate cause of the crisis which undermined German democracy. But mass unemployment alone did not lead to the victory of nazism. Generally speaking, the unemployed tended to stay loyal to their marxist party allegiance — many of them apparently leaving the ranks of the SPD (German Socialist Party) for the more radical Communist Party. What the crisis did was to renew the feelings of fear and antipathy latent among wide circles of the German population since the beginning of the republic. It also brought with it severe economic problems for the middle class — bankruptcy for farmers and businessmen, fear of worklessness for skilled workers and clerical staff who were usually immune to such threats, restricted opportunities and prospects for professional people.

The Nazi Party was in a unique position to exploit this situation. For years it had been harping on the evils of the Weimar republic. It had never been compromised by collaboration with the regime. Its leaders were new men not obviously representative of any class or economic interest: its appeal was classless. Above all it — like the German Communist Party — was a party of youth. Its leaders were young men, most of whom had fought — or even been too young to fight — in the war. It is sometimes suggested that the nazi voter was not conscious of any material reason to vote for the National Socialist Party, but that he was overwhelmed by a dazzling system of propaganda. This is quite untrue. Nazi propaganda was only effective among those already receptive to its message. The printed word, for example, was never handled well by the nazis. *Mein Kampf* — Hitler's political testament — was a symbol of loyalty rather than a genuine source of instruction to those who bought it. As for the party press, its journalism was of very low standard and its circulation derisory. It has been estimated that in 1932 the nazis had more party members than people buying their newspapers. The most damaging attacks on the Weimar republic came from other sections of the right-wing bourgeois press — the most obvious example being the Hugenberg concern.

Once a general disenchantment with German parliamentary democracy had established itself the nazis were able to exploit the fact that they were the most persistent, reckless and flamboyant precursors of a new order. They also had the advantage that they did not promise any steps in Germany which might really frighten any major sector of the population. Only the Jews, social democrats and communists had anything to fear from a nazi victory. The more genuinely revolutionary aspects of nazi policy, for example their contempt for legal processes and their hostility to the Christian religion, were not clear to most voters. The party could thus appeal to those who wanted to see a stronger, authoritarian state, and those who wished to see a transformation in German life which might offer them something better than the austerities and uncertainties of that critical era.

For these people the party's propaganda machine was well designed to impress: parades, mass meetings lit by searchlights and torches, speeches at which applause was carefully regulated and opposition absolutely forbidden, posters screaming hostility to Germany's enemies abroad who were bleeding her to death and her enemies at home who were betraying the nation for their own personal gain. Above all, literally as well as metaphorically, there was Adolf Hitler, flying from city to city in Germany with electoral energy that none of his opponents could match. The nazis, whatever may be said against them, did possess more dynamic activists — and more of them — than any other party.

Hitler never received a majority of the votes at a general election. He was called to power as the result of a presidential decision. It is, however, fair to point out that as leader of the largest German party he had some right to demand that power should be entrusted to him.

Once he had achieved office he soon demonstrated that the spirit, and in some cases even the letter, of a parliamentary constitution had little significance for him.

It has often been remarked upon that the doctrine of national socialism as set out by the party's theorists did not coincide with the administrative practice of the Third Reich. In the social sphere the reverse of what the nazis promised sometimes seemed to be happening. For example, the nazis claimed to favour rural life as against urbanization. They required more land for the settlement of German farmers. They were supposedly supporters of an independent peasantry, and in the breakthrough of 1930 many of their early successes came in rural areas such as Schleswig-Holstein where small farmers were faced with bankruptcy. Yet in the

Third Reich the drift from the country to the town increased rather than diminished. Within three years the public-works programme, with its emphasis on military expenditure, created a serious and quite unexpected shortage of labour, especially skilled labour. Production costs for farmers rose faster than the prices of their produce. As for the settlement of new peasant communities, the Weimar republic did more to settle townsmen on the land than the Third Reich.

Then again the independent businessman and craftsman, for whom nazi propaganda expressed concern, was by the nature of things less able to profit by the large-scale contracts offered by the government in its public-works programme than the big business enterprises for whom nazi ideologists evidently had less sympathy. The expansion and concentration of great industrial enterprises was not checked by the advent of fascism in Germany; on the contrary, the pressure of the government's economic programme hastened this development.

Even the status of women, and it was a *völkisch* maxim that their place was in the home, could not be entirely safeguarded by the new regime. At first it was easy to alleviate unemployment by removing women from the labour market, but such idealism was less easy to sustain when an acute labour shortage developed, and when conscription compounded other demands on the male labour force.

It also became clear that many of the figures most closely associated with ideology in the party were not going to make a great impact on their country's political life. Gottfried Feder, the economic expert, was given a state secretaryship in the Ministry of Economics but was rapidly ejected from this position by a completely orthodox, if ingenious, banker-economist, Dr Hjalmar Schacht. He ended his career as a professor of economics in the Berlin Technical University. Alfred Rosenberg, the party's leading specialist on racial questions and metaphysics, was not able to impose a new Germanic religion on the nation. For many years his foreign policy section of the Nazi Party did not seem to exercise much influence, and when in the war he was appointed Minister for the Occupied Eastern Territories, he was unable to compete with the authority of Himmler's SS in the

framing of policy towards subject populations. Another
theorist, this time in the field of law, Hans Frank, was never
able to persuade Hitler to draw up a new legal code to fulfil
the party's promise to support German common law. Hitler
had no taste for laws of any kind; they might be used to
restrict his power. Frank, who had defended Hitler at his
trial in Munich in 1924, was not made Minister of Justice
as he might have expected. This post was held until 1942
by Gürtner, a member of the German National People's
Party.

Coupled with this apparent disregard for dogma in practice
was the evident disinterest shown by many of the leaders in
doctrinal subjects. Hitler himself is reported to have told
Hermann Rauschning that the Nazi Party's social programme
was a 'great landscape painted on the background of our
stage'. It was for the masses. 'It points the direction of some
of our endeavours, neither more nor less. It is like the dogma
of the Church.' This latter comment was scarcely reassuring,
since Hitler only admired organized religion for its techniques
of mass manipulation; never for its Christian message.

Yet when all these points have been taken into account it
does not seem reasonable to ignore the extent to which the
nazis did achieve the ideological goals which they had set
themselves during their thirteen years in opposition. The first
part of their programme, the union of all Germans and the
equality of Germany with other powers, was virtually a
reality by the summer of 1939. Certainly the Nazi Party had
gone farther towards realizing pan-German dreams than any
other form of German leadership in modern times. The
German army had been reorganized and vastly expanded. The
German population was protected from the so-called Jewish
danger by the Nuremberg laws, and Germans of Jewish racial
origin were being treated as inferior citizens.

As for social policy, there had been setbacks, but there had
been attempts to realize the nazi programme, and there had
been successes too. A number of measures taken at the beginning of the nazi era were designed to strengthen the small
businessman and farmer against big business competitors.
Restrictions and taxes were imposed on department stores,
the training and qualification of skilled artisans were made

more rigorous, and early public-works schemes were designed mainly to benefit smaller contractors, though as the economy developed and rearmament became a more pressing question so the advantages of large industrial enterprises became more obvious. As for farmers, they were organized into a grandiose sounding, nationally directed agrarian estate — the *Nährstand*, or community of food producers. Small farmers received a moratorium on rural debts and a new inheritance law which secured their lands in their own family. Food prices were held up by restricting imports, and although the real problems of farmers — irrational land distribution and uneconomical size of holdings, lack of capital and lack of technical education on the land — were scarcely touched at all, the status and security which many farmers felt were lacking under the Weimar republic seemed to have been restored under the Third Reich.

Big business certainly profited more from nazi economic programmes than did the farmers or the small retailers or craftsmen. But the wealth reaped from rearmament contracts was paid for by the need to acquiesce in interference by the government in the fields of investment, overseas trade and finally labour policy. Big business prospered, but its real independence had been far greater under the Weimar republic which many of its leaders had purported to despise.

Even the industrial working class, whose political organizations were very quickly crushed by the nazis and whose political leaders had been liquidated, imprisoned or driven abroad, could feel in 1939 that the nazi promises about a *Volksgemeinschaft* had not been entirely without foundation. The national socialist state was not their state, but it took a lot more notice of them than ever the old German empire had done. To be a worker was no longer to be a member of a dangerous, alienated group, creating his own sense of community within the Social Democratic or Communist Party. It was to be a member of the Labour Front, to be flattered in the press, to be offered mass jollity in the form of *Kampf durch Freude* and government-sponsored benevolence on the part of employers competing for nazi industrial honours as leaders of the *Volksgemeinschaft*. Above all, there was work, even if real wages were low. The Third Reich was not a workers' state, but it at least gave higher status to working men than the empire of Wilhelm II had done.

Of course the achievements of the Third Reich had been gained at terrible cost. On the domestic front this meant a concentration of power in the hands of the nazi leadership. This is connected in the public mind with the well-known expression *Gleichschaltung*, 'co-ordination'. The impression is sometimes given that fascism in Germany established an all-pervasive — or totalitarian — system which had been carefully planned to the last detail before Hitler became Chancellor. It is certainly true that within eighteen months of being given the leadership of a coalition government Hitler had destroyed all political opposition, rendered parliament a cipher, subjected the means of public expression to his party's control and neutralized or liquidated possibly dangerous interest groups such as the trade unions (abolished) or the employers' associations (co-ordinated). It is also true that before the nazis came into office they had set up planning organizations designed to facilitate national socialist policies once they had achieved power. But although there is no doubt that the will to power existed everywhere in Hitler's party, the beginnings of the Third Reich were marked by a great deal of improvization. Hitler's method was to give his subordinates in various spheres the opportunity to establish themselves as best they could. If, like Goering, Goebbels and Himmler, they succeeded, well and good — if, like Feder, their programmes proved impracticable and aroused too much opposition from powerful social groups, they were dropped.

The Third Reich was characterized by tendencies rather than systems. For example there was never any systematic constitutional reform which established a new order in Germany. The Weimar constitution was simply undermined by a series of arbitrary acts thinly camouflaged as emergency legislation. The most important of these were the decree 'to protect the people and the state', issued on 28 February 1933 after — though not simply as a result of — the Reichstag fire, and the Enabling Act passed by the Reich parliament on 23 March 1933. The first enabled the police authorities to imprison persons suspected of treasonable activity or intentions. Established as a short-term emergency act to combat a supposed communist conspiracy, it continued in force for twelve years. The second enabled Hitler to promulgate laws as decrees without reference to parliament. Once again this was presented as a temporary measure, but the power put into Hitler's hands was never relinquished until he designated Admiral Dönitz President of the Reich on 29 April 1945.

Despite talk of a national revolution when the nazis came to power there was no major purge of the civil service, nor did the professional party men necessarily find themselves entrusted with administrative authority. The most obvious cause of this was the fate of the SA. Attempts by its leader to press the government to incorporate his forces into the regular army finally led to his destruction in the purge of 30 June 1934. The army remained free from party interference in the sense that it retained its military and apolitical character: it did not escape from Hitler's control. Soldiers took a personal oath to Hitler in 1934, and in February 1938 he became their commander-in-chief.

In the civil service a number of officials of obviously republican sympathies were dismissed and Jewish officials were progressively eliminated. But in the central administration there was no great purge. Instead, there was an influx of professional men into the nazi movement. Between January and April 1933 tens of thousands of officials and teachers joined the party. This did not mean that a career in the bureaucracy was impossible without a party card. Roughly half of the central administration's officials were not party members. Only in new organizations — like Goebbels' propaganda ministry or the Labour Front — did party membership alone offer a great deal of scope for professional advancement. The most powerful force to grow up within the Third Reich — Himmler's SS — was also a purely party-orientated organization, but its members showed a higher standard of professional qualification and even social status than was normal in the party as a whole, and particularly in the relatively plebeian SA.

For most of his period of rule Hitler utilized the old machinery of the German state but subjected the most important sectors of it to his will by placing them under the control of men personally loyal to him. When Himmler became head of the German criminal and political police in 1936 he ran affairs from his own headquarters and his main assistants — like Heydrich — were loyal SS men. Foreign affairs were conducted mainly by officials and diplomats who had served their country under Ebert and probably Wilhelm II. But many major steps in diplomacy ran counter to the instincts of the old-line Foreign Office men, and they were frequently bypassed in important matters. Ribbentrop's Party Bureau on Foreign Affairs was a jealous rival of the old Foreign Office, and was able to trade on Hitler's dislike of upper-class diplomats. This illuminates a characteristic of nazi rule — the tendency to run competing agencies in harness so that a number of choices remained open to the leadership in any field of policy. Of course, this also strengthened the position of Hitler *vis-à-vis* obstructive elements within both party and state administrative machines.

These overlapping and often apparently contradictory elements in nazi administration made it — and still make it — difficult to assess where power lay in nazi Germany, and to what end policy was being directed. It is obvious that Hitler was able — by his refusal to formalize arrangements within the power structure, and his preference for arbitrary acts or *ad hoc* decisions — to keep the direction of foreign and military policy very much in his own hands. (This was not so obvious at the time — witness the widespread belief outside Germany that Hitler was the pawn of capitalists or military men.) The use to which he intended to put this position is not always so easy to determine, but there is no good reason to suppose that he ever relinquished the utopian fantasies of Germanic power which had borne him along during his years of struggle in the 1920s.

There were, however, periods of quiet. To an outside observer in the autumn of 1934, Germany might have seemed to be through the most extreme phase of national socialist revolution and entering upon an era of stability. The most socially disaffected element in the nazi movement, the SA, had been effectively neutralized by the Röhm purge at the end of July. This series of gangster-type killings without any legal justification was greeted by conservative Germans with relief as heralding a return to normal methods of government. Hitler was able to brush aside the implications of his crime in a way which Mussolini might have envied had he possessed foreknowledge of it at the time of Matteotti's murder. In foreign affairs a crude nazi attempt to subvert a foreign government — that of Dollfuss in Vienna — met with failure. It was again made clear that nazis could not expect success without state assistance.

The elimination of the SA as a serious factor in German political life also coincided with a modification in the campaign of terror waged against Hitler's political opponents under the emergency decrees. The eclipse of the SA assisted an already established tendency to abolish many of the semi-official concentration camps and torture centres set up by the SA and SS during the early months of Hitler's rule. The whole concentration-camp system was originally a haphazard growth, resulting from a combination of political venom among the paramilitary elements in the Nazi Party and a serious overcrowding of normal prisons as the result of police arrests under the emergency laws. The fact that the SA and SS were classed as police auxiliaries exemplified the manner in which the normal apparatus of the state and the political armies of the party were intermingled at an early stage of the Third Reich's development. In 1934 the number of camps was reduced and their organization regularized.

On the face of it, Germany had survived a violent political upheaval — in which parliament, parties, unions and politically organized interest groups had been destroyed or neutralized — without serious social difficulties. The civil service and the army were still much as they had been. Business was still conducted in the old way. There had been no damage to property except that belonging to left-wing political parties or Jews.

But the nature of Hitler's movement had not changed. It was consolidating itself after a series of rapid advances. On the home front for instance — and I use the word front advisedly, since the Nazi Party always spoke and often acted as though it were at war in peacetime — arbitrary arrests continued, though less frequently. The political police, now under the control of Himmler and being co-ordinated with the SS, was still perverting the course of justice by arresting politically undesirable people without respect for the law courts. The legal theory enunciated to support such measures was the claim that Hitler's will was the expression of the nation's will and must be treated as law. This was not only a far cry from Frank's projected code of Germanic common law: it was at variance with all other legal traditions. Attempts by the Ministry of Justice to resist Himmler usually failed because Hitler supported his party colleague. Hitler was not interested in justice, and the SS was a loyal instrument of power.

Similarly the changes in concentration camp adminis-tration regularized those institutions and made them part of German life. Within a very few years they were again to be expanded. Even before the second world war the organiz-ation of terror represented by the Gestapo and the concen-tration camps was on the upswing, keeping pace with the increasingly aggressive tone of German propaganda, with the rising crescendo of Germany's four-year plan and the success-ively more radical demands of her foreign policy. Here again there was no real break in policy, although it is not necessary to believe in deliberately framed plans of aggression brought painstakingly to maturity.

The fact is that Hitler and his colleagues stated from the outset of their period in office that it was their intention to rearm Germany. They did this at great speed. To do it they broke international agreements in a manner alarming to professional diplomats, they took strategic risks which alarmed their military advisers, and they placed great strains on the economy which led to the resignation of their most intelligent economic expert — Hjalmar Schacht. At the end of this process there occurred a war. It was perhaps not the war which Hitler had always intended. For one thing it lasted much too long. For another Germany lost it. But it is diffic-ult to imagine that the feverish energies unleashed in an advanced industrial state like Germany in the 1930s could have gone on being whipped up along nazi lines without military conflict. Had foreign responses to nazism been different Hitler might indeed have hesitated before risking war, but in that case the whole momentum of his movement would have been checked, and it is likely that the latent social and political rivalries within the Third Reich would have caused its whole system to crumble.

The war itself, when it came, undoubtedly radicalized nazi policy, since it released it from the need to fear either foreign opinion or the remnants of opposition at home. With Germany at war the most extreme *völkisch* objectives could be pursued both internally and against enemies abroad. The most obvious example of this new opportunity being grasped is to be seen in the administration of occupied eastern territories. This gave the nazis an opportunity to implement their theories of German colonization, territorial expansion and racial supremacy unhampered by the need to conform to existing patterns of society or administration. A conciliatory policy towards Russian populations, in particular, might have won the nazis considerable support, but they preferred to treat the Slavs as biologically inferior specimens and the Russian nation — quite apart from its bolshevik government — as a threat to German security.

The most obviously extreme but logical development of nazi theories was of course the elimination of the Jews. Here again, the war had the result of releasing Hitler from all restraints, and he could pass from the phase of treating the Jews as aliens to the one in which they could be totally liquidated. It was a result quite consistent with the objectives the nazis had always set out for themselves. But it was a good deal more than most Germans expected when they voted for the nazis in 1933.

To sum up, German fascism was characterized by a romantic desire to create a new form of political organization which would avoid the conflicts common to industrialized societies. At the same time this organization should exploit the most modern techniques in war, politics and domestic economy in order to develop its power. Here German fascism exhibited a parallel with Germany's own social development, in which backward political forms and nostalgia for a mythical past were combined with extremely rapid technical progress. The theories which underlay German fascism were already current, though not predominant, among discontented middle-class elements in Germany before the first world war.

They were openly irrational and laid great stress on the racial unity of the Germans. They sought to reform society by stressing that unity and defending it against the supposed assaults of socialism and world Jewry. The war itself sharpened the differences within Germany over the future of the Reich and mobilized support for *völkisch* ideas. The defeat which followed increased the receptiveness with which many middle-class Germans viewed these concepts. In Hitler the nazis found a man capable of expressing the hopes and resentments of this movement with unexampled clarity and of endowing it with an unflinching will to power. Once in possession of that power German fascism utilized but did not seek to strengthen the apparatus of the state. Instead a multiplicity of agencies — some state, some party and some a mixture of both — enabled the nazi leaders to impose their will on the nation. The result was administrative chaos which would only avoid serious rupture by a policy of action. That policy brought German fascism initial successes and final disaster.

Had Hitler won the war it is not entirely clear what form his new order in fascist Europe would have taken. One thing is certain: the Germans would have wielded the power and other peoples would have been their slaves or satellites. Although Himmler's Waffen-SS contained foreign recruits, the Germans gave little genuine encouragement to nationalist allies in neighbouring states. Hitler obviously had a vision of a Europe colonized by Germany, with perhaps the western and northern countries having a separate but subordinate existence. Smaller nations would be blotted out. In discussions about other nationalities he did indicate certain general and rather obvious preferences — the Slavs and the Greeks were going to fare worse than the Scandinavians, for example — but national coexistence or collaboration were alien concepts to him. He was interested in power for Germany alone.

References

1 G. Ritter, 'The historical foundations of the rise of national-socialism', in *The Third Reich*, UNESCO Publication, London, 1955, 381.
2 ibid., 397.
3 A. Hitler, *Mein Kampf*, Munich, 1939, 200.

5

AUSTRIA

◆

K. R. Stadler

Austrian fascist movements, inspired and financed from abroad, played a fateful part in the history of the First Republic (1918-38): one wing undermining and eventually overthrowing the parliamentary democratic system in 1934, the other seizing this opportunity and paving the way for the German invasion and the temporary extinction of the Austrian state. The latter was the Austrian branch of Hitler's NSDAP (National Socialist Party), orientated towards Germany and often unfavourably compared with the 'pro-Austrian, patriotic' Heimwehr movement which, though orientated towards Italy, is represented as the valiant defender of Austrian independence. This view is at best a mis-leading over-simplification; for even though many Heimwehr men fought the nazi danger in the last phase, neither move-ment was patriotic in the sense that it wished to defend Austrian independence; it was simply a choice between vassalage under German or Italian rule.

At various times, and on various issues, these two strands of Austrian fascism met, intermingled, borrowed from each other, combined or fought each other. Both showed certain national, i.e. Austrian, characteristics which makes it difficult to be certain of the degree of 'patriotism' in each. It is com-monly assumed, for instance, that Austrian nazis desired only to be Germans. But this was true neither of the respectable, 'legal' section of the party (typified by Seyss-Inquart), nor necessarily of the underground militants many of whom resented the complete disappearance of Austrian traditions and institutions after the German takeover, as we know from

the captured German documents. On the other hand we have
evidence of Austrian Heimwehr men learning Italian and
visiting Italy for a first-hand experience of their fascist ideals
— and this at a time when the oppression of the South
Tyrolese moved the sympathies of the whole civilized world.
Both movements had their political ancestors in the Habsburg
monarchy, both derived from social and national forces
operating in the heartland of the empire, and both found
their *raison d'être* in the Peace of St Germain and the
Austrian state it produced. It is therefore necessary for an
understanding of Austrian fascism to sketch in its historical
background.

The roots of Austrian fascism lie in the multinational
empire with its incessant nationality struggles and in the profound economic changes which, in the last decades of the
nineteenth century, produced great social tensions leading to
the formation of the popular mass parties of the left — the
Social Democrats — and of the right — Schönerer's Pan-
German Party in the Sudetens, and Lueger's Christian Social
Party in Vienna. The right-wing parties contained many
features which impressed the young Hitler, as he acknowl-
edged in *Mein Kampf*; his ideological debt was almost
entirely to Schönerer, while in Lueger he saw the ideal
modern mass leader. Yet no greater contrast could be
imagined than between the plebeian Austrian, clerical and
demagogic, and the aristocratic pan-German with his anti-
clerical, anti-Czech and anti-semitic obsessions: an early
example of the eclecticism which was such an important
element in Hitler's mental make-up.

While Schönerer and Lueger, each in his own way, prepared the ground, it is in the period of the First Republic
that we see the growth of what must properly be called
fascism — national socialism on the one hand, and 'clerico-
fascism' (Gulick) or 'Austro-fascism' (Eichstädt) on the
other. For they represented, in Ernst Nolte's definition of
fascism, 'the most successful branch of right-wing extremism'
and combined, 'in varying proportions, a reactionary ideology and a modern mass organization' (H. Seton-Watson).
They were activists without a coherent philosophy or ideology, anti-revolutionaries with a nostalgia for the past: the

monarchists looking back to the glories of the old empire, the national socialists an even longer way to the origins of a Teutonic master-race. They were all ex-soldiers — veterans of the Habsburg armies or of the German free corps, Kapp *putschists* and soldiers of fortune. At first they were without political influence, an irritant rather than a factor in Austrian politics. The crisis of July 1927 marked the turning point when the Christian Social Party 'adopted' the Heimwehr, a decision which led inexorably to civil war in February 1934 and the extinction of parliamentary democracy. In that period even the Austrian NSDAP managed to increase its membership from a mere 4500 in 1928 to 43,000 in 1933. However, as a rival to the Heimwehr, and because it engaged in terrorist activities, the Nazi Party was banned in 1933, and after the unsuccessful *putsch* in 1934 in which Dollfuss was killed and Mussolini rushed troops to the Brenner, its fortunes reached a very low ebb. (It was then that Hitler decided on an 'evolutionary' way to settle the Austrian question; but this is another story.)

The last phase of independent Austria, the 'Christian Corporate State' period from 1934 to 1938, opened quietly enough: with the socialists and the nazis driven underground, Schuschnigg's 'Fatherland Front' organization was in sole control of the country's destinies. With the dismissal from the government of Prince Starhemberg, the Heimwehr leader whose political (and private) peccadilloes had become intolerable, and the absorption of his organization in the federal army, it seemed that the merely authoritarian wing of the conservative camp had won the struggle against the fascist wing. But this victory was short-lived; in the same year — 1936 — Schuschnigg concluded the notorious 'July Agreement' with Hitler which provided for the penetration of the 'Fatherland Front' by nazi and pro-nazi elements and for the peaceful *Gleichschaltung* of Austria. After the Berchtesgaden meeting with Hitler, into which he had been tricked by Papen, Schuschnigg at last realized the danger Austria was in, but being rebuffed by Mussolini gave in without a fight. The German invasion on 11 March 1938 was the result of authoritarian policies enforced by fascist methods; Austro-fascism had paved the way for nazi fascism.

This was the historical and political setting in which Austrian fascism developed and operated. If we now examine its nature we notice immediately that, apart from tactics or symbols, its characteristics are in no way peculiarly Austrian, but are of the kind we meet in several, or all, fascist movements in Europe. Following George Mosse's classification of fascist characteristics, in which he discovers significant differences between west European and central and east European movements, we find Austria with a foot in each camp: her fascism is predominantly bourgeois, and the Heimwehr espoused the corporate state idea, both typical of 'western' fascism. The racism and anti-semitism of the NSDAP, however, is a characteristic of the central European tradition of race-orientated nationalism. In this essay I intend to examine the nature of Austrian fascism under the following five headings:

(1) attitudes to socialism
(2) anti-democratic ideology
(3) anti-semitism
(4) nationalism and revisionism
(5) attitudes to Germany.

Anti-socialism

As a reactionary, anti-revolutionary movement Austrian fascism met with complete rejection from the left, on matters of principle as well as on particular political issues. This was true not only of the more bourgeois Heimwehr, but also of the nazis in spite of the misappropriation of the word 'socialism' in their party's name; and it may explain why neither branch ever succeeded in making any significant inroads into the ranks of organized labour. Thus the circle closes: the social background of the founders of fascism determines the social composition of the movement a generation later.

Admittedly, the anti-socialism of the nationalists had a working-class background when, in the 1880s, the first *deutschnationale* workers' and journeymen's clubs were founded in Bohemia and spread to Moravia and Silesia. Originally neither trade unions nor of a political character, they

developed into a form of protective association against the
flood of cheap Czech labour which was attracted by the
process of industrialization. Their political influence was
slight even when their 'Association of German Journeymen'
had become the 'German Workers' Party' in 1903: they had
three seats in the *Reichsrat*, and three in the Moravian Diet,
before the Great War. Their 'socialism', based on the writings
of Rudolf Jung, was an amalgam of reformist — and even
marxist — ideas and racist-nationalistic slogans. With the
growth of the Social Democratic Party and genuine trade
unions they became increasingly isolated, appealing more
to white-collar workers, shop assistants and clerks and pan-
dering to their snobbish convictions that they were superior
to the 'proletarians' who allowed themselves to be exploited
by Jewish leaders. They opposed socialist ideas of the class
struggle, workers' solidarity and internationalism with fancy
notions of the 'people's community' and the superiority of
German over Slav. The separation of the Sudeten lands from
Austria made matters even worse after 1918, for the loss of
however slight a working-class element isolated the Austrian
NSDAP still farther from the common people. A party whose
'ideological basis' was described by one of its historians as a
mixture of Jung's social reformism, Riehl's ideas on land
reform and profit-sharing, Gottfried Feder's monetary-reform
scheme and Hitler's anti-parliamentarism, overlaid with anti-
semitism and borrowings from Italian fascism, was not likely
to make much impression in post-revolutionary Austria.

The anti-socialism of the Catholics was of a different kind.
Buttressed by a papal interdict on membership of socialist
organizations, and with a respectable record of social-
reformist teaching (notably the work of Vogelsang who had
inspired Lueger), Austrian conservatism presented a more
plausible alternative to marxist socialism than national socialism ever did. It had a genuine working-class following, small
but loyal, which supported the authoritarian policies of
Dollfuss and Schuschnigg but held aloof from the extremism
of the Heimwehr fascists. And it is the latter we are princi-
pally concerned with, and their backers — the Christian
Social leadership and the Church.

In a different context F.R. Allemann has remarked that

'for the right the fear of socialism (or of what it takes for socialism) is an even stronger activating force than nationalism itself.' This was true of the Austria of the 1920s where the Heimwehr represented the extra-parliamentary arm of the bourgeois parties and was used to shore up their tiny majority over the socialists, to defend the urban bourgeoisie against the proletariat and the conservative countryside against the socialist towns. That the Church should have lent its support to such dangerous policies was due not only to the general 'ambivalence' of organized Christianity towards fascism which Ernst Nolte notes, but to the situation in Austria of which Hugh Seton-Watson writes:

> Austrian Catholicism abandoned oligarchic for demagogic procedures with the rise of Karl Lueger's movement, yet can hardly be said to have much modified its reactionary political outlook. [1]

Whatever we may think in retrospect of the character and achievements of the Austrian revolution of 1918, to contemporaries it seemed a genuinely revolutionary situation with all the opportunities and dangers this implied. To the socialists it was a time when the collapse of the old order presented them with the chance to nationalize key industries and services, to introduce long-delayed social reforms and to establish strong bastions of working-class influence and control. Their radical language and behaviour, which prevented the growth of an influential communist movement, frightened the bourgeois groups which found themselves threatened politically and economically. The aftermath of war – radicalized soldiers returning home from the war fronts, marauding bands of hungry townspeople, the state of lawlessness and violence – led to the formation of volunteer defence corps as guards for homes and farms in the country districts, and workers' and factory guards for similar purposes in the towns. The former were controlled by right-wing leaders, the latter by socialists, and both were in possession of arms that had belonged to the imperial forces. The Allied demand for the surrender of these arms was sabotaged as there was still fighting to be done: notably in Carinthia against the Yugoslavs, and in the east against Hungarian free corps seeking to deny to Austria the province of Burgenland.

Unlike the Republikanischer Schutzbund, the defence corps of the social democrats which was a highly centralized organization, the Heimwehr was in effect a federation of provincial associations, each mirroring the characteristics and political conditions of its *Land*. In consequence, it lacked any central authority or leadership. Its *Bundesführer* was little more than *primus inter pares* and each provincial leader was free to pursue his own policies and offer his services to the highest bidder. (Inevitably, this led to frequent quarrels which revealed the jealousies among the would-be saviours of Austria; but while this is common to all fascist movements, it must be stated that similar divisions in the Austrian nazi camp never revealed quite such unsavoury conditions — German headquarters were able to impose closer control and stricter discipline.) The result was that in eastern Austria the Heimwehr tended towards the Christian Socials, whereas in provinces like Styria, with a strong pan-German tradition, the nationalist element prevailed. This latter influence was further reinforced in the western provinces by the close contacts with German right-wing organizations whose force Ludwig Jedlicka acknowledges:

the sequel to the use of these voluntary formations was the first big expansion of the Heimwehr. It developed into a paramilitary organization for the defence of Austria against foreign enemies, but also against 'marxism' as the foe within, and this, in its turn, led to significant political, military and ideological relationships with similar movements in Germany. [2]

On these relationships the German archives which have been available to researchers since the second world war have shed a great deal of light. We now know not only of unofficial links between military leaders and political conspirators on both sides of the frontier, but also of official funds — including German Foreign Office subsidies — finding their way into the coffers of fascist units in Austria.

In the meantime, Hungarian archives have also yielded interesting material: they prove not merely extensive transfers of Hungarian money to the Styrian Heimwehr, but

eventually even to the central leadership of the Christian
Social Party in Vienna which pledged itself to remove the
socialists from the government, to reduce their influence in
the country, and to seek a peaceful solution of the Burgenland issue with Hungary. Early on in these negotiations
contact was made with Bavarian terrorist organizations like
that of Orgesch who provided money, arms and leadership
for the struggle against the 'Reds'. As it happened, the coalition government in Vienna broke up in November 1920,
but the Heimwehr, the monarchist Frontkämpfer and — less
important — the nazi Vaterländischer Schutzbund continued
as the strong arm of the bourgeois parties against the socialists, now in opposition. Their opportunity came when, on 15
July 1927, Viennese workers clashed with the police in the
course of a demonstration. Bitter street fighting developed,
with eighty-nine people killed and many more wounded; and
although the Social Democratic Party bore no responsibility
for the course the demonstration took, the crisis provided the
fascists with a cause and a slogan.

It is worthy of note that these events coincided with
renewed Hungarian intrigues against the Little Entente
and attempts to disturb the good relations between Austria
and Czechoslovakia. At Easter 1928 Premier Bethlen discussed plans with Mussolini for a Heimwehr *putsch* in
Austria, and the Duce offered one million lire and arms to
foist a government upon Austria that would take the country
into the Italian-Hungarian revisionist block. But no amount
of foreign money could compensate for the basic weakness of
a movement that was unpopular and riven by fierce rivalries,
until Mgr Seipel, a Catholic prelate and Federal Chancellor,
gave it official recognition and public respectability. Under
constant pressure from Mussolini to 'settle accounts' with the
Austrian socialists who were the last remaining obstacle to a
fascist-dominated central Europe, successive chancellors
moved ever nearer to the brink of the abyss, and in February
1934, with Chancellor Dollfuss providentially (or inten-
tionally?) away in Budapest, the Heimwehr laid its plans for
the overthrow of democracy. For the next four years the
socialists — who had represented 42 per cent of the electorate
— existed as an underground movement under conditions of

harsh illegality; but even at the height of the crisis before the German invasion, when Schuschnigg consented to talk to their spokesmen about a common front for Austrian independence, it was at the request of the democratic wing of the conservatives and against the advice of the fascist elements. Their anti-socialism proved stronger than their patriotism.

The struggle against democracy

Since fascism represents the most reactionary and obscurantist ideology in the first half of the twentieth century, it goes without saying that it was irrevocably opposed to any form of democracy. In Austria this meant opposition to the parliamentary democracy which was established in 1918 on the ruins of the Habsburg monarchy and which had made possible the rise of the labour movement to a position of strength in the state. In the beginning fascist organizations of all kinds had argued fiercely among themselves whether or not to boycott elections and thereby demonstrate their contempt for democracy; or else simply to conceal the ludicrously small support they enjoyed in the country.

Since the Austrian Nazi Party in the early 1920s had become a branch of the German party, its anti-democratic ideology needs no further examination. But the Heimwehr movement is rather more interesting because of the thin mantle of ideological respectability provided by the universalist philosophy and *Ständestaat* theories of Othmar Spann, professor of sociology at Vienna University. This Catholic neo-romantic set out to oppose the teachings of Adam Smith and Ricardo with his own vision of the 'true state', in which the individual only counted as part of the whole and where *Formaldemokratie* was replaced by 'corporate (*ständische*) democracy'. This attack on liberal and socialist concepts appealed to both the conservative and the nationalist camp where it was accepted as the ideological justification for their anti-marxism. The nazis soon lost interest in Spann's ideas, however, because they conflicted with the totalitarian claims of Party and Leader; but the *Ständestaat* became the political goal of the Heimwehr and eventually of the Fatherland

Front, and in fact provided the name for the pathetic constitutional structure which Dollfuss established in 1934.

However, what historical interest the Heimwehr has does not derive from its ideological pretensions but from the role it played in Austrian politics — with the active support, be it noted, of the conservative leadership:

> Since the state authorities have proved too weak, and the parliamentary system unworkable, we shall have to consider ... extra-parliamentary means to cut the Gordian knot. If necessary, by brute force [3]

as their journal *Die Heimwehr* wrote on 10 August 1928. Their attitude was stated clearly in the 'Oath of Korneuburg', the political and ideological platform of the movement, adopted at a rally on 18 May 1930:

> We repudiate western parliamentary democracy and the party state!
> We are determined to replace them with government by corporations [*Stände*] and by a strong national leadership which will consist, not of the representatives of parties, but of the leaders of the principal *Stände* and of the ablest and most reliable leaders of our movement. We are fighting against the subversion of our *Volk* by marxist class struggle and liberal and capitalist economics.
> We are determined to bring about an independent development of the economy on a corporate basis. We shall overcome the class struggle and replace it by dignity and justice throughout society. [4]

This programme was meant — and admitted — to be completely fascist in conception. What its implementation would have meant was spelled out by Field Marshal Bardolff as president of the Deutsche Klub in Vienna, after a series of lectures by Spann, Heimwehr leaders, a representative of the German Stahlhelm and other reactionaries: the *Volksstaat* of the Heimwehr would change the constitution radically, make extensive use of plebiscites, reorganize parliament, simplify (and thereby effect savings in) the administration, change the franchise and the press laws, take the federal army out of politics, etc.

Bardolff, however, as befitted his military status, was opposed to the idea of a Heimwehr *putsch* and any activity that would lead to armed conflict with the state executive; but this was before the Korneuburg rally. His associates were anti-parliamentarian not only in words. In September 1931 the Styrian Heimwehr under Dr Pfrimer attempted its own 'march on Vienna' which inevitably failed; the time was not yet ripe. But their conservative protectors saw to it that Pfrimer and his eight associates were acquitted by a jury in the subsequent trial at Graz. After all, the government had known of Pfrimer's plans, and while hoping that he would desist had been toying with the idea of a constitutional *coup* themselves if the general elections failed to result in a two-thirds majority for the bourgeois parties. They were bitterly disappointed, for the elections confirmed the Social Democrats as the strongest single party in parliament, while the 'irresistible people's movement' of the Heimwehr polled less than a quarter of a million votes and returned eight members in a house of 165, most of them at the expense of the Christian Socials.

Parliament is no longer the centre of political gravity. We are the ones who make decisions now, we — the storm battalions of the Heimwehr. The time for talking politics is past!

Thus Prince Starhemberg, leader of the Heimwehr and — Minister of the Interior! But worse was to come: the great depression shook the Austrian economy to its very foundations; and at the same time, in the rivalry between fascist groups, the one least inhibited and most irresponsible was bound to win the race. In the local elections of April 1932 held in six of the federal provinces the nazis increased their share of the vote to between 15 and 20 per cent of the electorate, a success which was due to the virtual destruction of the smaller parties, heavy losses of the Christian Socials, and marginal losses even of the Social Democrats. Part of the Heimwehr — as for example the whole of the Styrian organization — got on the bandwagon and fused with the NSDAP, the rest, under Starhemberg and Fey, allied themselves with Chancellor Dollfuss whose bourgeois coalition rested on a majority of one in the federal parliament. This did not stop their intrigues, however. We now know of a secret meeting, on 24 June 1932, between Starhemberg, Pabst (military adviser of the Heimwehr, after an earlier career on the German general staff, involvement in the murder of Rosa Luxemburg and in the Kapp *putsch*), the Italian *chargé d'affaires* and the secretary of the Hungarian legation in Vienna. The subject of their deliberations was no less than a *coup d'état* against Dollfuss: a violent one if Dollfuss formed a coalition with the socialists, and a more gradualist one if he did not. Pabst claimed that he had the approval of the German NSDAP for a joint Heimwehr-nazi move, while Starhemberg counted on further support from Mussolini to consist of both money and arms.

If this plot against Dollfuss seems to bear out the assertion that 'he had no intention of becoming a dictator' (Jedlicka), we must at the same time bear in mind the extent to which Dollfuss had become dependent on Mussolini and the promises he had made to his protector about the destruction of the Social Democratic Party, the abolition of parliamentary democracy and the establishment of a corporate state system. These facts have been known since 1948 when the 'secret correspondence between Mussolini and Dollfuss' was published in London. It was a triangular struggle for power in Austria; in addition to the nazis, there was the Starhemberg wing of the Heimwehr aiming at an openly pro-Italian fascist solution, while Dollfuss preferred the refinement of corporate state ideas based on the papal encyclical *Quadragesimo Anno*. The effect was the same, and in order to keep his agreement with the Duce (and to steal the nazis' clothes?) Dollfuss repudiated not only 'marxist socialism', but also the democratic and liberal ideologies of the past. Seizing the opportunity of a deadlock in parliament in March 1933, Dollfuss started on the road to an authoritarian regime which might well have come about peacefully if some socialist activists had not been provoked into armed resistance by the Heimwehr in February 1934.

As a postscript on Starhemberg, who may be said to have personified the nature of Austro-fascism, it should be noted that at a time when he was already receiving aid from Italy

and was urging the Chancellor to adopt a firm line against
socialists *and nazis*, allegedly to protect Austrian independence, he also negotiated with the German NSDAP and was
even received by Hitler in February 1932. The documents
published by Kerekes [5] merely confirm, in this respect,
what Starhemberg, that soldier of fortune, had disarmingly
confessed, years earlier, in his 'memoirs'. After his brief
period of stardom (1933-6) he was dismissed by Schuschnigg
and retired sulking to his tent. The crisis of February 1938
presented him with his last opportunity: he offered himself
to Hitler as a worthy alternative to Schuschnigg — an offer,
however, which was not accepted. Having been let down by
Mussolini, and rejected by Hitler, he next embraced the cause
of western democracy and was seen for a while in the
uniform of the Free French Air Force, until he decided to
quit Europe. The end of the war saw him return to claim his
property — one of many similar 'victims' of nazi aggression.

Anti-semitism

Anti-semitism, writes P.G.J. Pulzer, the historian of its
political consequences in Germany and Austria, was

> a 'spontaneous' product, arising out of a particular situ-
> ation, not a creed foisted on the public from above by an
> unscrupulous ruling class. [6]

We have encountered its first stirrings in the pan-German
movement in the Sudeten lands, which were paralleled on the
conservative side in the demagogic opportunist utterances of
Lueger ('*I* decide who is a Jew' [7]). It had its roots in the all-
pervading nationality struggles of the monarchy, in the social
structure of its bourgeoisie, and — last but not least — in the
traditional religious anti-semitism of the Catholic Church.
The only consistently philo-semitic party after the decline of
liberalism, the Social Democrats, tended to dismiss anti-
semitism, perhaps too lightly, in Bebel's (or Kronawetter's?)
words as '*Sozialismus der dummen Kerle*'. For bourgeois
parties a measure of anti-semitism was almost obligatory; in
their manifesto of 1918 the Christian Socials proclaimed:

> The corruption and power mania of Jewish circles ...
> forces the Christian Social Party to call on the German-
> Austrian people for a most severe defensive struggle against
> the Jewish peril. Recognized as a separate nation, the Jews
> shall be granted self-determination; they shall never be
> masters of the German people.

And hardly less vicious was the Pan-German Party:

> The party ... is in favour of a campaign of enlightenment
> about the corrupting influence of the Jewish spirit and the
> racial anti-semitism necessitated thereby. It will combat
> Jewish influence in all areas of public and private life.

Before long the anti-semitism of the Christian Social Party
was moderated and remained an undercurrent rather than
avowed policy. This may well have been due, in part, to the
fact that the party attracted a number of very rich Jews who,
as bankers and industrialists, sought protection against the
policies of the socialists.

But the situation changed with the growth of national
socialism in Austria and the obvious appeal of its anti-Jewish
propaganda: and rather than oppose it, the conservatives
preferred to cash in on this sentiment.

> We Germans gladly encounter the Jewish people and its
> national religion with full respect; we wish to see them
> protected, but also to protect ourselves ....
> In future [the Jews] will have to leave us to ourselves in
> our own concerns ... in our national culture they will not
> be allowed to have their say except as guests.
> The religious German must decisively reject baptism as an
> 'entrance ticket' for the Jews.

Thus Emmerich Czermak, chairman of the Christian Social
Party, in 1933; and it is worthy of note that while the
language is moderate, at any rate compared with contemporary nazi statements, the opposition to the Jews is based *on
race*, which even baptism cannot change. In the period of the
corporate state, campaigns copied from Germany under the
motto 'Germans, do not buy from Jews!' were conducted by
prominent officials of the 'Fatherland Front', Jews were ex-

pelled from various organizations, and it required some courage publicly to oppose this new trend; at any rate, there is no
record of a single prominent conservative protesting against
this revival of anti-semitism in the Catholic camp. On the contrary: even the Catholic labour leader Leopold Kunschak, a
hard fighter and basically a decent man who was then at odds
with Schuschnigg and strenuously opposed the fascist Heimwehr, is now known to have accepted financial aid from the
Reich for his Freiheitsbund. According to Papen, Hitler's
ambassador in Vienna, the result was a strengthening of the
anti-semitic line pursued by Kunschak's group.

In all this, the ambivalence of the Church towards fascist
ideologies again played its part, some dignitaries coming out
with openly anti-semitic statements, others remaining silent
when they should have spoken out. When challenged on the
un-Christian nature of anti-semitism, Catholic apologists
sometimes contended that they were not opposed to Jews,
but to 'Jewish' materialism, atheism, marxism; and some
bright publicist coined the term 'anti-Judaism' as the
Christian version of anti-semitism. It was difficult to decide
in March 1938, and made little difference to the Jews
anyway, whether the perpetrators of pogroms acted on
grounds of anti-semitism or of anti-Judaism.

Nationalism and revisionism

This aspect of the characteristics of Austrian fascism is rather
more complex, and it is necessary to distinguish between the
nationalist revisionism of the nazis and the purely political
revisionism of the Heimwehr. The position of the Austrian
NSDAP was fairly clear: it considered Austria and its people
an inalienable part of the German race and Reich; its revisionism embraced the lifting of the ban on the *Anschluss*, the
recovery of the lost borderlands, and the acquisition of
additional living-space. As well as generally xenophobic, it
was particularly anti-semitic in Vienna, anti-Yugoslav in
Carinthia and Styria, anti-Czech in Lower and Upper Austria,
although, not surprisingly, it dropped its earlier anti-Italian
line on orders from Berlin, which did not do it much good in
the Tyrol!

In contrast to the nazis, the Austro-fascists were anything but nationalists. They were nurtured in the Habsburg tradition in which, theoretically at least, there were no conflicting national interests because all nations were equal in the eyes of the dynasty. German-speaking Austrians therefore became pan-German nationalists with Schönerer, socialist internationalists with Victor Adler, or else remained loyal subjects of the Kaiser with a belief in the supranational mission of the monarchy; but there were no Austrian nationalists then. Nor could these same people develop a spirit of Austrian nationalism after the collapse of the empire: either because they rejected the republic altogether and hoped for the restoration of the Habsburgs, as did the monarchists; or because they dreamed of a Catholic federation embracing Bavaria, Austria and Hungary, the hope of reactionary romantics in the Christian Social Party; or simply because they desired a fascist *Mitteleuropa* in which they would provide the missing link in Mussolini's Rome-Budapest axis. This, of course, was the attitude of the dominant section of the Heimwehr, whose substitute nationalism was revisionism and who resented the parvenu nations that had grown up around them and which, with the aid of the Little Entente, prevented the realization of their hopes. Never before has the venality of small men with delusions of grandeur been quite so pathetically revealed as in Kerekes' book; and neither have the machinations of successive Hungarian governments, the intrigues against their neighbours and their interference in Austrian affairs been so well documented.

Like the national socialists, the Heimwehr was selective in its likes and dislikes; we have already noted the ambiguous position its leaders adopted in the Burgenland question when they first conspired with Budapest. Similarly, where Italy was concerned, the South Tyrol issue became an absolute taboo once Mussolini had committed himself to massive support of Austro-fascism. Oddly enough, it was the Duce who first broached the subject to Count Bethlen at Easter 1928, when he offered the Heimwehr one million lire and arms provided it was willing to seize power in the near future: 'When this has been done, I am prepared to negotiate with the new government improvements in the situation of the German

minority in South Tyrol.' On Grandi's advice this was speci-
fied to mean a government in which Steidle would have the
decisive voice, provided the latter gave a written undertaking
never to raise the issue in public, officially or otherwise.
Steidle — Tyrolese himself — readily pledged his word; and it
was not for want of trying that his pledge was never put to
the test. [8]

The nazis on the other hand were bound by party discipline
to obey Hitler's decision that a relatively small issue like
South Tyrol must not be allowed to damage the good
relations between the two fascist nations. Nevertheless, there
were rumblings of anti-Italian sentiment throughout the
period, and they almost reached crisis proportions in 1939
when Hitler 'liquidated' the South Tyrol problem by means
of a transfer of population to the Reich. Even the Tyrolese
Gauleiter himself, according to a 'situation report' of
Himmler's SD, had some harsh words for his fascist allies:

> If there are still people in Italy who believe they need
> not be satisfied with the frontier on the Brenner pass
> and talk about a frontier in the Karwendel mountains,
> it might likewise occur to us to speak of a frontier at
> Salurn [Salorno]. [9]

However, the odd indiscretion or violation of discipline apart,
both the nazi and Austro-fascist leadership proved repeatedly
that their nationalism and their revisionism were extremely
elastic concepts and more useful as demagogic slogans than as
precepts for practical politics. In any case they were totally
irrelevant to Austria's real interests; to define and reach
general agreement on these, however, would have required a
measure of national consciousness and patriotism which was
sadly lacking on all sides, a lack which may well have been
the result of the ambivalence of most Austrians towards
Germany.

Yet mention must be made of one manifestation of a
genuinely Austrian national conviction shared by both
fascist movements: it related to Austria's 'mission' in the
Donauraum. Whereas other fascist movements produced
visions of a remoulding of Europe on racial or corporate
authoritarian lines, or even of a completely 'new order' for

Europe, the provincialism of Austrian fascism never raised its sights above and beyond the old Habsburg monarchy, that is to say towards the south-east and towards northern Italy. Reference has already been made to the monarchist hopes of a Habsburg restoration and the romantic dream of a Catholic federation of Bavaria, Austria and Hungary. After 1933 a number of Catholic writers who were forced to flee Germany settled in Vienna, and their experiences lent urgency to the speculations about an alternative to the pagan nazi Reich. This was found in an almost metaphysical concept of a new Reich, Catholic, mildly reformist, and based on the alleged traditional virtues of Austria in the ordering of relations among different nationalities, but without reference to such mundane matters as political realities, frontiers or constitutional arrangements. Now these men were by no means fascists themselves, but their acceptance of the *Ständestaat* turned them objectively into allies of the Austro-fascists and with their woolly philosophy provided the educated elements in the Heimwehr with the ideology which the Starhembergs were incapable of producing.

The special skill in diplomacy which Austrians have always prided themselves on played its part in the thought-processes of Austrian nazis, too. There are several references to it in *Hitler's Table Talk*, [10] ranging from grudging admiration for the Habsburgs to praise for Seyss-Inquart's rule in Holland. In 1940 Neubacher, first nazi mayor of Vienna, was sent to the Balkans as ambassador extraordinary 'because he was an Austrian', and the *Südost-Europa Gesellschaft* in Vienna became the focal point for the Reich's penetration of the south-east. And after Badoglio's 'betrayal' of the Axis, in September 1943, Hitler was persuaded to agree to the extension of the Reich to the borders of 'Austrian Venetia' (the province itself to become a German satellite), while Goebbels noted in his diary how the annexationist appetite of the Austrian *Gauleiters* grew as the situation in Italy deteriorated. Both contemporary utterances and postwar apologetics suggest that the more imaginative and articulate among the Austrian nazis did have a vision of a 'new order' in south-east Europe which the Reich was to impose, and they were to have been its planners and leaders. It was not the least of

their complaints that Hitler did not give them enough scope
— or enough time.

Austria and Germany

When the Austrian National Assembly in November 1918
unanimously declared, 'German-Austria is a constituent part
of the German republic', it did so because it could see no
future for the small and impoverished remnant of the old
empire. Since this was the hour of triumph for nationalism,
and German Austrians could expect little sympathy from the
former subject races, it is not surprising that they, too,
should seek safety with the German people, as well as economic viability. But the *Anschluss* they envisaged was not the
unconditional surrender of 1938, but a fraternal union in a
federal state. Once this was ruled out by decision of the
Allies, and the League of Nations had provided a financial
basis for the new state, the demand for an *Anschluss* became,
as Renner once put it, 'an academic question'.

The social democrats at the time saw in the *Anschluss* the
fulfilment of the liberal democratic hopes of 1848, the
coming together of the Austrian and German working classes
in a great social republic set on a socialist course. Developments in the Weimar republic soon disillusioned them, and
without any hesitation they dropped the *Anschluss* clause
from their party programme when Hitler came to power. The
Christian Socials, too, who had been much more divided over
this question, were not prepared to complicate relations with
the Allies, on whose good will the very survival of Austria
depended, by insisting on a measure about which they had
reservations of their own. After all, to most Catholics
'Germany' was a great Protestant power, fashioned, led and
officered by 'Prussians', and memories of 1866 still rankled
with them. By inclination and by tradition they were anti-
German rather than pro-German; they had accepted the
Anschluss idea as a way out for Austria and they continued
to pay lip-service to it, but it was a real issue only for the
Grossdeutsche Volkspartei, the pan-German bourgeois splinter group which was eventually swallowed up in the rising
tide of national socialism. Yet, for reasons that are difficult

to gauge, every single party to the right of the socialists included racial, nationalist elements in its programme and terminology, insisted on its *Deutschtum* and on Austria being a branch of the German *Volk* — nazis as well as monarchists, urban conservatives as well as anti-clerical farmers' leagues. This national line was used not merely 'for the record', but also as a stick with which to beat the unpatriotic internationalist socialists, and it is not surprising that it should have become an element in Austrian fascism, with disastrous consequences for the country's future.

The pro-German attitude of the national socialists needs no further stressing; it was the Austrian nazi party's *raison d'être* to work for the absorption of their country in the Reich — with themselves in positions of power and control, of course. We have already noted their disappointment when the *Anschluss* was followed by the appointment of large numbers of Reich-Germans to key posts in the party and the state. What is rather more baffling is the inability of Austro-fascists and authoritarians to understand that their ritual protestations that Austria was but part of the *Deutschtum* were eroding what little national consciousness existed. It began in 1920 with the Frontkämpfer Association defining its nature and aims:

> It is Aryan in character, stands outside party politics, and has no truck with international subversive elements such as social democrats and communists.
> Its ideal is the unification of the entire German *Volk*. [11]

Similarly, the Heimwehr leader Steidle explained in 1928 why his organization refused to recognize the twelfth of November, the date of the proclamation of the republic and Austria's national holiday: it had been celebrated by Austro-marxists and by

> the enemies of the German people, when they had trampled underfoot the Germans and prevented their unification .... We do not reject the state; on the contrary, we accept it because we want to imbue it with our spirit, rebuild it in accordance with our ideas, and reconquer it for the German *Volkstum*. On this piece of earth where we

happen to live we shall have to prove whether this part of the German *Volk* is still viable or whether it will have to perish like a dead branch. Fate has endowed us members of a great and richly talented nation with … a territory of our own where we can prepare for our high mission …. Our mission may well be that Providence has appointed the *Südmark* [of the Reich] to determine the future and and the fate of the nation, just as on a previous occasion the *Nordmark* did, when the German *Volk* had been forced on its knees.

And the 'Oath of Korneuburg', which we have already quoted, spoke of the determination of the Heimwehr 'to serve the whole community of the German *Volk*' and asked each member 'to realize and to proclaim that he is one of the bearers of a new German national outlook'. This, of course, was the time when Starhemberg negotiated a pact with Gregor Strasser of the German Nazi Party who offered him financial support for a 'national front' in Austria consisting of NSDAP and Heimwehr — an offer which the Prince describes at length in his memoirs. Two years later in Berlin, in a lecture to the 'National Club', he still avowed his pan-German conviction: 'Repeatedly and with heavy emphasis he stressed the *Deutschbewusstsein* of the Heimwehr, but at the same time he tried to impress on his audience that the citizens of an independent Austria could also be very good Germans'. [12]

The same ambivalence, only less excusably, governed the actions of the conservative authoritarians. Schuschnigg's comment on Dollfuss — 'a catholic pan-German' — applied with equal force to himself and characterized his policies in those fateful years. While it may be understandable that in his search for a more broadly based coalition against the socialists Dollfuss in May 1933 authorized negotiations with two nazi leaders, and inserted in the programme of the 'Fatherland Front' the ominous words of Austria's mission in central Europe 'for the future good of every German', it must be remembered that within fourteen months he paid with his life for his folly; what is rationally inexplicable is the subsequent behaviour of his successor, Schuschnigg. It had never been fully realized that the 'July Agreement' of 1936 between Hitler and Schuschnigg, which provided for the inclusion of several nazis in the cabinet and defined Austria as a *deutscher Staat*, was not forced upon Schuschnigg but represented his own idea of a solution, as we now know from the published German documents. It was in April 1936 that he first mentioned the possibility of recognizing the 'national opposition' in a closed circle of friends (one of whom immediately informed Papen), and asked his chief of cabinet for a list of suitable names. One can imagine the delight in Berlin; Hitler even offered to meet Schuschnigg and others if this were desired, but it proved unnecessary: Schuschnigg needed no further prompting, and fate took its course.

Even the 'leftist' labour wing of the 'Fatherland Front' proved no wiser than its university-trained leaders. We have already noted how Papen succeeded in making political capital out of its anti-semitism; under his influence — and that of nazis who had infiltrated into prominent positions — it even committed itself to a pro-nazi, pan-German policy, thus reversing the process which Pulzer noted, according to which pan-Germanism was 'the ideology which increasingly provided the impulse to political anti-semitism'. Points for a political platform at a May Day rally included '*rapproche-ment* with the Reich' and an 'understanding with the Austrian national socialists on the basis of Austrian independence'. In May Papen was able to report to Hitler that the leaders of the Freiheitsbund 'are completely following our line'. Staud, its leader, is said to have refused Czech money offered on condition that his organization 'adopt an anti-German attitude'; Papen comments:

> This further shows the necessity of our continuing, as before, to support this movement financially .... Our connection with the Freiheitsbund, especially with its leader, Staud, is already so intimate that I have been asked which personalities would be desired by the German government in the event of ministers from the national opposition being included in the cabinet. [13]

Even allowing for the fact that Papen is not the most reliable of witnesses, and that Kunschak and Staud — like Schuschnigg — were at no time crypto-nazis, but patriots of sorts and according to their lights, the evidence of their shortsightedness is nevertheless damning. Their hostility to socialism was greater even than their love of country, and rather than work for reconciliation on the basis of a democratic *Staatsidee* they all engaged in intrigues with one or both of the would-be rulers of Austria. Even within hours of the German invasion, in March 1938, Austrians were asked in Schuschnigg's ill-fated plebiscite, to vote for an Austria 'free *and German*, independent and social, Christian and united'.

The leaders of the 'Fatherland Front' paid dearly for their mistakes in German jails and concentration camps, which they shared with socialists and communists. It was this experience which produced the unity and national consciousness of the Second Austrian Republic.

References

1   H. Seton-Watson, 'Fascism, right and left', *Journal of Contemporary History*, 1 (1), 1966, 185.
2   L. Jedlicka, 'The Austrian Heimwehr', *Journal of Contemporary History*, 1 (1), 1966, 129.
3   ibid., 139.
4   L. Jedlicka, 'Zur Vorgeschichte des Korneuburger Eides', *Osterreich in Geschichte und Literatur*, 7 (4), 1963, 150.
5   L. Kerekes, *Abenddämmerung einer Demokratie. Mussolini, Gömbös und die Heimwehr*, Vienna, 1966, 100.
6   P.G.J. Pulzer, *The Rise of Political Antisemitism in Germany and Austria*, New York, 1946, 330.
7   ibid., 204.
8   Kerekes, op. cit., 10.
9   K. Stadler, *Osterreich 1938-1945 im Spiegel der NS-Akten*, Vienna, 1966, 324.
10   H.R. Trevor-Roper, *Hitler's Table Talk 1941-1944*, London, 1953, 263, 344.
11   Jedlicka, 'The Austrian Heimwehr', 130.
12   Kerekes, op. cit., 100.
13   *Documents on German Foreign Policy*, series C, vol. V, London, 1966.

6

HUNGARY

◆

J. Erös

The characteristics of the Horthy regime

Two popular views are current about the character of the Horthy regime which dominated Hungary from 1919 to 1944. On the one hand, it is regarded as an old-fashioned, conservative or even reactionary regime, dominated by landed aristocrats and titled bureaucrats — a suitable ally for Hitler's Germany or Mussolini's Italy, but internally a non-fascist and non-nazi regime of traditionalist Christian gentlemen who may have been 'wrong' but were 'romantic'. On the other hand, the Horthy period is seen as constituting the first fascist-racialist regime in central Europe, whose founders — Admiral Horthy and his terrorist-propagandist officers and journalists — invented nazism or were at least the pioneers of fascism and of that new European order which Hitler and Mussolini were later to establish. Is it not true that for these two men of destiny Horthy was an irreplaceable pillar of the new European order? Hitler himself spoke of the 'Horthy myth' which he, Hitler, wanted to preserve at all costs. Even more: Horthy's long-time political associate and prime minister of the early 1930s, General Gömbös, was the first central European politician to predict, seven years before it emerged, the formation of the Rome-Berlin axis which was to dominate 'the new map of Europe'. So how can one talk of an anti-fascist Horthy regime?

Reality is of course much more complex. Neither of these

extreme and over-simplified judgements will do. The Horthy regime had from beginning to end a *dual character*, and all its important institutions and ruling groups were divided between a fascist and a conservative wing, not to speak of the floating groups in the middle. This was true of the members of parliament who, from 1922 to 1944, formed the unified government party. It was true of the civil service, the army, the various powerful armed security services, and the 'patriotic associations', as well as of the nerve centre of the regime, the secret societies. The history of the regime is the history of the struggles between these two wings in the various institutions — struggles which usually ended in compromises, continuously made and unmade, compromises which are only partially revealed by the changing composition of the cabinets and the personalities of the prime ministers, for the cabinet was by no means the only government of the country. The army, which escaped civilian control, was the instrument of the Regent, Admiral Horthy, whose position in turn depended on the support of the army. The Regent, manoeuvring between the military and civilian centres of power, was the decisive political force, through his ability to balance one wing against the other and keep a foot in both camps. Horthy himself was a counter-revolutionary officer of 1919 vintage and a member of the more well-to-do section of the landed nobility, connected by ties of friendship and later by marriage to the landed aristocracy. Hence both camps hoped he would be *their* leader and only the extremist groups — the revolutionary national socialists on the right, the republicans and socialists on the left and the most militant monarchists in the middle — were from time to time in conflict with him and his regime. Yet they all attempted to influence him time and again.

Miklós de Horthy, one-time member of Francis Joseph's military cabinet and the last commander-in-chief of the Austro-Hungarian navy, was a fairly realistic man with an international outlook. He knew that as head of state of a small and economically weak country he had to obtain the support of the dominant European powers. Hence, he was not impervious to foreign pressures and advice. Until 1930 he listened (up to a point) to the western democracies; from then onwards it was fascist Italy and nazi Germany which had to be placated and won to the cause of Hungary, as seen by Horthy. Finally, by 1943 it was again the western democracies and even the Soviet Union which had to be appeased. But that was to be the end. The system, as sensitive to events as a seismograph, was finally shattered and destroyed by the earthquake which swept over the Danubian plain in 1944.

The dual character of the regime can be traced to its origins. Many of its most characteristic institutions, leaders, and dominant ideologies emerged already during the summer of 1919 in the provincial capital of south-east Hungary, Szeged. The region was protected from the Red Army of the communist-socialist coalition government of Budapest by a buffer of French occupation forces. But the various anti-communist and anti-democratic groups who gathered in Szeged to prepare for the reconquest of Hungary were far from united. The three most important groups were the ex-officers of the Austro-Hungarian army, the aristocratic landowners and the unemployed civil servants of old Hungary. The former officers had shared the same experiences of war service, followed by humiliating and stringent economic difficulties, to which had been added persecution at the hands of rebellious soldiers and revolutionary workers and intellectuals. The aristocratic landowners had shared some of these experiences, but they did not have the same background of professional humiliation. Indeed, these men seldom suffered economic hardship. Finally, unlike the ex-officers, they could look forward to prosperity and economic security once the 'sanctity of private property' — a favourite slogan among the landowners — was restored. The civil servants, escaping from Red Budapest or from the vast territories detached from the kingdom of Hungary by the Paris peace conference, had by training a more legalistic outlook than the officers, and hence in their political attitudes were nearer to the group of aristocratic landowners. On the other hand, the economic insecurity of some of the civil servants made them sensitive to the extreme ideas of the military. Significantly, Admiral Horthy, Minister of Defence in the new 'national' government and soon commander-in-chief of the slowly emerging new 'national army', was on equally good terms with both the aristocratic politicians in Szeged — such as Counts Paul Teleki and Gyula Károlyi — and the less socially prominent officers, such as Captain Gömbös, Secretary of State for Defence, and Captain Paul de Prónay, the commander and organizer of Special Squads.

These squads were formed exclusively from politically reliable officers with the task of fighting the opponents of the Szeged groups by direct action methods, that is by kidnapping and secret or public executions, always without appeal to 'clumsy' legal methods and courts. It is wholly legitimate to call these men professional right-wing conspirators, because they had spent most of their time since the collapse of the old army in conspiratorial political activities against the succession of democratic, socialist and communist-led governments in Budapest. When they formed their squads in Szeged, the members were selected on the basis of political skills, which included abilities as propagandists and security agents. These squads worked more or less harmoniously at this stage with the aristocratic ministers and their associates. Their main protectors and political inspirers were Admiral Horthy, Captain Gömbös and the Chief of Staff, General K. Soós de Bádok. It was the latter who gave the order to Captain Prónay to create a *tabula rasa* in all towns and villages which his men were to occupy. This unwritten order implied swift execution of all supporters of the Red regimes. As the leading cadres of the Communist Party had fled to Austria during the first days of August, it was mainly workers, peasants, social democrats and radicals who were exposed without defence to this wholesale slaughter.

The right-wing officers and politicians who had gained control of the Szeged power machine soon found allies in all Hungarian cities. The natural allies of the more radical wing were the middle-class groups, especially those who had suffered economic deprivation. The allies of the conservative politicians were the big and medium landowners, including the clergy, and certain bankers and industrialists, driven by the excesses of the revolutionaries toward the conservative right. Some of these were gathering in Vienna, where Count István Bethlen, their future protector, was organizing the anti-revolutionary forces. Thus the distinctive outlines of both the more cautiously conservative and the adventurous extreme-right wing of the counter-revolutionary movement were already taking shape in the decisive months of the tragic year of 1919.

The picture was complicated by the fact that the conservative wing was divided between the royalists (or 'legitimists' as they were called) and the opponents of the Habsburg dynasty. At this stage the legitimists had some support among the officers. The division between legitimists and their opponents corresponded roughly to the division of the old Hungarian ruling classes into a west-Hungarian (usually Catholic) and an east-Hungarian (mostly Protestant) group. Count Bethlen, a Protestant aristocrat from the east (Transylvania), was a moderate anti-legitimist; Captain Gömbös, the Lutheran military politician, was an extreme nationalistic opponent of the Habsburgs, now the leader of the most intransigent section of the anti-legitimists. Admiral Horthy befriended them both. He also trusted another Transylvanian aristocrat, Count Paul Teleki, who shared — although with certain reservations — most of Count Bethlen's conservative-nationalist ideas. It was these three men who forged the so-called 'Unified' governing party out of the political groups emerging from the elections of 1920, notably the Christian National and Smallholders Parties. The Unified Party 'governed' from 1922 to 1944; that is, most of the time it supported the prime minister and party leader chosen for it by the Regent. Nevertheless, its members were politically not without power and in their parliamentary groupings reflected the division of the regime into moderate conservatism and fascistic, racialist, dictatorial extremism. But in spite of serious disagreements on social and constitutional issues, the leaders of both wings of the party upheld the same ideology, or rather the same political formula — the 'Christian-national' principle.

The slogan of 'Christian-national' politics goes back to the early months of 1919 when, in opposition to the republican regime of Mihály Károlyi, Count Bethlen founded the first 'Christian national' party to counteract the international principles and 'materialistic' outlook of those left-wing social democrats and trade unionists who then dominated the government. The slogan 'Christian' as used in Hungary also suggested racialism. The German term *völkisch* is untranslatable. There was an undoubted influx of German and Austrian *völkisch* ideas in 1919, mainly through the agency of the half-assimilated German minority, living in Hungarian towns and penetrating its army as well as the professions and civil service.

The leaders of both wings of the Horthy regime interpreted these principles as implying the rejection not only of left-wing socialism and communism but also of liberal democracy. Pacifism and anti-militarism was another enemy and was identified with freemasonry on the one hand and the international labour movement on the other. Yet whilst the conservatives were apologetic about their moderate anti-semitism and upheld the principles of parliamentary rule and respect of individual rights, the extremists declared themselves intransigent racialists and enemies of the rule of a 'liberalistic' parliament. They were willing — as events soon showed — to form alliances with the German racialist and dictatorial groups emerging in Berlin and Munich, whose long-term aims were inconsistent with Hungarian national interests. They also preferred violent action against both the internal and external enemy. The conservatives, in contrast — once the dirty work had been carried out efficiently by the officer squads and their civilian counterparts, the patriotic strong-arm groups — preferred to return to the traditional Hungarian policy of cautious authoritarianism. This policy was compatible with the existence of a tamed parliament, such as emerged from partially controlled elections. The conservatives wished to defend the regime by drastic legislation, a strong police force and efficient civil servants rather than by the uniformed or non-uniformed rowdies who had helped them suppress the socialists and democrats.

Lastly, a 'national' policy was equated by all supporters and leaders of the counter-revolutionary regime, as well as by its opposition on the extreme right, with the restoration of Hungary to the old, pre-1918 frontiers. The officers, the conservatives and the racialists alike accepted as the final and supreme aim of Hungarian foreign policy the restoration of

the thousand-year-old Hungary in its integrity. This irredentist propaganda had a decidedly millenarian overtone and
promised both social and economic salvation for the Hungarian masses. Thus, it played a similar role to the social-
imperialist propaganda of the precursors of fascism in Italy
and of Hitlerism in Germany — even if the territorial objective was less ambitious. But an empire it was to be, or as the
Hungarian Catholics preferred to call it, a 'realm' — the realm
of St Stephen, first king of Hungary.

The various groups and wings of the counter-revolutionary
movement were united not only by the same, albeit ambiguous, ideological formula, but also by a variety of common
organizations. These organizations showed many original
traits and characteristics — traits which are decidedly 'modern' and not simply inherited from traditional monarchical-
bureaucratic absolutism. At the same time one needs to
notice that these forms of organization were not yet fully
fledged, mature, fascist or Hitlerite forms of political organization and leadership. The totalitarian system of single-
party government dominated by the messianic-demagogic
leader could never establish itself in Hungary (unless one
wished to describe in this manner the short-lived Szálasi
regime, which was nothing but a façade for direct German
military rule). The Horthy regime began and until its end
functioned as a pluralistic system of competing groups and
organizations forming an uneasy coalition, yet at the same
time engaged in non-violent struggles with each other.

The white terror

The atmosphere of conspiracy surrounding many of the
important organizations of the regime is a most odd characteristic. The historian could find two reasons for this preference of clandestine work among both the civilian and
military leaders of the organizational structure. First, the
founders of these organizations originally entered into
politics as members of small conspiratorial groups, preparing
armed insurrections against the leftist regimes. Secondly,
they had fantastic notions about the political and social

power of freemasonry under liberal or radical democratic regimes, which they believed needed to be combated by similar methods.

Hence, already in Szeged, a small circle of military conspirators and some civilian collaborators decided to set up an 'anti-masonic' secret society, which would have its tentacles in all important public and private organizations. The initiators of this plan were members of a small group of military conspirators known as the circle of the twelve captains. Its most prominent members were Captain Marton, Captain Kozma and Captain Gömbös. The circle started its activity as early as the beginning of 1919 in Budapest, where it successfully infiltrated a legal and seemingly loyal organization of republican officers. In January 1919 it succeeded in making Captain Gömbös president of the association, the so-called MOVE (Hungarian National Defence Association). Gömbös and his friends turned this organization into a centre of anti-government activity, so that it was soon suppressed. The twelve captains then dispersed to organize underground movements, finally to emerge together in Szeged during the decisive weeks. There they were connected with the revival of the MOVE — now also open to civilians with the right qualifications — and with the setting-up of such semi-secret societies as the Blood Brotherhood of the Double Cross and the more important EKSZ. The latter was a mock-revival of Hungarian tribal society, run by a committee of seven 'tribal chiefs' — the most important of whom, at a later stage, was Captain Gömbös. The EKSZ was formally established in November 1919, after the entry of Admiral Horthy and his army into Budapest. The immediate task of this secret society would seem to have been to influence the parliamentary elections in such a way as to assure a majority in support of Horthy's candidature for the post of regent. And assured it was, thanks to the organizing activities of Captain M. Kozma, chief of the propaganda department of Horthy's High Command, who directed the intervention of the military during the election period to influence the selection of candidates, especially in the country constituencies. Even the relatively moderate Christian socialist Prime Minister, K. Huszár — accepted by all parties as a constitutionally minded man — was induced to

declare that 'Bolshevism was the offspring of radicalism and
social democracy'. Hence, the leftist candidates could be
freely persecuted, as responsible for bolshevism. (This was
the period when train-loads of political undesirables left
Budapest for the provincial internment camps). Not surprisingly, the majority of the first Hungarian parliament to be
elected by secret universal suffrage was reliably right-wing.
Whether it was also solidly behind Horthy we shall never
know, as Prime Minister Huszár frankly told the parliamentary leaders that Horthy had to be elected to the regency or
else parliament would be dispersed by the military.

The secret societies and patriotic associations gave loyal
support to their 'invisible leader' and protector, the Regent,
for years to come. Yet, in day-to-day administration, the
influence of Gömbös became stronger as time passed. He
made effective instruments out of the proliferating paramilitary associations, which were co-ordinated by the secret
societies, capable not only of harassing the enemies of the
regime (including the legitimists) but also of mobilizing
popular support for himself once his ambitions to become
leader of the regime emerged. The strong-arm squads raided
social democratic and liberal newspaper offices, clubs and
trade unions in the early stages of the Horthy regime. But
they were also used to organize popular demonstrations in
support of their favourite leader, Gömbös, who, during his
premiership, addressed them from a balcony in the style of
Mussolini. The political career of Gömbös was cut short by
his premature death in the autumn of 1936. From then on
the secret societies and paramilitary associations became a
fighting ground between those more or less moderate ruling
statesmen, who had the confidence of the Regent, and the
friends and pupils of Gömbös, who made feeble attempts to
revitalize these organizations, in order to establish that one-
party state and right-wing dictatorship which had been the
final aim of Gömbös. But during this struggle the MOVE was
disarmed and the EKSZ became paralysed. Consequently the
organizational centre of rightist dynamism shifted elsewhere.
By 1937 it could be found in the ranks of the right wing of
the government party. But the right-wing members of parliament did not have enough political weight without the

support of the right wing of the army, which, during the premiership of Gömbös, became a decisive political force. At the same time the influence of Germany began to increase. So the pressure began to come simultaneously from the army, from the extreme right, both inside and outside the government party, and last but not least from Berlin. After the occupation of Austria this last influence loomed especially large.

Thus we see the emergence of definite periods in the evolution of the Horthy regime. The first period can be described as the period of the white terror — when the prime ministers (István Friedrich, K. Huszár and finally S. Simonyi-Semadam) were unable to control the activities of the irregular sections of the army or of the secret political branches of the regular army. In the second period Prime Minister Teleki began the process of 'consolidation'.

The period between July 1920, when Count Paul Teleki became Prime Minister, and May 1922, when Count István Bethlen organized an election managed by a conservative administration, can be described as the period of transition from the era of white terror to the age of consolidation and the rule of law — Hungarian-style. Already in this period of transition the alliance of the Regent and his more moderate generals with the anti-legitimist wing of the aristocracy began to take shape as the decisive force. Teleki initiated the policy of resisting both the extreme right and the militant legitimists, without relaxing pressure against the extreme left. Not without assistance from courageous liberal members of parliament and from the press, Count Teleki began to restore the ascendancy of the civilian authorities over the officer detachments and racialist associations. This process was completed by Count Bethlen.

The Bethlen era

The greatest danger to their policy was represented by the special squads of the army which were well armed and expanding in numbers. These organizations, however, had inner weaknesses which made the victory of the Regent and his conservative prime ministers inevitable. There was, first of all, the fact that not only the lunatic fringe of the detachments but their psychopathic centre could justly be accused of pursuing their own economic interests with methods more appropriate to a protection racket and criminal gang than to a 'unit of the reserve of the gendarmerie', as these semi-military squads were now called. Secondly, the leadership of the detachments was deeply divided between legitimists and anti-legitimists, between friends and enemies of Gömbös, so that many were deprived of the most effective defence: the support of the *apparat* of Captain Gömbös. Finally, their addiction to violence and direct action was regarded as dangerous both by the aristocratic politicians and by Horthy. The latter realized by now that the abolition of parliament and a takeover by the commanders of the squads might precipitate military intervention by Hungary's suspicious neighbours. Moreover, the foreign policy of the extreme right was the immediate invasion of Czechoslovakia and armed intervention in Austria; Horthy and his advisers realized that this was dangerous and 'premature'. The political line on which Horthy, the regular army officers, the aristocrats and the political leaders of the Christian National Union and the Smallholders Party agreed was that there would be *neither restoration of the Habsburgs nor dictatorship by the extreme right*. Hence, the leaders of the special detachments who wanted either one or the other of these solutions had to go. It was a line which was particularly attractive to the members of the Smallholders Party, who were sworn enemies of the Habsburg solution.

Until summer 1923 Gömbös himself supported this political line. Only then did he realize that Bethlen, whom he had helped to win the elections in 1922, was much too liberal and too conservative for him. Yet he had only to stay for five years in the political wilderness. Gömbös and his friends proved politically more adroit than the commanders of the special squads: they remained 'respectable' and socially acceptable reserve forces of the regime, holding the key positions in the secret societies, in the patriotic associations and also in certain sections of the army. However, when Gömbös formed his own parliamentary group of seven 'racialists', he exposed himself, at the next election, to political defeat and isolation, which forced him to change his tactics and return to the government party. Thus until 1931 Count Bethlen and his conservative friends stole the limelight, having built up a remarkably stable political system.

Under this system there existed a curious relationship between the politically powerful governing classes and the economically leading social classes. The Bethlen group successfully claimed the right for the 'historical classes' to monopolize power. By 'historical classes' they meant the strongly nationalistic and anti-Habsburg wing of the landed aristocracy and their allies: the lesser nobility who, either as civil servants or as owners of middle-sized estates, guaranteed the success of Bethlen's 'united' government party at election time and upheld social order between elections. This dedication to the conservation of social order at home was paradoxically combined with a policy of subversion of the international order. No direct actions were planned but contacts with Mussolini were established and his support was assured for plans of territorial revision. At the same time groups hostile to the established frontiers were financed in the neighbouring countries and money was forged in great quantities to provide the funds.

The Catholic, legitimist aristocracy and the mainly Jewish industrial and banking circles accepted the claim of the 'historical classes' to lead and rule. In exchange, they were consulted on matters of financial and economic policy and enjoyed the unchallenged right to run the large estates and industrial enterprises as seemed to them most profitable. They also obtained protective tariffs, price subventions and, not least, protection against demands for radical agrarian reform and industrial unrest. A stable currency and a balanced budget were established with the assistance of the League of Nations and of the financial centres of Europe and the USA. All this fully satisfied the otherwise powerless monarchical aristocrats and liberal industrialists. On the other hand, one should not forget that both these groups had great influence on the daily press and on the cultural life of the country, besides possessing of course their own powerful professional organizations.

In a sense the Catholic high clergy was itself a section of the big landowner class, for ecclesiastical property constituted an important part of the Hungarian system of big estates. Not unlike the Catholic aristocrats, the bishops were often ardent legitimists. Under the Bethlen system they enjoyed — like their lay counterparts — economic power and cultural influence, but very slight political power. The Catholic-inspired political parties were small and divided between principled legitimists, taking up postures of opposition, and flexible Christian socialists (or, as they were called, members of the Christian Economic Party) who supported Bethlen and his successors 'from the outside'. Some sections of political Catholicism even operated *within* the government party. Catholic groups enjoyed decisive political control only on the local government level, notably in Budapest. It is not surprising that when the struggle between conservatism and national socialism became more acute, most of the Catholic leaders supported the conservative front, whilst their mass base was being undermined by national socialist propaganda. But that was only to happen at the end of the 1930s. During the Bethlen regime political Catholicism and the Catholic-dominated sections of the education system greatly contributed to the stability of the structure established by the Calvinist politician Count Bethlen.

This structure, however, was stable only on the surface. Once the European agrarian and financial crisis brought wheat prices down and blocked the source of new international credits, the Bethlen regime was bound to collapse. The suppressed political and social dissatisfaction made the return of the extreme right to power, even if not to total power, inevitable. C.A. Macartney, whose book on Hungary — *October Fifteenth* — must be regarded as a classic whether one likes it or not, has analysed this process in detail and convincingly.

However, a word of caution must be added, lest one assume, from reading the summary review of these events, that the men of the extreme right who assisted General Gömbös to become premier in 1932 were socially more advanced than the conservatives who resisted their bid for power. One has to remember certain historical facts in order to realize that those who worked for a tranformation of Hungary into a fascist and racialist country were not enlightened and principled crusaders for social justice; nor were their conservative and liberal opponents such anti-social reactionaries as they were depicted in the German and the Hungarian nazi press. One should not forget that it was Count Bethlen who restored to the industrial workers the right to establish trade unions and to obtain, within certain limits, political representation. Industrial workers' wages went up during the Bethlen regime, to a normal central European level, whereas during the white terror they had fallen deeply. Unemployment figures also fell, thanks to the economic and financial reforms introduced by Bethlen, who had systematically attracted foreign capital to finance the expansion of industry. Only in the field of agrarian reform were Bethlen and his friends ultra-conservative. But in the same field Gömbös and his friends were pretty vague and some of Gömbös' chief lieutenants were landowners with a very anti-social and money-grabbing reputation. The more extremist, 'revolutionary' national socialist leaders of the post-Gömbös era were of course more radical in their promises of agrarian reform. Yet their practical understanding of the problem was seriously limited by their romantic, mythological and pathological manner of thinking. What they had in mind was the establishment of a military-peasant 'estate' or 'corporation'. Nevertheless, they too relied on the support of certain 'anti-social' minded landowners and county administrators who started their careers in Gömbös' circle, and they too had to rely on Hitler in order to obtain power. And Hitler was a staunch supporter of the principle of productive and mechanized large estates, producing a substantial surplus to feed his cities and armies.

Yet, a serious weakness of the Bethlen system was created by the prohibition on state employees and agricultural workers to organize freely. They were at the mercy of the official, government-sponsored 'nationalist' unions and many developed into secret supporters of the more extreme national socialist groups.

Of course, the policy of industrialization as practised by

Bethlen before 1931 had advantages for the class of big landowners, as it absorbed more and more of the propertyless
farmers and agricultural labourers into industry. Hence, it
eased the pressure for land in the countryside. In practice,
the *absolute* number of Hungarians engaged in the agricultural sector did not decrease during the rule of Bethlen
and his successors, but the *percentage* of Hungarians engaged
in agriculture fell from 56 to 50 per cent between 1930 and
1937. So the pressure on the big estates during this period
did not increase, even if it did not fall. This was particularly
important once the prewar road of emigration to the USA
had been blocked. But no land-reform policy could have abolished agricultural over-population and under-employment
unless it had been combined with a much more energetic and
systematic long-term policy of planned industrialization. The
conditions outside and inside Hungary were not favourable
for such a policy.

In defence of Bethlen's policy one must add that he did
not neglect the development of social services in town and
country, concentrating mainly on education and health.
Several measures of social policy favouring employees,
workers and farmers, which were enacted during the 1930s,
were prepared during the last years of the Bethlen era, or
framed by conservative politicians who survived their mentor
politically, such as F. Keresztes-Fischer and Paul Teleki.

The great scandal of the Horthy regime was that no
provisions were made for the unemployed, except organized
charity. But the measure to abolish unemployment benefits
was introduced before the rise of Bethlen and was not
remedied by his successors. All in all, it can be said that
whilst the Bethlenites and their allies were moving towards a
policy of rational economic advance in the framework of an
internationalist economic system, their right-wing rivals were
hankering after distorted medieval ideas such as privileged
'estates', economic autarky and a pseudo-tribal organization
of social life. Behind all this mumbo jumbo there were,
however, two realities guiding most leaders of the right: subservience to the economic and military needs of nazi
Germany; and demands for economic privileges for themselves and their supporters — not the voters, of course, but

the members of the party militia and related organizations.
Events showed that in Hungary it was not the cultured upper-
middle class and the aristocracy which worshipped the most
reactionary ideas, but the alienated sections of the middle
classes and of the lower nobility, whether in or out of uniform.

The years of Gömbös

There was just enough social dissatisfaction and political unrest in Hungary during the years of the world economic crisis
of the 1930s to undermine the authority of the Bethlenites
and induce the Regent to promote General Gömbös from
Minister of Defence to the rank of Prime Minister in 1932.
With Gömbös some of the men and organizations connected
with the first, violent, crusading epoch of the regime were
swept into power, although enough conservatism survived in
the system to prevent them from gaining *unlimited* power.

The most important factor in the new situation was the
personality of the new Prime Minister. Although now a
moderate about the racial question, and fairly cautious in
economic policy, he had unlimited personal ambitions. Soon
anyone with ears could realize that he wanted to establish
a single-party state with himself as all-powerful, infallible
leader and dictator. He was of course often clumsy and
sometimes even ridiculous when he made his bid for absolute power — as, for instance, when he stated that 'it is
enough if there is only one clever man in the country'. He
also complained bitterly in public that 'there are powerful
leaders elsewhere', only he was not permitted to become
one, which he seemed to find both unjust and inexplicable.
But there was a simple explanation: his power base was too
narrow! Sandwiched between a jealous head of state and a
parliamentary party built up by Bethlen, he appealed in vain
to the patriotic associations, to the dissatisfied middle classes,
to the masses. His programme of social, political and racial
reforms was just not radical enough. And his appeals to the
workers to become 'nationalist' and discard their freely
elected leaders fell on deaf ears. In order to build up popular
support and a power machine, Gömbös authorized his old

fellow-conspirator Captain Marton to organize a nation-wide
'movement'. Its local organizers were dubbed 'vanguard
fighters' by Gömbös, which contributed to the general
hilarity surrounding this experiment of building a revolutionary mass movement from above, assisted by well-paid bureaucrats and respectable landowners. The racialist dynamism and
anti-Red fury of the early counter-revolutionary movement
were missing.

It is a curious thing that Gömbös, who was a racialist till
1928, became so moderate in this respect by 1932. The explanation lies in the fact that in 1928 Bethlen concluded a
treaty of friendship with Mussolini. From then onwards the
Duce became the source of inspiration for Gömbös. But he
rediscovered racialism later, when he established close contacts with the victorious German national socialist leaders.
Gömbös and his political friends had to make paradoxical
manoeuvres in order to remain 'defenders of the Hungarian
race' without indulging in anti-semitism, German-style. The
records of the cabinet meetings and the official papers of the
Gömbös era show pathetic and dangerous attempts by the
Hungarian leaders, including Horthy himself, to reinterpret
fashionable racialism in an innocuous and 'positive' way.
Racial defence in Hungary was to mean improving the health
of the Hungarian race by making marriages dependent on
medical certificates. Plans to sterilize the sick were also
discussed, but not pursued. What these men of power,
discussing a policy of racial hygiene, did not realize was that
if one starts with 'positive' proposals to strengthen the race,
as the highest value, then the door is opened to a more
radical interpretation of the same principle which leads
directly to the policy of racial discrimination. From this
point, as events were soon to show, it was only one more step
to the policy of deportations and extermination.

Supporters of Gömbös later suggested that if he had
survived as leader of a national socialist Hungary into the war
years, he would have prevented the spread of German
methods of racial defence to Hungary. But the evolution of
his idol, Mussolini, seems to disprove this hypothesis.
Furthermore, one should not forget his increasing infatuation
with the leaders of nazi Germany. Gömbös visited Hitler for

the first time in June 1933. (Gömbös was the first prime minister of any country to visit the dictator of nazi Germany.) He demanded markets for Hungarian products from Hitler and discussed foreign policy. Impressed but dissatisfied, Gömbös concluded a secret agreement with Goering, agreeing upon political and military co-operation, and in which Gömbös promised to establish within two years a system in Hungary similar to that which Hitler had established in Germany.

This agreement was never accepted by the Regent or the cabinet, so that when Gömbös died in October 1936 the agreement lost all political significance. On the surface Gömbös' policy failed. Nevertheless, he succeeded in modifying the balance of power in Hungarian politics in such a way that German influence could be effectively exercised in Hungary in the future. Gömbös had established strong economic and political ties between Budapest and Berlin and these were not dismantled by his successors. One of his most fatal moves was to make a colonel of the General Staff, D. Sztojay, Hungarian minister in Berlin. Furthermore, thanks to the purge of the higher echelons of the army and to the energetic management of the 1935 elections by two members of the circle of twelve captains (B. Marton, now general secretary of the government party and M. Kozma, now Minister of the Interior), right-wing, pro-German elements dominated both the army and the government party. The same was true of the gendarmerie, but less true of the police and of the civil service in general. Gömbös' friends could thus attempt to revive his policy with a certain optimism, even if the extra-parliamentary single-party movement had to be dismantled.

The year 1936 was the turning point in the evolution of the Horthy regime. Seventeen years of its existence were over, two-thirds of its total existence. Eight were still to come. By 1937 the character of the regime was there for all to see. The original leaders of both the conservative and the fascist wings were out of the way: Gömbös was dead and Bethlen had lost the leadership of his party for good. But these groups were still dominated by the pupils and successors of the once

powerful leaders. From now on for the remaining years of
the regime the two camps engaged in hostile co-operation,
interrupted by non-violent struggles. Horthy's power was in
the ascendant, both legally and politically. It was he who
survived Gömbös and Bethlen, it was he who chose their
successors and directed their policies — Hitler permitting.
But there was another factor, apart from increasing German
pressure, which the Regent had to take into consideration
more than the mood of parliament or public opinion. This
was the leadership of the army. The army by now was
increasingly radical and leaned towards national socialist
solutions in both internal and external policies. The main
aims of the army were rearmament and close military-
political co-operation with Germany, sugar-coated with
social and racialist reforms. Prime Minister Darányi, Gömbös'
first successor, and incidentally one of the 'tribal leaders' of
the top secret society, gave in to army pressure and in spring
1938 announced a programme of massive rearmament, to be
financed by taxation levied on big business. The army, it
would seem, was now anti-capitalist! The same Prime Minister also introduced the first legislative measures establishing
racial discrimination in the professions and in economic life.
These measures were continued and developed even further
by his successor B. Imrédy. The latter, both as a financial
expert with a European horizon and as a statesman who
claimed to follow a Catholic political philosophy, was
regarded as more moderate or more conservative than the
man whose place he took at the Regent's wish. But the high
hopes which the conservatives and liberals attached to this
change were dashed by Imrédy, who took a strictly pro-
German line when — just after the Munich conference — the
first Vienna award expanded Hungarian territory at the
expense of Slovakia. He also revived Gömbös' experiments
to base the prime minister's power on a party of militant but
respectable fascists and racialists and thus establish a dictatorship. This was to be his undoing and the real reason for his
fall, not the tragicomic disclosures concerning his alleged
Jewish ancestry. The text of the memorandum which the
conservatives and smallholders, led by Bethlen, submitted
to the Regent in January 1939 is clear evidence of the

hostility to this attempted new development and the reason for Imrédy's fall.

A reliable conservative and principled Hungarian patriot was to take Imrédy's place. This man was Count Paul Teleki. On the surface his premiership was successful — a third of Transylvania was allotted by the Axis leaders to Hungary in the second Vienna award. But his power was undermined by the manoeuvres of the army leaders, especially by the Chief of Staff, Henrik Werth. Horthy either would not, or could not, defend his prime minister against the fatal coalition of the Germans, the Hungarian army leaders and the right wing of the cabinet, which pressed for intervention in the war on the side of Germany.

The army

The army thus represented a strong political force already during the premiership of Teleki. Under Teleki's successor, L. Bárdossy, much less energetic and clearly anti-western minded, the army became even more powerful. From 1941 onwards, the institution of labour squads for politically and racially unreliable people was misused by the army to deport and decimate tens of thousands of racially or politically undesirable elements, including — besides Jews — social democrat shop-stewards, anti-German journalists and young Hungarian poets. Many thousands perished during the death marches or were starved to death or simply executed by non-commissioned officers, on the instructions of their superiors in the chain of command.

But early in 1942 the military overreached themselves when they organized mass executions in Yugoslav territories occupied by the forces of the Hungarian army and gendarmerie. Two months later the Regent again chose a Bethlen supporter as Prime Minister, both to put the army in its place and to open the way for armistice negotiations with the western democracies. This man was the true-born Hungarian nobleman and wealthy landowner Miklós Kállay. Under his premiership the excesses of the army were slowly but effectively eliminated and the censorship of the press somewhat relaxed. His efforts to obtain an armistice — after the victory

of the Allies in North Africa and after Stalingrad — became
frantic and were interrupted only by the invasion of Hungary
by Hitler's troops on 18 March 1944.

A right-wing government was now imposed on Horthy and
the Hungarian people by Hitler. It included a few conservatives tolerable to the Germans, but the bulk of the cabinet
was reliably pro-German. The right wing of the old government party shared the most important jobs with the leaders
of the new party of Imrédy and of the smaller national
socialist groups, such as the gendarmerie officer L. Baky or
the local official and organizer of 'scientific' research into
racial conditions, L. Endre. The cabinet was headed by D.
Sztojay, the former colonel of the General Staff and Hungarian minister in Berlin. These men presided over the surrender of anti-German politicians and half a million 'racially unreliable' elements to the SS and Gestapo. The process of total
nazification was only interrupted in July 1944, when Horthy,
with the help of the reliable sections of his army, turned
upon Endre, Baky and their gendarmerie and interrupted the
deportations and expropriations. Step by step the Regent,
listening to the advice of Bethlen, rid himself of the majority
of the pro-German politicians and started secret armistice
negotiations with the Russians. Not surprisingly Horthy was
arrested by German troops, striking on 15 October on
Hitler's orders, against the nerve centres of the Hungarian
capital. Endre and Baky, together with the Arrow Cross men,
now served as top administrators for the Germans, who in
fact controlled those parts of Hungary not yet occupied by
the Russian army. The success of the German operation was
greatly facilitated by the fact that in the decisive hours the
bulk of the Hungarian officers deserted their supreme commander, the Regent, and went over to the Germans. Perhaps
the Regent demanded too much of them — after all, they
were only acting in accordance with their deep-seated convictions.

The reader may ask himself how it happened that the
officers of the national army were so thoroughly indoc-
trinated by an extremist political ideology. The answer can
be found in the peculiarities of the Hungarian army. Many
officers were members of secret societies permeated by

racialism and hatred of the democratic labour movement. Moreover, the system of officers' training was given an ideological twist by instructors infected by nazi ideas. Thus General Beregffy, one of the members of Szálasi's right extremist cabinet in 1944, was for many years commander of the 'Ludovika' military academy. Finally, one must remember the influence of the Hungarian right-wing press, which enjoyed powerful financial support from the Hungarian or German authorities or from both. However, influential as the army leaders may have been, they were never able to establish that dictatorship which they often admitted to be their final goal. Thus they were obliged to act indirectly and put pressure on the Regent and his cabinet in order to implement their extremist policies.

More and more documentary evidence has been unearthed since the end of the war confirming the strength of army pressure and throwing light on the spirit of the officer corps, or at least of its powerful 'right wing'. First of all we have the memorandum drawn up by General Soós de Bádok, one of the 1919 organizers in Szeged of the national army and special terrorist detachments. The memorandum was submitted to the Regent in January 1938, after consultation with a great number of officers, of whom the most important was General Jenó Rátz, Chief of Staff and a figure trusted by the right wing of the army. According to this document (published by C.A. Macartney in his *October Fifteenth*, vol. I, p. 213), the army demanded measures to reduce Jewish influence in the press, in cultural life and in economic activities. In the last field, 'Christian' activities were to be strongly supported. The memorandum also demanded increased taxation and control of the big firms (by the army?). Employment was to be given to students who successfully completed their studies at university. 'All left-wing agitation' was to be mercilessly persecuted. But this measure, oddly enough, was to be coupled, according to the memorandum, with a 'juster distribution of land' and measures intended to protect the poorer classes.

The author of the memorandum added that only 'a government resting on an autocratic basis' could carry out these reforms speedily. Hence the Regent should run the country without parliament or at least with a parliament which had a strong right-wing majority. Consequently there should be freedom of organization for the forces of the right, including Szálasi's group.

A memorandum containing similar demands was submitted to Prime Minister Darányi at the same time by General Rátz. This memorandum was more clearly aimed at a massive rearmament programme. Darányi accepted it, without committing himself to a clear-cut system of dictatorship. Soon after, he was succeeded by another partisan of the two measures demanded by the army, B. Imrédy.

By early 1939, when Count Paul Teleki replaced him, Imrédy, together with his Minister of Defence Jenó Rátz, was working actively to build up a single-party state. With Teleki's succession, it seemed reasonable to believe that the drift to the right would be stopped. But this is not the impression one gets by studying the new Prime Minister's memoranda submitted to the Regent in the autumn of the same year. (The documents were published in a somewhat ambiguous English translation by M. Szinai and L. Szücs in Budapest in 1965 in the volume entitled *The Confidential Papers of Admiral Horthy*.) Prime Minister Teleki complained that 'in certain respects we have departed from a legal basis and begun to slip over to a certain military dictatorship, which, however, is exercised from below rather than from above'. He added that during his period of office he was made aware that there were 'two governmental machineries and two governmental systems' in Hungary, a legal one and a 'military regime spreading to practically all branches of civil administration, whose functions the lawful governmental system is unable to supervise and control'. He reminded the Regent that the participation of military persons in civil administration started in the days of the premiership of Gömbös. An untenable situation had been created by new powers of this kind given to 'military delegates' in civilian departments. Furthermore, the army was conducting commercial negotiations with Germany and also interfered in the process of foreign policy-making and negotiations. On the one hand, the generals demanded excessive sums for cars — sums which could be used to solve the most urgent social problems of Hungary; on the other hand, they incited the workers and interfered in the process of social policy-making in a demagogic way. He also complained about the interference of the army in the training of students at secondary schools and universities. The military spread an anti-Christian spirit and attempted to introduce 'the use of teenagers for a counter-intelligence service within the school, and even in their families'. Teleki claimed that these were 'symptoms of muddle-headed Arrow Cross ideas' which the officers were attempting to introduce into the education of youth. He added that a

> spirit has evolved in the body of officers, and especially in the General Staff, that is apt to impair the relations between the army and civilian society. This spirit is even today to some extent of Arrow Cross inclination, manifesting itself in a less overt form, yet existing in the way of thinking.

Finally, the Prime Minister explained that the principle of ministerial responsibility had been systematically violated because measures were being taken which affected government departments without the ministers' participation. Today, 'two parallel administrations' are 'hampering one another both in small and great matters'.

He concluded by demanding an assurance from the Regent that 'with respect to political activities' at home, 'or, more important, in foreign politics', the army and general staff 'should be subordinated to the prime minister' and the army should not 'interfere in departmental duties'.

On 3 April 1941, Paul Teleki committed suicide. His gesture was intended as a protest against the decision of the Regent to give way to the combined pressure of the Germans, his own generals and the right wing of the cabinet: the transit of German forces was to be permitted through Hungarian territory in their attack on Yugoslavia; Hungarian forces were to be mobilized and allowed to occupy northern Yugoslav territory. No logic-chopping about the timing and legal character of military intervention by the Hungarian army in the war can explain away this basic fact. Teleki's policy of neutrality towards the west and friendship with

Yugoslavia had failed — after it had been undermined by the manoeuvres of the same military leadership about whose political influence he had complained so bitterly a few months earlier. It is a historical fact that the Germans used their contacts with the Hungarian army leaders 'to put into motion political leadership' — as General Halder put it when he imposed pressure on Hungary to participate in the war against the Soviet Union. (See the diary of the German general attached to the High Command of the Hungarian army, quoted in Admiral Horthy's *Confidential Papers*, p. 183.)

The fascist groups

Important as the collusion between the right wing of the government party and the army leadership may have been, this was only one of the characteristics of the Hungarian political scene after the death of Gömbös. Another was the emergence of new, demagogic, plebeian, extremist national socialist movements. It was a new phenomenon, for both leaders and followers adopted an extremely anti-liberal attitude, not because of memories of the 'sins' committed by left-wing parties and governments, nor because of the hardships connected with the postwar inflation, but because they suffered social frustrations and economic insecurity in a deflationary crisis which they blamed on the conservative wing of the Horthy regime and on the 'racial enemy'. More important perhaps even than frustration and insecurity was the inspiring example of the triumphant German national socialist movement. Inspiration was followed by material incentives, in the form of financial and political assistance from Berlin, culminating in 1944 in the distribution of arms to the stormtroopers of the Hungarian extremist movements by the German authorities. Besides these new nazi features, these Hungarian national socialist groups also showed a few typically Hungarian features, already visible during the white terror — in particular, personal and organizational divisions and disagreements which split the extreme right into many groups.

There were three main groups which operated to the right of the right wing of the government party. The most 'moderate' and 'gentlemanly' group was led by Imrédy and General Rátz.

This group lacked mass support. It obtained thirty seats during the elections of 1939, but only thanks to the official support its members enjoyed in the safe constituencies of the government party. They only left that party in October 1940 to form an energetic opposition against the liberal-conservative and truly national policies of Teleki and M. Kalláy.

The second group was led among others by L. Baky. L. Baky had been a leading terrorist at Horthy's headquarters in Transdanubia in 1919; he was promoted to chief of the special branch of the Hungarian gendarmerie and entered politics in 1937 in the national socialist movement, as a retired major. But he remained on good terms with his former fellow officers in the gendarmerie, and was also well connected in Berlin, especially to Himmler. Being more demagogic than Imrédy, Baky and his group enjoyed some popular support — they obtained eleven seats in 1939 when the elections were secret and they had perhaps a hundred thousand party members in the autumn of 1944.

But the mass basis of the third group — the Arrow Cross Party — was more substantial. According to István Deák its membership fluctuated widely. The party had perhaps twenty thousand members in 1937; more than one hundred thousand at the end of 1940; and perhaps half a million in September 1944. But in between, especially in 1943 and early 1944, its membership was much lower. The reasons for the spectacular rise of the membership between spring and autumn 1944 can be found in the fact that the Germans and the Sztojay government brutally suppressed all left opposition groups, but treated the Arrow Cross with kidgloves, leaving it in a monopolistic position as the organizer of the opposition.

Looking at the social composition of Arrow Cross membership, it is surprising to find that the peasantry was underrepresented, with only 13 per cent of the membership in 1940. The middle classes were over-represented with 36 per cent — nearly half being army officers! Also over-represented were the workers, but it is fair to assume that these were mainly unskilled, unemployed or unorganized workers. The workers in the big industries of the Budapest region took an anti-fascist line in 1944: they boycotted the elections to fascist-type nationalistic works' councils in summer 1944 and later resisted the orders of the national socialist authorities to evacuate their factories and move into western Hungary. In 1939 thousands of communist sympathizers must have voted for the Arrow Cross; in 1944 they showed their true colours. The composition of the top leadership of the Arrow Cross was dominated by professional counter-revolutionaries of lower-middle-class origin, many of them ex-officers. This may explain the dominant role which the army played in the ideology and utopia of Szálasi. His dream-world Hungary which he dubbed the 'Danubian-Carpathian Great Father-land' was to be held together by the army, to whom all resources of the nation were to be subordinated.

The social background of the Arrow Cross leader had a certain similarity to that of Adolf Hitler. His father was a non-commissioned officer. Szálasi himself became a professional officer, fought at the front during the first world war and served under the republican and perhaps also under the 'Red' regime in 1918 and 1919. Going through the staff college of the Horthy army, he served in the counter-intelligence department of the General Staff. It was in the course of these activities that he realized that he was predestined to become the saviour of Hungary and of Europe. This fanatical convic-tion enabled him to take risks which his more cautious rivals avoided: he organized secret sections of his party, which armed themselves; he was uninhibited in his political, racial and social propaganda. Most of all he demanded total power for himself and his movement and was not afraid of risking lengthy prison sentences. Facing journalists who questioned his qualifications to be a political leader, he answered them by claiming that politics is the art of organization, an art which he had learnt thoroughly on the General Staff of the army. His lieutenants were also adepts of that art, although they learnt it elsewhere, probably in nazi Germany. One of his main lieutenants was, for instance, a white terrorist officer, Emil Kovarcz, who took part early in 1920 in the kidnapping and murder of two prominent social democratic journalists — B. Somogyi and B. Bacsó. (This was Hungary's Matteotti affair.) After a period as a teacher at the 'Ludovika' military academy in the early 1930s, Kovarcz became an

Arrow Cross deputy. Prosecuted for organizing bomb outrages, he escaped to Germany in 1940. In October 1944 — following the instructions of the SS — he organized an Arrow Cross rising in Budapest. After this he became 'Minister of Total Mobilization' in Szálasi's so-called government. Another organizer of armed party activities was K. Wirth, a renegade leader of a Christian socialist trade union. A newcomer to the ranks of the Arrow Cross organizers in autumn 1944 was Colonel Paul de Prónay, whom we met earlier as the most prominent leader of special detachments in the first phase of the white regime. All these men and their less famous associates were now freely applying their various talents as organizers, murderers and extortionists. So the white regime ended — as it had begun — *'dans le sang et dans la boue'*.

The period of German occupation, which began in March 1944 and ended — with the exception of western Hungary — early in 1945, gave various opportunities at different times to all three extreme right-wing groups to participate in power — if not in decision making, at least in the execution of policies framed by the Germans. At the same time they were engaged in a fierce fight with each other. It was only during the last months of 1944 that, under German pressure, they began to combine their forces. But by then it was too late. 'Total power' was never enjoyed by Szálasi nor by Baky or Imrédy or their various helpers who were all dreaming of 'leadership' in a national socialist Hungary.

All this again shows the failure of the fascist forces to achieve unity and establish a mature, totalitarian fascist political system. Hungarian fascism remained divided and was only partially successful. Yet it was operating in a pluralist system which did not quite exclude it from power. Hence, its impact on Hungarian politics and society was destructive and effective to a degree which is difficult to assess. The Horthy regime was certainly pluralistic, but hardly a liberal system. This is obvious from the fact that fascist forces operated so freely within a system which was built on an ideologically and politically corrupted army and gendarmerie, both of which were commanded by officers trained in the spirit of the white terror. Hungarian fascism was less

'mature', less 'modern' and less plebeian than fascism in Italy
and Germany — just as Hungarian parliamentarism was less
modern and less democratic than its German or Italian
counterparts. Hungarian fascism may have been backward,
semi-feudal and militaristic, but nevertheless it was an extremist, racialist fascism. Those who did not feel its destructive fury may deny this fact — those who experienced it have
to go on testifying to this truth as long as they live. It is
historically undeniable that during the Horthy regime fascism
and racialism were strong political forces, contained from
time to time, only to be unleashed at intervals. These destructive forces could be camouflaged, but never destroyed, as
long as the regime existed.

The miscarriage of totalitarian fascism in Hungary was due
to the fact that Gömbös, who was in his element in conspiratorial small groups, conspicuously failed when he attempted
to act as a charismatic leader of a nation-wide mass movement. Szálasi was more successful in the 'second phase' of
fascism, but was incapable of getting himself accepted by the
Hungarian establishment as Prime Minister — a necessary
step to transform his mass movement into an all-powerful
governing party. Horthy adamantly resisted all attempts to
force him to play the role of a Hindenburg. Hence, fascist
tendencies in Hungary had to ally themselves with the army
in order to attain their goals at least partially. Thus, Hungarian fascism which started as a military conspiracy ended as
a militaristic mass-movement.

Finally, we must ask the question: did Hungary produce that
type of fascist movement which turned against Hitlerism and
defended national interests against plans of German domination? Latin countries did produce such movements and in
this respect Hungary was nearer to the Latin countries than
to the Slav ones in which the resistance to nazism seldom
took fascist and racialist forms. Reviewing anti-Germanic
Hungarian fascist thought one must first of all mention the
mediocre novelist and brilliant propagandist Dezsö Szabó. He
started his career as a minor member of the pro-French
school of progressive Hungarian literature, but his choice of
French models and inspirers was rather unusual for that circle

of radical democratic intellectuals. His idols were Barrès and Péguy and probably Bergson and Maurras. By the time the left-wing revolution swept over Hungary, he had produced a novel in which he defended the true-born rural Hungarian, peasant or poet, against the forces of capitalism and urbanism. Hailed by the communists, he turned against them and switched from anti-capitalism to anti-semitism. He could have been the poet laureate of the Horthy regime, but very quickly he turned against the new 'establishment'. Szabó was deeply suspicious of both the conservatives and the Gömbös followers, the former as the opponents of the land reform he demanded, the latter as the conscious or unconscious tools of German racial imperialism. He was extremely vicious in his attacks on General Gömbös, deriding his claim to become 'leader' of a reborn nationalist Hungary. Szabó's one-man magazine was avidly read by Hungarian nationalist intellectuals and also by some of the more cultured members of the officers' corps. The seeds of a right-wing anti-German movement were sown by Dezsö Szabó, who also had a definite influence — not always a favourable one — on a new, rising generation of Hungarian populist poets, novelists and journalists. Whilst he mercilessly lampooned Gömbös and his friends as comic figures, he shuddered with horror when he described the rise of Szálasi and his men. He called the Arrow Cross movement 'the Hungarian variant of death'. By this he meant two things: first, that the establishment of a pro-German Arrow Cross regime would represent a mortal danger to the survival of the Hungarian race; secondly, that Szálasi and his men personified the Hungarian manifestation of that 'death-principle' which the black uniformed SS squads represented in Germany.

Szabó was not a practical politician and could not organize a political movement. Yet his influence, especially in undermining the authority of Gömbös and mobilizing anti-German instincts in young men on the right, should not be underrated. The attempts by more practical-minded right-wing politicians to mobilize anti-German racialist sentiment were only more effective on paper. There was, first of all, the so-called 'Order of the Brave' established by Horthy on the advice of his military chief of cabinet, Captain Magasházi, in

1920. (The *chef de cabinet* in question was, not surprisingly, a member of the group of the twelve captains.) The members of the Order of the Brave were recruited from the veterans of the first world war, and also from those who played an honourable part in the various irredentist risings and later in the second world war. They had to possess a gold medal of bravery and had to be men loyal to Horthy, ready to fight any internal or external enemy of his regime. Apart from the inheritable title of 'brave' (*Vitéz*), they received an inalienable plot of land which amounted to forty holds in the case of an officer but only to eight holds in the case of a non-commissioned officer (1 hold = 1.43 acres). The former gift did not satisfy the social ambitions of the officers, the latter grant was not enough to live on, but too much for dying. More substantial were the advantages which the members of the order enjoyed as active officers, civil servants or politicians. But special qualifications were needed for such careers — to be brave was not enough. In the end the order proved a broken reed — it was unable and perhaps unwilling to support Horthy against Hitler when the chips were down.

Another organization of the right which had anti-German tendencies was composed of shooting clubs and was called the Association of Turanian Hunters. The name itself shows that an effort was made to create a racialist ideology which would infuse 'fascist dynamism' into this paramilitary organization. The word Turanian hints at the racial origin of the ancestors of the Hungarians and carries at the same time an anti-German connotation, for the nazis claimed to be Aryans and — as all students of mythology know — Aryans and Turanians fought epic battles in legendary times. But nothing like this was to happen in the prosaic twentieth century. Under the premiership of Miklós Kállay the Turanian Hunters were especially favoured by the authorities and their membership reached probably several hundred thousand. The authorities hoped that the Turanians would use their weapons — if the call to arms came — against the Hungarian nazis or the Reds or even against the invading German army. But the call to arms never came — Horthy and his advisers decided in March 1944 to yield to the Germans without armed resistance. Kállay went into hiding, and the new pro-German government dissolved the Turanians and reorganized the Order of the Brave and similar right-wing anti-German organizations. All these movements ceased to count because Horthy never uttered the call to arms. That came from elsewhere, at a later date, from the leader of a military resistance movement which emerged in the autumn of 1944. His name was Endre Bajcsy-Zsilinszky. To mention him among the anti-German racialist and right-wing leaders may seem paradoxical, but the life history of this hero of the resistance justifies it. After fighting in the first world war as a courageous officer at the front, he joined the circle of racialist officers surrounding Admiral Horthy in the first phase of the counter-revolution. Elected member of parliament, he joined the Racial Defence Party of Captain Gömbös. As he took both his Magyar nationalism and his social reform principles seriously, he did not follow Gömbös into the government party, nor did he join the new national socialist movements. Instead he founded his own party, the National Radical Party, and demanded a radical agrarian reform as well as a democratic electoral law. In the late 1930s he became a member of the Smallholders Party and was the leader of its left wing during the war years. By now he was a national democrat of deep convictions and fought the army and gendarmerie when it attempted to implement genocide by direct action. He also attacked the foreign policy which led to Hungary's entry into the war on the side of Germany and was especially powerful in his attacks on the demands of the German minority for power. When the Gestapo raided his flat, on 18 March 1944, he received them with revolver shots. Wounded, he was taken to prison and liberated only in mid-October 1944. When the armistice policy of Horthy misfired and the Germans took over power for themselves (assisted by Szálasi's storm-troopers and by Baky's gendarmes) he began to organize the anti-German groups of the Hungarian army, preparing an armed rising. Betrayed, he was again arrested and brought before Baky's officers to be investigated. Finally, he and three of his fellow officers were executed.

At the time of his martyrdom German-occupied Budapest witnessed the emergence of a resistance movement inspired by Bajcsy and Szabó; the young officers, students and professional men co-operated with groups of workers who were organized by the parties of the left, united in a popular front. Soon various military targets, used by the German army, went up in flames. One of the objects to be blown up was the statue of General Gömbös, which his friends had erected in white marble on the banks of the Danube, in memory of his contributions to the creation of a right-wing Hungary. By now that creation was going up in flames.

It may be understandable if the author of this essay ends by reporting his personal observations while working (from 1931 to 1944) at a Budapest institute for popular education. Here the employees had the status of civil servants; half of them were university graduates, the other half had only secondary school education. The graduates were supposed to be actively interested in educational, scientific and cultural matters and usually were; the non-graduates performed important but less glamorous tasks in the clerical and administrative fields. The university graduates were as a whole — with one or two exceptions — ardent Hungarian patriots, who became more and more bitterly opposed to the policies of nazi Germany during the war years. The *majority* of these graduates had a Catholic outlook and probably voted for the lists of the Christian Economic Party, which supported the more conservative wing of the government. The *minority* was composed of Protestants and persons with a secularist outlook, vaguely 'populist' in politics. 'Populist' included both partisans of the budding democratic Peasant Party and men with a Hungarian racialist or even 'Turanian' outlook. Remarkably enough, some members of this group risked their lives and liberty during the last months of the German occupation in order to engage in underground resistance activities.

On 15 October 1944 the non-graduate clerical staff showed its true colours. Many of them (not including the strictly non-political women and again with one or two exceptions) had been for years secret members of the Arrow Cross Party. Interestingly enough, these men were generally disliked by the students and other members of the general public who came into contact with them; they were regarded as anti-social and narrow-minded. This seems to prove that a revolutionary movement can be rooted in social envy, without producing a sensitive social conscience in its supporters.

Finally, there were also 'uneducated helpers' employed in the institutions. Nobody seemed to care what their political opinions were. In fact they had none, apart from an instinctive and diffuse suspicion of the Germans as well as of the Russians. Most of them were of peasant origin and were intellectually formed by the Hungarian village and accepted the peasant belief that 'politics is the game of the gentlemanly tricksters'. I would be surprised if they would have changed their attitudes after 1945.

Similar observations undertaken among the conscripts of the army in 1944 confirmed the impression that the bulk of the masses of Hungary was untouched by the inhuman ideologies which were so loudly proclaimed in their name. They seem — thanks to their ideological immunity — to survive all ideological dictatorships, just as they have survived the rule of the 'historical' classes.

7

RUMANIA

◆

Zev Barbu

'Le Roumain est un animal nationaliste', writes the play-
wright Eugène Ionesco who once suffered at the hands of
Rumanian fascists. This is obviously an over-dramatization of
his own experience as well as a common form of fallacy
based on over-generalization. Such, or similar, statements
may, however, appear to be true in more than one sense.
There is first of all the language. Though it would be an exaggeration to maintain that the Rumanian 'nationalistic'
vocabulary is richer or more colourful than that of most
other European languages, it is nevertheless true that
Rumanians seem to have special inclinations towards using it.
Anti-semitic expressions, for instance, are so deeply ingrained
in the language that even Rumanian Jews often refer to each
other by the obviously pejorative term *Jzdan*. One can,
admittedly, take this as an adjustment symptom, as an identification with the oppressor, as B. Bettelheim would have it,
but before doing so it is useful to bear in mind that the
question of the relationship between prejudiced language and
prejudiced behaviour is by no means a simple one. Many
Rumanians may be guilty of the former, but not of the latter.

The second sense in which Ionesco's opinion may appear
to be true is more directly connected with the so-called
Rumanian character. Like most peoples who have lived for
a long period in a colonial or semi-colonial state, the
Rumanians suffer from a strong feeling of inferiority. Mainly

because of this they tend to establish their self-identity as individuals or as an ethnic group by strong negative references. In their behaviour, verbal or otherwise, they make it crystal clear that they do not like to be confounded with their neighbours, Hungarians, Bulgarians, Poles .... At this very moment their supreme endeavour is to demonstrate to the world that they are not Russians. This implicitly leads to a strong positive self-reference in their search for their identity. In the past, there were three main ways in which they inflated their self-consciousness as a nation, by stressing their Latinity, their Christianity and their traditional rural way of life. This demonstrative self-assertion should not be taken to mean that Rumanians hate foreigners, any more than most other nations. It is only that they lack confidence in their dealings with foreigners, and, because of this, fall easily into the extremes either of deference and respect or of rejection. In their contacts with foreigners the Rumanians start from an attitude, or rather a feeling of suspicion. This is, however, often no more than a working hypothesis by which they test differences and similarities with the final purpose of ensuring that they are accepted or acceptable.

Since this sheds direct light on one important aspect of anti-semitism, it seems relevant to mention a frequently voiced opinion, shared by the writer, that the Rumanians did not hate the Jews because they were Jews, but mainly because they were so 'different', because, in Rumania, the Jews were less assimilated than they were in Germany, for instance, or in many other European countries. As will be shown later, Rumanian anti-semitism was to a great extent a behavioural symptom characteristic of a non-differentiated society, of a homogeneous and closed traditional community in which a highly differentiated category of people is normally perceived as an out-group. To understand this, it is enough to mention that in Rumania the Jews were not only racially and culturally different: throughout the modern period, they became more and more identified with the commercial and urban section of society, i.e. with a group and way of life for which there was little if any room in a traditional peasant community. Thus, a great deal of anti-semitic feeling in Rumania was generated by a conflict between tradition and modernity. In Rumania, more than in most other European countries, the image of the Jew was closely associated with the image of the middle classes.

There is yet another point which explains, though it does not justify, Ionesco's dictum. This is the westernization of Rumania, which began in the upper strata towards the beginning of the last century and has been growing steadily since. As this is a kind of socio-cultural process which is better known in its Russian version, it is helpful to bear in mind that, in Rumania, it followed approximately the same course and had similar results. The modern intelligentsia of Rumania were a product of westernization and, similar to the Russian intelligentsia, disclosed in their development all the main symptoms of a marginal group. Until the last decades of the nineteenth century the Rumanian intelligentsia saw themselves as a progressive group whose mission was to transform a backward traditional community into a modern society on the model of France. This led, of course, to their gradual alienation from the native culture. Thus, already towards the end of the nineteenth century, one could see the first signs of marginality among Rumanian intellectuals who became aware that they belonged neither to the west because of their origin, nor to their native culture and society because of their education. The crisis was solved in a manner which has by now become a well-known phenomenon. Many Rumanian intellectuals began to reidentify with the people, with their traditional way of life and culture. This started off an intense process of revival, reappraisal and indeed exaggeration of native, hence specifically Rumanian, traditions, values and, generally speaking, Rumanian ways of life. The village and the peasant became symbols of honesty, sanity and primeval purity, the strongholds of national life. Christianity itself became a Rumanian virtue. From the beginning of the century, up to the second world war, the Rumanian cultural scene was dominated by 'populist' movements, literary, political and religious, so many hotbeds of nationalism and anti-semitism.

But, needless to say, neither nationalism nor anti-semitism should necessarily lead to fascism, a much more complex phenomenon, which can perhaps be defined as follows. It is first of all a type of social-political movement developing within a nationalistic, and often populist, climate of opinion. If a social movement is defined as a collective reaction to a 'problem', then the specific problem of fascism consists of a crisis of social solidarity and identity normally attributed to the decline of the traditional and ethnic characteristics of the community. Secondly, as a political movement fascism displays strong tendencies towards an authoritarian and paramilitary type of organization. Thirdly, it contains visible totalitarian elements in that the movement, or party, constitutes a concrete model, indeed an archetype, of society as a whole. Fourthly, as a model of society, fascism includes emotional revivalist and, on the whole, regressive forms of social organization. It is backward looking in that it uses traditional and often primeval symbols of social solidarity. The image of a primary group constitutes a central motivational force among the members of such a movement.

Now if the above definition is borne in mind, there was only one movement and one party in Rumania to which the term 'fascist' can be applied. This had various names corresponding to various stages in its development, but it was generally known as the 'Iron Guard'. It is, therefore, the Iron Guard that constitutes the basis of my present considerations of Rumanian fascism. Following the general theme of these essays I should like to make a twofold approach to the subject, a descriptive and an analytical one, thus preparing the ground for the central question with which this study is concerned — the national characteristics of Rumanian fascism. Before I do so, however, it is necessary to say a word about my sources and above all to complain about the difficulty encountered in this respect. Particularly scarce are the sources concerning the social composition of the Iron Guard in its various stages of development. For this reason it was necessary to lean, sometimes heavily, on data presented and often interpreted in previous studies of Rumanian fascism, and particularly those of E. Weber. Among Rumanian publications on the subject, L. Patrascanu's *Under Three Dictatorships* deserves particular mention. Though this study has a limited interpretative value, it has the merit of having been written by someone who witnessed most of the events to

which it refers. From time to time in the course of this essay
I have had to rely on my personal contact with and recollec-
tions of events. The re-reading of the political and autobiographical works of the leaders of the Iron Guard, Codreanu
and Motsa, added considerably to my understanding of some
of the most characteristic traits of Rumanian fascism. As far
as primary sources are concerned, however, it must be said
that most of the studies published so far, in Rumanian or
other languages, are on the whole under-documented.

The origins of Rumanian fascism can be traced back to
1919, and generally speaking to the period of social turmoil following the first world war. The first thing to be
mentioned, however, is that Rumania was not a defeated
country. Nor was she disappointed and frustrated as was
Italy. On the contrary, by a stroke of luck, Rumania came
out of the war somehow dizzy with her success: as a result of
the peace treaty of Versailles all the provinces in which the
Rumanians constituted a majority — Transylvania, Bucovina
and Bessarabia — were united in a new Rumanian national
state with a population of over seventeen millions. Thus
Rumanian fascism was not the outcome of national defeat.
This does not mean, however, that Rumanian fascism was in
no way the child of collective confusion and anxiety. As
recent studies of mental disorders and of suicide in particular
have shown, sudden riches and sudden poverty produce
similar results. If the analogy can be stretched so far,
Rumania found herself in the position of the *nouveau riche*,
with a territory five times bigger than that of the Old Kingdom, and with a population not only considerably larger,
but also highly heterogeneous in traditions and ways of life.
The problem, therefore, was one of organization and unity.
What were the unifying factors, and what was the basis for
consensus and solidarity in the new community? Questions
such as these aroused considerable anxiety. This was reflected
in the political situation of the country which was marked by
vague democratic populist ideologies and even vaguer democratic reforms — with one exception, the extension of
electoral rights to all males over the age of 21. The spectrum
of political parties was rich, colourful and highly changeable.
One structural feature, however, seemed to be constant: an

almost empty 'centre', with the large traditional political parties to the right, and a very small Social Democratic and even smaller Communist Party to the left. Electorally, there was no sign of political radicalization.

That the birthplace of the Iron Guard was Moldavia has its own significance. Ever since the creation of the first independent Rumanian state (1859) with its capital in Bucharest, the Moldavians have given signs of wounded pride. One way in which they showed this was by a retreat into provincialism and by slightly demonstrative nationalism. Even more significant is the fact that, at this period, Moldavia had a relatively large Jewish population, larger than that of any other Rumanian province. And last but not least was its geographical position adjoining Bessarabia, recently incorporated in the Rumanian state, and thus highly aware of and sensitive to the threat of communism. As will be seen later, communism as an idea and a threat from outside played a considerable part in the rise and development of Rumanian fascism, despite the fact that — unlike Germany or Italy — she never had a strong marxist party.

Historical circumstances apart, the Iron Guard owed its existence to one man who had been its indisputable leader for almost twenty years. This was Corneliu Zelia Codreanu. Though retrospective interpretations should always be taken with a grain of salt, there is hardly anything in Codreanu's biographical background which can throw serious doubts on the assumption that he had strong authoritarian traits in his personality. His father, a schoolteacher in a provincial town of Moldavia who became a well-known political figure, throughout his life gave unmistakable signs of strong disciplinarian impulses and heroic fantasies wrapped up in bombastic nationalistic language. The relationship between father and son is best illustrated by an incident which is often mentioned by the latter in his autobiographical writings. At the beginning of the first world war the father, despite his advanced age, volunteered for the army. This was a signal for the son, then a schoolboy, to leave home and wander for a few weeks from one military unit to another offering his services. He was refused and so returned home. Thus his first heroic 'flight' ended in disappointment. In this context, it is worth mentioning that before going to university he studied at the military school of Manastirea Dealul.

Though relatively little is known about Codreanu's relationship with his mother, one fact deserves special mention. She was of German origin, and this certainly had something to do with his demonstrative nationalism. As has often been suggested, his need for achievement coupled with a mystic faith in human will may also have come from her. One hastens to add, however, that Codreanu was not a 'voluntarist' in the sense in which Hitler was. If one wanted to size up his personality in a formula, one would say that he was a sentimental and mystic authoritarian. The paranoid streak in his personality reached theomanic proportions and the basic motif of his life was *Imitatio Christi*. Thus it was not the need for action that dominated his conception of the world and of man, but rather the need for faith and sacrifice. His image of Christ, which he avowedly took as the model of his life, was the Christ of *Theologia Crucis* rather than that of *Theologia Gloriae*. This reveals a characteristic aspect of the cultural background of Rumanian fascism.

Considerably more significant is the cultural environment of the formative years of Codreanu and the Iron Guard. In 1919, Codreanu started his student life in Jassy, the capital of Moldavia. From the start his cultural and political development was deeply influenced by Professor C.A. Cuza, a sort of Rumanian Julius Strasser, obsessed by the Jewish threat to the purity of Christian girls. Cuza was also a skilled demagogue and the inspirer and leader of a small political organization which consisted at the time mainly of students. The programme of the organization was nationalistic-racist and was centred around three main points: (1) The unity of all Rumanians in an ethnic national state from which foreigners were to be eliminated or where they would be deprived of positions of social and political responsibility; (2) the emancipation of the peasants, not so much through economic reforms, badly needed at the time, as through political education; (3) by far the best known point of the programme: the solution of the 'Jewish Problem'. In this context Cuza advocated the complete segregation of the Jews and anti-semitic violence as a means to this end.

Cuza was Codreanu's mentor of the right, but nothing that Codreanu learned from him was strikingly new. Cuza served mainly as a catalyst for his nationalism and anti-semitism. There was, however, in Jassy at that time, another political mentor, a much more interesting figure towards whom Codreanu throughout his life conserved a warm feeling of respect and admiration. This was a certain Constantin Pascu, a manual worker with intellectual and political aspirations, who managed to organize around himself a small group consisting of one lawyer, one priest, one student and about thirty skilled manual workers. To the extent that Pascu's group possessed any political programme, it can be described as a vague version of national socialism, with a strong emphasis on the first term. At any rate, what held the group together was an obsession, a sort of action-anxiety — the defeat and final destruction of the communist organizations which were apparently gaining ground in many local industrial enterprises. 'Apparently' is a key word here for, according to some views, communism — or rather the threat of communism — did not play any considerable part in the rise of Rumanian fascism. This may be so, but it is worth recording that Codreanu speaks about thousand-strong communist crowds demonstrating on the streets of Jassy. Though of short duration, Codreanu's membership of Pascu's group provided him with an excellent opportunity to learn and rehearse a role for which he soon became famous. It gave him his first opportunity to organize people and lead them into action, which in this case consisted of street demonstrations and fights. But above all he learned one thing which became a basic tactical principle of the Iron Guard, namely, that violence, organized and sustained violence, pays rich political dividends. Pascu's group specialized in strike-breaking activities and Codreanu excelled in this.

With this brief background, we can turn now to the rise and development of the Iron Guard. In a more detailed treatment of the history of this political movement it would be necessary to distinguish between its private and its public face, between the internal organization of the movement and the political programmes and electoral successes of the party. I should like, however, at least for the time being, to keep these two aspects together, not only because they are in reality closely interconnected but also because this leads me more directly to the main question — the particular characteristics of the Iron Guard. The main points in its history are as follows:

Between 1920 and 1933 the Iron Guard consisted of student groups organized outside the official unions, first in Jassy and then in the other three universities of the country, Czernovitz, Bucharest and Cluj. There was only a small minority in each university but all three were well organized and ready to use threats and other terrorist methods, so that they became an awkward and often dominant group at many student meetings. Their programme can be summed up in two points, violent anti-semitism demanding the application of a *numerus clausus* for the admission of Jews, and a vague Christian reformism. Much more important than their programme, however, was their way of life as individuals and as a group — their dedication, discipline and readiness for action.

The period between 1923 and 1927 can in many ways be considered as the period of political consolidation. In 1923, Codreanu and Cuza together formed a political party, the League of National Christian Defence, which, in 1926, won six seats in the Rumanian parliament. Two events of this period are particularly relevant for the understanding of Rumanian fascism. The first full proof of its violent nature and terrorist methods was given in 1923, when a student, a follower and friend of Codreanu, murdered a member of the organization on the assumption that he had contacts with the police. This brought to light the essential organizational and ethical features of the movement. For it appeared that the victim was previously tried and sentenced by the 'secret tribunal' of the organization, which also designated the executioner.* Expressions such as 'traitors' and 'heroes' as well as the 'blood baptism of the Guard' were used in this

* This was Ion Motsa, the son of an orthodox priest from Transylvania, famous for his nationalistic activities. Motsa had just returned from France where he was a member of Action Française, and soon became a great figure in the movement, normally referred to as 'the saint'. He died in 1936 in the Spanish war. He was the first translator in Rumania of the *Protocols of the Elders of Zion* in 1923.

context. Public opinion was certainly horrified, but also slightly mystified and fascinated, by such language and behaviour. So were the authorities who dealt with the events in what may be described as a paternalistic manner. The students involved in the murder, including Codreanu, were arrested, tried and finally sentenced. However, all this was done in a climate of empathetic excitement so that nothing prevented the offenders from posing as victims and even as heroes. This should be stressed because it played an important part in the formative years of the Iron Guard, and nothing can account for it but the prestige which intellectuals and students in particular enjoyed in the Rumanian society of the time.

The second event relates to Codreanu's life. During a short term of imprisonment, in 1923, he had his first vision: the Archangel Michael came to him and urged him to dedicate his life to God as revealed by the Rumanian Christian tradition.* A few years later (1927) he founded the Brotherhood of the Cross, an élitist body which he placed at the centre of his party. To indicate the nature of this organization it is necessary to mention that, apart from the Archangel's revelation, Codreanu was inspired by an old Rumanian tradition. Such forms of privileged and mystic associations, or rather communions, between two or more people existed and maybe still exist among Rumanian peasants. The association is highly ritualized and often those entering upon it have to taste each other's blood in order to become brothers, 'unto life and death'. The Brotherhood of the Cross conformed in many ways to this pattern of human relations in which the primary ties of blood are symbolically resurrected. The Brotherhood of the Cross was the mystic body of the Iron Guard, open only to the few and the elect. Those worthy of membership had to undergo a primitive ceremony, a *rite de passage*. They were summoned to a secret place, and after an incantational ritual which took place at a late hour of the night they made a formal vow pledging their life to the cause and the 'Captain'.

In 1926, as a result of a quarrel between Codreanu and

* In 1926 Codreanu murdered the prefect of Galatsi, Manciu.

Cuza, the League of National Christian Defence was dissolved, and in 1927 there came into being the first independent political organization of Codreanu's movement, the Legion of the Archangel Michael. This was a prototype of fascist organization. To start with, it had no political programme. 'The country is dying for lack of men and not for lack of programmes' were the words used by Codreanu at the foundation meeting of the Legion. If I may advance an idea, the *legionari* constituted a psychological rather than a political group: the basic trait of their organization was a state of mind. The main points in their programme were, 'Faith in God', 'Faith in the Mission' and 'Love for each other'. All these were 'cultist' in character, and required specific tests and trials and particularly specific states of mind. This is even more clearly revealed by the fourth point in their programme; 'Love of songs'. We shall return to this shortly, but for the moment it is enough to mention that music, vocal music above all, was a basic element of the *legionari*'s way of life. All their meetings started and ended in incantational rituals of song and often dance.

The Legion had a conspiratorial type of organization. The basic unit was the 'nest', a small group consisting of seven, rising to a maximum of twelve, members who called each other *camarazi*, a term which was used not by the Rumanian communists (who called themselves *tovaresi*), but by the Rumanian army. Above the level of the 'nests', the Legion consisted of a semi-military and semi-mystical organization with a rigid hierarchy. At the top was the 'Captain' and a small number of 'great commanders of the Legion'.

The 'nest' as the structural unit of the party was a model of totalitarian groups. Even the name was chosen to appeal to the needs of dependence and security of the young. In it, the *legionari* received their basic training, which consisted of some knowledge of the history and martyrology of the Guard, instructions about rules of conduct expected of them, and above all unconditional obedience to the Leader. The 'nest' had a monolithic internal organization, with all decisions made unanimously. Though in principle and overtly Codreanu was not against democracy in the same sense as Hitler, on the question of leadership he had always held extreme authoritarian views. 'I was a leader from the beginning', he often said, meaning that a leader should have obvious and compelling qualities which make election and, on the whole, formal delegation of authority unnecessary. Consequently the leaders of the 'nests' emerged eruptively, as Max Weber would put it; they were the obvious choice. Since Weber has been mentioned, it would be interesting to raise the question of the specific nature of their charisma. It was certainly not physical power, nor knowledge or organizational skill, but rather loyalty to the cause and a highly sublimated aggression, the aggression of Christ chasing the traders out of the Temple. They were essentially religious people with a Manichean vision of the world in which — following the example of their patron, Saint Michael — they were the angels of light. Since the mission of the *legionari* was nothing less than the moral regeneration of the nation, the distinctive mark of their leaders was a high sense of mission and martyrdom.

This throws light on one of the most characteristic organizational and psychological features of the Iron Guard. I know of no other fascist movement which inculcated in its members a deeper sense of personal dedication and sacrifice. To start with, one of the main élite groups within the Iron Guard was the so-called 'death team', consisting of young fanatics ready to kill and be killed. Their status and mission were highly institutionalized, or rather ritualized. It was said that they used to wear around their necks a tiny bag of Rumanian soil and that there was nothing in the world which they would not do at the sight of it. There were also other less magic expressions of their sense of sacrifice. Most outstanding in this respect were their songs with the mystique of death as the basic motif. Here are a few examples:

> *Legionari* do not fear
> That you will die young
>
> For you die to be reborn
> And are born to die
>
> For we are the death team
> That must win or die

> Death, only the *legionari* death
> Is a gladsome wedding for us.

Two powerful motifs of the mystique of death inflamed the mind of the *legionari*. One, explicitly stated in the last quotation, is traditional-native, constituting the central theme in one of the best-known Rumanian ballads, *Mioritsa*, where the hero threatened with imminent death overcomes his fear by comparing death to a wedding, the bridegroom being himself and nature his bride. It was often said that this was the 'typical' Rumanian attitude to death. Even more powerful is the other motif, the Christian mythology of resurrection and victory through death.

While the main slogan of the *legionari* was 'victory or death', this religious formula seems to reveal more adequately the deep motivation of their behaviour. The more and the heavier they had to pay for their murderous violence, the more they practised it. These are a few figures illustrating this tight chain of action which can be formulated either as 'kill and be killed', or 'kill to be killed'. Between 1924 and 1937 they committed eleven murders — mainly of important political personalities. During this period, however, over 500 *legionari* were killed, mainly by the police. Between April and December 1939, the year of martyrdom, some 1200 *legionari* were arrested, imprisoned and exterminated. To this, one should add another point, the significance of which can hardly be overestimated. In the summer of 1936, in one of Bucharest's hospitals, there took place an event which cannot be described otherwise than as ritual killing. It concerns Stelescu, a prominent *legionari* leader who had just left the Iron Guard and joined another nationalist organization. While he was lying in bed, a group of four *legionari* broke in and fired 120 shots at him. After that, they chopped his body in small pieces, danced around it and kissed each other.

How can one understand such a destructive and at the same time ritualized aggression? Professor E. Weber puts forward two interpretative hypotheses. The first refers to the autocratic and terrorist methods used by the Rumanian government and by King Carol in particular against the Iron Guard and against any radical non-conformist organization.

He compares the Rumanian regime of the period to that of pre-revolutionary Russia. Since terror normally breeds greater terror, the legionary violence was a reaction, perhaps an over-reaction, to the violence of authority. While not denying the usefulness of such a hypothesis, in this particular case it raises two points of difficulty. As mentioned earlier, Rumanian authorities did not always use harsh methods in their dealings with the Iron Guard. This is particularly true with regard to the early stage of the movement. The second point is more specific and refers to the difficulty of defining and testing 'provoked' behaviour. As far as my personal experience and observation goes, I find no conclusive evidence that the legionaries were provoked to violence. On the contrary, at any student meeting I attended in which *legionari* were present — and there were many such meetings — I could not help noticing that they formed a solid and visible group highly skilled in terrorist method. They provoked long before they were provoked. It is significant to note that they normally described their opponents, passive or active, as 'cowards'.

The second hypothesis put forward by Weber refers to the nature and meaning of legionary violence. The *legionari* were, admittedly, violent but — he is inclined to think — they were not bad people. A certain amount of evidence for this can be derived from Codreanu's writings and particularly from his paternal advice to his followers, where he urges them to use the 'right means' in their struggle against their opponents. Moreover, he praises and stimulates in them virtues such as honesty, integrity, purity, work and Christian faith. This is obviously so, but all this has to be seen in the right context. Leaving aside the more general question regarding the dis-crepancy between 'ideal' and 'real' behaviour, the first point to be noticed is that expressions such as 'purity of con-science', 'integrity', and 'righteousness' are the staple food of sectarians and authoritarians: this is the normal manner in which they rationalize their violence. As for the meaning and content of the concept of 'right means', it would be enough to note here that in all Codreanu's writings, the enemy — and this included everybody outside the Iron Guard — is de-scribed as 'corrupted' and 'doomed'. What the 'right means' can mean, in this context, is easy to guess. In fact Codreanu had a sectarian concept of morality, and the Legion can in many ways be described as a messianic salvationist movement. Its morality was that of a closed group: 'good', 'right', 'honest' were terms which it applied to whatever and whomsoever supported its cause.

It is now time to return to the political activities and success of the Iron Guard. As already mentioned, the League of National Christian Defence won six parliamentary seats in the election of 1926. This represented 120,000 votes. In 1931, the Legion of the Archangel Michael won less than 2 per cent of the electorate and according to the Rumanian constitution this meant no representation in parliament. One year later, however, it won five seats. This was the first serious warning of its political potential and the government reacted swiftly by dissolving the Legion as a political party. This allowed the legionaries to pose once more as victims. The proof is that, in 1937, when they were recognized again as a political party under the name 'All for the Fatherland', they gained sixty seats, representing more than 16 per cent of the electorate. This placed the Iron Guard in the second place — after the National Peasant Party — among the political parties of the country. In 1938, the organization was dissolved once more and its leadership decimated by the dictatorial regime of King Carol. Between April and December 1939, more than 1200 legionaries, including Codreanu, were arrested and lost their lives in circumstances which have remained to a great extent obscure. The official version was that they were shot while trying to escape. Although it never recovered from this blow, the Iron Guard appeared once more in the political arena. This was in 1940-1 when Rumania had for the first time a *legionari* government. It was in fact a coalition government of the military group of General Antonescu and the surviving elements of the Iron Guard under the leadership of Horea Sima. The coalition did not work, and after an abortive *putsch* and revolution, in early 1941, the legionaries were eliminated from the government and their leadership was again decimated.

The political career of the Iron Guard can be summed up in two points. First, between 1931 and 1940 it increasingly became one of the most important political forces in Rumania. Second, with the exception of Italian fascism and German nazism, it was one of the few wholly fascist movements to come to power and form a government. How can one explain this success?

In answering such a question, it is useful to recall one of the best known interpretative models of sociological studies of fascism. According to this model, fascism is a middle-class phenomenon expressing the interests of either the upper-middle class, i.e. their expansionist-imperialist aspirations as well as their apprehensions about the economic implications of liberal democracy, or the specific interests of the lower-middle classes in their struggle against 'big capital'. Sometimes these two hypotheses are combined, and the interpretative model is amplified with other variables, such as the level of industrialization of the community as a whole, and the degree of politicization of the masses and of the working classes in particular. The difficulty about applying such interpretative models to Rumania of the interwar period is that the middle classes were numerically small, as well as ideologically, politically and socio-culturally ill-defined. Something like 80 per cent of the population were peasants while the industrial workers constituted a tiny and poorly organized minority. The difficulty is increased when one takes into account the ideology of the Iron Guard with its systematic attack on urban bourgeois values and ways of life.

All this makes it necessary to abandon for Rumania, at least for the moment, the theoretical hypothesis regarding the middle-class element of fascism and to look more closely at the social composition of the Iron Guard at the levels of leadership, party membership and electoral support. Naturally it must be borne in mind that one is dealing here with an authoritarian organization; hence the level which counts most is that of leadership.

From the beginning, the leadership was dominated by two categories of people, intellectuals and youth. For lack of more adequate documentation, the best one can do to illustrate this point is to refer to the data offered by Weber from the analysis of two groups in terms of their occupation and age. The first consists of 215 legionaries interned in

Buchenwald between 1942 and 1944, the second of 32 legionaries executed at Vaslui in September 1939. Though for obvious reasons these cannot be considered as representative samples, the following figures seem to be indicative of both the composition of the leadership and the membership of the organization as a whole. Taking the two groups together, intellectuals represented between 40 and 50 per cent, including students who alone represented almost 30 per cent, professions and public servants. The average age in the first group was 27.4. Particularly young was the top leadership. For instance, in 1931 Codreanu was 32, Motsa 29, Marin 27 and Stelescu 24.

The question of the social origins of the Legion's leadership and its membership in general presents considerable difficulties. As Weber rightly points out, the middle-class element (state employees, professionals, and even tradesmen and shopkeepers) seems at first sight to dominate. But one particularly relevant point needs to be noted: their connection with the traditional rural population and way of life is direct, almost uninterrupted. Codreanu was the son of a schoolteacher and the grandson of a peasant, Motsa the son of a priest and grandson of a peasant. This applies to the leadership at all levels and on the whole to the so-called middle-class element of the Legion.

All this throws considerable doubt on the class membership, let alone on the class identity, of the legionaries. It is very likely that we are dealing here with a psychological rather than a social group. Most of its members were climbing up the ladder of social hierarchy in the direction of the middle class. But the point is that they had not yet arrived, they had not yet broken away from their rural traditional background. On the whole they were a marginal group and it was their condition of marginality rather than their class interests and consciousness which determined their political behaviour. What follows is an attempt to demonstrate this point.

The prominent part played by the intelligentsia in the history of the Legion can in itself be taken as a symptom of marginality, of classlessness, as Mannheim would put it. To this general condition can be added a series of more specific

ones. First of all, the kind of intelligentsia we are dealing
with belonged to an emerging, newly born society without a
clear sense of solidarity and identity, and certainly without a
stable system of stratification. Furthermore, they belonged
to a society in which the upper as well as the urban strata
were traditionally associated if not identified with outsiders,
Turks, Hungarians, Germans, Greeks and Jews. This says a
great deal about the social position, objective or subjective,
of Rumanian intelligentsia and of legionary intelligentsia in
particular. In reality they could not and did not belong anywhere, and escaped reality by inventing their society and
reference group. For example, Codreanu identified himself
with the 'people', an idealized community which he never
defined except in vague and abstract terms such as 'unity',
'purity', 'Christianity'. It was an unhistorical entity including
all Rumanians who had existed in the past and would exist in
the future. Even more characteristically, Motsa, after reject-
ing the corrupt social reality of his time, identified himself
with the 'old world', the legendary past of his nation. This is
an important point which should occupy a central place in
any detailed study of Rumanian fascism. The most one can
do here is to point out that the reference group of the legionaries, of the intellectuals in particular, was an imaginary one.
It was an ideal society in which the legend of an old traditional Rumanian community loomed large. The predominant utopian element in this image of society was of a moral
religious character, with brotherly unity and love as the basis
of communal life.

The only element which linked this image of society to
reality was the rural community of the Rumanian village. As
has often been said, the legionaries were 'idealists' in that
they struggled to maintain and indeed to introduce into
Rumanian society of the interwar period the morality and
social solidarity of a traditional community and primary
group. They were the arch-enemies of secularization, urbanization and industrialization. Moreover, they tried to maintain
— in an idealized form, of course — the elements of a pre-
market and pre-individualized society. Nobody who lived in
Rumania during this period can forget the eerie and anachronistic character of a legionary demonstration. It was some-

thing between a political protest, a religious procession and a historical *cortège*. The middle and indeed the core of the demonstration consisted of a well-organized body of young people in uniform — the 'green shirts'. It was normally headed by a group of priests carrying icons and religious flags. Finally, all this was followed and surrounded by men and women in national traditional dress. It is significant that the Captain normally appeared in traditional Moldavian dress, though the green shirt was the official uniform of the Legion.

To all this one should add that the leadership and to a great extent the membership of the Legion was young, a fact which certainly contributed to its idealism and marginality. Particularly significant in this context is the fact that the movement began in student circles. Apart from the *Sturm und Drang* characteristic of their age, the Rumanian students of the period suffered from the anxiety of prospective unemployment.

One can now turn briefly to the mass base of the Legion. As mentioned earlier, in 1937 the electoral support of the Legion represented 16 per cent of the total voting population. How can one explain this considerable success? Who were its supporters?

Previous attempts to answer such questions have pointed out three factors. Firstly, the legionaries used new electoral methods. They contacted regions, remote mountain villages, normally neglected by other parties; they also showed considerable skill in making personal contacts with the villagers. Secondly, most of the regions from which they derived their electoral support were poor. Thirdly, some support came from regions with a relatively large Jewish population, though on the whole these regions gave greater support to Cuza's National Christian League. To sum up, the Legion recruited its mass support from the rural population which was either neglected, politically and administratively, or economically poor, or both, as well as from a rural and urban population open in various degrees to anti-semitic propaganda.

Though essentially correct, such an interpretation may be misleading in one important respect — the economic status of the Legion's supporters. Poverty does not seem to describe their economic condition adequately. The peasants who joined the Legion and those who voted for it were not the poorest of the poor, not by Rumanian rural standards at any rate. For lack of adequate information I am compelled once more to use impressionistic methods. In a village in the county of Sibiu which I happen to know well, the first converted and the martyr of the organization was a certain Dimitri. When he joined the Legion, Dimitri was in his early twenties and poverty was not the crucial element, for the land holdings of his family were slightly above the average in the village. But Dimitri's father was an isolated figure, mainly because of his quarrelsome character, but also because he was by far the smallest man in the village. One of Dimitri's sisters suffering from a slight physical infirmity had an illegitimate child, an extremely rare event in the village. As a result two other sisters left home and settled down as housemaids in the nearest town. Dimitri was a very religious young man; he used to pray loudly and conspicuously in the village church. This may be an exaggerated portrait of a rural *legionari* but certainly not a wrong one. In most villages, those who joined and supported the Legion were the slightly odd characters, such as the blacksmith and the cobbler, or amongst the peasants those who for one reason or another were living on the fringe of the community. All this reinforces the view put forward in the previous pages: the characteristic traits of Rumanian fascism can only partly be derived from the social class and economic conditions of its supporters. At least as, if not more, relevant is a set of psychological factors, a state of mind, characteristic of individuals and groups suffering in various degrees and in various ways from lack of social integration and purpose.

8

POLAND

◆

S. Andreski

Semi-fascism against pseudo-fascism

The character of the groupings embattled upon the Polish
political arena on the eve of the second world war offers
interesting material for a comparative analysis of fascism
because many of the features which went together in the
classic Italian and German cases did appear but in incomplete
clusters on different sides of the line dividing the contestants
for power.

The regime set up by Pilsudski after his successful coup in
May 1926 was a military dictatorship of a relatively limited
kind: indeed, much more tolerant than Franco's regime (when
he was still in good health and fully in control) or the dictatorship of Papadopoulos in Greece, neither of which tolerated
opposition political parties or press; whereas in Pilsudski's
Poland opposition parties continued to function and had
deputies in the parliament, despite the use of the resources of
the state for pro-government propaganda, as well as some
fraudulent counting of votes. True, laws were rammed
through by various legalistic subterfuges which violated the
spirit if not the letter of the constitution, and by intimidation
of the deputies; but the opposition remained vociferous in
parliament as well as outside. Opposition newspapers often
used to make scurrilous attacks on Pilsudski and his assistants,
and although issues would be impounded and legally responsible editors often jailed the papers continued to appear.

Pilsudski was not a career officer but the creator of the Polish army. He received no military training and his first 'military' experience consisted of 'terrorist' actions as a socialist militant in the Russian revolution of 1905. On ethnically Polish territory such revolutionary activity had a very mixed character: partly it was an echo of what was happening in Russia, but many of the participants were motivated less by party or class solidarity than by the hatred of Russian domination. In later years Pilsudski told some of his ex-comrades that he saw no point in remaining in the Socialist Party once the tsar was overthrown and Poland had gained independence.

Regarding Russia as the chief enemy, at the beginning of the first world war Pilsudski organized a Polish Legion in Austrian Poland, hoping that a Polish kingdom under a Habsburg might be set up if the Russian empire were rolled back. However, after their victories over the Russians in 1916 the Germans felt no need to hold out this bait to the Poles; and, for resisting an incorporation of his Legion into the regular Austrian army, Pilsudski was sent to prison in Germany. When the Central Powers collapsed and insurgents were chasing the remnants of the German troops out of Poland, Pilsudski became head of state and the commander of the emerging army.

Like most other people, Pilsudski greatly underestimated the bolsheviks' capacity, and thought that a restoration of the old regime in Russia would constitute a greater danger to Polish independence. For this reason he delayed his attack on Kiev (designed to set up an independent state of Ukraine) until the bolsheviks defeated the White army of Denikin. Had this attempt been made while the latter was still advancing towards Moscow, world history might have taken a very different turn. As it happened, Pilsudski's march ended in a disaster and an invasion of Poland by the Red Army which was repulsed only at the gates of Warsaw by a risky outflanking manoeuvre.

In 1921 a constitution modelled on the French one set up a parliamentary government. Like de Gaulle almost three decades later, Pilsudski could not bear to play the game of parliamentary politics and withdrew from all his functions to his house in the country where he lived in impecunious circumstances, refusing to touch the pension granted to him.

From the viewpoint of comparative study it is essential to bear in mind that, in contrast to other personal dictatorships which eventually acquired certain features of fascism (namely, Salazar's in Portugal and Getulio Vargas' in Brazil), Pilsudski's most vehement enemies were to be found in the parties of the right, while he enjoyed a varying degree of goodwill from the parties of the left until more or less the last five years of his life. True, soon after his seizure of power he made peace with the landowning aristocracy which previously was hostile and afraid of his socialist associations, and from 1930 he faced a clear opposition from the parties forming the Centre-Left Alliance. The leaders of this alliance were unlawfully imprisoned and then exiled. None the less, the rudimentary nature of his ideology permitted the existence of a 'leftist' wing in his camp, which became even stronger after his death when the inheritors of power were moving in the direction of pseudo-fascism. The establishment of his dictatorship was certainly not designed to protect the upper classes or to forestall a populist revolution, as was the case with Franco in Spain or Pinochet in Chile. There was no danger of an uprising of the lower classes in Poland in 1926. On the other hand, it is true that the multiplicity of the parties, their shifting alignments and, above all, their spiteful factiousness could be viewed as damaging the cohesion and efficiency of the public administration and the army, and therefore as a grave danger to the national survival.

Like General Videla in Argentina when he put an end to the second Peronist regime, Pilsudski could plead with some justification that he had to save the country from the brink of chaos. True, it is by no means proven that things would not have got better without his intervention, and it is certain that his regime had equally grave faults though of a slightly different kind, but the fact does remain that, owing to unbridled demagoguery and factionalism, the country was governed badly, and that parliament was often a scene of unseemly rows or even brawls. It is also true that deputies (often very ignorant and greedy) interfered with the workings of the administration in a way which aggravated inefficiency and favouritism.

Apart from its lack of totalitarian inclinations, Pilsudski's rule differed from fascism in having no ideology apart from the cult of personality and a vague insistence on the need for order and national strength. Pilsudski had never been a demagogue and was leading no party when he seized power with the assistance of the officers who had been his subordinates during the wars. The only mass organizations which helped him were certain socialist trade unions who regarded him as a leftist and remembered his past as an activist in the revolutionary fraction of the Polish Socialist Party during the 1905 revolution. In fact the refusal of the railwaymen's union to transport to Warsaw the troops sent against him from Poznan tilted the balance in his favour.

Though undoubted master, Pilsudski refrained from taking up the post of either President or Prime Minister and until his death remained the Minister of War. The army and foreign policy were his sole real interests and on some issues pertaining to these matters he showed remarkable far-sightedness. For example, he never had doubts about the nazi danger, and when Hitler came to power he proposed to the French a joint preventive war which the latter refused to contemplate. He had no ideas on other aspects of public life; and when asked after the *coup* about his programme, he answered: 'We must bring a bit of order and honesty.' However, despite his personal honesty and indifference to money, his wayward wilfulness and lack of respect for law stimulated rather than impeded the spread of favouritism and corruption. He had absolutely no idea what to do about it beyond complaining that 'a lot of lice have climbed on my back'. In any case a few years after his seizure of power his health began to fail, and during the last two or three years before his death in 1935 he was a feared and irascible invalid who could still appoint officers of the state but was no longer able to check what they were doing.

So long as the Marshal lived, the regime exhibited no features pertaining specifically to fascism as distinct from other forms of authoritarianism. The ruling circle consisted of Pilsudski's old officers (now mostly ranking as colonels) and chosen top officials. They had no particular views on economic policy beyond a generally conservative orientation. Though only some of them were of aristocratic descent, they all soon acquired fairly close convivial contacts with the landed nobility and to a lesser extent with the wealthy bourgeoisie — which, it must be added, was very small and almost entirely Jewish, except in the western regions where it was mostly German. Although the policy of agrarian reform adopted by the defunct parliamentary government was not altogether discontinued, the division of big estates proceeded at a slow pace; and the general economic policy was conservative in the sense that no radical reforms were undertaken or even envisaged, and the rulers showed no special concern for the plight of the poor. It would be a mistake, however, to regard the regime as the tool of the bourgeoisie or even of the landowners. The former was too weak and alienated in virtue of its Jewishness, and the latter too ineffectual to govern the country through interposed tools. The predominant vested interest was that of the officer corps and the officialdom with their families. The military component had a clear ascendancy; and one of the most conspicuous results of the *cuartelazo* was the taking over of many of the most important civilian posts by seconded officers — analogously to what more recently happened in Brazil and Greece.

To obtain influence in parliament, and eventually control over it, Pilsudski ordered a pro-government party to be set up, baptized as the Non-Party Bloc of Collaboration with the Government — a name which well indicated its passive nature. Its membership comprised mainly people dependent upon the government for their livelihood — public employees of all grades and aspirants to such posts, with a sprinkling of businessmen hoping for a state contract or licence or a less severe treatment from the tax office. The embryonic ideology consisted of depreciation of the disorderliness of parliamentary rule, insistence on the need for a strong government and army, and persistent reminders that the old Polish kingdom perished through excess of freedom leading to anarchy.

In practice, the most conspicuous activity of the Non-Party Bloc (apart from the allocation of jobs) was public worship of the Marshal. This cult of personality was tied up with a genuine popular reverence for things military, fed by an intense nationalism which saw in the army the sole defence against rapacious neighbours. Although many people resented the insolent bearing of the officers and their interference in politics, they hesitated to criticize this pillar of national existence; and for this reason the Polish prewar regime enjoyed a larger measure of popular support than do the Latin American militocracies which are regarded by most citizens as tools of foreign economic domination.

To counteract a widespread preconception, I must stress that neither Pilsudski nor his heirs showed anti-semitic inclinations. On the contrary the imputations of philo-semitism served as the most effective weapons in the campaign waged against him by the National Party. The government had always tried to suppress anti-semitic outbreaks — very vigorously when Pilsudski was still alive — and only during the last two years before the war did their resolve on this matter begin to weaken.

Riding on the crest of a boom, Pilsudski's government was not without popularity during the first three years of its existence, and the enlargement of its parliamentary support in the 1928 elections was not entirely due to administrative pressure. A massive recourse to intimidation and fraud became necessary to retain these seats in the following elections fought in the midst of the great depression which hit Poland very hard indeed.

Shortly before he died Pilsudski promulgated in 1934 a new constitution (rather similar to de Gaulle's) which formally transferred many rights and powers from parliament to the president. In itself the constitution was not unsuited to the condition of Poland, and was not completely authoritarian, as the rulers remained under obligation to seek the approval of the electorate. However, it never became much more than a dead letter because (apart from frequent illegal abuses of power) it was supplemented soon after Pilsudski's death by an electoral ordinance which established a system of screening and selecting the candidates to ensure that the government would always win. The new electoral law in fact abolished elections, and created a legal foundation for an authoritarian regime, which, though still less oppressive than the dictatorship of Pérez Jiménez in Venezuela or Perón in Argentina was certainly much more dictatorial than de Gaulle's.

Becoming increasingly irascible and intolerant, Pilsudski ended his days surrounded by a crowd of unintelligent yes-men. At a loss when he died, and searching for something to replace his by then rather tarnished but still persistent charisma, they began to imitate the models which at the time seemed to represent the victorious trend of social evolution: namely, fascist Italy and nazi Germany.

Pilsudski had certainly been guilty of ordering illegal arrests and ill-treatment of his opponents — probably including a couple of secret murders. None the less, he felt uneasy about doing this, and used force with a great deal of hesitation and with restraint compared to what lay within his power. Encouraged, however, by the example of more 'progressive' states, his successors shed his scruples and set up a concentration camp. It must be added, however, that though evil enough, this camp was no forerunner of Auschwitz: the aim was not extermination but intimidation of political opponents and, seizing the opportunity, of economic criminals — mostly Jews whose crime consisted of taking money abroad without permission (which became necessary in the 1930s), but whose guilt was only 'known' to the police but could not be proven: for if the latter was the case they would have been sentenced by a court and sent to a normal prison. The inmates were imprisoned without trial on the basis of a decision of a police chief or of a *starosta* — an official similar to the French *préfet* or *sous-préfet*. The stay in the prison camp was usually short — normally not more than six months and often only three weeks — but the treatment was exceedingly cruel and, apart from brutal beatings, involved various forms of chicanery designed to undermine the victim's self-respect, such as limiting the time allowed in the lavatory so as to force him to soil his underwear. The staff consisted of policemen who had a record of admonishments or punishments for assaulting prisoners, and was commanded by a sadistic colonel, Kostek-Biernacki.

The imprisoned political opponents represented a wide

assortment: Ukrainian nationalists, Polish fascists, peasant leaders, communists, socialists, trade unionists, even conservative journalists guilty of disrespectful remarks about the character of one of the potentates.

The other most important innovation of Prime Minister Slawoj-Skladkowski (a colonel with a degree in medicine but the mentality of a sergeant-major) was the creation of a motorized riot police, whose helmets had the same shape as those of the *Reichswehr*, and who soon had an opportunity of proving their mettle by terrorizing the peasants in the southern regions who refused to pay the oppressive taxes.

On the walls of all public buildings the dead Marshal began to be flanked by President Moscicki (hitherto a figurehead) and the new Marshal Rydz-Smigly — a very mediocre man who had been Pilsudski's obedient hireling. With time the latter moved gradually to the fore as the prime object of a cult of personality which, though meeting less resistance, always remained rather artificial in comparison with the genuine devotion which his many followers had felt for Pilsudski.

Ideologically the pro-government party (now renamed the Camp of National Unity) remained confused, and so disorientated that for a short while some of its organizers even toyed with marxist phraseology. The only sure point (on which a large part of the nation followed it) was a devotion to the army, that is, to militarism. Efforts were made to build up the pro-government youth organizations, but the results were merely quantitative, and amounted to gathering a large number of careerists or indigent students seeking a sojourn in a summer camp with free food and transport. Indoctrination in reverence for the governmental trinity (the dead Marshal, the new one and the President) was intensified and teachers (especially headmasters) culpable of tepidity were dismissed and replaced by more ardent adorers. None the less, these efforts failed on the whole to conjure up fanaticism and mass hysteria, and as far as intensity of feelings was concerned the only analogies to the *Hitler Jugend* or the Rumanian Iron Guard could be found among the opposition youth movements.

Perón's party had also been organized from above, when

he was already in the saddle, but in contrast to the 'Camp of National Unity' it had succeeded in stirring up widespread and genuine enthusiasm for *justicialismo*. Moreover, whereas the Polish government's party consisted almost entirely of white-collar state employees to the almost complete exclusion of manual workers, Perón's egalitarian demagogy (made credible by a few measures of real levelling) secured him a mass following among the labourers.

The predilection for regimentation led the rulers to introduce numbers and uniforms for secondary-school boys, although the increasingly time-consuming and harsh part-time military training in all educational institutions for boys over sixteen was at least partly dictated by a genuine desire to strengthen national defence. Despite the growing oppressiveness of the regime, the opposition parties continued to operate legally, with the exception of the Communist Party, membership of which was punishable by imprisonment for five years. The trade unions conserved their full independence although they were harassed and their members ran the risk of being beaten by the police during strikes. Outspoken enemies of the regime continued to teach at the universities (which unlike the schools had a large autonomy) and vociferously hostile newspapers continued to appear, though under harassment. Even more: in some universities and colleges the strong-arm men of the semi-fascist and fascist opposition youth movements were able to intimidate their pro-government colleagues and even professors, and fought battles with the police which on some occasions lasted several days. On the other hand a citizen could be imprisoned for two years for saying something to an official which could be interpreted as an insult, although the treatment of the public in government offices was very rude. It was, however, easy to get in and out of the country, or to obtain foreign publications.

The Polish regime was never fully or even half fascist in any acceptable sense of the term: it had not grown out of a movement, it had no doctrine advocating a new social or even political system, its mass organization was created bureaucratically from above, and was never used for street fighting or suppressing strikes or keeping opponents at bay — a job left to the police. It had no equivalent of Hitler's storm-troopers or Mussolini's blackshirts. None of the leaders was a charismatic demagogue. In career and personality they resembled Argentina's Ongania or Brazil's Castello Branco rather than Hitler, Mussolini or Doriot.

Rather than to nazi Germany or fascist Italy, prewar Poland offered more analogies to Franco's Spain; although here too there were a number of important differences – the most obvious being that the Polish dictatorship was much more tolerant of independent organizations and more liberal with regard to the dissemination of ideas and the censorship of the press. Secondly, the Spanish fascist party – the Falange – formed a part of the ruling establishment whereas in Poland the semi-fascist National Party (SN) as well as the smaller, more fully fascist, Radically National Camp (ONR) were hoping to overthrow the regime, although it is true that a splinter group of the latter party did for a while ally itself briefly with the government in 1937 when Colonel Koc was pushing the government party – the Camp of National Unity (OZN) – in the direction of more complete fascism. The third important difference was that in Spain the army was regarded as the engine of internal repression whereas in Poland it enjoyed the genuine affection of the mass of the nation, though not, of course, of ethnic minorities. No contrast could be more striking than between the sullen reactions of the scanty spectators at a military parade in Madrid, and the ovations from large crowds which used to accompany such occasions in Poland. Though opposed to the excessive power and privileges of the officers, even the socialists were not anti-militaristic, as under the circumstances only somebody who favoured a renewed subjugation of Poland by one of its neighbours could have been hostile to the army as such.

The fourth important difference was that the Polish dictatorship enjoyed no special favours of the Church, which on the whole preferred the opposition National Party and was a bit worried about Pilsudski's Calvinist background, socialist past and Jewish friends; whereas the modicum of allegiance which the Spanish military rebels and their landowning allies did manage to find among the masses during the civil war was due entirely to the Church's blessing of their claim to defend the faith against the godless republicans. Throughout its duration pietistic docility was the only part of the ideological support of the Spanish regime which had any motivating force among the common people. In Poland, had the fight been between the socialists and the others, the clerical issue might have become a bone of contention. As it was both the government and its two strongest opponents — the National Party and the People's Party (known abroad under the more descriptive name of Peasants' Party) — were not only willing but eager to leave the Church in control of souls, vied with one another in piety, and all welcomed priests into their ranks. Consequently the Church did not have to choose between the main contestants for power and could concentrate its ire on the marxists and the liberal free-thinkers.

The fifth difference between prewar Poland and Franco's Spain was that the ideological component which could be called fascist (as distinct from militarist or simply authoritarian) was even weaker in the Polish regime, which never had a wing attaining to the programmatic articulation of the Falange or the Opus Dei. As we shall see in a moment, there existed in Poland at that time a party calling itself Falanga, but it was in violent opposition. Furthermore, the Polish rulers have never made any attempts to set up a corporativist economic system, and such measures of economic interventionism as exchange and import controls instituted in the 1930s were dictated by a pragmatic concern about the desperate position of the balance of payments.

In comparison with Horthy's Hungary the aristocracy had much less power in Poland, where there was no counterpart to Count Károlyi. Contrary to the opinion generally held abroad, very few of the colonels who ruled Poland were of aristocratic origin. Pilsudski himself was a minor squire, but the ancestry of his successor, Rydz-Smigly, was so obscure that his enemies whispered that he was the son of a Ukrainian peasant woman and an Austrian gendarme. Foreign names like Beck or Bartel, or peasant ones like Koc or Rydz, indicate that their bearers were no aristocrats. Only in the diplomatic service and among cavalry officers did the noblemen predominate. All in all, the Polish regime on the eve of war could be characterized as an authoritarian, highly militaristic, pseudo-fascist bureaucracy.

The most dangerous enemy of the regime — that is, the enemy most capable in the short run of infiltrating the important posts and organizing a coup — was the National Party, which started its life under the name of National Democracy, and during the parliamentary era before 1926 offered more analogies to the Indian Congress than to Mussolini's blackshirts. Its founder, Roman Dmowski — like Pilsudski of petty-squire ancestry — was a political intellectual like Nehru or Thomas Masaryk rather than an uncouth rabble rouser like Hitler or Doriot; and his writings are on a higher intellectual plane, and in a more educated style, than those of Mussolini or Primo de Rivera, not to speak of the nazi outpourings. In his outlook and manner of expressing his views he resembled most closely the elders of Action Française such as Charles Maurras, but especially Jacques Bainville with whom he shared a fear and dislike of the Germans. He transmitted this attitude to the National Party, including its new fascist wing, which remained throughout its existence warmly pro-French and militantly anti-German, and used to accuse the government (especially when Colonel Beck was Minister of Foreign Affairs) of cowardice or even treason in their negotiations with the western neighbour. Vying with each other in patriotism, the government and the National Party jointly fanned nationalist fervour to such a degree that, regardless of what they thought about Poland's chances of defending itself, the leaders could not imitate Dr Beneš and accede to Hitler's ultimatum.

Apart from general chauvinism, the National Party appealed first to anti-semitism, and secondly to the resentment against the privileged bureaucrats, which was particularly strong in the western regions where it combined with the protest against discrimination in favour of other parts of the country. The party's economic programme was *poujadiste avant la lettre*: protection of small traders and producers against the rapacious bureaucrats and big business which was in the hands of Jews and Germans — which explains the confluence of *poujadisme* and chauvinism. Far from preaching the desirability of dictatorship — hardly a profitable line to take in a country which was already enjoying the benefits of this method of conducting public affairs — the party clamoured for the resurrection of democratic liberties and for honest elections. In fact, the *Führerprinzip* never became the party's official doctrine; nevertheless in its organization and the content of its propaganda, as well as the manner of conducting it, during the 1930s the party — and especially its youth movement — fell deeper and deeper under the spell of fascism.

As in most of the world, the great depression of the 1930s radicalized all political groupings in Poland; and the sliding of the National Party towards pugilism and subversive preparations was intertwined with the growing oppressiveness of the regime in a relationship of mutual stimulation.

Mussolini had many admirers in Poland both on the government's side and among its enemies; and the attractiveness of his ideas was further enhanced by Hitler's spectacular career and his success in rapidly raising Germany's power and international status. Not that the Polish admirers of Hitler were pro-German. On the contrary, without drawing a rebuke from their elders, the younger leaders of the National Party proclaimed as their goal a reconquest of all the lands which had ever been ruled by the Polish kings; which on the west meant the present frontier on the Oder and Neisse, with of course East Prussia incorporated. The party emblem was the sword of Boleslav the Valiant who at the beginning of the eleventh century established the frontier of his kingdom beyond the Oder. It is surprising how many people regarded these aims as practicable, particularly as they also included pushing the eastern frontiers of Poland to Pskov and the Black Sea. The last thing which these imperialists expected was that the first part of their programme of territorial expansion would be carried out by Stalin at the price of annexing the eastern territories of prewar Poland. Their attitude to Hitler was one of admiration for his skill and pluck, coupled with an intense desire to do for Poland what they believed he was doing for Germany: that is, to create a monolithic militarized state which could beat the Germans at their own game. Naturally, this was also the avowed aim of the more extreme splinter group, the Radically National

Camp, although in practice this faction played down the issues of foreign policy, and concentrated on baiting and waylaying Jews.

Unfortunately from the viewpoint of the National Party's goals the state comprised large ethnic minorities which added up to over one-third of the population. As far as the Ukrainians, Byelorussians and Lithuanians were concerned, the plan of these Polish double patriots was to apply to them the same medicine which the Germans had tried on the Poles before 1918 — forcible assimilation. Efforts in this direction — consisting of curtailments of non-Polish-language schools and publications — were repeatedly made by the administration, but the National Party and its more extreme splinter groups accused the ruling circle of being treasonably timid. As regards the Jews, they regarded a policy of assimilation as undesirable even if it were practicable — which they believed it was not.

Wherever there are large masses of densely settled Jews there exists between them and the *goim* a barrier of endogamy and a certain degree of mistrust and mutual disdain, or at least condescension, often coupled with expressions of enmity — open on the part of the majority, veiled on the part of the minority. However, in traditional eastern Europe this barrier entailed no questioning of the Jews' right to a place in society. In Poland the idea that it might be possible to get rid of the Jews appeared only at the beginning of the present century, and became widely popular only in the 1930s when it was the main plank of the National Party's propaganda; the other contribution of the party to the socio-political climate being an interest in ancestry regardless of the professed religion, which manifested itself most conspicuously in an assiduous search for Jewish grandmothers of prominent political opponents. This preoccupation, it must be added, was suitable only for people of fairly humble descent because it was chiefly among the nobility and the intelligentsia of several generations' standing that Jewish ancestors were to be found. It might be remarked, incidentally, that if one goes by so-called racial traits, it is quite evident that very many central European aristocrats have a much closer genetic relationship with the ancient semites than most of the generals of the Israeli army whose physical appearance is typically Slav. Polish novels contain many references to an 'eagle-like nose' typical of a highly-bred, martial nobleman; and it is clear that this genetic feature is not indigenous to this part of Europe and can only have been imported from the Near East. Almost needless to say, the protagonists of racial purity took no cognizance of such trivia.

Given what could be foreseen at the time, the solution which the National Party proposed for the Jewish problem was as wild as the idea of the frontier on the Oder: namely, a transplantation of the Jews to Palestine. The only Jews of whom the National Party approved were the zionists; and although some of their followers whispered about killing the Jews, the party planners drafted elaborate memoranda on how to organize Jewish emigration, working out how many ships and railway wagons it would require, and how many could travel overland and how many by sea. Some even suggested that Poland should take over the Palestinian Mandate and send troops to carve out a Jewish state. The most common slogan on the placards carried by anti-semitic demonstrators was 'Out to Palestine', although in practice the main efforts were directed towards reducing the entry of the Jews into lucrative professions such as medicine and law, keeping them out of the higher posts in the army and civil service, undermining their superior competitive power in business by harassment, and limiting the number of Jewish students at the universities. The official aim of the National Party was to limit the number of Jews to 10 per cent of all students (which was the percentage of Jews to the total population), but the hotheads hoped to debar them altogether from higher educational institutions.

As the deepening crisis made *laissez-faire* capitalism appear less and less workable, the National Party gravitated more and more towards the idea of a corporativist economy on the Italian model, but with a strong *poujadiste* streak. The National Party had never been a pretorian guard of capitalism (to use Kautsky's expression), firstly because the capitalists were either Jews or Germans — and therefore unsuitable allies for a chauvinist party — and secondly because neither big business (such as there was) nor the estate owners had any need of an additional guard, as they were quite well protected by the arm of the authoritarian state. Consequently, in contrast to the Italian *fasci*, the strong-arm squads of the youth movement were never employed to intimidate the workers or tenants and suppress strikes. Indeed, since breaking the windows of Jewish shops was one of their chief occupations, and since most shopkeepers were Jews, the activities of these militants could at a stretch be called anti-capitalist. Another important difference from Italian fascism (and even more nazism) was the clericalism of the National Party, which with fair success tried to outbid the government in piety and ultramontane proclamations, and thus to enlist the powerful force of devotionalism on its side.

To assess justly the ideals and the appeal of a corporate state we must divest ourselves of the pejorative emotional resonance which the word 'corporativist' has acquired through being bandied by regimes which lost a war in addition to committing atrocious crimes. The first thing to remember is that until Keynes published his *General Theory* in 1936 nobody offered a diagnosis of the economic crisis which suggested an effective and reasoned remedy, and that the most successful policy against unemployment at the time was the one pursued under Hitler's aegis by Hjalmar Schacht 'playing by ear'. As *laissez-faire* capitalism was obviously not working, most people agreed that it had to be replaced, the only question in dispute being by what. And here the choice was limited to some form of confiscatory collectivism inspired by marxism on the one side, and on the other some form of regulation by partnership between government and private producers organized in cartels, guilds and corporations. One did not have to be a lunatic or a criminal to opt for the latter solution, particularly if one had property or a good job to lose in the event of a revolution. There is no necessary connection between corporativism and concentration camps; and in any case Mussolini's corporativism was largely (and Hitler's entirely) a sham covering pure despotism. Furthermore, although 'corporativist' has become a dirty word, the economic structures of present-day western Europe have evolved in a direction which does not diverge very far from what the academic protagonists of corporativism envisaged in the 1920s and early 1930s.

Whereas the role of the National Party in society and politics was very different, in the realm of paraphernalia its imitation of the Italian and German models became almost complete. Step by step the increasingly influential youth wing introduced into the old party of black-coated notables brown shirts (though pinker than those of the nazis), the jackboots, the goose-step and the nazi salute. Unlike the *fasci* or the SA, however, these cohorts were prevented by the police from carrying weapons. Moreover, in contrast to its latter-day models, the party had no charismatic rabble-rousing leader, although at least one of the younger chiefs was moving into that position. The old intellectual politician Roman Dmowski remained the titular head until his death shortly before the war, but he was quite unfit to lead uniformed stormtroopers.

In western Poland the National Party enjoyed the support of the large majority resentful of Warsaw bureaucrats. As this was the only region where commerce was in the hands of the Gentiles, the local traders liked a party which promised to keep out the Jews; and in any case they were attracted by its *poujadiste* economic programme. Only in these provinces, moreover, were the peasants prosperous and self-respecting instead of being underdogs; and consequently, only here were they attracted in mass to a party which tried to integrate them with the artisans, the petty traders and the out-of-office intelligentsia in opposition to the grasping bureaucrats. In central Poland the National Party made some headway among the artisans and the emerging class of Gentile small traders, but not so much among the industrial workers, most of whom adhered to the Socialist Party. In southern and to a lesser extent central Poland the majority of articulate peasants supported the People's Party. There were many other parties — the Ukrainian nationalists, Jewish socialists, marxist peasants and so on — but none of them had much influence. It must be noted, however, that owing to the government's recourse to fraud and intimidation in the elections, even before the new system of screening candidates was introduced, the returns at the polls did not represent the true measure of popular support which the various parties enjoyed.

The National Party's following among the intelligentsia was largely a question of ins and outs: the well placed being mostly on the side of the government, whereas students and graduates without connections, and therefore with poor prospects for a good bureaucratic post — but whose piety or non-proletarian background deterred them from socialism — flocked to the youth movement, and prepared to over-throw the government. They were equally attracted to the programme of eliminating Jewish competition for white-collar employment. The underlying condition of these motiv-ations was that the production of diploma holders greatly exceeded the demand — though not necessarily the needs which could not translate themselves into monetary offers.

There were hotheads who found the National Party too moderate — too much under the influence of elderly professors, lawyers and parsons, and perhaps not eager enough to give positions of leadership commensurate with their merits to young firebrands, who consequently broke away and founded a Radically National Camp, which advo-cated more violent direct action and even terrorism. A small splinter group of similar persuasion called itself Falanga, to accentuate its feeling of kinship with its Spanish prototype. Though small in absolute numbers, these factions made a great noise and had a big following among the students. They were accused of a few political assassinations, but their chief activity consisted of organizing student riots and assaults on Jews. They were believed to be collecting weapons. Some of their leaders were put into the government's concentration camp.

The Radically National Camp resembled the Rumanian Iron Guard in its readiness to resort to violence but not in its devotionalism, being in fact much less clerical than the National Party, and in this respect more like the Italian fascists or the nazis. On the other hand, in the social orgins of its members it was much less demotic than either the Iron Guard or the nazis and more like the French Cagoulards or the Spanish Falange. As with Action Française, its propa-ganda and activities had fewer populist undertones than those of the nazis, not to speak of the thoroughly populist Iron Guard.

There was thus a curious constellation of forces on the Polish political arena on the eve of war. The parties expressly vowed to the interests of the poorer classes — the People's Party and the Polish Socialist Party — though in existence and enjoying wide sympathies, were effectively kept down by the police; while the Communist Party was banned and in any case weakened by its subservience to the national enemy, as well as by the extermination of its best leaders during Stalin's purges. The open struggle for power was waged between a pseudo-fascist, militarized bureaucracy and a semi-fascist party of anti-semitic and ultramontane chauvinists.

During the last few months before the war the internal quarrels somewhat abated, dampened by the rising wave of unrealistic martial fervour. No doubt the Germans wanted no equivalent of Quisling in Poland, but the fact remains that none of the Polish fascists and semi-fascists turned into one, and many fell resisting the invasion or in the underground army, or perished in the concentration camps. Given their treatment of the conquered, it was not surprising that the nazis found collaborators (whether for hounding Jews or any other purpose), not on the basis of ideological sympathies but among individuals of generally low moral fibre, lacking any sense of honour, and particularly susceptible to the promptings of cowardice and greed.

9

FINLAND

◆

A. F. Upton

Finland was one of the European countries where fascism came very close to a successful seizure of power in the early 1930s, though it was her good fortune to survive the danger and preserve a democratic system of government intact, through the strains and stresses of war and defeat, down to the present day. It is probable that the near success of fascism in Finland is closely linked to the fact that in its beginnings it was a natural development of the native nationalist tradition, and owed little or nothing to international fascism, while its later adoption of the outward trappings of fascist orthodoxy added nothing to its strength, and may indeed have weakened it. But it follows that for any understanding of developments in Finland, it is necessary to be aware of the basic features of the history of the Finnish nationalist movement.

From 1809 to 1917, Finland was an autonomous Grand Duchy under the tsar of Russia. It was a predominantly rural society, in which Finnish was the language of the vast majority of labourers, share-croppers, and small independent farmers, but which had been endowed with a native, Swedish-speaking ruling class of landlords, burghers and officials. During the course of the nineteenth century there had developed a typical romantic-nationalist movement built round the claims of the Finnish language. The political father of Finnish nationalism, Snellman, was deeply indebted to

German idealist philosophy, whose ideas and ideals provided
the movement with its intellectual backbone, and left the
emergent Finnish intelligentsia with a powerful pro-German
orientation which it has never lost. As the movement for the
development of the Finnish language grew, there was
collected a body of folk poetry, the *Kalevala*, which was to
become the Finnish national epic. By an accident of geography the richest finds were made over the frontier in Russian
Karelia, and as research developed, further pockets of
Finnish-speaking peoples were discovered, scattered over
northern Russia as far as the Urals. These discoveries were to
leave a fateful and, some would argue, baleful legacy to
Finnish nationalism.

The early nationalist movement was naturally directed
against the hegemony of the Swedish-speaking minority and
their culture, but in the 1890s internal divisions were overshadowed by a change in Russian policy. Hitherto the
Russian government had respected the constitutional autonomy of Finland; now they launched a policy of crude russification, involving open violation of the legal and constitutional rights of the country. This inevitably swung the
nationalist movement round towards a policy of resistance
to Russian aggression and, at a very early stage, there
emerged an activist minority, dedicated to underground
conspiracy and the use of violence, which ran sometimes
parallel, sometimes at odds, with the constitutional non-
violent resistance of the majority.

Resistance to russification left two abiding characteristic
features of Finnish nationalism, of which the first is a hatred
of Russia that quickly took on a racialist character. The
nationalists saw the Russians as Asiatic barbarian oppressors,
the hereditary enemies of the Finnish race and culture.
Against this enemy, history and divine providence had called
the Finnish nation to defend western and Christian values. In
this way the nationalists discovered Finland's place in the
great scheme of European history, and her manifest destiny.
The second characteristic was the tradition of activism, the
taste for extra-legal direct action, for underground conspiracy, and for solutions by violence.

This simple emerging pattern was complicated in the last

years of the nineteenth century by the emergence of Finnish socialism, a product of the industrialism that had come to Finland after 1870. The Finnish workers' movement quickly adopted marxism in its most doctrinaire forms, scorning Bernstein's revisionism, adhering to class war and revolution. Thus, while the socialists and the bourgeois nationalists shared a common enemy in the tsarist oppressor, so that some co-operation between the movements inevitably developed, as a general rule the socialists rejected all contact with the domestic class enemy, while as good international-ists they began to seek contacts with the Russian socialist movement. It is true that during the crisis of 1905-6 the socialists and the nationalists managed to work together in forcing liberal reforms on the Russian government, but this co-operation was short-lived, and even renewed Russian oppression after 1907 did not heal the breach between the socialists and the nationalists — their mutual hatred of Russia was no stronger than their distrust of one another.

When war broke out in 1914, all Finns recognized that Russian military defeat might be Finland's opportunity, and the bolder spirits set about preparing for any eventuality. The activist wing of the nationalists, with some socialist support, negotiated with the Germans a scheme for training Finnish volunteers in the German army, who would then become the spearhead of a future Finnish national rising. These were the *Jägers*, of whom there were about two thousand fully trained in Germany by 1917. After the Russian February Revolu-tion, the activists began to plan a revolt, in close collabor-ation with the German authorities. But the socialists, who in the parliamentary elections of 1916 had won an absolute majority, found themselves in a strong position when parlia-ment was allowed to meet by the Russian provisional government, and lost what interest they had ever had in co-operating with Germany, while their radicals perceived a chance to carry through a revolution that would secure independence of Russia and victory in the class war at one blow.

In these circumstances tensions built up inside Finland through 1917. They were sharply boosted when first, in fresh parliamentary elections, the socialists lost their majority to the bourgeois parties, and then the Russian October Revolution encouraged the socialist radicals to defy the verdict of the electors, and emulate the bolshevik example. But the socialists were split, and hesitated fatally, while the new bourgeois government declared independence on 6 December, and it was not until late January 1918 that the socialists sought to take power by an armed *coup*, which precipitated a civil war. In this, the Reds were assisted by Russian weapons and technical advisers, and the Whites by German military aid, and it was the latter who emerged victorious in May 1918 and, together with their German allies, indulged in the bloody repression of the vanquished Reds.

They also tried to strike back at Soviet Russia, and to expand the frontiers of the new state by seizing eastern Karelia and the Kola peninsula, at first, under P.E. Svinhufvud as Regent, with German backing, then, under the pro-entente Mannerheim, the White commander in the civil war, with Anglo-French backing. But the Allies could not persuade the Russian Whites to agree to pay the territorial price which the Finns were asking in return for intervention in the Russian civil war. Thus the proposed territorial expansion of the republic was frustrated, and after Mannerheim's defeat in the presidential election of 1919, it was dropped as official policy. But nationalist activists, with the acquiescence of the Finnish government, were allowed to mount two incursions into Karelia in support of anti-Soviet elements there, the last in 1922. But these were defeated. When official Finland made peace with Soviet Russia at Tartu, in October 1920, the best that could be secured was a promise of autonomy for Soviet Karelia, a promise that was to be fulfilled in a manner that was not anticipated. The activists rejected the peace treaty from the outset, while the more moderate right accepted it grudgingly as an unfortunate necessity. Thus Finland was endowed with one of the most promising ingredients for a fascist movement, a *terra irredenta* in Karelia, whose loss could be blamed on the feebleness of the democratic regime which had negotiated the 'shameful' treaty of Tartu.

The circumstances in which independence had been gained

dictated the shape of postwar Finnish politics. Within the Finnish left, the defeated Red leaders had retired into Russia, where in August 1918 they formed the Finnish Communist Party. The socialists who remained in Finland, and survived the White terror, re-formed a Social Democratic Party, still marxist, but of the revisionist brand. This party, which was legal, slowly recovered strength and usually held about sixty seats in the 200-member parliament, but the bourgeois parties mostly continued to treat the social democrats as political outlaws, and would have no open dealings with them, while the communists attacked them bitterly as traitors to the socialist cause.

The Communist Party was regarded from the beginning as an instrument of bolshevik imperialism, a tool of Moscow, and a treasonable conspiracy. It was formally adjudged an illegal organization in Finland, and any of its members who fell into government hands got long terms of imprisonment. But it proved difficult to repress the communists. In the first place they enjoyed a secure base just over the frontier, across which men, money and propaganda flowed freely. But what was worse was that Soviet Karelia, in a mockery of the provisions of the treaty of Tartu, was indeed given a measure of independence, and became the private colony of the Finnish Communist Party, which they could develop as the nucleus of a future Soviet Finland. It needs no imagination to guess how this situation affected the nationalists in Finland, above all the resentful and frustrated activists.

But in the second place, the communists continued to attract a strong popular following as the true heirs of the defeated Reds, and this enabled them to infiltrate and control the Finnish trade union movement through most of the 1920s, to contest elections through front organizations, publish newspapers, run a youth movement. The first of their front organizations, the Finnish Workers' Party, was dissolved in 1923, only to be replaced by the Workers' and Peasants' Alliance. Through these movements the communists held between twenty and thirty seats in parliament, and controlled many municipalities. This blatant defiance of the clear intention of the law was a further gross provocation to the right, and did little to encourage respect for the law in general, or for the governments which apparently lacked the power to enforce it. The social democrats, who suffered more directly from the communists than anyone, still felt bound to defend their activities on general democratic principles, exposing themselves to charges of collusion.

The forces of the right were organized politically in the Kokoomus (Coalition) Party. This party had from the beginning adopted an ambiguous attitude to the new republican regime; it had been monarchist in 1918, and still hankered after a strong executive which would be above party politics. The party was fanatically anti-Russian and enjoyed the open support of Finnish big business. Further, it had the open or implicit support of many of the leaders of the victorious Whites. Svinhufvud was an open supporter, and he had never been reconciled with the parliamentary regime; as late as 1936 he was telling the German ambassador that it had grave deficiencies, and needed at least to be offset by a strong leader at the head of the executive. Similar views were held by the leading military heroes of 1918, like General Walden, organizer of the new Finnish paper industry and a pillar of the Kokoomus, whose views were known to echo those of his close friend Mannerheim, though the latter would never deign to be formally associated with a political party. These men, the White grandees of 1918, made no secret of their contempt for party politics, their impatience with the feebleness of the parliamentary republic, their belief that all socialists were traitors and hirelings from Moscow, their conviction that the final reckoning with the bolsheviks was yet to come, and their regret that the job had not been finished properly after 1918. Thus the founding fathers of the new state tended to express rejection of their offspring, because it had failed to follow the paths they had pointed out for it, and the Kokoomus Party tended to echo their sentiments. The mood was described by one of them in 1931 as follows:

Out of the game and powerless, embittered and distrustful, the men of 1918 withdrew into their shells. They had a dim perception that what they had won was now being thrown away by a kind of treason. They had no faith in the politics of compromise.

This left a very narrow base for the parliamentary regime to operate from. There were the Swedish People's Party, a pressure group dedicated to preserving the rights of the Swedish-speaking minority, the small Progressive Party which represented the liberal bourgeoisie and the intelligentsia, and the agrarians representing the small independent farmer. Since the anti-parliamentary groups — Kokoomus and communists — controlled between them nearly fifty of the 200 seats, and since the centre parties dare not enter into formal coalition with the social democrats, who had a further sixty seats, the parliamentary situation did not encourage the formation of strong governments. The regime could just survive, basically because there was tacit co-operation between the social democrats and the centre parties. But it was a survival marked by a depressing series of short-lived coalition ministries. In these circumstances it was most creditable that the governments of the 1920s managed to wind up the civil war by a general amnesty, enfranchise the share-croppers and tenant farmers through radical agrarian reform, institute universal compulsory primary education, eradicate illiteracy, raise standards of public health, find new markets for Finnish exports to replace the lost Russian market, and preside over the reconstruction of the Finnish timber and paper industries which was transforming the economy. The achievement is impressive, but its political base remained undeniably precarious and narrow and, as events proved, at the mercy of any serious setback.

Against the background of the parliamentary game which they despised, the forces of the right entrenched themselves in movements and organizations of a kind different from the orthodox political party, leaving the Kokoomus to fly their flag in parliament. The most important of these was the Suojeluskunta — Defence Corps — hereafter referred to as the SK. This was a volunteer militia first raised by the activists before 1918, and retained after the war. Although largely armed and financed out of government funds, it was an autonomous organization, whose officers were elected by the membership from the parish level to the national commander-in-chief. It also controlled its own membership, and socialists of any kind were rigidly excluded, so that the SK was in effect a private army at the disposal of the right, regarding internal security as its first function. In addition the SK gave the right a nation-wide organizational framework, while its annual congresses provided a platform on which conservative and nationalist views were freely aired. Over wide areas of the country, the local SK and its officials exercised a condominium with the duly constituted organs and officials of the republic.

The second major institutional embodiment of the Finnish right which developed in the 1920s was the Akateeminen Karjala-Seura — the Academic Karelian Society — hereafter referred to as AKS. This began as a student society in the university of Helsinki, founded by activist students who had taken part in the expeditions into Karelia in the immediate postwar period. Its original aim was to stimulate continuing interest in the Karelian question, and to organize relief activities among Karelian refugees, but it quickly grew to be the leading student organization. It was a masonic type of society with a carefully controlled membership, and those admitted were subjected to an examination and had to pledge unconditional obedience to the Society. By 1926 the Society had infiltrated all the student bodies, and in the 1930s could count on about 80 per cent of the vote for its candidates in all student elections. Postgraduate membership was developed, and a nation-wide network of branches established.

AKS became another undoubted power in the land, for the great majority of Finnish-speaking students enrolled, and were subject to the systematic brain-washing and discipline which was the heart of the Society's activity. This was important, because in Finland virtually the whole ruling class is university trained, so that the civil service, the officer corps, the professions, the writers and journalists, the managerial class in industry, and the teachers were predominantly men and women who had subscribed to the ideals of the AKS, and tended to project those ideals on the community at large. Only the minority of socialist students and the Swedish-speaking students stood out against the AKS, so that the pressure for conformity was very strong, and the ideas of AKS became the accepted norm for the educated Finn.

The ideology of AKS was strongly nationalist, and politically reactionary. It stood of course for unyielding resistance to communism at home and abroad, and linked this with its aspirations towards the territorial expansion of Finland at Russia's expense expressed in the idea of *Suur-Suomi* (Greater Finland). In its more sober forms the idea was that in the inevitable European showdown with communism, Finland would have the chance to annex eastern Karelia. In its more expansive forms it envisaged taking the Kola peninsula, incorporating Estonia and Ingria — the region round Leningrad — and the pockets of Finnish-speaking peoples in northern Russia, which would produce a Finnish great power stretching to the Urals. The Society advocated extreme linguistic and racial nationalism, it was totally hostile to the Swedish-speaking minority, opposed any Scandinavian orientation of Finnish culture or politics, opposed the League of Nations and disarmament, and increasingly came to reject political democracy. Here foreign borrowings became evident in the concept of democracy as a degenerate form of government unsuited to a strong and vigorous nation, and inevitably producing weak and corrupt government. The AKS particularly rejected the party system, since it regarded all parties as corrupt interest groups, while it preached a national unity transcending all internal divisions. A modern Finnish commentator has remarked that 'the Society was born before nazism and fascism, but it belonged to the same family.' It must be stressed that AKS was never an overtly political movement, and that its activity and influence were confined to the university-trained élite, but within that sector of Finnish society AKS was promoting an intellectual and psychological climate favourable to right-wing, authoritarian concepts.

A very different kind of organization which emerged in the 1920s was Vientirauha (industrial peace), financed by big business, and dedicated to combating aggressive trade unionism. This organization maintained a roster of volunteer strike-breakers, willing to go anywhere where industrial strife broke out. Vientirauha recruited chiefly in Pohjanmaa, the province bordering on the northern part of the gulf of Bothnia, which had been the cradle and power house of the White movement at the beginning of the civil war. The region was dominated by small independent farmers, who had fallen victim in the nineteenth century to the more extreme forms of Lutheran pietism, and mixed this in with a fiery nationalism, and a local tradition of fierce, lawless violence. Socialists were damned as townees, enemies of private landowning, and atheists, and, since 1917, as hirelings of Russia. Here it was easy to recruit young sons of the farms, pay them a retainer, and keep them as industrial ever-readies. They needed the cash, and enjoyed the adventure, and paid strike-breaking became an acceptable auxiliary occupation of the region. The first figurehead of Finnish fascism, Vihtori Kosola, was a recruiting agent for Vientirauha in Pohjanmaa, who rose to be the area organizer and treasurer of the organization. Kosola was himself a farmer from the region, and he made himself so valuable to his employers that they seem to have overlooked some very curious accounting on his part in 1928.

Looking back over the scene of Finland in the 1920s one can see much that was conducive to the emergence of a fascist type of movement. On the one side, the right, the self-conscious heirs of the victorious Whites, felt bitterly that somehow they had been cheated of the fruits of victory, that there were accounts still to be settled, and while scorning traditional politics, they built up their strength, especially through the SK, for the day of reckoning that was surely coming. On the other side were the communists, in many ways a mirror image of the right, openly dedicated to reversing the verdict of the civil war, blatantly building up their forces over the frontier, openly backed by Soviet Russia, brazenly mocking the law by their political and industrial activity inside the country. In these circumstances a renewal of violence was never far away, for in Finland, unlike many parts of Europe, the communist bogey was no figment of the imagination, but a hard and menacing political reality.

Yet no fascist movement emerged. It is true that one can find plenty of individual approval of Mussolini as a strong man who knew how to deal with communists; the AKS often cited Italy as a model of national regeneration, the Kokoomus approved of him. The rise of German nazism was also noted with approval in many places on the right, where

Weimar Germany was felt to be deplorably weak, and men longed for the re-emergence of a strong Germany that would be a counterpoise to Russia. But this was all, and it seems to illustrate the truth that Finland is stony ground for foreign ideologies in some respects. Isolated by geography and language, given to introspective brooding on their own special problems, the Finns have tended to be scornful of patent solutions for their difficulties imported ready-made from abroad. They do not accept that anyone from outside could teach them much about what directly concerns themselves. Italy was a distant country of which the average Finn had no direct knowledge and little interest. Fascism, as it emerged in Finland, was a home-grown product; what it came to borrow from international fascism were only the superficial trappings.

The economic depression came to Finland early and was affecting the vital timber trade by 1928, immediately producing a crop of industrial disputes in which the communists and Vientirauha clashed forcefully. As unemployment rose there was increasing evidence that the communists would be the immediate beneficiaries of working-class discontent, and their propaganda showed that they sensed a decisive struggle had begun. The right reacted by calling on the government to take defensive action, but although the government was willing to respond by new anti-communist legislation, it could not get it through parliament, since any major measures would have to take the form of constitutional amendments, requiring a two-thirds majority, and the social democrats alone, even without the twenty-eight communists in parliament, were enough to block this. In these circumstances, the thoughts of the right turned naturally towards direct action.

Through the summer of 1929 tension rose steadily, as the communists ran a campaign against the alleged danger of imminent European war directed against the Soviet Union, with processions and mass meetings. They announced that on 1 August they would hold a great peace demonstration in Helsinki, and various organizations of the right, above all the SK, announced that if the government did not ban the demonstration, they would stop it themselves. The government yielded, and at once became the focus of a communist-inspired campaign over its denial of the basic rights of citizens, pursued through questions in parliament and rallies up and down the country. The extremists on both sides were plainly looking for a showdown, and in November 1929 it began.

The communist youth organization scheduled a week-end school at the town of Lapua, in Pohjanmaa, and a hotbed of right-wing activism, main centre of recruiting for Vientirauha, home town of Vihtori Kosola. Although the occasion was perfectly legal, and had police permission, it was in fact a deliberate provocation. Trouble began as soon as the delegates began unloading at Lapua station on 29 November, many wearing red shirts worn outside the trousers, Russian fashion. Some of them, it being the week-end, and this a centre of pietism, held an anti-religious meeting in the street, and were there set upon by local people, beaten up, and stripped of their shirts, the police making no attempt to intervene. When the meetings of the school began, those attending were roughed up, the meetings subjected to constant interruption, with a certain amount of wild shooting around the meeting place, and again the police stood by, until the school broke up in disorder.

In direct response to this, at a meeting on 1 December in Lapua, the so-called Lapua movement was born. Its defenders always claimed that it began as a spontaneous movement of protest by the good citizens of Lapua, that it was the answer of the honest patriotic farmers of Pohjanmaa to the communist threat to their way of life. The evidence, scattered though it is, does not sustain such a theory. From its very inception the Lapua movement had plenty of money and a nation-wide organization behind it. The evidence is that all through 1929 the organized right in Finland — that is, the Kokoomus Party, the big employers' organizations, and the SK — had been preparing something like this, and that the Lapua meeting gave them just the excuse they wanted in just the right place, for in Lapua they could draw on the services of Vientirauha and its hirelings for the violent stuff, while at the same time being able to rely on genuine popular local support. The great protest meeting of 1 December has all the marks of a put-up job, and was in fact managed by Vienti-rauha. The chief of Vientirauha, Martti Pihkala, himself a prominent member of the Finnish employers' organizations, was busy behind the scenes, Tiitu, one of his local organizers, took the chair, and Kosola made the keynote speech.

In this speech, which was enthusiastically endorsed by the meeting, Kosola demanded that all communist activity be effectively repressed, and said that it would never be done properly under the existing system; therefore the time had come for the people to act for themselves. He went on:

> it is a waste of time to send delegations ... it would be better to send riflemen to Helsinki ... it may well be that the whole present form of government and the parliament-ary system will have to be sacrificed.

He called on the Finnish farmers, the backbone of the nation, to rise up and put an end to the futile posturings of the Helsinki politicians.

Thus Kosola emerged as Finland's strong man, yet it is impossible to believe that he was much more than a puppet. Kosola had no national standing before 1929; though he was locally powerful in Pohjanmaa, he displayed no marked political or oratorical talent, did nothing that would give him a claim to be regarded as a major political figure in his own right — basically he remained what he had been before 1929, the hired agent of Vientirauha. He fitted the bill because he made a plausible figurehead for what was supposed to be a farmers' movement, because he could be manipulated, and because when the time came for the real leaders of the right to take the stage, he could easily be set aside. Even the movement itself in its more euphoric moments did not seriously contemplate that Kosola should take over the running of the country.

The meeting of 1 December was then imitated all over Finland, similar speeches were made, similar resolutions passed, and on 15 March 1930 a congress was held at Lapua to launch a national movement. This set up a national co-ordinating body, Suomen Lukko — Finland's Lock, dedi-cated to the struggle with communism, and aspiring to become a national front of the right. The first committee had an agrarian politician and editor, A. Leinonen, as chairman, two bankers, I. Kaitera and I. Koivisto, Martti Pihkala of Vientirauha, the big industrialists Walden and Haarla, as well as Kosola and the Lapua leaders. The theme of its programme was the need for direct action, the need to meet force with force. Haarla spoke of a new round in the civil war, and of 'a conflict much bloodier than 1918'. Suomen Lukko succeeded in spectacular fashion, almost all the institutions of the right joined it, including the AKS, and in the course of 1930 it seems to have enjoyed the support of a great majority of non-socialist Finns, and was a genuine popular mass movement. The congress also launched the two key slogans of Finnish fascism, 'Finland awake' and 'we do what we will, others do what they can'.

From the beginning, President Relander and the government sought to appease the Lapuans, and announced that it would bring forward new anti-communist legislation. But the first instalment, a new press law introduced in March, failed to get the necessary two-thirds majority. The response of the Lapuans was immediate and forceful. At the end of March, about seventy men, some of them armed, attacked the printing presses of the Vaasa paper *Työn Ääni*, a left-wing socialist paper, and burned the building. The communists at once raised the matter in parliament, which on 3 April voted by 101 to 91 that legal proceedings should be instituted against those responsible. The narrow margin in this vote shows how far the right was already prepared to condone direct action; the Kokoomus deputies and their press in particular openly welcomed and excused the violence as a proper response to parliament's refusal to pass the press law. A. Palmgren, a Kokoomus deputy and head of the Finnish employers' organization, made a speech welcoming the action of the Lapua men, and declared that his organization stood solidly behind them.

When the Vaasa chief of police proceeded to arrest a leading mobster in Lapua, a crowd gathered at once outside the police station and forced his release. But a number of men were brought to trial in Vaasa in April, charged with the attack on *Työn Ääni*. However, from the start of proceedings the court was surrounded by a crowd that rose to over 1500;

the leading lawyer for *Työn Ääni* was seized as he left the building on the first day, driven off to Lapua, and not released until he signed a promise to withdraw from the case. The Lapua activists put out a statement signed by over seventy persons including Kosola, claiming that they had organized the attack on the press, and drove down to Vaasa in a triumphant motorcade to present their statement to the local prefect. The accused at the trial were then given nominal sentences and released, while no proceedings were taken against those who had caused the disturbances during the hearings. The prefect at Vaasa now asked the government for the support necessary for restoring order, and when this was refused, resigned; his successor, in order as he claimed to prevent further disturbances, closed down all the local left-wing newspapers.

Thus encouraged, the Lapua movement at once stepped up its pressure on the government, and at a further congress in April decided to organize a farmers' march on Helsinki to demand the full implementation of their programme. But immediate attention concentrated on shutting down the communist press, and when in June the movement threatened to use force against all such papers, the government issued an order to the prefects to close them, although this was clearly illegal. When the government's policy was debated in parliament on 1 July, the Minister of Justice publicly defended his refusal to restrain the illegal behaviour of the Lapua men, and concluded, 'the communists had practiced illegalities under the shelter of the law: now they are being shown how, through illegality, legality is being reinstated'. Parliament endorsed the government's action with a vote of confidence.

But their conversion came too late, for Lapua had decided to get rid of the existing government and put in its own nominees. As soon as the popular success of the movement had become clear, the real leaders of the right hastened to climb on to the bandwagon, and proceeded to use it to carry out their own takeover of the government. Svinhufvud travelled to Lapua and declared that the movement was a divine blessing on the fatherland, the Speaker of parliament made his pilgrimage to what was fast becoming a holy place and gave his endorsement, and a stream of public figures followed their example. The Lapuans agreed that Svinhufvud should form a government to carry out their programme, and in June they bluntly told the president and ministers to make way. When the ministers demurred, the Lapuans told President Relander that if he did not dismiss them and call on Svinhufvud, the government would be overthrown by force. They were with difficulty persuaded to give him a day or two to consider the matter, after which Relander capitulated. Despite the vote of confidence in parliament on 1 July, the ministry resigned and Svinhufvud became Prime Minister, and at once introduced new anti-communist laws into parliament.

Lapua now turned its attention to this body, and on 5 July, almost certainly with the connivance of the government, armed men broke into the parliament building and kidnapped two communist deputies from a meeting of the constitutional law committee. Svinhufvud, instead of taking steps to assert the authority of parliament, immediately asked for the suspension of the communist deputies, and then arrested them. Even so the social democrats stood firm against the new laws, and with the handful of bourgeois liberals who stood with them could still prevent a two-thirds majority. So Svinhufvud dissolved parliament.

The next step was to ensure that after the elections there would be an adequate majority for the new laws, and the whole campaign turned on this. The government did its part by suppressing the communists, their presses were closed, their leaders put in prison, and their organizations broken up. The rest was left to the Lapuans who were given a free hand to intimidate and terrorize the opposition.

Their campaign really opened with the farmers' march on Helsinki, the arrangements for which had been made in Lapua at a meeting on 20-1 June. A delegation was chosen to lead the march and present its demands to the president, and although this delegation contained a handful of farmers to keep up appearances, the bulk of the delegates reflected the real forces behind the movement. There were seven bankers, four priests, three factory owners, two officers, two lawyers and a police official. The organizers had been in touch with the Italian ambassador, A. Tamaro, who seems to have been enlisted as technical adviser, which is one of the few established examples of direct contact between the Finnish and foreign fascist movements. Once the Svinhufvud government was installed, official assistance was given, two General Staff officers were detached to help with the logistics, while the whole organization of the SK was at the movement's disposal. Public figures gave their endorsement of the march and its declared programme, even the aloof Mannerheim came out with a statement of support.

Consequently the march, which had been conceived originally as a demonstration to force the hand of a reluctant government, was turned into a national festival of the right. Early in August some 12,000 men, a quarter of them armed, marched through Helsinki and were given a solemn public reception by Relander, Mannerheim, Svinhufvud and the government. President Relander, in his address of welcome, thanked God for the patriotic upsurge which the marchers represented, Svinhufvud assured them that all their demands would be met, and communism in Finland would be stamped out for ever. The marchers then dispersed without further incident.

The summer and autumn of 1930 saw the high peak of Lapua violence, coinciding with the general election campaign. The movement, which became a formal registered organization in September, with Kosola as chairman, was technically a farmers' society dedicated to education and enlightenment; it was not a political party, and did not present candidates in the election. Its energies were concentrated on intimidating the surviving opposition, the social democrats and those few bourgeois progressives who refused to be carried away on the tide of enthusiasm for the movement. The first murders had occurred in July when two radical socialist politicians were killed: in one case, an overzealous police official who was investigating was called off on orders from Helsinki; in the second, which involved Kosola's son, no legal proceedings were begun for more than a year, and when the murderers were at last brought before a court, they were released after a hearing in camera. This travesty of justice proved too much for the then Minister of Justice, who ordered a fresh trial, which resulted in prison sentences for the accused.

But murder was not the characteristic weapon of the Lapuans. They went in for a lot of general violence, breaking up meetings, attacking newspaper offices, forcing local social democratic organs to close down by intimidation. But their speciality was kidnapping. The favourite form was to seize an opposition politician, or a trade union official, or an editor, take them to the Russian frontier, beat them up, and then dump them over the border — this appealed to the Lapuan sense of humour. If the victims were released, or when they managed to get back, provided the Soviet authorities did not proceed against them as spies, they were warned by Lapua to stay out of public life in future. During the summer and autumn of 1930 over a thousand members of local government bodies, social democratic party branches, public agencies, trade unions, staffs of newspapers, even candidates and former members of parliament, including the deputy Speaker, were the victims of abductions, and the authorities did nothing to protect potential victims or to track down the perpetrators. In October, twenty self-confessed kidnappers went as a delegation to the Ministry of the Interior, including several leading officials of the Lapua movement, one of them a High Court judge, and were assured by the Minister that if they did find themselves before a court, they could count on sympathetic consideration.

It was in face of this rampant intimidation, connived at by the legal authorities, that the election was fought. The opposition rallied round the figure of J.K. Ståhlberg, the first President of the Republic, who emerged from retirement to campaign for the constitution and the law. Ståhlberg immediately became the target of the most venomous Lapua abuse, for nobody could accuse him of being a hireling of Moscow. Inevitably, on 14 October, a group of armed men kidnapped Ståhlberg and his wife, and drove them towards the Russian frontier, clearly intending to leave them on the other side, but at the last moment the kidnappers lost their nerve and released them. This was going too far even for Svinhufvud's government, and legal proceedings were begun against the attackers, who had made no effort to conceal their identity.

The two chief figures were General Wallenius, then Chief of the General Staff, and the secretary of Suomen Lukko, and these, with their subordinates, were brought to trial and given prison sentences, but Wallenius was acquitted on appeal.

It was therefore not surprising that the election of 1930 was a triumph for the right. The Kokoomus jumped from twenty-eight to forty-two seats, which in Finnish terms is a landslide, but the social democrats, who must have picked up votes from the suppressed communists, hung on to sixty-six seats, just one short of a blocking third. When the new parliament met, the so-called Lapua laws were rapidly passed, giving strong new emergency powers to the president, sweeping powers for the government to close down offensive associations and publications, and revising the electoral laws so as to disfranchise anyone adjudged to have been a member of an illegal organization. The local electoral boards were given wide discretion to decide who fell into this category. Taken together, the laws were ample for the prevention of communist political activity, and in fact, with their aid, it was almost completely repressed; the Communist Party inside Finland in the 1930s was reduced to a tiny, hunted underground, incapable of any effective political action.

Svinhufvud and the grandees of the right had now got all they wanted from the Lapua movement, and would have been obliged if it had gracefully retired into the background and left them in control. But they found, as others have before and since, that having gone for a ride on a tiger, it was not so easy to get off again. As soon as the elections were over, Svinhufvud began to make speeches about the need to return to legality now that the aims of the movement had been met, but the Lapuans could quote against him speeches of his as late as 28 September, when he had described Lapua violence as 'right, necessary, and therefore to be supported'. They could also cite Mannerheim's appeal of 30 September to all patriotic citizens to give support to the 'selfless, patriotic endeavours, which have been launched into public life through the influence of the Lapua movement'. It was understandable that the Lapuans had acquired a rather high valuation of their own significance.

But for the moment there was no open breach between the

Lapuans and the grandees, for there was one more hurdle to be jumped, the presidential election due in early 1931. In this Svinhufvud stood as the candidate of the united right, with full Lapua support, against Ståhlberg, the choice of the social democrats, and many of the agrarians, on a platform of a return to legality. Although the new electoral law, and continuing intimidation, all worked for Svinhufvud, he was eventually elected by the smallest possible margin in the electoral college, 151 votes to 149, and this may have been swayed by the public intervention of the SK, which sent a delegation to the electoral college declaring that the SK would not tolerate any other choice but Svinhufvud.

With the presidency safe, Svinhufvud truly had no further use for Lapua and, as the established governing authority, began to find its defiance of the laws a nuisance. Svinhufvud was the last man to tolerate sharing authority, but Lapua had got into the habit of claiming to dictate policy to the government. The movement was now working out the next stage in its policy. It had acquired a national journal, *Aktivisti*, and in the pages of this one can trace the evolution of a full fascist programme. Chunks of ill-digested material from foreign fascist books and papers filled its pages, on the domestic front it now demanded the suppression of the social democrats, as the first step towards the abolition of party politics. It also adopted a fully fledged programme of anti-semitism, peculiarly absurd in Finland, where Jews are numbered in hundreds and are an utterly insignificant group. But *Aktivisti* claimed that the bolsheviks were financed and directed by international Jewry, and that bolshevism was essentially a Jewish ideology. In the realm of foreign affairs, the movement took up the extreme programme of AKS. In January 1931, *Aktivisti* published an article about the coming European crusade against Russia.

When it comes — and it surely will come, it must come — then we can really create a greater Finland — then the day will come when Finland's eastern frontier is the Urals, and when Finland, as a great power, will be an important factor in world politics.

Through 1931, Svinhufvud and Lapua drifted apart. Svinhufvud's new government, and in particular its new Minister of the Interior, von Born, made a conscious effort to re-establish legal authority, though progress was slow, since Svinhufvud was keen to avoid any confrontation. The courts continued to show marked partiality to any Lapua defendants who appeared before them, and when, for instance, von Born ordered that the social democrat meeting-house in Lapua should be restored to them, after it had been illegally seized by the activists, the Lapua leaders replied publicly, 'the building is closed and is staying closed.' The Minister had to give in, something of a stalemate was developing between the government and Lapua, and once more the movement was contemplating breaking it by resort to violence.

The decisive development was the emergence of General Wallenius, who in 1931, as soon as he was acquitted of the charges arising from the Ståhlberg kidnapping, was elected secretary of the Lapua movement. He found the presiding genius within the movement, now that the respectable backers were increasingly withdrawing, was Minna Craucher, who seems to have been a high-grade prostitute, with convictions for fraud but a marked talent for persuading monied men to give funds for the cause. Wallenius found that under the Craucher regime some half-baked plans for a coup had been formed, originally timed for November 1931. This sort of thing did not appeal to Wallenius' professional military mind, and he began a thorough shake-up of the movement which involved, as a first step, getting rid of Craucher, with whom a bitter feud developed. Then, once Wallenius was in control, he set about planning a real coup, in which the key role would be played by the SK under Lapua direction. When the time came, the Lapua leadership would call on the SK to mobilize and take over the country. At the same time the movement would demand the resignation of the government, and this would be facilitated by the Kokoomus ministers resigning at once. Then a government of national unity would be formed, but for this some figurehead was needed, for though Wallenius was willing to become prime minister himself, ideally he wanted Mannerheim to come forward as the supreme leader.

By December 1931, the knowledge of the coming coup

was so widespread that the social democrats put down a question in parliament. The government replied that it was aware that secret preparations were being made, that money was being raised, and that there had been subversion of the SK and the army, but they were watching events, and did not believe there was any immediate danger. However, in his address to parliament at the beginning of 1932, Svinhufvud referred openly to the danger, and once more appealed for an end to violence and illegality.

The evidence suggests that Wallenius had been thinking of late February 1932 as a date for his coup, and it is likely that a meeting of the Lapua leaders in Hämeenlinna, set for the last week in February, was connected with this. Then on 11 February Craucher intervened when she went to the authorities and told them about the projected operation, supplying some convincing supporting evidence. Wallenius' reaction seems to have been to postpone everything, but for some reason, part of the original plan went off on schedule.

The occasion for the rising was to have been a meeting held at Mäntsälä by a leading social democrat, M. Erich. Mäntsälä was well placed for a coup, being a small country town close to the capital, a convenient jumping-off place for a march on Helsinki. The local Lapua leaders and the SK had demanded that the authorities should forbid Erich's meeting, and von Born, recognizing a challenge, refused and ordered the police to give the meeting protection. On the evening of 27 February, a crowd of about 400 men, mostly local SK with their weapons, surrounded the meeting place, fired shots, defied police orders to disperse, and then took over the town. As soon as he heard the news, Wallenius hurried down from Pohjanmaa with 200 armed men, and at first clearly tried to persuade the Mäntsälä men that they had mistimed it, but then realized that it was too late to draw back, for already the local SK units were mobilizing and drifting into the town. So he put out a proclamation in the name of the men who had gathered at Mäntsälä, in which they demanded an end to all marxist activity, and the dismissal of von Born. The proclamation concluded:

Marxism must be put down or else we shall first destroy

the government and its representatives who are protecting it. The government can send its police to suppress us, but we shall meet them with arms in hand, ready for victory or death.

Thus Wallenius challenged the government to a trial of strength, and the government accepted the challenge. The army commander, General Sihvo, was confident of the loyalty of his troops, and the government ordered him to draw a cordon between Mäntsälä and the capital.

The next day, 29 February, the leaders of the Lapua movement officially endorsed the revolt, and issued an ultimatum to the government in Kosola's name, demanding its immediate resignation and the adoption of new policies — otherwise they would not answer for the consequences. At the same time the leadership moved to Mäntsälä and called their supporters to take arms. But it was at once apparent how they had been caught off-balance, for their plan went off at half-cock. Only part of the SK answered the call, some six thousand assembled at Mäntsälä, and in one or two places — of which Jyväskylä, an important communications centre in the middle of Finland, was the most significant — the local SK took over the functions of government, closed down the local social democratic organs and press, and arrested those who protested — but the general take-over of the provinces that had been planned failed to materialize. Similarly the Kokoomus ministers in the government were caught unprepared, and they split; two obediently resigned when Kosola issued his call, but the other two stuck with their colleagues. This helped the government to stand firm, and they answered Kosola by declaring the Mäntsälä gathering an insurrection, and ordering the arrest of the leaders. Svinhufvud, however, seems to have been less keen on a showdown, and was busy trying to negotiate a settlement. During 1 and 2 March he discussed with the rebels the possibility of forming a government under Wallenius and the suppression of the social democrats, to which he personally had no objection, but only if Mannerheim would come forward as a national leader. Mannerheim was willing to see a new government formed, but declined to be personally identified with it. Then his friend Walden was sounded, but he, as always, would go no further than Mannerheim.

So, on 2 March, Svinhufvud threw in his lot with his ministers and resolved on suppression. He issued a proclamation taking over command of all armed forces, including the SK, and ordered all SK members to return home, promising legal immunity for them if they obeyed. Malmberg, the elected commander of the SK, refused to read the order over the radio, so Svinhufvud broadcast it himself, and it seems to have been an impressive performance and gave the death blow to the revolt. He induced Martti Pihkala to go to Jyväskylä and persuade the rebels there to give up, which he did by reading them a stern lecture on discipline and respect for constituted authority. On his return he sent in a bill to the government: 'To suppressing one revolt — 1000 marks.'

The leaders at Mäntsälä now perceived that the game was up. They were faced by a determined government which had retained the allegiance of the army and regained that of the SK, whose planned rising had been a total failure, while Mannerheim and Walden had done a Pontius Pilate act on them, and refused to endorse the movement as they had done in 1930. There was nothing left but to negotiate terms of surrender. This took until 6 March, when it was agreed that the rank and file could go home, but the outlawed leaders must surrender and stand trial. Thus the revolt ended without bloodshed, and in November 1932 legal proceedings were initiated against the chiefs of the rebellion, though they did not come to an actual public trial until 1934. Then they were adjudged guilty of aiding and abetting an insurrection and given very light prison sentences, two and a half years being the longest. The principals, Wallenius, Kosola, and twenty-three others were released with suspended sentences.

The summer of 1932 saw the Lapua movement give a few dying kicks. On 7 March, Craucher telephoned a newspaper and said that she had valuable testimony to give, but that her life was in danger. The editor warned the police, who afterwards said they had difficulty in finding her. When they did she had been murdered, and the assassin, when brought to trial, was adjudged insane, though he alleged he had been commissioned to do the job. The truth about the Craucher murder has not been established, but the Lapua leaders certainly had strong incentives for silencing her.

There were other incidents; a revolt by the local SK in Sääksjärvi in the summer was serious enough to cause Svinhufvud to use his emergency powers, and in July there was a plot to kidnap several ministers, call out the SK, force Svinhufvud to release the Lapua leaders and let them form a government. The plot was betrayed and hastily cancelled, but one part went off when armed men broke into the house of the Minister of Defence, Lahdensuo. He defended himself with a revolver, and the attackers fled, leaving him unharmed.

It was clear that the government would proceed to suppress the Lapua movement by having it declared an illegal organization, and to forestall this it was decided to form a new, overtly political party. The founding congress was held on 5 June 1932, and it took the name of Isänmaallinen Kansanliike — Patriotic National Movement — commonly referred to as the IKL. The programme of the party says quite explicitly that it adheres to the aim of the Lapua movement, and in fact the leadership was simply transferred, though since Kosola was in prison the chairmanship was to be kept for him on release. But most of the leaders of the new party had in fact been implicated in the Mäntsälä revolt, the most prominent being B. Salmiala, and the priest V. Annala. The IKL developed into a proper fascist party, it adopted a blackshirt uniform, blue-black banners, and organized a uniformed youth movement, the Sinimustat — Blue-blacks — who were trained for physical combat. The main planks in the programme remained suppression of the social democrats, anti-semitism, an end to party politics, hostility to the Swedish-language minority, and a chauvinist foreign policy. At first the party fought elections in alliance with the Kokoomus, and in their first election, in 1933, they won fourteen seats.

Despite the formal disbanding of the Lapua movement, the forces that had backed it were still strong. They succeeded in having their revenge on General Sihvo, whose firm conduct had done more than anything to defeat them, much to the disgust of many fellow officers. A campaign was mounted

questioning his professional competence, and his enemies got
the ear of Svinhufvud, who agreed to Sihvo's dismissal
without bothering to consult his ministers. There was a
public outcry, and the government had to negotiate Sihvo's
resignation and find him a face-saving job as inspector-
general.

Even so, in retrospect, it is clear that the Mäntsälä revolt
was the beginning of the end for the fascist movement in
Finland — it had made its bid for power and failed. The
reasons for this failure are partly tactical: the *coup* went off
prematurely, and forced the Lapua leadership into hasty improvization. Once the SK failed to rise, and the army stood by
the government, there was no chance of a takeover by force.
But there were deeper reasons for the failure at Mäntsälä.
The movement had been betrayed by its original sponsors.
What had guaranteed success in 1930, and was fatal in 1932,
was the change in the attitude of the grandees of the right,
the men of 1918, like Mannerheim, Svinhufvud and Walden,
men with sufficient stature nationally to make a Lapua
regime credible if they chose to endorse it. Their ambiguity
and reticence in 1932 killed the revolt, just as their endorsement, making Lapua the legitimate heir of the White movement of 1918, would have saved it. Without the chieftains of
1918, Lapua could not be the truly national movement
which it claimed to be, and had to opt for the alternative
role of a political party on the right wing of the Kokoomus,
and bolster this up by borrowings from the international
fascist movement. This is the significance of the transformation into the IKL. The grandees had used the Lapua movement in 1930 when it suited their purposes and helped them
to re-establish their authority; they broke it in 1932 when it
presumed to challenge the way in which they were exercising
it.

In the history of Finnish internal politics, 1932 was a
decisive turning point. In December, a new government was
formed under Professor T.M. Kivimäki, which was the
longest-lived and the strongest government in the republic's
history. Its advent coincided with the beginnings of economic
recovery. Both agricultural and industrial production began
to rise, unemployment fell to a tolerable level, and the

government, with the aid of orthodox economic and financial programmes, presided competently over the economic revival, so that Finland became the famous country which paid its debts. The government was helped by an advantageous parliamentary position, for after the Mäntsälä affair it stood committed to bringing the fascists under control, and it was clear that only its success in this stood between the social democrats and their probable repression by an antiparliamentary regime. Therefore, although the Kokoomus was in opposition after Mäntsälä, Kivimäki had the tacit support of the social democrats, and his parliamentary position was probably stronger than that of any preceding government.

The threat of violence was still very much present in 1933, an election year in Finland. On one side the IKL was demanding the suppression of the social democrats, on the other the latter were demanding the putting down of the IKL and a drastic reform of the SK. The Kivimäki government was seriously considering taking legal proceedings for the suppression of IKL but finally decided against it, so sporadic violence and brawling between the IKL and the socialists continued to disturb public life; but the government kept it within tolerable limits, in the belief that the situation would gradually improve itself.

This view proved to be correct, and a major factor was a growing rift between the IKL and the Kokoomus. After the 1933 election, in which the IKL got its fourteen seats in parliament, it broke its electoral alliance with the Kokoomus Party, and its deputies acted as an independent political group; as they indulged in ever-growing extremist behaviour, based on the worst European models, their respectable bourgeois allies increasingly drew back from defilement. The fourteen deputies caused a sensation early in the new parliament when they all appeared wearing blackshirt uniforms, and proceeded to outrage their fellow deputies by provocative and unparliamentary behaviour, accompanied by an extremism of abuse and vilification in their speeches that caused deep offence. The IKL spokesmen declared that when they took power, the professional politicians would be put out of business, and if necessary behind barbed wire; they affirmed that hatred and violence would continue until the party system was smashed; they told the Minister of Justice, in a parliamentary debate, that he would end his days shovelling dirt (a euphemistic translation) in a concentration camp. Since the general tone of Finnish public life tended to be rather Victorian, particularly in conservative circles, this kind of behaviour was deeply offensive, and it was significant that in 1933 the Kokoomus elected as its chairman J.K. Paasikivi, a moderate and realistic politician, who led an active campaign to bring the Kokoomus back into the constitutional camp. By 1936 his efforts had succeeded, the Kokoomus, the voice of big business and finance, had broken completely with the IKL, and ended its flirtation with policies of direct action. It still opposed any move to suppress IKL, still grumbled furiously about the weaknesses of the democratic system, about the failure to rearm, and still wanted a foreign policy friendly to Hitler's Germany, but it had at last accepted as inevitable the parliamentary republic.

In 1934 the government took two major steps to restrain political extremism, the first of which was a new law against groundless incitement. Under this law, propaganda which brought the government or constitution into contempt or offended morals or common decency could be suppressed, and with its aid some of the more irresponsible IKL publications were temporarily suspended. The second measure was the so-called 'shirt law', which forbade the wearing of unauthorized uniforms in public, and declared private uniformed organizations illegal. The IKL, and especially its young activists in the Sinimustat, persistently defied this law, and further embarrassed the government by becoming involved in a fascist *coup* in Estonia in 1935, so that although the authorities were now displaying a new firmness and determination, the IKL got away with a lot of minor infringements of the law. This may have helped to give them, and others, an exaggerated impression of their real strength, so that the elections of 1936 came as a real shock.

In this election, Finland had its own version of a popular front, an electoral alliance between the social democrats and the agrarians on a programme of safeguarding democracy and social reform. Although the IKL held its fourteen seats, the new allies dominated parliament, and a very reluctant Svinhufvud had to see the Kivimäki government toppled, and a strong coalition of the left installed. In the following year the new alliance put forward the agrarian Kallio against Svinhufvud in the presidential election and won. Svinhufvud had to retire into private life. The new regime was now ready to hit back at the fascists; in 1938 they got a court order dissolving the Sinimustat, which was promptly re-formed as the Blackshirts. In November 1938, legal proceedings were begun against the IKL itself, on the grounds that it had continually acted illegally and that it was in fact a continuation of the condemned Lapua movement. The case was decided in the High Court in May 1939, when the court ruled that although the IKL had undoubtedly been guilty of illegalities, these were not sufficient to warrant suppression. The government then began appeal proceedings, but these were still pending when war broke out, and were allowed to lapse.

Even so, there is every sign that after 1936 the Finnish fascists were in decline. It is true that there was in Finland a widespread welcome for the revival of German power under Hitler, but this was mostly based on old-fashioned balance-of-power considerations; the business community had a lot of trouble and unpleasantness in arranging trade with Hitler's Germany, and even on the right it was commonly asserted that good relations with Germany in no way implied acceptance of Hitler's ideology. The most direct echo of nazism was to be found in the Swedish-language minority, cut off from the IKL by the language issue. There, a few extremists perceived that the Swedish-language Finns might qualify as Aryans, and that in this way nazism could offer some compensation for their minority status. Men like C.A. Gadolin, with his periodical *Svensk Botten*, became outspoken admirers of Hitler and the Axis, but even within their own community they were a lunatic fringe.

In fact the success of the Kivimäki government, the economic recovery and the democratic victory in the elections of 1936 and 1937, which readmitted the social democrats to a full place in public life, had at last secured and made viable the parliamentary republic. Mannerheim reflected this changed situation by adapting his own position to it; he now became an advocate of national conciliation, and even entered into relations with the social democratic leaders. With the communists still firmly suppressed, Finland in 1939 was a model of prosperity and stability, and it is no surprise that IKL support slumped in the election of 1939, when they were cut down to eight seats in parliament.

When the war came, it dealt the fascists a further cruel blow. For in the Winter War, the long awaited showdown with the bolshevik enemy, Finland's main sources of outside support were democratic Sweden, France, and Britain, while nazi Germany was virtually the ally of the Soviet Union. Mussolini was friendly, but in no position to help. The Finnish right, building on the national tradition of pro-Germanism, had always found it easier to put over Hitler as a model than Mussolini, and their sense of betrayal in the Winter War was traumatic. The IKL virtually lapsed into inactivity, and hid itself for shame.

However, with Hitler's triumphant conquests in 1940, and the *rapprochement* between Finland and Germany which became evident after August 1940, fascist morale began to recover. A symptom of this was the emergence of new fascist groupings, which appeared against the background of a growing debate on Finland's place in the Axis new order in Europe. They tended to argue that if Finland wanted a worthy place in the new order, she should adapt her institutions to the prevailing ideologies.

Among these groups there appeared a Finnish National Socialist Party, which was a straightforward copy of the German model, and ran quite a considerable press campaign in the autumn of 1940, but seems to have had a minimal response. Other groups propagated a specifically Scandinavian brand of totalitarianism; such were Teo Snellman's Vapaa Suomi — Free Finland — group, and Räikkänen's Gustav Vasa movement which projected the great Swedish king as a prototype Hitler. None of these new groups seems to have represented much more than a few enthusiasts grouped round a periodical, their political influence was insignificant, and was commonly dismissed as such in the official press, for the government tended to frown on them as disturbers of national unity.

In October 1940, the IKL organized a congress, inevitably at Lapua, for all groups sympathetic to the new order in Europe, and succeeded in drawing up a manifesto, calling on the country to prepare itself to take its place in the new Europe then being born. But this attempt to form a common front of totalitarian parties was a feeble gesture, there was no real substance behind it, and the official press brushed it off as empty posturing. Soon after this the IKL lost its freedom of action when, in January 1941, it agreed to enter a new coalition government of national unity. One of the leaders, the Lutheran pastor Annala, became a minister, but there was a price to be paid. The IKL had to agree to stop its attacks on the social democrats and the parliamentary system, which in effect muzzled it and deprived it of most of its *raison d'être*.

Naturally, when Hitler attacked the Soviet Union in 1941, and Finland joined in, new vistas seemed to open for the fascists. Briefly it appeared as though the dream of *Suur-Suomi* was going to be realized under Hitler's patronage, and much of the energy and propaganda of the IKL concentrated on this theme. Its spokesmen became as bold in their claims as the official censorship would permit, but it was a last moment of triumph, and by 1942 it was clear it had been as illusory as the earlier ones. It is significant that when the Germans were recruiting the Finnish SS battalion in 1941, although individual members of IKL were involved, the movement as such played no part, and there seems to have been no official contact between it and the German Nazi Party. Indeed, the weakness of Finnish fascism in the 1940s can perhaps best be illustrated by what happened when Ribbentrop flew to Helsinki in June 1944, to stop Finland from making a separate peace with Russia. In the car from the airport he asked the German ambassador if there were not even a few hundred dedicated Finnish fascists who might be used for a pro-German *coup*. The ambassador had to confess that he doubted if there were any at all.

With the provisional peace treaty of September 1944 the development of Finnish fascism came to a full stop, since article eight of the peace treaty required Finland to dissolve all fascist organizations, and prevent their being re-established.

Under this clause, the IKL, the smaller totalitarian groups, the AKS, and above all the SK, were dissolved. It would be rash to assert that the spirit which lay behind these movements has entirely disappeared in Finland even today, but as a political force the movement which came so near to success in the early 1930s is dead.

When we look back on the history of the Finnish fascist movement, it seems clear that it owed its strength to its local, native roots. History and geography had combined to produce a Soviet Russia which embodied both a national and ideological enemy, and also, through the civil war in Finland, forces in the country ready to respond to the double challenge. By contrast with these factors, ideological fascism, a remote and foreign phenomenon, seems to have been of marginal significance. As long as the Lapua movement was solidly based on the tradition of the activists and White Guards of 1918, and could plausibly represent itself as their direct successor, it was powerful, but when, as the IKL, it became more and more openly identified with the ideas and practices of international fascism, its strength ebbed, and even the triumph of Hitler in Europe did not produce any significant revival in Finland. Just as many Finns in the 1930s and 1940s were pro-German without being nazi, so they could admire the idea of strong anti-communist government without being fascists. The Finnish fascist movement arose as a genuine response to a communist threat that was no figment of the imagination, but a real force with its centre of power tantalizingly close, but untouchable, just over the frontier. But once this menace had manifestly been brought under control, the impulse behind the movement weakened, and the borrowed trappings of international fascism, which the movement came to adopt, were left as an increasingly empty shell, a façade with nothing very substantial behind it.

10
NORWAY

◆

T. K. Derry

About a fortnight before his execution, the Norwegian fascist leader, Vidkun Quisling, gave the following answer to a private visitor's inquiry about his relations with Hitler. 'You must not misunderstand me if I express myself plainly. I was the leader of a small people in a weak country. In power politics I was dependent upon Germany and Adolf Hitler, but in political ideas I regarded Hitler as my subordinate and my instrument.' Thus Quisling to the very end saw himself in the centre of the scene. And even now history has not reduced him to his true dimensions. In 1940 his name provided a heaven-sent alternative for the clumsy term, 'fifth columnist': within a week of the German invasion of Norway *The Times* led the way with an item about 'quislings everywhere'. In 1964 a 'Life', in which he was portrayed as a 'prophet without honour', received a degree of attention never accorded to any serious study of Norwegian politics. But to understand fascism in Norway, it is first necessary for us to try to understand Norway.

In the first place, we have to do with a very small people of three millions spread over a territory as large as the British Isles. Parliamentary government dates back to the much venerated constitution set up on 17 May 1814, which is associated with the separation from Denmark in that year; a triumphant nationalism found further expression in the dethronement in 1905 of the House of Bernadotte, which for ninety years had been kings of Norway as well as Sweden. The completely independent Norway of the early twentieth century was, however, a country without any wide political ambitions — neutral in the first world war; an early and enthusiastic member of the League of Nations, where their national hero, Fridtjof Nansen, figured as the spokesman of humanity rather than of any narrowly Norwegian cause; more than content with its position in what was often advertised during the 1930s as the 'peaceful corner of Europe'.

At the same time, it should be noticed that the social and economic structure of this small people, while broadly resembling that of its west European neighbours, had two special features. One was the entire absence of any territorial nobility or even aristocracy, comparable to the great landed families which influenced political development elsewhere, for better or worse. The other was the belated onset of the industrial revolution, for Norway had no coal but abundant sources of hydro-electricity. The growth of machine industry after 1900 brought a rising standard of living to a country which always depended upon imported foodstuffs for its well-being. But it also brought about the uprooting of a part of the rural population, the growth of a navvy class, and some spasms of the social malaise which had been so widely characteristic of English life a hundred years earlier. Accordingly Norway, which lacked so many other prerequisites for fascist movements, was affected very rapidly by the influences of the Russian revolution. In 1918, when the rest of the world was at war, soviets of workers, and in a few cases of soldiers, made a temporary appearance. In 1919-21 the Norwegian Labour Party was the only one in western Europe which adhered firmly to the Comintern.

Against this background we may now attempt to delineate the features of a rather shadowy fascist movement as it existed in Norway down to the second world war. The foreign influences, from which much of its ideology was naturally derived, seem to have been German rather than Italian. Apart from vaguely eulogistic references to Mussolini as a strong man who had put down strikes and established social harmony, a single Oslo newspaper, *Tidens Tegn*, was the only regular source of propaganda favourable to the new developments in a country with which Norway's ties were not particularly close. Germany, on the other hand, had a language and literature with which many Norwegians were familiar, and an educational system on which theirs was in many respects modelled. Visits of nazi propagandists to Norway can be traced even before Hitler's accession to power, and the converse is also true — Quisling's leading associates included men who had been frequent visitors to national socialist Germany.

One example is A.V. Hagelin, who joined Quisling in 1936 and was Minister of the Interior in his wartime regime; he had spent twenty years in business, chiefly in Dresden. Another is his adviser on points of law, a philosopher of rather modest attainments, named Herman Harris Aall. He had steeped his pen in anti-British sentiments as early as the first world war, and by 1939 was in receipt of a considerable subsidy from Berlin for an office in south Sweden, from which he was to spread a very tenuous doctrine which he called social individualism. This has been represented as Admiral Canaris' counterblast to national socialism, designed to sweep through Scandinavia first and afterwards to blow Hitler himself from his perch. But Aall was active in keeping Quisling's name before his German masters, and was in due course promoted by him from the forlorn hope in Sweden to a chair of jurisprudence in Oslo University.

Among native sources of fascism we may name first the disrepute into which parliamentary government for a time fell through its structural weaknesses. Down to the end of the first world war a system of single-member constituencies was used, which in 1918 — the year when events in Russia had roused great expectations among Labour supporters — produced a paradoxical election result. With an increase of votes cast in its favour, the Labour Party received one fewer seat than after the previous triennial election. Moreover, their total representation was fifteen, as compared with fifty-one seats secured by the government party (Liberal) for about the same number of votes. The inevitable sequel was the adoption of proportional representation, under which no party secured a majority at any election. In a country where

the members of the legislature are strictly representative of
their locality; where members of the government, on the other
hand, may be chosen by the prime minister from outside the
ranks of the legislature (in which they sit and speak but do
not vote); and where parliamentary discords are not held in
check by any power of dissolution — durable coalitions were
hard to construct or maintain. Accordingly, we must picture
a series of minority governments, with limited resources in
personnel and still more in voting power, struggling to tackle
the problems — especially the overwhelming economic
problems — of the interwar period.

A programme of direct action had a considerable appeal to
the peasants of the big valleys of eastern Norway, who were
very hard hit by the fall in prices of farm products, especially
the timber from which a third of their profits came. In the
1920s a newly formed Agrarian Party campaigned with much
more outspoken bitterness than the conservatives against the
growth of trade unionism as a new and highly unwelcome
intruder on the rural scene. It championed Norway's ancient
claims in Greenland — ultimately disallowed by the Hague
Court — with a romantic enthusiasm suggestive of *mare
nostrum*. When the party held office in 1931-3, and still more
after its fall, when some of its leaders considered the possibility of forming a new government which would try to rule
in defiance of the parliamentary majority, its tone was very
like that of the openly unconstitutional Lapua movement
among the farmers of Finland. It seems significant that the
former agrarian Prime Minister was to receive a ten-year
sentence for collaboration during the German occupation of
Norway.

As regards the industrial situation, many of the factors
which might stimulate the growth of fascism in Norway were
the same as elsewhere. Although the Labour Party definitively broke with Moscow in 1923, when the communist
minority set up a party of their own, its aims were still in
principle revolutionary. When King Haakon in 1928, because
of its electoral success, called upon it to form a minority
government, a genuine run on the banks was one main factor
in its overthrow after only eighteen days in office. In
1919-31 Norway, like many other countries, suffered from a

series of big strikes and lockouts, in which the feelings of the workers were aroused against the 'bourgeois state' by the use of the law to enforce contracts and, more especially, to protect strike-breakers from violence. The bourgeoisie, for its part, never forgot the earlier link between the Labour Party and the Comintern, and believed all the more firmly in the nefarious activities of 'Red Guards' because they were hard to trace.

But in two respects at least, Norwegian society may be regarded as particularly vulnerable. Having been a poor country for so long, she lacked strongly based and highly developed credit institutions: the already mentioned occasion in 1928 was only one of several when the collapse of the currency might easily have been precipitated. At the same time, and partly for the same reason, the forces for the maintenance of law and order were very thin on the ground. In 1931, for example, a single riot (at Menstad) was held by the Minister of Justice to have rendered the State Police for the time being useless. His private calculation was that he had only 620 soldiers with whom if necessary to supplement the Oslo police force; beyond this, he would have to depend on all the uncertainties of a call-up of army conscripts.

The earliest organization, in which some features of fascism made a tentative appearance, was an anti-strike weapon called Samfundshjelp, which in 1920 began to solicit support from banks and employers' associations. While its main activity was to protect the public against the withdrawal of essential services, it also acted to some extent as a police reserve and, in one or two towns at least, a part of the membership was recruited and trained as a paramilitary force. Its presiding genius was a cavalry colonel. But since no threatened marxist coup ever caused this organization to demonstrate its true strength, which remains therefore highly conjectural, for the present purpose perhaps the most interesting feature of Samfundshjelp was its membership from 1921 to 1930 of the institution in Switzerland sometimes known as the 'international anti-comintern entente'.

From a political standpoint, however, more weight should be attached to the establishment in 1925 of the 'non-party', but definitely anti-marxist, Fedrelandslaget or League of the

Fatherland. Its founders included Christian Michelsen, the Grand Old Man of Norwegian political life, who as Prime Minister twenty years before had successfully broken the tie with Sweden. And its early members included Nansen, who (with the possible exception of his fellow explorer Amundsen) was the only Norwegian citizen with an international renown. If they had lived longer — they died in 1925 and 1930 respectively — it is possible that the new society's widespread propaganda for stronger government and a united front against the Red Peril would have had important results. In 1930 it had 412 local branches, whose total membership was alleged to exceed 100,000, fed upon a diet of nationalist sentiment, proposals to increase the defence budget, and a general demand for more effective national leadership. But in the later 1930s the movement lost ground, partly at least because its weekly, *ABC* (Anti-Bolshevik Clubs), combined its championship of the corporative state with an undiscriminating enthusiasm for the Hitler regime in Germany.

In March 1931, another ingredient in the ideology of fascism can be traced in Norway in the Nordisk Folkereisning, a society which was to preach the superiority of the Nordic race, pointing to the Scandinavian founders of the Russian state as a convincing and significant illustration of the dogma. The movement was virtually stillborn, for within two months its leader obtained office, re-emerging from the tasks of government two years later with schemes for a much larger and more definitely fascist organization. That leader was a Major Vidkun Quisling, who gave a new stamp to an already existing Norwegian fascism.

A brief reference to his earlier career may justify the claim that Quisling was a fascist leader *sui generis*. Four centuries of respectable and unadventurous ancestors; an upbringing in a quiet country vicarage; academic ambitions always crowned with success; patriotic enthusiasm determining the choice of a military career; and a passing-out examination from the military high school with the highest marks achieved in the century or more of its existence. In 1911, at the age of twenty-four, this exceptionally promising officer entered the General Staff, where he was allotted Russia as his special field of study, which in turn gave him three different openings. In 1918 and in 1920-1 he served for short periods as military attaché in Petrograd and Helsinki, and for a rather longer period in 1927-9 as a Norwegian Legation official looking after British interests in Moscow — for which he received an honorary CBE. In the second place, his familiarity with Russian conditions brought him two appointments under Nansen in his relief work and a third, directly under the League of Nations, for a similar purpose. Finally, for nearly four years (1926-9) Quisling had a private business job in Russia, in connection with a north Russian timber concession operated by a fellow Norwegian, Frederik Prytz.

But in spite of these promising beginnings, Quisling came to look upon society with the sense of personal grievance which lay at the root of so much fascist leadership. One turning-point was his decision to stay on in Russia in 1923, when he was refused further leave from his duties as an officer of the General Staff. This effectively blocked his further military career, with the result that, finding himself temporarily without employment, in the winter of 1924-5 he compromised his political integrity by an attempt to induce politicians of the extreme left to employ him as an organizer of Red Guards in Norway.

The other turning-point was his experience in 1931-3, when the Agrarian Party, holding office for the first time, short of military connections, attracted by Quisling's racial views, and welcoming his supposed expertise in international relations, appointed him as their Minister of Defence. For this unexpected chance in a position of authority under a parliamentary regime revealed all too clearly that the gifts of absorption and application which had made him a distinguished examinee and a successful attaché were not coupled with gifts of political management, either in his own department of defence or in cabinet discussions or in parliamentary debate. Quisling achieved nothing for his country's defences, which were in a parlous condition; the second of the two prime ministers under whom he served longed to extrude him from his government; and his freely flung accusations of treason made him anathema to the Labour Party whose supposed interests he had once offered to serve. By

March 1933, when the agrarians lost office, he had been proved to be a liability rather than an asset to any democratic political party.

Two months later, Quisling re-emerged at the head of a new party, Nasjonal Samling, the National Unity movement, based on the leadership principle — with himself as leader. In considering how this could happen, it is important to bear in mind that the notion of some kind of anti-marxist crusade was congenial to some persons of influence, as had been made clear to Quisling at social gatherings. In such circles the hatred shown by the Labour Party made Quisling something of a hero, especially as the deployment of military and naval units after the Menstad riot was erroneously supposed to have been initiated by him in his capacity as Defence Minister. Moreover, Quisling's propaganda could combine in a kind of cloudy rhetoric a number of ideas of varying appeal.

Mention has already been made of the Nordic race myth, which he seems to have imbibed from Prytz during their business association in Russia. This had been developed in Quisling's book, *Russia and Ourselves*, of which an English translation was published by Hodder and Stoughton in 1932. The curious may find there a full exposition of the anti-communist theme, which he was accustomed to develop in his attacks on Labour. By this time he had also appropriated part of the doctrine of the corporative state, proposing to reduce the power of the Norwegian parliament by super-imposing a House of Corporations representative of economic interests. Since 1933 was the year of Hitler's triumph, it is hardly necessary to add that the example of a new era in Germany was freely quoted. But for an English audience it is important to notice that, ever since the death of Nansen three years before, Quisling had built upon his association with Nansen in his Russian relief work — which was never as personal and intimate as he claimed — to represent himself as the heir to that great man's ideas and leadership. He had never dared to suggest this in Nansen's lifetime, and while there may have been some effect on the ignorant, Nansen's friends were outraged.

Its original backers looked to Nasjonal Samling to establish its influence initially at the polls, and in this it failed signally.

The system of proportional representation offered a slender chance to a new party. NS did its best to form electoral alliances, most notably with a direct-action movement among the smaller peasantry, which employed a system of boycotting reminiscent of the Irish Land League in order to prevent forced sales of mortgaged farm property. But the failure of NS was quite overwhelming. In the general election of 1933 they secured 2.2 per cent of the votes, which gave them no seats, and next year their participation in local elections yielded only twenty-eight places in the local councils of the entire country. By 1935 the movement had 15,000 members and a network of nine papers (mostly weeklies), but in the following general election their vote showed an absolute numerical decline of 1200 and a percentage reduction of 0.4 per cent. In 1937 the local elections witnessed a final rout, for only seven seats were left in their possession. By this time influential backers had deserted *en masse*, and when the European war broke out two years later Quisling was a discredited leader, supported by a handful of personal associates and a minimal following confined to particular districts, and totally lacking the financial resources for any further nation-wide propaganda.

In at least two respects Quisling's failure resembles that of Sir Oswald Mosley. Returning prosperity made the conflict between capital and labour less menacing, so that extreme solutions were no longer called for. At the same time, some inkling of the savageries perpetrated by German fascists against political opponents and the Jews was penetrating into other countries, and made the shortcomings of democracy seem comparatively trivial. The acceptance of a planned economy by all important parliamentary parties was also a stabilizing influence in both countries. But in Norway particular importance attaches to the ending of the long period of political uncertainty in 1935, when the second Labour government abandoned the last vestiges of its revolutionary traditions and formed an alliance with the agrarians. Bartering support for farm prices and a tax system which favoured farm interests for acceptance of a not too advanced socialist programme in industrial life, the Labour Party secured a parliamentary majority. This was confirmed by the

1936 election, and when the Germans invaded Norway in 1940 the Labour government was in its sixth uninterrupted year of office.

We must now turn to consider the national characteristics of fascism in wartime Norway. During the seven months of Norwegian neutrality Quisling was almost a one-man fifth column. Having so largely lost his basis of domestic support, he built eagerly upon his earlier, rather tenuous associations with the Germans. His motive at the outset was not, in all probability, purely selfish: it was not irrational for him to believe that the Norwegian government was playing into the hands of the Allies, especially the British, and he may even have imagined quite genuinely that there was some secret agreement for letting them into the country. With that degree of self-justification he contacted in succession Rosenberg, Raeder and Hitler himself, trying in vain to put over the idea of a political *coup* in Norway, to be engineered by him with German support. The pretext was to be the alleged unconstitutionality of parliament in sitting for a fourth year under a law which it had itself passed substituting quadrennial for triennial elections. But the Germans were more interested in the size and determination of his following, of which he was unable to present a convincing picture.

In the new year Quisling's visit to Hitler was rewarded by a subsidy, which enabled him to revive his party propaganda. But the German decision to forestall a hypothetical Allied landing by an invasion of Norway was kept a close secret. Six days before it took place, a German staff officer interrogated him in Copenhagen about the state of Norwegian defences; but even then it is unlikely that he was told anything, though he may have guessed a lot. Neither the army commander nor the German minister in Oslo had any instructions to coordinate the invasion with a Quisling *coup*. But on the fateful morning of 9 April 1940, the representatives of Raeder and Rosenberg in the Norwegian capital made immediate contact with him, enabling the power vacuum, created by the precipitate withdrawal of the government to avoid capture, to be used to his advantage. With their help Quisling was able by the same evening to broadcast the news that he had formed a government of his party supporters in friendly relations with the Germans. Several of his fellow 'ministers' refused to join him in his act of treachery, but Hitler approved the *fait accompli*. Thus the war situation gave new life to a thoroughly discredited fascist leader and a party which had long been on the verge of extinction.

The immediate consequence was the embitterment of Norwegian feeling by this stab in the back, which predisposed the king and the lawful government to continue what seemed to be a rather hopeless effort of military resistance. After a week the Germans dismissed Quisling from office in a belated and unsuccessful attempt at pacification. At the end of their two months' campaign, with the whole country under their military control, the Germans further explored the possibility of doing a deal with representatives of the regular political parties, while reserving some share of authority for Quisling's NS as the party which was both in ideology and interest firmly tied to their own fortunes. But in mid-September 1940, when Britain's chances of survival were beginning to improve, the other Norwegian parties escaped from an agreement which they saw would give increasing power to Quisling, and were immediately banned.

For the remaining four-and-a-half years of war Nasjonal Samling, with Quisling as its highly publicized Leader, held office under the Germans; at first they were on a kind of probation, but in February 1942 Quisling was given formal authority as Minister-President. Neither the German army commander nor the civilian Reichscommissar, Terboven, regarded him as competent or his party as a worthwhile ally; but as long as Quisling kept within the limits of authority which Hitler thought him fit for, it was too dangerous an undertaking for any German to try once more to dislodge him. Thus within certain limits we can speak of a native fascism let loose in wartime Norway. Yet it must never be forgotten that what we are examining was a strictly subordinate regime, quite unable to achieve the change of status which Quisling most desired, namely, the termination of military occupation through the negotiation of a peace treaty with Germany.

But to find the national characteristics of this fascism is

not easy. It was, almost by definition, anti-British and pro-German, but only its anti-Russian gestures appear to have been to any large extent spontaneous. About 7000 Norwegians were recruited for service on the eastern front — about one-eighth of the number of loyalists secretly in training for their own war of liberation — and propaganda about the peril to Europe from the east was fairly well received. The same cannot be said about anti-Jewish propaganda, to which Quisling gave special support in an address at Frankfurt in March 1941. Though at that time he professed to be advocating their removal to a place of settlement outside Europe, the support which he and his party subsequently gave to the rounding-up of the Norwegian Jews for deportation to German concentration camps has always been regarded by the Norwegian people in general as one of the very darkest stains on their record. Many risked their lives in bringing a substantial proportion of Jewish families across the border to safety in Sweden.

It is possible that there was some element of genuine national appeal in the continuous vaunting of the superiority of Nordic man and the leadership principle over the parliamentary systems of the effete democracies. In most social groupings — the Church, the teaching profession, the trade unions, the sports clubs and so forth — the opposition to such ideas was very effective, but there are indications that local government institutions (under the control of Hagelin) were penetrated to a significant extent. The national romanticism fostered by the Agrarian Party had not lost its charm for the inhabitants of remote valleys, who shared Quisling's lifelong passion for the medieval sagas and were not always quick to see the absurdity in such pretences as the identification of his strong-arm men with the *hird* which attended the saga-kings.

Nasjonal Samling rose from a membership of about 7000 in 1939 to a maximum of 43,000 in November 1943, and they represented only the hard core of collaborationism. In Norway as elsewhere, collaborationists, whether accepting a fascist party label or not, were influenced by a variety of non-ideological motives. In a small country, with a long history of subordination to foreign rulers, it was in any case tempting to accept the German 'new order' in Europe as a fact, without feeling any personal obligation to examine the moral or political principles on which it might rest. A special incentive to do so was provided in some instances by personal disappointment over the failure of Britain to match promises with performance during the two months' campaign in 1940. More often it was provided by a deep-rooted appreciation of German culture, such as was felt by the novelist Hamsun or may be presumed in the scientist Skancke, Quisling's Minister of Education, who had been trained at Karlsruhe. And if collaboration in general meant a secure livelihood in difficult wartime conditions, party membership offered a career. Quisling himself had been almost without visible means of support; as Minister-President he pocketed about £30,000 a year. Lesser men of course received lesser rewards, but a career in NS offered profit, power, and a spurious dignity to people normally left in obscurity: cranks, adventurers, social misfits, and occasionally sadists.

Since the picture just given must be broadly applicable to the wartime experience of many occupied territories, it may be desirable to inquire in conclusion whether there are any special features in the Norwegian treatment of the fascist problem when the war ended. Two points may perhaps be made. The trial and execution of Quisling attracted world-wide attention, partly because of the enigma of his character (did any other major fascist leader end up by offering his services in the Church?); and partly because it preceded the trials at Nuremberg. Viewed in perspective, he seems a less significant figure than he did then – and by no means a representative Norwegian fascist. The other, possibly less familiar point is the thoroughness of the postwar investigations conducted by the Norwegian courts of law.

About 90,000 persons – more than twice the maximum membership of NS – had their actions during the occupation examined by the police. Of these, twenty-five were eventually executed, mainly for murder, torture, and aggravated acts of delation, Quisling being one of a total of no more than three persons whose death was exacted primarily as the price of high treason. But there were 18,000 prison sentences, of which one-fifth were for more than three years, and another 28,000 persons were fined or deprived of civil rights, which for many of them meant loss of employment. Making every allowance for subsequent acts of amnesty, this is a formidable total for a country of three million inhabitants. To some extent the explanation lies in the marked Norwegian respect for law, which very largely excluded private acts of vengeance but also made it impossible for known illegalities to be glossed over. A deeper explanation may, however, be tentatively suggested.

In 1940-5 the traditions of parliamentarism, nationalism, and neutralism, on which (as was said at the outset) prewar Norwegian life was based, had all been outraged. Painful experience had shown the hazards to which the independence of a small country is exposed. One of those hazards was the existence of a political movement willing to collaborate with a potential enemy. However slight its native roots, however chequered its earlier history, and however limited its practical achievements as a treasonable institution had been, such a movement was bound to receive a punishment related to the unknown future. Unknown — but for Norwegians today, fascism appears to have been a temporary and rather trivial aberration of alien origins and character, while the constitution of 1814 remains the palladium of their national liberties.

11

DENMARK

✦

Malene Djursaa

Danish nazism had no roots and left no traces. It was a fifteen-year parenthesis in Denmark's political life which few would have noticed but for the wider significance borrowed from the German neighbour and 'protector' of 1940-5. During the German occupation Danish nazi parties expanded their membership considerably in relation to prewar numbers, but never commanded more than at the most 1 per cent of the population as members, or 2 per cent as voters. No Danish nazi party ever held a position of even partial power, either before or during the German occupation.

Despite this overall insignificance, no less than twenty-nine self-proclaimed nazi parties came and went in the period 1928-45. Most of these need not detain us long, however, as they were short-lived and very small. For most, accurate membership numbers are not known, but figures exceeding three digits must have been a rarity. Neither are ideological differences between these small parties of much interest, as they were almost exclusively regroupings of the same people, in which personal animosities and ambitions played a larger part than ideological variances of the German model which they all shared.

One of these twenty-nine parties was formed in 1928, thirteen during the 1930s, and fifteen during the occupation. If one does not operate with too lax a definition of fascism, antecedents during the 1920s were quite insignificant and were themselves imported, on the Italian model. Worth a mention perhaps are E.N. Møller's blackshirt Nationalkorps from the 1920s.

The search for Danish relatives of interwar fascism has in particular focused attention on the Conservative Party's youth branch KU (Konservativ Ungdom, with about 30,000 members at its strongest) and on the farmers' organization LS (Landbrugernes Sammenslutning, about 40,000 around 1936-7), with which the political party Frie Folkeparti, later Bondepartiet, sympathized. And certainly connections between LS, KU and Danish nazism can be established, firstly visible in some overlap of members and leaders, secondly in an attempt during the occupation to form a joint pro-German government of LS and DNSAP, which was the largest Danish nazi party. All the same, KU and LS were not fascist organizations, and 'semi-fascist' is a meaningless term. KU 'flirted' with fascism in the 1930s, and adopted some of its external style. During this period it experienced a considerable growth, and there are indications that it attracted much of the potential nazi support from the younger urban middle class during these years. By the end of the 1930s, however, KU's flirtation with nazism had once more cooled.

As regards LS, this was first and foremost an economic farmers' organization, whose political sympathies were directed by trading pragmatism. When this pragmatism no longer suggested Danish nazism as a useful ally, relations between the two organizations diminished and henceforth existed primarily through the connections of both with the Germans, for whom they were potential rather than active tools in the power game.

In the Danish jungle of political parties, the best guide to the extent of Danish fascism remains the number which called themselves fascist or national socialist, i.e. twenty-nine parties in seventeen years. Of these, only DNSAP (Danmarks National-Socialistiske Arbejder Parti) achieved any numerical significance, and it was the only one to take part in national elections. Many of the other nazi parties were splinter groups from DNSAP, or were at some time amalgamated with it, which means that most Danish nazi party members must at some time have been members of DNSAP. Moreover, as the only nazi representative at the polls, aside from the German minority party in South Jutland, DNSAP must have absorbed most of the nazi votes. Hence to all intents and purposes this party may be considered representative of interwar Danish nazism, and the following story of DNSAP may be read as the story of Danish nazism in the period.

Ideology and organization

Denmark's National Socialist Workers' Party, DNSAP, was founded by Captain Cay Lembcke on 16 November 1930, two months after Hitler's large electoral victory. The first programme was an almost direct translation of the NSDAP's twenty-five points. In 1933 Lembcke was replaced by Fritz Clausen as leader of the party, and the twenty-five points changed to eight points, in a vaguer formulation of essentially the same substance. Hence ideological divergence from the German model was always slight.

The party organizational structure was also scrupulously copied from Hitler's NSDAP. Hoping to achieve the same results by the same means, DNSAP treated its German model as a magic formula to be observed in the smallest detail. Numerous layers of the pyramidal party structure divided the numerically modest membership. Its symbol was the swastika, and names and abbreviations were as far as possible transfers from Hitler's organization, or nostalgically outmoded Danish equivalents. As in Germany, all units and sub-units had their own flags, emblems and badges, ranks and degrees, salutes and honours, oaths of allegiance and vows of vengeance. The four main membership branches were 'ordinary' party members (PM), women members (KM), the paramilitary corps (SA) and the youth groups (NSU/NSUP). Attempts to create a number of affiliated trade and cultural associations met with little success.

Numbers

Although by far the largest of the Danish interwar nazi parties, DNSAP was always small. After a slow start, it reached about 5000 members by the outbreak of war in

1939. The German occupation of Denmark in April 1940 precipitated an inflow of new members, and the party peaked in March 1943, just before a general election, with approximately 21,500 members, or 0.5 per cent of the population of four million. This election was a big disappointment for DNSAP which, despite German backing, only managed to retain its usual three seats in parliament. Straight after the elections, membership numbers fell steeply, and German military reverses further accelerated the exodus from the party. Although many were trapped in their party allegiance by the sharply defined 'them-and-us'-awareness of war and occupation, only 12,600 remained as members of DNSAP by the end of the war. By this time, approximately 39,000 different individuals had been members of DNSAP in the fifteen years of its existence.

Social composition

Who were these 39,000 members of DNSAP? Postwar opinion commonly classed them as society's dregs and criminals, traitors to the national spirit through personal moral failings. Sociological investigation cannot refute this judgement, but neither does it support it in any way. In class terms first, the 39,000 Danish nazis were an almost exact microcosm of Danish society at the time, with a perfectly representative proportion coming from the middle and lower-middle class. On an occupationally based nine-point class scale, the party's adult men are distributed almost exactly like the adult men in Denmark's population at the time. Second, although at times some occupations were more strongly represented in the party than others, DNSAP's overall occupational distribution also diverges little from that of Denmark's population in 1940. Third, 'declining' or 'threatened' occupations were not more strongly represented in the party than others. Fourth, an examination of members' previous political allegiance has shown that they were recruited from right- and left-wing parties in proportions which correspond to national election figures, and that they had been sociologically quite typical members of these parties. Fifth, Karl O. Christiansen's work on postwar

collaboration trials shows that the Danish nazis' educational
and familial background was not unfavourable when compared to a 'normal' population. Sixth and last, Christiansen uses the indices of unemployment and income levels
before and after recruitment to collaboration to conclude
that opportunistic motives do not appear to have played any
important part among the Danish nazis.

Not only the tenacity with which the 'outsider' definition
of the country's native nazis survives in Denmark, but also
the widely accepted view of fascism as a middle-class movement justify this emphasis on the Danish nazis' normality in
so many sociologically measurable aspects. From this
normality follows, first, that Danes can no longer write off
the 1-2 per cent native nazis as simply deviant, and their
existence as nothing more than a slight blemish on an otherwise spotless national record. Secondly, it raises a query
about the established and generally accepted tenet of the
middle-class base of fascist movements. It is true that in the
early years of DNSAP's existence the middle classes predomi-
nated among the members, as is presumably the norm for
new political parties. The DNSAP vanguard consisted especially of the rural middle class of independent farmers.
Unusually for a new party — not just a new fascist party
— the young DNSAP was organizationally based on the
country districts and some provincial towns, and only later
became a predominantly urban party with the main weight in
the capital. This shift of emphasis was probably occasioned
by a reversal during the German occupation of the relative
conditions of the rural and urban economies. Going back to
the great crisis of the early 1930s, Danish agriculture had
been hit particularly hard, especially in South Jutland — the
border region to Germany — where DNSAP was strongest.
Conditions for Danish agriculture improved in the late 1930s,
and the occupation offered large possibilities for food
exports to Germany. For industry, however, the occupation
meant shortage of materials and widespread unemployment.
Also of importance in the party's shift towards an urban
character was the move to Copenhagen of the headquarters
(and hence of the biggest propaganda drives), as well as the
greater physical presence in the capital of the German

occupying power, with resultant chances for party members of economic gains.

Simultaneously with the rural to urban trend, the membership was undergoing a middle- to working-class shift. Since this class trend was observable in both country and town districts it was not only, as one might think, an effect of the rural-urban trend. At the end of the fifteen years, the party's class divergences from the national average had been evened out, the party's average entry figures being very close to the distribution of the Danish population in the 1940 census.

I have stressed those aspects of the party in which it was typical of its parent country, but thereby untypical of other fascist parties. But the reverse is also true. In line with other fascist parties, DNSAP included relatively many young people, and few women (21 per cent). However, it is open to question whether these two features are typical not so much of *fascist* parties as of *new* parties. Support is given to this notion by the fact that, as the party aged, it gradually came to include a greater proportion from the higher age-groups, and more women. Urban women especially were recruited during the occupation, but country women also increased their share. A simultaneous growth in the youth branches of the party suggests that much of the party's recruitment in later years took the form of 'inter-family' or 'closed-circle' enrolment of existing members' families, natural enough given the background of increased isolation and ostracism which the nazis experienced during the occupation. The extent of this isolation can be seen in the fact that by the 1943 elections, the party counted only twice as many votes as registered members, as compared with six times as many in 1939.

That the membership of DNSAP was far from constant over the years has already become apparent in this outline description. The main developments can be summarized as: (1) a move from the country and the provincial towns towards the capital; (2) a move from the higher social classes towards the lower, on average a 'normal' distribution; (3) an increase of both rural and urban, but especially urban, women's representation in the party; and (4) an ageing of the party membership caused not by the recruits getting older, but by the young members leaving again more rapidly.

Table 1   DNSAP membership by social class (compared to Danish population)

Social class	Denmark 1953-4 Svalastoga study	DNSAP entries**			
		Average	1930-5	1936-9	1940-5
Upper-middle and above:	3.9	3.4	3.5	4.5	3.2
Middle-middle:	8.0	7.1	8.6	6.6	6.9
Lower-middle:	30.0	30.6	35.0	33.8	28.8
Upper-lower:	34.0	33.7	34.5	31.6	33.9
Middle-lower and below:	24.5	25.2	18.4	23.4	27.3
Total % (approx.):	100	100	100	100	100
Cases*:	4000	2551	437	381	1733

* Men of 21 years and over.   ** 10% random sample.

Table 2   DNSAP membership by age group (compared to Danish population)

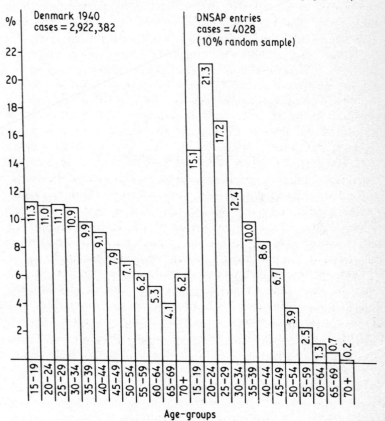

Age-groups

Source: M. Djursaa, *DNSAP-danske nazister 1930-45*, Copenhagen, 1981.

The leaders

In DNSAP's complex party organization, over 7 per cent of all entrants became leaders. These differ from ordinary members in a number of respects. One of the more pronounced differences is that leaders were of a higher social class than members, with a high proportion of self-employed; another that their class-distribution remained constant through the years while that of the members changed towards the lower classes. Further, leaders were older than other members, included fewer women, and remained in the party twice as long. Finally we know that the DNSAP leaders' involvement in their society was greater than ordinary members' on a number of counts: namely membership of clubs and associations, trade unions, tenure of honorary posts, and previous association with other political parties.

None of these listed differences can cause surprise, and they are differences which we could intuitively expect to find in any political party. The value of stating them here is that our intuitive assumptions have in this case been empirically proven.

Geographical distribution

DNSAP was never very evenly spread over the country. Some areas remained almost unaffected, notably Bornholm (which is a physically isolated island), the thinly populated West and North Jutland counties, and Svendborg (Funen) and Holbæk (Sealand) counties, whose few members on the other hand remained comparatively long in the party. The record-holders in party faithfulness were the extreme north and the South Jutland counties, the latter also having the highest ratio of party members to total population. Other districts with a relatively strong DNSAP support were East Jutland, Lolland-Falster and some Sealand counties, especially the capital with surrounding district.

Explanations of many of the differences in the party's geographical distribution are little more than speculations. The virtual absence of nazis on Bornholm and in West Jutland could perhaps be due to geographical isolation, or perhaps to cultural differences in the case of the West Jutland fishing communities which possessed a strong puritanical tradition. The location near Ålborg, Thisted and Ribe of German fortification works and industries seems to have strengthened DNSAP during the occupation in these areas, as was seen most consistently in the election results of 1943. Political traditions also seem to have played a part, as DNSAP did not manage to get a foothold in those rural districts where more than one strong agricultural party was established prior to the appearance of DNSAP. This was true of Thisted, Holbæk and Svendborg counties. On a local level, exceptional DNSAP strength in particular parishes or clusters of parishes can often be attributed to the influence of individual local party leaders or local VIPs known to sympathize with the party.

South Jutland

One region stands out from all the others. From first to last, DNSAP's undisputed stronghold was in South Jutland, North Schleswig to the Germans, the region which was under German rule between 1864 and 1920 when a plebiscite drew the border just north of Flensburg. In 1943, 4.5 per cent of the region's voters supported DNSAP, against 1.8 per cent in the rest of the country. Even within this region, however, the party's support varied considerably. Of the four counties its strongest was Åbenrå, and within this county especially the parishes around Bovrup, where the headquarters were located from 1933 to 1940, and where the party leader Fritz Clausen was the local doctor. In 1943, DNSAP set its all-time record when 28 per cent of all registered voters in Bovrup gave the party their support.

Bovrup was clearly exceptional, even in South Jutland, but taken as a whole the region's DNSAP members joined earlier, and in greater numbers, and stayed longer in the party than in any other part of the country.

There are specific economic and political explanations of DNSAP's special position in South Jutland, but they can be seen as specific effects of one general circumstance, namely the transfer of the region from German to Danish sovereignty in 1920.

In the case of South Schleswig and Holstein, which remained under German rule during the nazi regime, Heberle has pointed to the importance of a breakdown of the region's traditional liberal farmers' organizations in allowing the nazis to fill the organizational void. A direct parallel to North Schleswig (South Jutland) cannot be drawn, either in the political or in the economic part of Heberle's analysis — but in a much wider interpretation of his thesis it can be argued that the transfer of the northern part of Schleswig to Danish sovereignty in itself constituted a 'breakdown' of its whole economic, political and institutional structure, which paved the way for nazism.

In the economic sphere, the region after 1920 had a different market, different competitors and different creditors. The South Jutland farmers had fallen behind the strong technical and organizational development of Danish agriculture, and catching up was expensive. Not only this, but the change of nationality itself had been economically unsettling, as German inflation and Danish reflation played havoc with loans and capital. As a result of such factors, agriculture in South Jutland suffered much more than the rest of the country from the postwar crisis, which in turn made it more vulnerable to the more general crisis of the early 1930s. That the South Jutland farmers also became more vulnerable to nazi propaganda is suggested by the fact that DNSAP's greatest support in the region was always found in its rural districts.

In the political sphere, South Jutlanders were offered a new set of alternatives by the Danes, but naturally it took time before the individual's loyalties to one or another party could become fixed. Hence the region's voting pattern was very volatile in the interwar period. Continued agitation between the region's Danish- and German-minded population groups ensured that the nationality of a vote was still seen as more important than its political colour, and economic as well as nationalistic issues gave rise to a number of 'protest movements' in the 1920s and 1930s. Against this background, it makes sense to see South Jutland's DNSAP as one within the spectrum of the region's protest movements.

Although the new border had been drawn on the basis of

a plebiscite, it was of course unavoidable that national minorities became stranded on both sides of the border. From 1933 the German minority in South Jutland had its own nazi party, the NSDAP-N, openly affiliated to Hitler's NSDAP. This was a rival, not an affiliate, of DNSAP, which did not recruit among the German minority. NSDAP-N's strong *heim ins Reich* propaganda, as well as economic and cultural battles between the two nationalities centring on land and schools, contributed to widespread uncertainty regarding the region's future nationality, especially after Hitler started rolling over the map of Europe 'liberating' German minorities. The majority of the South Jutland population were committed to German or Danish nationality — but some remained on the fence, dubbed 'piebalds' by committed nationalists. For these piebalds, the uncommitted and the nervous in the battle of nationalities, DNSAP could appear as a political insurance broker, offering Danish nationalism on a German model — the very combination which ruled out any co-operation of DNSAP with the Danish nationalist movement in the region.

Why Danish nazism failed

The leader

The prominence of the leader in fascist ideology invites an explanation of fascist parties' success or failure in terms of their leader's personal charisma. Accordingly the overall ineffectiveness and failure of DNSAP has often been ascribed to Fritz Clausen's personal shortcomings, epitomized in the ironical wartime saying 'God save the King and Fritz Clausen', the best guarantors of national virtue.

Certainly Fritz Clausen was not a very convincing leader-figure. He was fat and not particularly intelligent-looking, drank somewhat excessively, and unlike the King did not cut a very dashing figure when portrayed on a white horse. But he was probably the best man the party had, and an objective estimation of his effectiveness as party leader does not yet exist.

Besides, we don't need the person of Fritz Clausen to explain the failure of nazism in Denmark — rather, economic and political explanations vie with each other to produce a richly over-determined case against its feasibility.

General pre-conditions of fascism

Some major points in the programme of the German NSDAP were anti-parliamentarism, anti-democracy, anti-communism, anti-semitism, nationalism and social reform, and it is in the German population's response to these that the mass following of the NSDAP is most commonly explained.

In Denmark, nazi parties adopted the same programme, but conditions were so vastly different that no easy response could be found in the Danish population. Parliamentary democracy had been introduced to Denmark in many slow stages, but it had stood its decisive test in a constitutional crisis in 1920. By the time DNSAP had had time to form its organization in the 1930s, parliamentary democracy had been seen to work through good as well as bad times and commanded a high level of confidence, very different from Germany, where the first democratic government was identified with defeat and poverty.

The Danish government, and with it the parliamentary system, was further strengthened by the role it had been able to play during the depressions. It was lucky in that both the post-war and the 1930s depressions were relatively mild in Denmark, but this was also seen to be a result of the Social Democratic government's extensive countermeasures of social reform. The significance of this for the chances of nazism was recognized by Best, the German plenipotentiary in Denmark during the occupation, who reported home that 'a social revolution is not necessary in Denmark and is therefore without effect as a point in the programme of Danish national socialism.'

The remaining programme points of the NSDAP fared little better. As regards anti-semitism, Danish Jews were few, only about 6000, and in any case highly integrated with the Danish population, who were not commonly conscious of ethnic or cultural differences between themselves and Jews. Even Best concluded that the influence of Jews in Denmark was small, and that they could best be proceeded against individually.

The other nazi arch-enemy, the communists, were just as inconspicuous in Denmark as the Jews. Even in the 'semi-revolutionary' atmosphere of 1920 the Communist Party obtained barely 4000 votes and no elected candidates. In 1932, it had two members elected to parliament, which increased to three in 1939 — but clearly the Communist Party could spark off no 'tide of Red fear' for DNSAP to utilize.

Political space

The weakness of the communists seems to be connected to the weakness of the nazis also in the sense that the existing party constellation was seen to cater for most vested and organized interests of both right and left. Two groups, each of two established parties, had become a working tradition in the formation of minority governments, yet remained sufficiently flexible to negotiate political settlements across the traditional alliances at the depth of the depression in 1931-3. These four parties had effectively filled the political space and left neither extreme right nor extreme left any room in which to manoeuvre. The new extremists were 'latecomers on the political scene' (Linz), in Denmark's case a scene not characterized by crisis or serious instability. What instability and dissatisfaction there was during the early 1930s, DNSAP was unable to exploit effectively, as it was formed too late to achieve the practice and adaptation of organization and ideology which NSDAP went through in the 1920s.

Imitation versus nationalism

The issue of nationalism was a particularly thorny one for DNSAP, bound up as it was with its imitation of a German party, the issue of the border with Germany, and finally Germany's occupation of Denmark.

In the first place, Denmark in the 1930s was not very receptive to nationalistic propaganda. It had not been on the losing side in 1918 — had not even participated — and had just had the issue of the border settled to most people's satisfaction with the return of South Jutland in 1920. Besides, the Danish nazis' professed nationalism was considered not quite credible, being so closely modelled on the German NSDAP. In the 1930s, Fritz Clausen made concerted attempts to prove his party's independence of Germany, claiming 'Nordic' origins for the swastika and corporativism. At the same time, however, he was speaking of the 'racial unity between Danes and Germans, which transcends national differences', outraging Danish nationalists by accepting a few members of the South Jutland German minority into his party, and earning the distrust of South Jutland nationalists by his attempts to avoid the politically explosive border issue.

When the Germans occupied Denmark, the nazis' credibility as Danish nationalists was of course totally destroyed, and they came to be regarded as the Germans' lackeys, outright traitors to their own country. Some, of course, did collaborate. But popular belief and official findings notwithstanding, there is every reason to believe that the party did not act as either political or military fifth column for the Germans before April 1940. It is unlikely that the Germans would have wanted it, surprise and secrecy being essential to the success of their military strategy. But it is equally unlikely that the Danish nazis would have wanted to act the part. Although they copied programme, walk, uniform, emblem, organization, rhetoric and actions from their German idol, although they — unsuccessfully — courted German connections in the 1930s and tried to get the Germans to accept DNSAP as a 'brother party', the party was nevertheless an unwilling protégé of the occupying power, for in the nazi programme nationalism was important, and taking this over meant a declaration of independence. The balancing act between the two countries had always been difficult. With the occupation, it became impossible. Treated as traitors, many Danish nazis accepted the Germans and collaborated. With this step and not before, imitation became servitude.

Public opinion before the war

Even this overview of some 'traditional' pre-conditions of fascism does not exhaust the obvious explanations of

DNSAP's failure to achieve a mass following. In particular, the big neighbour to the south was both DNSAP's strength and weakness; its strength in that the party owed its very existence to its German model — and in that it gained many of its followers among those who admired the 'vitality' and 'order' at first seen to characterize the new German government. In these early years, while Hitler was building roads rather than armies and appeared to be creating an economic miracle, the general attitude to Germany included much approval, and Denmark's tiny group of native nazis were tolerated, with a slight smile perhaps. They were too few to be taken entirely seriously, and were still very much a localized countryside phenomenon.

But as the tide of opinion towards Germany turned, so also did that towards Denmark's native nazis. Demonstrations against the swastika and all it stood for began already in 1933, and as Hitler's aggressive militarism became increasingly apparent, the old fear of the enemy of 1848 and 1864 revived. The fear was fuelled by the German minority's demands to return to Germany, although these demands were never backed by Hitler.

From the growing fear of Germany followed a growing fear of Denmark's native nazis. But the measures taken to curb their growth were on the whole characterized by restraint and good sense. A ban on uniforms imposed in 1933 was aimed primarily at KU's fascist 'flirtation' (mentioned earlier) and at the German minority's paramilitary corps, but it equally restricted the DNSAP-corps' publicity-effect of goosestepping in long boots. The press contributed by following Mae West's maxim that 'all publicity is good publicity' and voluntarily starved the native nazis of news coverage — probably the most effective countermeasure of all.

DNSAP during the occupation

Evidently, the results of this public disregard were good, for the nazis remained a tiny minority. But with the occupation in April 1940, DNSAP assumed an importance out of all proportion to its numbers, as ideological kin to the Germans.

'Norwegian conditions' were also feared in this respect, for the Norwegian NS, which was even smaller and less well organized than DNSAP at the start of the occupation, assumed a government role after only a few months.

The same thing could have happened in Denmark. DNSAP hoped for and expected it to happen, others feared and expected it. But it did not happen, and the reasons why are of the utmost interest, since the only realistic possibility the party ever had of achieving power was as a puppet government under the Germans.

The reasons for the limits of German support changed and evolved over the five years of the occupation, but a constant factor was the fact that the Germans were only really interested in DNSAP as a component in their postwar empire, and as a wartime arrangement much preferred the constitutional government to remain. At the very start of the occupation, they had particularly pressing grounds for this preference, for Denmark (together with Norway) was the first component of a package deal which the Germans were planning to make with a number of small countries. In exchange for 'protection', the Germans promised to respect the sovereignty of the country. This promise was made flamboyantly in April 1940, for the benefit mainly of the USA, which was coming up to election time. With a stake in the success of the isolationists, which would mean only limited help to England from the United States, Germany had to keep her promise to Denmark for a while, although she was the only country to have accepted the 'offer'.

Besides, there was another consideration in these early months, for the Danish government had agreed to negotiate with Germany on a customs and currency union. In the late summer of 1940 these negotiations fell through, and the Danes were also beginning to wake up to some measure of resistance, as yet passive. As the Germans at this time were still hoping for a speedy end to the war, the idea of giving DNSAP the government through a coup first became relevant around September 1940, about the same time that Quisling was allowed to walk into government in Norway.

DNSAP was alerted to the possibility of a coup and fully expected it to happen. It even set the date, for 17 November.

In the end, however, the Germans changed their minds, informed DNSAP that it would have to wait, and told it to concentrate on getting a larger following in the meantime.

Why was the coup 'postponed'? A major reason appears to have been the inflexible opposition of the King to an unconstitutional government. From their Dutch and Norwegian experiences the Germans knew the importance of the monarchy in the enforcement of control. Only if the king agreed could a nazi government have the appearance of legality, and without his agreement the Germans knew that a forcible *coup* would spark off too much unrest, meaning that they would have to move in valuable military personnel to keep order. This could not be risked, for the emergence of German plans to attack Russia meant that the expected end to the war was no longer immediately in sight. Military considerations appear to have been in the foreground in the Germans' decision to call off the coup.

DNSAP suffered considerably from the disappointment, and a number of breakaway groups were formed at the beginning of 1941.

The last question to be answered is why the postponement of the coup became the abandonment of the coup — for it seems that the Germans genuinely did not abandon the idea till much later.

One factor undoubtedly was that the Germans became increasingly disenchanted with Fritz Clausen as a leader and did not want to have to deal with him in a situation of even partial power. But the main reason was quite simply that the Germans were getting what they wanted from the existing government. So long as the 'protectorate' required the presence of relatively few soldiers and continued to supply the essential foodstuffs, the Germans saw no reason to introduce any disturbing element for the sake of ideological kinship. Military, economic and diplomatic considerations fluctuated in importance, but always the arguments for continued negotiation came out strong.

In 1943 the situation changed again. Active resistance was growing rapidly, and in the summer a series of large popular strikes swept the country. Since law and order were obviously breaking down anyway and the government resigned, this would seem to be the natural moment for the Germans finally to give DNSAP the government. They did not do so, as DNSAP had by then already been abandoned as a serious component in the power-constellation, even before its humiliation in the March elections of the same year.

This election was the big event behind the vagaries of fortune in 1943. DNSAP had expected up to nineteen seats, the Germans had been sceptical if hopeful, but when in the event DNSAP only managed to retain its usual three seats, the Germans' patience gave out. If three years' financial support for propaganda could not make the party grow, they concluded that nothing would, and that it was best left alone. Political support had been scant for some time before the election, and the German SS had in February 1943 established the Schalburg corps as a substitute for DNSAP, which could no longer supply the desired front-line soldiers. After the elections, even most financial support ceased, and DNSAP was definitely out in the cold, at least for the duration of the war.

In the last two years of the war DNSAP was without political importance. They were years of dissolution, internal leadership quarrels, fragmentation and membership decline, interspersed with efforts to clean up the party and start again. These efforts meant that the nazis did not retreat from public awareness, and both Danish and German minority nazi party members figure heavily in postwar collaboration trials.

Fascism's 'second wave'

If the person of Fritz Clausen is unnecessary to explain the failure of nazism in Denmark, so perhaps are the other listed part-explanations, involving absence of pre-conditions or particular social and political obstacles. However interesting, however right, in a broader comparative context these should perhaps be relegated to a position of 'sufficient but not necessary explanations'.

Denmark was just one in a series of west European countries which started their fascist attempts late, in fascism's 'second wave' of the early and middle 1930s. All these second-wave parties were imitations of Germany, some more slavishly than others. And all failed to gain a mass basis for their imported ideology.

The Norwegian NS (Nasjonal Samling) was another such second-wave imitation party. But despite many cultural and economic similarities between the two countries, a socio-logical comparison of their nazi parties has shown these to have been widely different in their social composition. However, instead of concluding that the failure of imitation parties has to be accounted for individually, we could also choose to see the two Scandinavian nazi parties' divergence from each other — and particularly the Danish party's demonstrated 'typicality' compared to its national society — as indicating a common failure to appeal strongly to any particular class or group.

In Denmark's case at least, this reflects the apparent absence of solid collective motives, either social or economic, for people to become nazis; rather, it looks as if Danish nazism was a matter of individual ideas and feelings, individual ambitions, individual connections and efforts.

This raises the much broader question of the exportability and mutability of nazism. A further reduction of the previously discussed ideological components of nazism leaves three vital ingredients:

1 A purely *ad hoc*, improvised, unsystematic and short-range economic programme — which by the very nature of this description cannot be immediately exportable.

2 A purely visceral, systematic anti-semitism, the export-ability of which would be conditional on the prior exist-ence of a strong anti-semitic tradition, merely needing to be systematized. In Denmark, anti-semitism in the 1930s was much too weak to fulfil this condition.

3 A comprehensive aggressive militarism, exportable to the more powerful countries, but hardly to the small and militarily weak ones — like Denmark and Norway — which made up the bulk of fascism's second wave.

In this assessment, only anti-semitism remains as a likely candidate for successful export to other countries.

Time, or rather the lack of it, could be yet another under-lying factor in second-wave imitation parties' failure to achieve a mass base. Firstly, these parties often found the political space already filled. Secondly, they had too little time to create organizations which could effectively exploit the radical reactions to the economic crisis. Thirdly, they had too little time to attempt an adaptation to local conditions of such of nazism's ideological components as might prove exportable.

12
GREAT BRITAIN

✦

R. Skidelsky

British fascism is associated above all with the name and personality of Sir Oswald Mosley. There had been a few fascist groups in the 1920s. The British Fascists, founded in 1923 by Miss Rotha Lintorn-Orman, was an extreme right-wing body, disproportionately staffed by generals and admirals, and dedicated to unrelenting struggle against bolshevism. The Imperial Fascist League had been started in 1929 by Arnold Spencer Leese, a retired veterinary surgeon and specialist in camel diseases. An anti-semitic publishing company, the Britons, founded by Henry Hamilton Beamish, dated from 1919. These groups had virtually expired by the early 1930s, though the IFL, reduced to a few dozen members, maintained a raucous, anti-semitic presence throughout the decade. In 1937, William Joyce and John Beckett formed the National Socialist League, a breakaway from Mosley's movement. It attracted about one hundred members.

We are left with the British Union of Fascists, founded on 1 October 1932. It campaigned for almost eight years, before being dissolved on 23 May 1940. Although it never came near to power, and in fact never won a single parliamentary seat, it was, for most of that period, a definite factor in British domestic politics, and may, at its peak, have had a membership of between 30,000 and 40,000. Its importance was almost entirely due to the outstanding qualities of its leader and founder, Sir Oswald Mosley. The first part of this essay will deal with Mosley's career and personality. Then I shall give an account of the BUF itself, before turning to the wider question of fascism and the British political culture.

Mosley's career and personality

The salient facts of Mosley's career up to the time he formed the BUF are as follows. Born in 1896, the eldest son of a wealthy and prominent Staffordshire county family — his grandfather was the original of John Bull — he was educated at Winchester and Sandhurst. One of the earliest volunteers to the Royal Flying Corps, he was invalided out of the war in 1916, after a spell in the trenches. Elected MP for Harrow in 1918 on the Coalition Unionist ticket, he crossed the floor in 1920 in protest against the Black and Tans; in 1924 he joined the Labour Party. When Ramsay MacDonald formed his second Labour government in 1929, Mosley, then thirty-three, was appointed Chancellor of the Duchy of Lancaster with special responsibilities for unemployment. In May 1930 he resigned from the government, after the rejection of his Memorandum on unemployment policy. In February 1931 he quit the Labour Party and formed the New Party with a handful of his parliamentary colleagues. This was wiped out at the general election of October 1931 which returned a massive 'National' majority. In the following year, after a visit to Italy, Mosley launched the British Union of Fascists.

Certain features of this story help to explain Mosley's characteristic attitudes to the problems of his day. Politics was far from being his natural vocation. He was born into the squirearchy, or minor aristocracy. This class had traditionally provided local, not national, leadership: in its three hundred years as a leading country family, the Mosleys had sent only two backbench MPs to Westminster. Mosley himself grew up in a feudal world, unconnected with industrial England. His education was completed at Sandhurst, not Oxbridge. He thus entered parliament without the benefit of a modern political apprenticeship — an émigré from a dying enclave of old England, with something of the attitude of a professional soldier.

Probably he would not have come into politics at all but for the first world war. The war ended the Mosley connection with rural Staffordshire. Even more important was the experience of war. His experience in the air and in the trenches worked on a powerful imagination, giving him a vision of an England reborn, and instilling a hatred of the 'old gangs' who had blundered his country, and Europe, into an appalling bloodbath. Martial values, and wartime organization, might be applied to build a 'land fit for heroes'. The chivalry of air combat might create a more durable basis for European conciliation than the calculations of old-fashioned diplomacy. Mosley desperately wanted to become an air ace. Instead he crashed his aeroplane at Shoreham, before his adored and adoring mother. This probably saved his life, since he was soon afterwards invalided out of the war. But one feels that thereafter he always needed to prove to himself that he was a hero.

For the 22-year-old Mosley, the parliament of 'hard-faced men' was a disillusioning and also misleading experience. The disillusion lay in the failure to build a new world, and the all too depressing prevalence of old political habits and ideas. Idealistic hopes for a reconciling peace, and an effective League of Nations, foundered in the machinations of politicians and diplomats. European statesmen were exploiting, so it seemed to Mosley, the sacrifices of the soldiers in order to pursue the projects of nineteenth-century imperialism – in Russia, the Middle East, and the Ruhr. The Amritsar massacre, and Lloyd George's use of the Black and Tans in Ireland – the issue on which Mosley broke with the coalition – seemed to display the same unregenerate attitudes. Finally, the economic collapse of 1920-1 put paid to immediate hopes of a 'land fit for heroes', ushering in instead a decade of mass unemployment.

Mosley's experience of coalition politics misled him as much as it depressed him. The war had disrupted the two-party system. Politics between 1918 and 1922 were dominated by the attempt to construct a new 'centre' party from the bits and pieces of historical Liberalism, allied to 'patriotic' Labour and 'moral' Conservatism. Mosley was involved in a couple of such attempts, the lead being taken by his patron, Lord Robert Cecil. The dream of a non-ideological, non-class party of the centre never left him. The Conservatives, he told Lord Robert, had sold out to the 'bourgeois profiteer'. Socialists, on the other hand, were too concerned with 'ultimate issues'. Although the leftward evolution of his own ideas, plus the failure to establish a viable centre party, was to carry Mosley into the Labour Party in 1924, he was basically out of sympathy with this redivision of politics into Labour and Conservative. He failed to appreciate its deep sociological roots. He continued to believe that beyond Westminster there was the potential movement of the war generation awaiting the kiss of life. His experience in holding Harrow twice as an Independent strengthened this conviction. And his success at Westminster itself in elegantly hopping from one group to another fed the illusion that party commitments were as fragile as his own.

But Mosley was not just a politician of war-nostalgia. He was determined to give his 'middle way' some intellectual content. Mass unemployment (of 10 per cent of the labour force in the 1920s) gave him his chance. The result was his pamphlet *Revolution by Reason*, written in 1925 with his Labour Party friend, John Strachey.

It was a striking attempt to break new ground, intellectually and politically. Orthodox and socialist thought on unemployment alike took its stand on the old political economy inherited from the nineteenth century, the central contention of which was that there could never be a general glut — that is a general insufficiency of demand. The problem, therefore, must lie in some disturbance in proportion. Business spokesmen, and most orthodox economists, argued that as a result of better trade union organization wages (and therefore the costs of production) had become too high for full employment. Socialists tended to argue the reverse: that wages (and therefore consuming power) were too low under capitalism for the purchase of a full-employment output. Both sides therefore tended to explain the mass unemployment of the 1920s in terms of a maldistribution of rewards to the factors of production. The situation was to be remedied either by lowering real wages or — in the socialist version — by redistributing income from the rich to the poor, which was held to require in the end the public ownership of the means of production. The solution, in either case, involved class struggle — which the moderate leaders of both main parties shrank from, particularly after the experience of the General Strike of 1926. Mosley's break with this line of reasoning comes out in the following key statement in *Revolution by Reason*:

> At present Socialist thought appears to concentrate almost exclusively upon the transfer of present purchasing power by taxation, and neglects the necessity for creating additional demand to evoke our unused capacity which is at present not commanded either by the rich or by the poor. [1]

The influence of Keynes on this formulation is obvious, though Mosley went further than anything Keynes was actually proposing at the time. What he advocated was that, under the cover of a floating exchange rate, the budget should be unbalanced to the extent necessary to raise actual production to the level of full-employment production. The struggle over the distribution of the existing product would be replaced by a joint sharing of an expanded product.

Revolution by Reason had little resonance in the 1920s, even on the left. Both its intellectual daring and its conservative implications were lost on Mosley's contemporaries. It was for a later generation to discover in Keynesian 'demand management' the intellectual basis for 'consensus' politics. Yet Mosley's later political evolution cannot be fully grasped unless one realizes that he believed he had discovered the way out from the 'dogfight between Capital and Labour' — a basis for a positive consensus to replace the Baldwin-MacDonald politics of 'decency' which, by refusing to push intellectual premises to logical conclusions, bought political peace by betraying the hopes of the war generation.

At the time it was not Mosley's programme but his political style which attracted (mainly unfavourable) notice. Mosley broke ranks not with his search for mass consent, but with his methods of communicating with the mass mind. This first came out during the rowdy by-election in which he was returned to parliament as Labour MP for Smethwick in

December 1926. The conservative press found something deplorable in the spectacle of an aristocrat, the son-in-law of Lord Curzon, who spent his amply provided private life in beautiful houses and a 'jet set' of fashionable artists and writers, inflaming the passions of the mob. The contrast between Mosley's 'reason' and his 'populism' was thus established quite early in his career. Mosley excelled on the public platform. At his best, he had an almost unique ability — perhaps only Joseph Chamberlain is comparable — to bring technical economic arguments to life for a mass audience. Only by investing reason with passion could popular support for progress be mobilized in an era of mass democracy. Much more could be said about Mosley's 'high road' and 'low road'. Here it is sufficient to note that Mosley's power of platform appeal, his ability to generate excitement and devotion, blinded him to the extent to which modern political support is institutional, not personal. He came to believe that the basis of political power lay in the response of large audiences to stirring speeches, rather than in the habitual loyalty to parties. He came to prefer the theatre of politics to its substance; which is, perhaps, another way of saying that deep down he wanted to be a legend rather than an achiever.

As Chancellor of the Duchy of Lancaster in MacDonald's second Labour government, Mosley set to work with a high sense of destiny: 'Before we leave this mortal scene, we shall do something to lift the burdens of those who suffer .... We of the war generation are marching on.' [2] In practice, Sir Oswald marched straight into the impenetrable wall of Philip Snowden's orthodoxy at the Treasury. There was simply no money, declared the Iron Chancellor, to lift the burden of suffering from the increasingly large number of unemployed. As the world depression deepened, Mosley bombarded the ministries with lucid, but unavailing, memoranda. Finally, he decided to amalgamate them into one big Memorandum, and send it to the Prime Minister.

The nation, he told MacDonald, must be mobilized for a supreme effort. He proposed a small 'war cabinet' serviced by a 'think-tank' headed by Keynes; a protected home market, with government money for modernizing the older, and developing the newer, industries; a £200 million programme of centrally organized public works; and a great increase in the public debt to provide the money. It was a nationalist programme to fight the depression. When it was rejected, Mosley resigned office. 'I perhaps misunderstood you when I came into the Labour Party,' he told MacDonald. [3] Eight days later, on 28 May 1930, Mosley defended his alternative before a packed House of Commons, in one of the most remarkable speeches ever delivered to that assembly. He ended:

> What I fear more than a sudden crisis is a long slow crumbling through the years ... a gradual paralysis, beneath which the vigour and energy of this country will succumb .... What a fantastic assumption it is that a nation which within the lifetime of everyone has put forth efforts of energy and vigour unequalled in the history of the world, should succumb before an economic situation such as the present. If the situation is to be overcome, if the great powers of this country are to be rallied and mobilised for a great national effort, then the Government and Parliament must give a lead. I beg the Government tonight to give the vital forces of this country the chance they await. I beg Parliament to give that lead. [4]

In the next few months Mosley's oratory reached new heights as his fortunes waned. A speech to the Labour Party conference at Llandudno in October 1930 was rapturously acclaimed; but the party managers were able to stave off the challenge with some ease. Meanwhile, Mosley was convinced that history was at last living up to his sense of drama. The party system which thrived in normal times would surely break up under the impact of the impending collapse of the world economic system. The moment had come to revive the 'centre party' ideas of 1919-22. Mosley's programme for fighting the depression was designed to reunite the scattered and frustrated survivors of the 'war generation'. Surely the Tory and Liberal ex-officer politicians of his own age, like Harold Macmillan, Oliver Stanley, Walter Elliott, Henry Mond and Archibald Sinclair, could be brought together with his Labour supporters, John Strachey, Aneurin Bevan and W.J. Brown, into a new Mosley Party?

It was, in fact, a non-politician from the prewar generation who gave Mosley the decisive push. Mosley's conversations with the young Tories had led nowhere; his attempt to form a 'Manifesto Group' in the Labour Party had petered out. But then, early in 1931, the car manufacturer, Sir William Morris, handed him a cheque for £50,000 (about £500,000 in today's values). On 28 February 1931 Mosley launched the New Party. Six MPs — five Labour, one Conservative — resigned their Whips at the same time.

The New Party reflected the diverse strands of Mosley's personality and experience: the search for a political framework adequate for his ideas, the instability of the party system, his conception of himself as a man of crisis, his penchant for the dramatic gesture. The most interesting statement of its early political purpose is contained in an article by C.F. Melville, which appeared in the journal *Fortnightly Review* in May 1931. The central assumption of the New Party was:

> The trouble is not that we have a class war so much as we have a class deadlock. The deadlock must be unlocked. We shall try to do something towards unlocking it.

Melville found strong similarities in the policy, though not in the methods, of the 'German and English movement':

> Both movements are in effect National-Socialist parties which, while appealing to the working masses, attract to themselves the support of the industrialists; thereby becoming the protagonists ... of industry versus banking finance.

Thus, Melville thought, 'Sir Oswald Mosley and his associates propose to help both industrial capital and the industrial worker to their mutual benefit,' a policy which suggested to him the Mond-Turner conversations of the later 1920s. His prognosis of the New Party's future was not pessimistic:

> It is obvious that the New Party hopes — and it seems to me to have a good chance of eventually realising this hope, provided it can succeed in reconciling the many aims and as many interests which it represents — to become the

principal magnet for a new 'Centrum' in British party politics .... In this sense it cuts right across the old arguments about *Left* and *Right*.

Although the New Party started out, in Strachey's words, as 'an entirely Utopian appeal for social compromise', sociological forces, as well as Mosley's conceptions and temperament, had already started to push it towards fascism before Mosley formally adopted the label. The fundamental sociological fact was that Mosley started his 'centrist' career with the organized forces of Labour ranged against him. This estrangement was completed by the New Party's intervention at the Ashton-under-Lyme by-election on 30 April 1931 which was generally considered (wrongly) to have handed the Labour seat to the Conservatives. At meeting after meeting, New Party speakers faced organized disruption from Labour and communist militants. Mosley's response was to organize a 'private army' of stewards, initially un-uniformed, and trained by the Whitechapel boxer Ted Kid Lewis. At the same time, Mosley observed to Harold Nicolson, his most prestigious non-parliamentary supporter, that 'The main response we are getting ... comes from the younger Conservative group.' Thus the hostility of organized Labour, Mosley's pugnacious response to it, and the nature of the New Party's grass roots support, all pushed the party towards the right.

However, the crucial point is that Mosley did not want to be there. To John Strachey's question — whether to come down on the side of working-class revolt or ruling-class reaction — Mosley replied 'On neither side'. He would not become a communist, or return to the party of 'predatory plutocracy'. The movement towards fascism arose essentially from Mosley's refusal to choose between left and right in a situation of mounting social crisis. Rather, it seemed to him that fascism was the natural legatee of the centre party idea. It was based on the notion of having a government strong enough to control both communism *and* predatory plutocracy, while using the power of the state to build the higher civilization which would put both out of business. Such was the direction of Mosley's thoughts in the final months of his parliamentary life.

Whether he would ever have carried these ideas to their logical conclusion had the New Party retained a parliamentary base is open to question. As it was, the parliamentary side of the New Party (already diminished by the desertion of W.J. Brown, Oliver Baldwin and John Strachey) was obliterated in the general election of October 1931. From the point of view of building up a parliamentary following, Mosley's timing had been disastrous. He assumed that the economic crisis would force the Labour and Conservative parties into an unholy alliance to defend the pound, leaving the field free for a true 'national' alternative. MacDonald and Baldwin did their bit by joining up to form a National government on 24 August 1931 — the consensus of 'decency'; but MacDonald failed to carry the Labour Party with him. Thus the two-party system was not broken. Opposition to the National government still had its natural focus in the Labour Party. The New Party, along with other splinters, became a political irrelevance. But its very collapse in the general election of October 1931 convinced Mosley that parliamentary centrism had to give way to a grass-roots variety. On 1 October 1932 he launched the British Union of Fascists from the remnants of the New Party and deserters from existing fascist organizations, campaigning for a 'Greater Britain'.

The British Union of Fascists

Mosley's policy for winning power, expounded in his book *The Greater Britain* (1932), was a recapitulation and development of the proposals and arguments of his Labour and New Party days. It consisted of three parts: an economic argument designed to show why Britain must extricate itself and its empire from the crumbling international system in order to realize the postwar dream of a high-wage, full-employment economy; an argument for an 'executive' system of government capable of decisive action and free from detailed parliamentary control; and the proposition that the new system of political economy could be brought about only by a new political movement (fascism). The economic argument is an adaptation of Mosley's original ideas of 1925 to the world economic collapse of 1929-32; the argument for 'executive' government and a new 'type' of politician, first formulated in the Memorandum and New Party proposals for a small 'war cabinet' to organize the fight against the depression, reflects Mosley's experience of government in the minority Mac-Donald administration; the argument for a 'new movement' develops Mosley's old dream of a 'centre party' of the war generation. The distinctively new element was the linking of the economic argument for greater national (and imperial) self-sufficiency with the prospects for world peace. 'The measure of national reconstruction already described', Mosley wrote, 'involves automatically a change in our foreign policy. We would be less prone to anxious interference in everybody else's affairs, and more concentrated on the resources of our own country and Empire.' [5] Essentially this remained the programme for the rest of the decade, though its presentation became increasingly populist. The 'international economy' was progressively personalized in terms of 'alien' or 'Jewish' financiers; parliamentary democracy became the domain of the corrupt 'old gangs'; Jewish interests, too, were preventing peace by making bad blood between Britain and Germany. The idea of dictatorship also became more explicit, with electoral choice reduced to an 'occupational franchise' for an advisory parliament, and national referenda in which voters could reject the ruling set of fascist ministers, leaving the monarch the task of choosing a new fascist prime minister. There were also proposals for a 'corporate' reorganization of industry, with the government settling any dispute: strikes and lockouts were to be abolished. 'In such a system,' Mosley wrote, 'there is no place for parties and for politicians. We shall ask the people for a mandate to bring to an end the Party system and the Parties. We invite them to enter a new civilisation.' [6]

The BUF was an expression of sociological optimism, not a response to sociological pressures. The main hope was that in time of crisis, comparable to war, sectarian loyalties, rooted in class, would give way to a rallying of 'patriotic' Britons behind a non-class, non-sectarian movement. The initial situation of economic collapse seemed favourable. Further, before starting the BUF, Mosley had assured himself of the support of Lord Rothermere, the press proprietor; a promise fulfilled in January 1934, when the *Daily Mail* and its sister papers came out for the 'blackshirts'. The publicity boost created a minor bandwagon in the BUF's favour in the first six months of 1934, its membership peaking at between 30,000 and 40,000. There was no special concentration by the BUF at this stage on target areas or target groups. Members were joining from all round the country at a satisfactory rate. Nevertheless, it seems clear that in the 'Rothermere' phase, the membership was heavily middle-class, Mosley attracting what Baldwin called 'ultra-montane' Conservatives, offended by the consensus of decency and stagnation. Noticeable also was the attraction of the movement to young people, which was to remain a permanent feature.

Nor, in this period, was the BUF seriously organized for electoral politics. The official myth was that it would come to power in a violent situation — probably resisting a communist attempt at takeover. The organization was to be based on a number of big headquarters in the main urban areas (the main one was 'Black House' in Chelsea), organized as military barracks, in which squads of uniformed blackshirts would live and train for the great day. Their other function was to provide support for the platform, as Mosley and the BUF speakers put the fascist appeal to audiences which often contained fiercely hostile sections.

This phase of British fascism ended in the disorders of the Olympia meeting of 7 June 1934, after which Lord Rothermere backed out. Also, by 1934, the first real impact of economic recovery was starting to be felt. The BUF shrank as rapidly as it had grown.

The second phase — from the summer of 1934 to March 1937 — marks the beginning of a more orthodox attempt to win power, based on a national party headquarters staffed by 140 full-time officials, the rudiments of a constituency organization, and a series of campaigns directed at particular areas, groups and themes. This phase was marked by a much higher degree of centralization. The military model was retained, though military aims were abandoned. Local fascist bigwigs, who had tried to organize independent satrapies,

were removed, and their groups brought under the control of
Neil Francis-Hawkins, Director-General of Organization, and
a system of National Inspectors. Ward and action units were
established as the basis of constituency organization. (By
1938, the BUF was ostensibly organized to fight about eighty
seats.) The whole system, intended to provide an unbroken
chain of command from the Leader at the top to the
humblest active member, was in practice riddled with
personal jealousies and divided jurisdictions. Supreme policy
was made in a Policy Directorate, but little is known of its
working. It seems that the usual friction prevailed between
the bureaucrats who valued the organization as an end in
itself, and the political propagandists, William Joyce, John
Beckett and Arthur Chesterton, who wanted a more daring,
risk-taking, propaganda appeal, based on anti-semitism. On
the whole, Mosley sided with the administrators. Curiously,
the conservative elements in the BUF, represented by the
ex-military men, proved as bad for its image as the anti-
semitic radicals: for it was their love of uniforms and elaborate organization for violence which helped turn the parliamentary politicians against the BUF in 1936.

In the summer and autumn of 1934 the first systematic
attempt was started to concentrate propaganda on certain
regions and groups. In the autumn of 1934, Bill Risdon,
an ex-ILPer, was sent to 'open up' Lancashire, home of the
ailing cotton industry. The ex-miner and boxer 'Tommy'
Moran went to the South Wales coalfields. John Beckett
concentrated on the Tyneside. Rural areas (the BUF had
intervened in the East Anglian 'tithe war' of 1933) were
assiduously wooed. From late 1934, too, dates the growth
of support in East London, where the BUF started to champion Gentile grievances against Jewish immigrants.

Although the BUF tried to win support in the depressed
textile and coalmining industries, its main *class* appeal was
directed towards the petty bourgeoisie and the unorganized
sections of the working class. On the one hand, it directed
its propaganda at the 'small man with his independent firm
[who] is caught between the upper millstone of trustification
and the lower millstone of socialisation'. [7] On the other
hand, it exploited the grievances of shop assistants, cinema

usherettes, barmaids, servants, etc., particularly where these could be shown to be exploited by big Jewish employers.

Finally, throughout the 1930s, the BUF tried to pick up support through single-issue campaigns — the 'Mind Britain's Business' campaign of 1935, connected with the Abyssinia crisis, the 'Stand by the King' campaign of 1936, and the Peace campaign of 1939.

By the mid-1930s, the BUF's presence on the political stage was giving rise to severe problems of public order. From the moment he broke with the Labour Party, Mosley had had to face militant opposition, to which he reacted by organizing his 'private army' of uniformed stewards who travelled round with him to meetings, and whose presence in turn offered a provocation to his opponents. In forming the BUF, Mosley adopted a creed and livery hateful and offensive enough to a section of (especially) left-wing opinion to ensure the further development of active hostility. The opposition was generally mobilized, co-ordinated and directed by the Communist Party, which saw in fascism a threat, a competitor, and a chance for its own growth. The announcement of a BUF parade and meeting in a large urban centre would be the signal for a 'counter-demonstration' at or near the vicinity, which often led to violence, with the police in the position of defending the fascists against their enemies. Indoor meetings were protected by fascist stewards, but these meetings, too, were penetrated by opponents determined to prevent the speech from being made. Few large BUF occasions in the main urban and industrial centres escaped some violence in the 1930s, though elsewhere the fascists were relatively unmolested. The most famous disturbance took place at the Olympia stadium on 7 June 1934, when the bulk of an audience of 12,000 watched, disgusted or admiring as the case may be, the efficiency (or brutality) with which the stewards ejected several hundred demonstrators.

Politicians and the police tended to attribute the violence to the provocation of the fascist uniform (initially a black shirt tucked into grey trousers: later a more elaborate affair with jacket, boots, breeches, belt, cap, etc., worn as a privilege of rank or service). This was a superficial analysis: what fascism stood for was provocative enough; and violence did not die with the end of the uniform. It was also widely argued that provocation was deliberately used by the BUF as a tactic to gain publicity, or to impress opinion with fascist ruthlessness in dealing with the 'Reds'. There is something in this, but it is exaggerated. Marches were intended primarily to advertise meetings and as an activity for members. Insults directed by fascist speakers at hostile elements in their audiences generally arose out of the context of the meetings themselves. To try to assign responsibility for the violence is probably a pointless exercise: Mosley claimed the right to propagate a creed which was sufficiently offensive to ensure militant opposition. Violence flowed from this basic dynamic. Nevertheless, some fascists and communists no doubt enjoyed violence for its own sake; and passionate politics released instincts which in more tranquil times are confined to football matches.

At the heart of the BUF's confrontation with its opponents in the streets and halls of urban Britain lay its clash with the Jewish community, particularly in East London. This requires some consideration.

Mosley himself had no known personal history of political or cultural anti-semitism. At the start of the BUF he declared that 'anti-semitism forms no part of the policy of this Organization, and anti-semitic propaganda is forbidden.' It is easy to conclude that his later espousal of political anti-semitism (although he has always rejected the charge) was purely opportunistic — an attempt, from late 1934 onwards, to re-establish a declining movement by exploiting a base prejudice. The fact that the only place where the BUF succeeded in winning a mass following was in East London with its large Jewish community of first and second generation immigrants lends support to this interpretation. But the story is more complicated than this. East London fascism was a fairly spontaneous growth. Its leader, 'Mick' Clarke, was not a BUF officer sent to 'open up' a new area, but a native East Ender who saw in the BUF an effective instrument for ventilating deeply rooted local Gentile grievances against East London Jews, ignored by the established political parties in the area. Gentile East London with its combination of tiny businesses, sweated workers, lack of trade-union organization, appalling slums, and a strong local Jewish capitalism, found in the BUF a 'natural' political vehicle; and the BUF's growing involvement in East London in turn coloured its whole political stance. The conventional interpretation also ignores or minimizes the role of Jewish anti-fascist militancy, stimulated by Hitler's victory in Germany, but also dating back to the post-Russian Revolutionary connection between East London Jews and communism, in making the BUF as a whole 'Jew-conscious'.

Having said this, there remains a substantial element in the BUF's anti-semitism which cannot be explained either by reference to the anti-fascist opposition offered by Jews themselves, or by the existence of local anti-Jewish grievances in East London. Anti-semitism was the nearest thing fascism ever had to an all-embracing ideology, capable of rivalling those of liberalism and marxism. It provided a comprehensive explanation of social ills, in terms of a malign Jewish dynamic, which in the modern world has had the appeal of religious faith to a small minority of intellectuals and fanatics. In other words, it has provided the devotional core which any mass party needs to stay afloat in lean times; and was, in fact, the only ideology available for a movement like fascism. Mosley himself, it is clear, never accepted the anti-semitic ideology; but he increasingly picked on Jews as the main targets of his denunciations. There are a number of reasons for this, which are listed in no definite order of importance (we cannot, after all, be sure what went on in Mosley's mind). Firstly, he needed some anti-semitism to retain the 'devotional core' — his militants and tireless propagandists. Secondly, he clearly saw the propaganda utility of concentrating all his fire on a single opponent. The masses required both something to love and something to hate, he is alleged to have remarked. They could not be taught to hate capitalism, since Mosley only wanted to control it, and anyway hoped for business donations. Nor could simple, straightforward anti-communism deliver the support of the non-socialist radicals. Anti-semitism was a way of being radical without being communist. It was an ideology of radical nationalism; and Jews were just prominent enough in the activities fascism denounced (international finance and communism) to give the imputation that they dominated in these spheres a superficial plausibility. Thirdly, but linked to the second point, Mosley deliberately used anti-semitism as the chief weapon in his peace campaign. The avoidance of another European war was a genuine political commitment dating back to his first days in parliament; reinforced, but not caused, by his later sympathy with the fascist powers. How far he actually believed that Jews constituted a powerful, or dominant, war lobby is impossible to say; but he increasingly categorized them as such. Finally, although Mosley, and probably most of his followers, had no previous history of anti-semitism, this is not to say that they were not liable to react to Jews anti-semitically under certain conditions. The potential for anti-semitism is deeply rooted in European history and culture, based on the predominantly unfavourable stereotype of Jews which is the inheritance of the Jewish diaspora in Christian Europe. It only needed the active opposition by 'foreign' Jews to his political projects — he once referred to hecklers as the 'sweepings of the ghetto' — to activate Mosley's dormant anti-semitic prejudices.

So how can we sum up the BUF's turn to anti-semitism in the mid-1930s? It had a definite sociological basis in East London. Beyond this, it seems to have been a calculated attempt by Mosley to achieve a propaganda coherence or edge, made possible by an inability to think of Jews in the mass as either fully British or indeed fully human, once Jews had started to impinge on his politics.

The second phase of British fascism ended in the East London 'battle of Cable Street' on 4 October 1936, the passing of the Public Order Act two months later, and the mixed local election results which the BUF chalked up in three East London boroughs in March 1937. These events marked the climax of the BUF's rowdy penetration of East London and the government's reaction to it: the Public Order Act banned political uniforms and gave chief police officers the power to ban marches in their areas for up to three months at a time. This political blow to the movement's *élan*, coupled with its failure to win local power in

East London, produced, or perhaps merely brought to a head, an internal crisis, financial, ideological and political. In one afternoon, Mosley sacked over a hundred full-time officials of his inflated headquarters staff. The emphasis thereafter was on decentralization and local initiative. Despite this, financial solvency was not restored. Except for the money provided by Sir William Morris, Lord Rothermere and Mussolini, Mosley had never received large donations. Now the supply of funds virtually dried up, and he had to spend £100,000 of his own money to keep the movement going in its last two years. Significant for the BUF's ideological complexion was Mosley's dismissal of Joyce and Beckett, who, together with A.K. Chesterton who left about a year later, formed the radical anti-semitic group in the leadership. By this move, Mosley repudiated the strategy of full-blooded anti-semitism; and in fact anti-semitism thereafter tended to become less important. To the political crisis there was no immediate solution, and it became more acute in the months ahead, with falling membership, and the closure of propaganda outlets, as the Metropolitan Commissioner used his new powers to ban fascist marches in East London, and as municipal and private owners withheld permission for the BUF to use their halls for meetings.

The last phase of BUF activity was dominated by the 'peace campaign' of 1938-40 which brought the movement fresh support, a new vigour, and, perhaps, a new integrity. For the first time since he launched British fascism Mosley was able to identify with a cause which had deep roots in English radical politics, though under peculiarly unrewarding conditions. The BUF — which had advocated rearmament for the sole defence of the British Empire, but otherwise wanted non-interference in European affairs — now made strange contacts with the pacifist fringe; and for a time it seemed as if Mosley might emerge as leader of a 'peace front'. In July 1939, the BUF staged its last great rally at the Earls Court Stadium, Mosley declaring that 'a million Britons shall not die in your Jews' quarrel'. But events were now moving too swiftly and Mosley was reacting too slowly to the new possibilities. The BUF was too much identified with nazism for it to be able to mobilize the powerful peace sentiment under its own banner; and Mosley was not prepared to abandon fascism for the cause which now claimed his allegiance. After the outbreak of war on 3 September 1939 Mosley was still capable of getting an enthusiastic response in East London to his call for a negotiated peace; but BUF candidates fared miserably in a number of by-elections. With the opening up of the war in the west and the fall of Chamberlain's government, British fascism was doomed. On 23 May 1940, it was disbanded under Regulation 18B. Mosley and 700 of his supporters were interned as security risks. It was ten years, almost to the day, since his resignation from the second Labour government.

The BUF and the domestic political context

Between 1932 and 1940, the BUF failed to establish itself as a serious contender for power. Nor did it have much prospect of improving its position without the support of a German victory, though had war been avoided, fascism would no doubt have remained a larger factor in British and European politics than proved to be the case after 1945. For most of the 1930s, the BUF was about the same size as the Communist Party, larger in the early 1930s, perhaps a little smaller at the end, when it may have had about 20-25,000 members. Clearly fascism had only a limited scope for growth in Britain. Why was this so?

The reasons for the BUF's failure can be grouped under four main heads: firstly, its own tactical mistakes; secondly, the nature of the British political system; thirdly, the character of the British social structure; and fourthly, the economic and international context in which it operated.

The BUF's chief tactical failure was its inability to prevent itself being saddled with responsibility for violence and public disorder. This led not only to the passage of legislation specifically designed to cripple it; but also to the progressive closure, through informal, local or police pressure, of its main propaganda outlets. In short, Mosley failed to solve the tactical problem posed by unrelenting left-wing opposition. His boast that his strong-arm methods had 'secured free speech' was in fact the reverse of the truth: because by the late 1930s all the big halls were closed to him, and he was not allowed on the radio or to write in the press. (The BUF only got the Earls Court Stadium through a last-minute cancellation.) The blackshirts won the 'battle of Olympia' itself, but lost the propaganda war which followed, as well as Lord Rothermere's support. The 'battle of Cable Street', contrary to legend, led to an *increase* of fascist strength in East London; but it also led directly to the passing of the Public Order Act and the ending of fascist processions in East London. How Mosley should have handled his tactical problem is difficult to say. He seemed to face an unenviable choice of being ineffective or brutal. He would have done better had he learned earlier the lesson he tried to impart to his followers after the war, that 'You win not by the punches you give but by the punches you duck.'

The BUF's mishandling of the problem posed by its opposition undoubtedly limited such scope for growth as it possessed in Britain. But this does not lie at the heart of Mosley's political failure. What decisively constrained fascism's advance was not its lack of ability to exploit favourable opportunities, but the lack of favourable opportunities to exploit.

The British political system was a crucial barrier. There are three aspects worth noting here. Firstly, there was an absence of political ideas favourable to fascism such as existed on the European continent. There was no *nationalist* ideology of the kind developed by Corradini in Italy. There was no anti-semitic ideology of any importance. Overt racialism was frowned upon. Social imperialism was dead. 'Chesterbelloc' provided only a tiny trickle of Roman Catholic social thought. In short, liberalism remained the hegemonic public philosophy, with socialism as a somewhat deviant branch; there was no resonant set of anti-democratic, or anti-liberal ideas, waiting to be taken up by a fascist movement, as was the case elsewhere. This situation was reflected in the paucity of intellectual support which fascism received. In so far as the younger intellectuals rejected liberalism, they turned to marxism. Fascism, by contrast, had few intellectual fellow-travellers, and they tended to be isolated, eccentric figures: Ezra Pound, Wyndham Lewis (for a time), Bernard Shaw (in certain moods), the novelist Henry Williamson. There was no fascist equivalent of Trinity College, Cambridge.

Secondly, the British parliamentary system was politically very efficient. Dangerous situations did not produce a crisis for political institutions as they tended to do on the continent. Even when the world financial crisis shook the two-party system in 1931, it did so in a way which did not help Mosley. Those who would normally respond to a straight-forward 'patriotic' appeal to save the nation had the National government; those who wanted reform and reconstruction could still pin their hopes on a Labour Party purged of its collaborationist leadership. The instinctive cleverness of the political arrangements which got England through a dangerous decade is astounding. Certainly, the sheer *political* competence of the English parliamentary system in this period is remarkable.

Thirdly, Mosley assumed that the failure of the British political system to cope with the economic problem would bring it down. He forgot the other half of the equation. The stability of a political system depends not only on its efficiency in solving problems, but on its *legitimacy*, the respect in which the system is held. People who love and respect their institutions are less likely to change them in haste. German democracy collapsed in 1933, not just because the economic crisis was too severe, but because the Weimar republic had too few supporters. Eventually even legitimacy will succumb to inefficiency, but it takes a long time.

Other political explanations of Mosley's failure are less convincing. The British, it is said, hated anti-semitism. At the level of the élites, this may have been so; and, in so far as anti-semitism led to the closure of propaganda outlets, it was counter-productive. But at the mass level it is doubtful if Mosley was harmed by his attacks on Jewish financiers, though outside East London they did not win him a mass following.

There has always been a certain tension between élite and popular levels of British politics which Mosley tried to exploit in the 1930s, as he did in his populist Labour Party days. But a combination of a party system seen to be effectively competitive on economic issues, a National government which satisfied the patriotic feelings, and a governing class capable of co-opting able dissidents with all the skill of the old Roman senatorial order, served to keep the political system legitimate for the mass of voters.

The social basis of British democracy was also much more secure than in many European countries. This, too, put a decisive limit on the growth of British fascism.

The crucial point is that there was no important social group which was not adequately represented in the existing political system. British democracy arose out of social competition. The competition in feudal times between the monarchy, the great nobles and the towns established the original balance of the British constitution. In the eighteenth and nineteenth centuries there was the competition between the aristocracy and the middle classes which in turn let the working class into the political system through successive extensions of the franchise, as each side sought to establish a mass following. As a result of this long development, every important social group acquired a stake in the system and a share in running it. Because access was relatively satisfactory, individuals retained strong attachments and loyalties to the institutions which represented them at the centre: their political parties, trade unions, pressure groups, etc. In the language of political science, they were not available for 'mobilization' by new movements. Robert Benewick writes, 'Fascism's ultimate dilemma was the presence of a sense of community which at one and the same time contained and was nurtured by competing interests and loyalties.' [8] This was the social basis of the successful MacDonald-Baldwin politics of accommodation and decency.

Mosley tried to overcome this dilemma by building a coalition of gentry, small men providing services (traditionally to the wealthy) and 'deferential' and 'patriotic' workers, urban and rural: a coalition based very much on the social structure of the Staffordshire estate in which he grew up; a traditional coalition put together from the 'losers' of modernization, whose numbers he hoped would be swelled by progressive economic failure. And he did recruit from all three groups, but not enough. Mosley did not win significant support from the gentry class which remained attached to conservatism. There was quite a strong ex-officer element in the BUF; but, on the whole, the military section of the population — those who had served in the regular forces — found their outlets either in their own organizations, like British Legion, or in Conservative patriotic organizations, like the Primrose League. More importantly, the British army was stationed abroad, and had adequate outlets for its fascist values in ruling the empire. Fascism did recruit among small shopkeepers, furniture makers, tailors, etc. These were the people who gave fascism social space to grow all over Europe. But in Britain, the world's most advanced (or senile) industrial economy, these intermediate groups were less heavily populated than elsewhere, and had been more effectively absorbed by the main parties. Mosley's biggest failure was to win substantial support from the working class. The loyalty of working-class people to the Labour Party and their trade unions proved unshakeable. Sections of the working class gave him support while he was in the Labour Party, but their support was not transferable. Fascism's pickings were meagre: some Conservative Lancashire working men and women, a few servants and shop assistants.

Nor did the strategy of trying to win support through minority politics offer better prospects. There were too few deprived, isolated, ethnic or religious minorities, unrepresented, or under-represented, in the British political system: East London, where the BUF was able to exploit communal tensions, was an obvious exception. There was clearly some potential for this kind of politics, as the post-1945 successes of Scottish and Welsh Nationalists show, as well as the Protestant and Catholic politics of Northern Ireland. But at the time these national and religious issues were dormant. British fascism was anyway not equipped to exploit them, and anti-semitism only had a strong appeal in East London (especially in north-east Bethnal Green, site of an earlier Huguenot immigration). One minority somewhat susceptible to fascist propaganda was the Irish Catholics. British fascism did disproportionately well in this group. But it was small beer.

Finally, we must look at the economic context. Even though Mosley was wrong in thinking that his chances of

success hinged on the severity of the depression, he was right
to suppose he would gain from profound economic distress.
His greatest miscalculation was to suppose that economic
collapse was inevitable. In doing so, he seriously underestimated the underlying strength of the British economy.
The marxist analysis was that capitalism's need to 'withdraw'
concessions from the working class in order to restore profitability would shift working-class allegiance from Labour to
communism. Mosley's hope was that the same crisis would
shift a section of the bourgeoisie and working class towards
an anti-communist movement which stood for a system of
national and imperial economy promising full employment,
high profits and high wages. In fact what occurred was a
gradual movement of opinion towards the concept of the
Keynesian-Welfare state which would make both communism
and fascism unnecessary. But this took place in an economic
environment insufficiently stimulating to produce success
for violent remedies. And the lack of communist growth in
turn weakened the rationale for the fascist alternative.

What is striking in retrospect is the shallowness of the
British depression and the speed of recovery from it in the
absence of any deliberate fiscal stimulus. British unemployment, 2.9 million at its peak in late 1932, was half Germany's
and a sixth of America's at the same date. From 1933
onwards there was a steady recovery (briefly interrupted in
the winter of 1937-8) so that John Stevenson and Chris Cook
in their recent study, *The Slump*, could conclude that 'most
people were better off by 1939 than they had been ten years
earlier.' [9] Between 1933 and 1937 inclusive, the British
economy grew at 4 per cent a year, unemployment fell from
22.8 per cent to 9.5 per cent, output and real wages rose
above their 1929 level.

The relative mildness of the British depression was caused
by a number of factors. There was a substantial, though
unintended, fiscal stimulus in the worst years, arising from
the fact that government spending did not fall as fast as government revenue. (For example, in the depth of the depression,
the real value of social services and unemployment benefits
was going up owing to the failure of government economies
to match the fall in the cost of living.) Secondly, Britain's

external position held up relatively better in the depression years than that of either Germany or Japan. In the period of collapsing world economy, the legacy from the past, in the form of captive empire markets and income from foreign investments, helped keep up demand. (The imperial connection, which made Britain a 'satisfied' power, also undercut the kind of appeal to unsatisfied foreign ambitions which fascism was able to exploit in Germany and Italy.) Specific policies of the National government, notably protection and cheap money, helped produce a 'home market' recovery. Finally, the remaining slack was taken up by the rearmament programme after 1937.

The resilience of the British economy damned Mosley's much more strenuous plan for securing British prosperity (as it had Joseph Chamberlain's campaign for tariff reform) and by the same token gave British fascism an unfavourable domestic context, unlike in Germany where the national socialists could integrate the problem of mass unemployment with their nationalist, anti-Versailles, anti-reparations propaganda in an explosive mixture.

Summary

Oswald Mosley saw his mission in politics as to create a policy and political framework capable of expressing the ideals of the war generation. He was much more successful in the former than in the latter. His Keynesian approach to economic problems in the 1920s could have made Keynesianism a more powerful political force sooner had he stayed in conventional politics. Instead, he saw the economic and political crisis of the early 1930s as a chance to realize his dream of a new party of the centre. The failure to achieve this at Westminster threw him back on the grass-roots alternative which, given his own background and temperament, the nature of his recruitment and opposition, and the emergence of fascism as a European-wide phenomenon, was bound to take the form of an attempt to establish a British fascist movement. The logic of the fascist struggle itself — its need for an ideology capable of holding together the militant core and unifying the disparate elements of its appeal, the nature of the opposition it aroused, and its sociological possibilities (and limitations) — drove Mosley into the politics of violence and anti-semitism. But although this discredited him, it was not the cause of his political failure. In reality, the whole project of trying to establish a new centre party, capable of drawing off substantial support from the existing parties of the right and left, was misconceived in the British context of the time. It underestimated the inventiveness and resilience of the political system in the face of crisis, and the congruence between existing arrangements and the values and aspirations of the main social groups. It also banked on a far greater degree of economic collapse than in fact occurred, or was plausible to expect. As a result, British fascism failed to establish a mass base, except in East London; and never became a serious contender for power, though, partly because of its nuisance value, partly because of the fear it inspired, and partly because of Mosley's own charisma, it remained an element in everyone's political calculations. The final impression left is of a tragedy of wasted talents, rather than of a real danger to British democracy.

References

1 O. Mosley, *Revolution by Reason*, a pamphlet read to the ILP summer school at Easton Lodge, August 1925, 16-17.
2 Quoted in *Labour Magazine*, 1 May 1929.
3 Quoted in T. Jones, *Whitehall Diary*, vol. 2: *1926-1930*, London, 1969, 259.
4 Parliamentary Debates (1930), Hansard, vol. 239, col. 1372.
5 O. Mosley, *The Greater Britain*, London, 1932, 140.
6 O. Mosley, *Fascism*, London, 1936.
7 Quoted in *Action*, 21 May 1936.
8 R. Benewick, *Political Violence and Public Order*, London, 1969, 305.
9 J. Stevenson and C. Cook, *The Slump*, London, 1977, 5.

13

BELGIUM

✦

G.Carpinelli

A phenomenon like fascism in Belgium can be measured, and its boundaries marked, in various ways, each leading to quite different conclusions. If one takes into consideration (as we shall be doing) all the political movements with fascist tendencies in Belgium between the two wars, the fascist phenomenon is of considerable size. If, to estimate its maximum dimensions, we use electoral figures — which, despite their limitations, still retain a definite indicative value — then we can note figures not far short of 20 per cent in 1936 and still over 12 per cent in 1939. These are notable percentages, higher than those of the Italian fascist deputies elected with the proportional system in 1921.

Nevertheless, if one adopts more precise criteria, one cannot assign to the fascist groupings in Belgium as much space as would be warranted by the 1936 electoral result. One needs to make certain distinctions, which tend to reduce the significance of the fascist phenomenon. A first distinction is one generally accepted, albeit expressed in different terms — that between 'essential' fascism and 'accessory' fascism. It allows us to isolate the case of the Flemish nationalist movement which, reorganizing itself in 1933 on partially new bases, inserted barely disguised fascist objectives into its programme. This movement, which took the name of Vlaamsch Nationaal Verbond (VNV, Flemish National League), was motivated in its concrete political action above all by regionalist or federalist concerns; the fascist tendencies, although not of a purely theoretical nature, still only played a somewhat secondary role in overall practical policy. This contrasts with the activities of other movements, like Rex, Verdinaso or the Légion Nationale, in which fascist-type objectives played a fundamental part.

A second distinction can be made between 'disguised' fascism and 'open' fascism. Fascist tendencies did not always show themselves in a clear and immediately recognizable form, a fact that has led to notably divergent appraisals by scholars of the overall importance of the fascist phenomenon. There could be no doubts about the fascist character of movements like Verdinaso and the Légion Nationale. The very fact that these movements possessed a paramilitary organization, which played a major role in their internal structure, was already highly significant. But the declarations of Verdinaso and the Légion Nationale were also very explicit. Thus in 1932, for example, Verdinaso wrote openly in favour of dictatorship, stating clearly that it wanted to end parliamentary democracy. The Légion Nationale even made public its presence at a sort of fascist international congress, organized at Montreux by the CAUR (Committees of Action for the Universality of Rome), and made no bones about identifying itself with the ideology of Mussolini's regime, at least until 1938 when it broke away for reasons of foreign policy. But although these movements were able to develop on an organizational level, they never gained a mass base.

The Rexist movement, on the other hand, which achieved relatively widespread popularity, officially adopted a moderately authoritarian position during the period of its most rapid expansion, between late 1935 and mid-1936. It stated that it wanted to gain power on the basis of 'sufficient unanimity' [1], that it intended to maintain parliament, even if with restricted functions, that it proposed to uphold freedom of association, etc. The VNV can be characterized in similar manner: not only did its fascist tendencies play a purely secondary role in the party's practical politics, but they were expressed in ambiguous manner (even if they could be read clearly by the *cognoscenti*: but public opinion does not consist just of *cognoscenti*). In the 'diet' (*landdag*) of 6

May 1934, Staf De Clercq, the VNV *leider*, publicly made a declaration of principle: on the institutional plane, the party's objective was the creation of an organic popular state 'in which popular participation and control would not be empty words', a state which had nothing to copy from 'Maurassism, Italian fascism or Hitlerism'. [2] Analogous ideas were asserted by the 'theoretician' of VNV, H.J. Elias, in two articles in the party daily, *De Schelde*, in October-November 1934. But an ideology cannot be judged simply in terms of what it states; it is also necessary to see what it makes possible in practice and what it hides. From the point of view of practical efficacy, the ideology and the public image of Rex in the first half of 1936 and of VNV until 1940 were infinitely more dangerous (according to their adversaries) or more useful (for their supporters) than the proclamations and uniformed marches of the Légion and Verdinaso. Given the state of public opinion, a dose of authoritarianism could still seem acceptable to many; but an excessive dose, such as dictatorship imposed by violence, tended to be rejected at once by the overwhelming majority. Hence from the point of view of suitability of ideology to practical aims, if the aim of a fascist movement is not simply to impose a dictatorship through violence but to set up a mass reactionary regime, Rex and VNV were *more* fascist, more effectively fascist, than the Légion Nationale and Verdinaso.

Equally, one needs to take into account a movement's practice, its undeclared philosophy emerging from its behaviour, from the facts. Anyone who had taken the trouble to compare the statements with the facts of the Rexist movement of 1936 and of VNV could have noted the disquieting premise to a markedly authoritarian vocation. The internal structure of Rex in 1936-7 was in no sense democratic. It is described in the following manner by J. M. Etienne, who judged that Rex was *not* a fascist movement at that time:

The organization of the party is not democratic. The principle is the authority of the leader, with devolution of responsibilities at successive levels. Degrelle appoints the main leaders, who in turn appoint their subordinates. The lower rank is responsible to his superior, who can rescind his appointment at any moment. In practice and by statute there is no provision for intervention from below. Orders come from above; in a word, everything is dependent on Degrelle, absolute and uncontested leader .... Rex has a political council, which meets several times a week under the chairmanship of Léon Degrelle, but its role seems to be purely consultative. [3]

As for VNV between 1933 and 1936, although its parliamentary group was in the hands of the moderately authoritarian wing, the party machinery was in good measure under the influence of a definitely fascist clique.

It is not surprising that the most important movements with fascist tendencies in Belgium should have displayed a sort of residual respect for the parliamentary system and democracy — in Rex's case only for a certain period, but with VNV until 1940. The parliamentary regime had functioned uninterruptedly and properly for a long time in Belgium. From 1830 until 1914 political liberties had never been suspended or suppressed. It is true that the introduction of universal male suffrage in 1919 had made it more difficult to put together parliamentary majorities. From the point of view of the ruling class, parliament had become a less docile instrument, not so easy to influence and control. But the ruling class had other 'legal' instruments through which to make its influence felt. In 1926 and 1935, at particularly critical moments, exchange speculation had bent the will of a parliamentary majority that was opposing the centres of real economic power in the country. But in general such trials of strength were superfluous. Parliament was attuned to public opinion, not least for reasons directly related to the relatively small dimensions of the country. As the *Times* correspondent noted on 12 November 1936: 'railway communication in Belgium has been so speeded up that practically all deputies are able to go to their homes in the provinces every evening and return to Brussels in good time the following afternoon.' [4]

This political system had managed to overcome the test of

the first world war without experiencing upheavals. In 1919 the Catholics had lost the absolute majority they had held in parliament since 1884. But after the war no new parties had emerged capable of posing a serious threat to the overall supremacy of the pre-1914 parties. The communist breakaway had had little success; only in the 1930s was the Communist Party to develop beyond the stage of a faction, sinking roots in a small but significant segment of the working class. Universal suffrage had changed the relationship of forces within parliament, but the fundamental political groupings remained the same: Catholics, socialists and liberals — in the language of Belgian politics significantly called the three 'traditional parties' — continued to get about 90 per cent of the votes between 1919 and 1932; the figure is all the more striking if one bears in mind that elections were based on the proportional system, hence not automatically excluding minor political groups.

Rex and VNV were phenomena of the 1930s. In the period from the end of the first world war until the early 1930s, fascism was only characteristic of small movements without a mass base: the Légion Nationale, founded in 1922, but becoming more clearly fascist after 1926 under the leadership of Paul Hoornaert; the Jeunesses Nationales (1925-32), created by Pierre Nothomb, who had started up similar initiatives in the past. In 1918 Nothomb had founded a Comité de Politique Nationale, with support from various sectors of the establishment; its aims were to pressurize the diplomatic actions of the government and so push towards the creation of a 'greater Belgium' (oddly enough at the expense of Holland, a country which had not taken part in the war). But the issue of territorial claims was soon closed, and in any case did not really interest public opinion. Despite the patriotic infatuation aroused by the war, nationalism — an entirely new phenomenon in Belgium — was never a popular cause. Even in the 1930s it was not nationalism that explained the success of authoritarian tendencies, at least in the French-language community.

The Légion Nationale initially was a veterans' grouping; in the 1930s it had between 2000 and 4000 members. The Jeunesses Nationales never got more than 2-3000, for the most part pupils of Catholic colleges. Both movements had a paramilitary organization, but they paid dearly for their restricted social mix: they remained completely remote from political life, that is from the continuously renewed possib-ility of expressing opinions and taking the initiative on specific, immediate problems of broad interest. The Légion took part in the general elections of 1925 and 1932, with hopeless results. Pierre Nothomb, too, was regularly defeated so long as he remained a leader of national-fascist organiz-ations; subsequently, in 1936, he was elected as a senator for the Catholic party.

The weight of fascist tendencies in Belgian political life of the 1930s was an entirely different matter. In those years there were two organizations which acquired (Rex) or retained (VNV) a mass base. Only in a very minor sense were they rivals, as VNV turned exclusively to the Dutch-speaking community, whereas Rex (although it managed to find some supporters among the Flemish) moved in the social area represented by French-speaking Belgium.

The Flemish nationalist party, of which VNV was the main heir, had gained 5.9 per cent of the votes in the 1932 elections, without losing its democratic image. In 1936 VNV got 7.1 per cent. Rex only appeared on the political scene at the end of 1935: on 24 May 1936 it gained 11.4 per cent of the votes. Fascism, practically non-existent in the Belgian political universe of 1932, four years later was to be found in the shape of two groupings which between them won the support of 18.6 per cent of the electorate. In a sense, this progress was more apparent than real. During the electoral campaign, VNV had done its best to retain the votes of the old Flemish nationalist base, by insisting on themes such as federalism, the interests of the middle classes and peasants, and anti-militarism. Rex was a wholly new phenomenon, whose physiognomy in certain respects was still unclear in the first half of 1936. But even so, the growth in support was remarkable. Its causes were immediate, particularly the electoral campaign waged by Rex, and especially by its leader Léon Degrelle, attacking collusion between politics and high finance. But there were also less immediate premises and one deeper cause. Two elements helped to create the situation in which the rapid developments of 1936 became possible: firstly, the transition to direct political action of fascist tendencies which had long existed within both the Flemish nationalist movement and the Catholic 'world'; secondly, the economic crisis of 1929, with its social and political repercussions.

The less immediate premises relate to the origins of VNV and Rex. VNV had emerged in 1933, uniting most of the groups which previously had formed the Flemish nationalist movement. It was the end result of a process by which a political force with an initially wholly democratic physiognomy was transformed into one ultimately capable of adopting para-fascist positions. The democratic character of the Flemish nationalist movement of the postwar years was real but fragile, in that it was based neither on a fully worked out ideology nor on a political or union structure. The 'party' in reality was a grouping of notables. Its specific object was the legal introduction of federalism in Belgium, with autonomy for Flanders. Between 1919 and 1925 it rose from 2.6 per cent of the votes to 3.8 per cent (in Flanders from 5.2 to 7.7 per cent).

Already by the mid-1920s the democratic ideals of the nationalist leaders no longer represented an absolute rule. There was one flamboyant exception in the person of Joris Van Severen, a Flemish nationalist deputy from 1921 to 1929. At the beginning of the 1920s Van Severen still displayed a political profile on the left; but by 1924 he had begun to change direction sharply, discovering inter-class 'solidarism', which condemned 'every social organization based on class'. In 1926 he stated his new objectives clearly and publicly: the creation of a great Dutch (pan-Holland) state, corporativism, and the seizure of power through the formation of militias.

Van Severen was among the promoters of an initiative in 1927-8 which was to show clearly for the first time the particular vulnerability of Flemish nationalism to authoritarian ideas. The initiative aimed at creating a unified organization of all the groups which made up the Flemish nationalist movement. The league which was formed did not last long. But its programme, ultimately accepted by all the groups, made play with the idea of the organic state and 'solidarism'; political democracy as a fundamental principle was left in the background. This attempt, a failure in 1927-8, succeeded in 1933 in the form of VNV.

Various elements were responsible for the final success of the organizational reunification in VNV, with its accompanying authoritarian stance. The journal *Jong Dietschland* (1927-33), which offered outside support to the movement, supported 'solidaristic' nationalism; it was influential among some groups of intellectuals and was extremely widely read by Catholic students. The social composition of the Flemish nationalist electorate was no longer the same: between 1919 and 1932 the urban, lay, progressive element failed to grow numerically; the expansion of the movement in this period was located exclusively in provincial or rural circles, among the petty bourgeoisie and peasants. Van Severen helped to push the overall evolution of the Flemish nationalist movement in an authoritarian direction by founding his own organization in 1931 – Verdinaso (VERbond van DIetsche NAtionaal-SOlidaristen, 'league of the national-solidarists of Dutch tongue'). The ideas were more or less those he had already proclaimed in 1924 and 1926. Members of the militia and sympathizers were often recruited among students. For the Flemish nationalist movement, which was going through a period of great ideological and organizational confusion, Verdinaso represented a rival, but at the same time a model in terms of its discipline and of the type of solution to which it pointed.

In the 1932 elections the Flemish nationalist movement dropped slightly in votes, from 6.3 per cent to 5.9 per cent; its deputies fell in number from eleven to eight. Herman Vos, leader of the parliamentary group and also the main spokesman for the movement's lay, progressive tendencies, lost his seat. The setback at the elections strengthened the demands for the reorganization of the movement. The problem was brought to the fore again by the call to found a National Flemish League (VNV), launched in April 1933 by the well-known nationalist and former deputy, S. De Clercq. In the discussions that followed, an active and determined minority managed to impose its own line. This minority

consisted in part of people identifying with the journal
Jong Dietschland, in part of a group working in Van
Severen's province, West Flanders, which did not intend to
leave him the monopoly of fascism and the pan-Holland
solution. The central nucleus and majority of the nationalist
movement had relatively little inclination towards authoritarianism, and basically wanted a federal solution to the
Flemish problem within the framework of the Belgian state.
These 'moderates' found themselves forced to choose
between a less rigid type of organization together with the
democratic group of Anvers, and a more rigid one with the
fascist wing. They chose unification with the fascist group
mainly because they thought it crucial to strengthen their
organization, even in an authoritarian sense, whereas they
regarded the ideology as purely subsidiary.

Staf De Clercq announced the foundation of VNV on 1
October 1933. This new unified organization of the
nationalists proposed 'to work for the liberation of the Flemish people and the promotion of the Netherlandish popular
community'; [5] it also wanted a new social and economic approach, and was opposed to liberalism and marxism.
In 1934 an anonymous pamphlet (*De Dietsche Volksstaat*)
was published to propagandize the principles of the new
party. It was written by H.J. Elias (a 'moderate') and spoke
of an 'organic' democracy, in which the responsibilities of the
state and parliament would be transferred for the most part
to corporations, the 'organs' of society. The creation of VNV
was symptomatic of a general tendency of Flemish nationalism to move away from democracy, as could be seen in the
decision of Herman Vos not to enter the new organization,
but to join the socialist party. S. De Clercq was chosen as
leider of VNV not because of his leadership qualities, but as
a neutral element acceptable to the various tendencies. In
fact De Clercq moved progressively closer to the fascist
grouping.

From 1934 Verdinaso began to follow a tortuous doctrinal
path, which took it progressively further away from Flemish
nationalism. It never queried its basic authoritarianism, but
the contours of the state it hoped for were redrawn several
times. Up to 1934 the aims of the movement were *Dietsch-*

land en Orde (a Dutch-speaking country and order); in 1934 the territory to be unified in a single state consisted of Belgium, Holland and Luxemburg; in 1937 only Belgium and Holland were mentioned. Verdinaso launched grandiose projects which bore no relationship to the exiguous forces on which the movement could rely. It did not participate in elections, but the most successful diets (*landdagen*), in 1936 and 1937, were only attended by about 15,000 members and sympathizers — and the annual diet represented the peak of the movement's organizational effort. The branches created in Holland and then in Wallonia remained of little importance, as the movement continued to be overwhelmingly Flemish.

Under the ideological cover of the great nationalisms predicted by Van Severen, the role of Belgium was revamped step by step, which was to prove fatal. Already in 1936 this tendency had begun to show itself quite clearly; by 1938 the projected union with Holland had been redimensioned and pushed into the background. 'Order in Belgium' now became Verdinaso's main goal. The nationalistic objectives which Van Severen outlined and modified with doctrinaire formalism between 1934 and 1937 did not correspond in any way to widespread feeling among the masses, but were rather indicative of the social isolation in which Verdinaso found itself. The direction taken in 1938 was more realistic, but in adopting it Van Severen had turned about too radically from his previous positions to retain the support of ordinary folk in Flanders. After 1937 he lost a not indifferent segment of his original Flemish nationalist supporters, without compensating for this by increased support in Wallonia and Brussels.

Flemish nationalism was one of the areas within which the new fascist tendencies of the 1930s had been able to take shape and mature in their initial and most obscure phase. The other area was that of the Catholic world, especially reactionary Catholicism. An entire wing of the Catholic right had never really accepted the postwar shift towards democracy, particularly the introduction of universal suffrage. Such Catholics found expression in various publications and associations — *Le XXe Siècle*, journals like *La Revue Catholique des Idées et des Faits* and *La Jeunesse Nouvelle* (later entitled

Pour l'Autorité), the Belgian Federation of Catholic Students — which found an obvious and firm reference point in the ideas of Action Française until 1926. After the Vatican condemnation of Action Française in that year, explicit references to Maurras were dropped, but identification with the content of the political position symbolized by Maurras did not automatically vanish. In the 1920s this reactionary attitude was of no importance in political life. It existed on the fringe of the Catholic party, which was reproved in muted manner of excess indulgence, without the critics daring to push their dissent to the limit of a clear break and the creation of a rival grouping. But the intellectual content of this tendency was incomparably superior to that of the Belgian fascist organizations of the 1920s. It did not merely echo the ideas of Action Française; it adapted and re-elaborated them, creating something original in the Belgian context. This can be considered as the deepest stratum of the cultural hinterland backing the Rexist movement in the 1930s. Particularly significant in this sense was the group — initially of intellectual ex-combatants — that published the journal *Pour l'Autorité* (1924-32) and founded a 'League for the Restoration of Order and Authority in the State' (1925-31). Its natural area of influence and growth was among Catholic university students, especially at Louvain. It tried without success to promote a 'doctrinal renewal' of the Catholic party, on the basis of ideas that tended to weaken the more broadly democratic development of parliamentary institutions since the war. *Pour l'Autorité* did not suggest abolishing universal suffrage, but proposed introducing a series of 'political reforms' which would have worked against the consequences of universal suffrage and even against political liberties: strengthening of the executive, restriction of parliamentary prerogatives, a degree of corporativism. Its constitutional objectives were very similar to those (officially) proclaimed by the Rexist movement in 1936. One precise proposal of *Pour l'Autorité* is to be found in the 1936 Rexist programme: family suffrage, by which the father was to be given supplementary votes equivalent to the number of his minority-age children.

The Association Catholique de la Jeunesse Belge (ACJB),

of which the Rexist movement was initially a derivation, also
formed part of this area of Catholic reactionary tendencies,
although it possessed its own particular characteristics. It was
not concerned with politics in the strict sense. As an organ of
Catholic Action it was subject to ecclesiastical authority,
with a role not to be confused with that of a party. But the
political ideology that circulated or surfaced through the
language or behaviour (not to speak of the 'purely' doctrinal
disquisitions) of ACJB was conservative or reactionary in
nature. The chaplain-general, Mgr Picard, also had specific
sympathies for Italian fascism. While keeping primarily to
religious issues, ACJB grew steadily to dimensions far beyond
those hitherto achieved by any *political* grouping of a reactionary kind: about 60,000 young people attended the 1927
congress of Liège; in 1931 at Brussels the propaganda slogans
forecast the 'congress of the 100,000'. Even if one discounts
exaggeration in these figures, it is clear that by 1930 ACJB
was able to reach a public of some tens of thousands. Initially
the recruitment of members was restricted mainly to
students, but then it broadened out to young farmers, traders
and craftsmen. But the working class lay outside the area controlled by ACJB: the Jeunesse Ouvrière Chrétienne evolved,
from 1925 to 1927, in a totally separate manner. ACJB
had another characteristic which was destined to favour the
successive development of Rexism: it gave rise to a great
desire for purity, and to an extreme form of activism directed
towards the Christian reconquest of society as its exhilarating
ultimate goal, but without any clear practical half-way or
immediate goals. In this sense a gap existed, which Rexism
was to try and fill in its own way.

In the 1925 encyclical *Quas primas* Pius XI had celebrated
in theocratic tone the regality of Christ on earth. The idea of
Christ King had particularly enthused the chaplain of ACJB,
the then abbé Picard. And from 'Christus Rex' the ACJB
publishing house acquired the name Rex. Mgr Picard called
the 24-year-old Léon Degrelle to direct Rex editions in 1930.
A law student, Degrelle was ideologically a product of the
reactionary culture that permeated young Catholic circles at
Namur and Louvain in the 1920s. His extreme ambition can
be seen in his attitude towards ACJB of which he wrote in an

article in *XXe Siècle* on 6 November 1929: 'In ten years the youth has become a giant. In another ten years the giant will take pride of place at the very heart of our country.' [6]

In 1932-3 Rex editions launched a series of publications, not all financially viable; indeed, from the financial point of view this type of activity proved disastrous, with losses two-thirds greater than revenue by the summer of 1934. But from the propaganda and organizational point of view the result was very different. By December 1933 the most important of the periodicals, *Rex*, had achieved a circulation of 37,000 copies. Even more, the publishing house formed the focal point for a youthful grouping, separate from but parallel to the Catholic Action movement. By 1934 Rex existed as a 'Catholic movement of action', and Degrelle was able to organize a meeting at Charleroi with 7000 participants. The first consistent nucleus of the Rexist movement, not yet fully political, had taken shape in less than two years. Degrelle could never have achieved such a result if he had not been able to exploit the organizational network of ACJB and even the parish structure: Rexist periodicals were sold in church porches.

In February 1933, with the authorization of Mgr Picard, Degrelle had begun to publish a political weekly. As he explained in *Rex*: 'We shall serve the Catholic party with all our strength, by criticizing or encouraging it, while waiting to conquer it.' [7] It was a similar programme to that of the reactionary Catholic right of the previous decade, but with a far more aggressive charge.

In the meantime, the effects of the economic depression were also making themselves felt. The crisis began late in Belgium and in a less acute form than elsewhere, but was prolonged. Production fell by over a third; unemployment reached its peak at the beginning of 1935. From the winter of 1931 until March 1935 successive Catholic-liberal governments followed deflationary policies. Among the many banks forced to close their doors were two, tied respectively to the Catholic and socialist parties. Many small and medium-size industries found themselves in difficulties through shortage of credit. In the retail trading sector, the growth in the number of outlets had led to overcrowding, while the competition of the department stores made itself felt. It was in these circles that the corporativism of both Rex and VNV in 1936 found a receptive audience: demands were made for restriction of entry to the sector, for limits to the growth of the department stores, etc. The peasants had also been severely hit by the crisis, as agricultural prices between 1929 and 1934 fell by about a half.

The deflationary policy not only proved ineffective, but was difficult to put into practice uncompromisingly without adopting a hard line against the working-class organizations. It was pursued with considerable conviction at the Ministry of Finances and was subsequently defended by the Flemish Catholic, G. Sap (who in 1936-8 was an informant — perhaps Degrelle's main one — on political-financial 'scandals'). But it was clearly and definitively abandoned in March 1935 when, despite the resistance of the conservative Catholics, a government of national unity was formed by the three traditional parties, with the Catholic P. Van Zeeland as premier. It was a government distinctly more to the left than its predecessors, which included socialists and assigned a central role to the democratic Catholics, thus confirming the new balance of power unfavourable to conservative forces.

The Rexist movement acquired an ever clearer political shape precisely in this period after March 1935. For over a year the situation in the country remained ambivalent, marked by a tendency towards greater economic prosperity, but also by the survival of dissatisfactions originating in the period of the crisis. The economic policy of the Van Zeeland government favoured a progressive expansion of industrial production, with a relative reduction of unemployment; but the return to profitability was less visible in the retail trade and agricultural sectors than in industry. The new government began its activities by devaluing the franc by 28 per cent on 31 March, which, among other consequences, led to a fall in real wages and salaries. Endemic lack of confidence, already generated by the years of crisis, now worsened.

It was possible to judge the effects on public opinion of both the economic crisis and the political developments of March 1935 in the Brussels by-elections of 14 April 1935. The socialist P.-H. Spaak, whose resignation a month earlier had caused the election, gained 48.6 per cent of the votes and was re-elected. There were no candidates for the Catholic or liberal parties, which obviously influenced the results. The Flemish nationalist S. De Clercq received 13 per cent of the votes. But even more significant were the 45,700 votes — 18.4 per cent — which went to a candidate new to politics, a businessman ruined by the crisis, who headed a shadowy royalist party, with a programme proposing dictatorship and propaganda denouncing 'scandals' and promising to double stipends and salaries. The episode revealed a widespread sense of discontent expressing itself politically outside the traditional parties.

The social consequences of the economic crisis are also of some importance in explaining the success of the Rexist movement before 1935. But until that date Degrelle's main problem was the need to avoid a rupture with the Church, so as not to deprive the Rexist movement abruptly of its essential quality as a Catholic movement. Hence the evolution towards a more direct form of political action was relatively slow. The attacks against collusion between politicians and high finance had already begun in the Rexist press in 1934. The social significance of such a campaign was well described many years later by a Catholic leader, G. Hoyois, who followed closely the development of early Rexism: Degrelle

> chose the best moment to present himself as public prosecutor. How many people, especially of the lower-middle class, felt weighed down! How many bore an inner resentment! A voice had finally been raised to free their conscience, to give vent to their bitterness by actually naming the guilty. To denounce politicians in receipt of dividends, when so many workers of all sorts were tightening their belts, was a real stimulus towards the disinterested reform of the state! [8]

In November 1935 Léon Degrelle finally launched into independent political action on a grand scale. From then on, the press began to take increasing interest in Rexism. On 2 November 1935 Degrelle, surrounded by a substantial body of followers, interrupted the Courtrai congress of the conservative wing of the Catholic party with a violent speech.

This first episode already displayed a deeply characteristic trait of the Rexist movement's campaign during the elections of May 1936: the attack against politicians, described as corrupt and without authority, was in reality directed primarily against the conservative elements of the Catholic party. In its initial nucleus the Rexist movement represented the revolt of young Catholics, aligned on reactionary or fascist positions, against the old conservatives acting as the natural and historical leaders of their environment. And ultimately the conservative Catholics were those politically most damaged by the Rexist attacks; some abandoned politics; others were not re-elected in May 1936. It was above all the conservative francophone wing of the Catholic party that paid for the Rexist electoral gains; the number of democratic Catholic deputies remained unchanged at the 1936 elections.

On 11 November 1935 Rex held its first large-scale political meeting at the Sports Palace at Brussels. The theme was: 'Catholics, come to Rex, Rex is the future'; the press estimated that at least 15,000 attended. On 20 November the Church openly distanced itself from Rex. But while it could disclaim any responsibility for Degrelle, it was unable to block the development of a movement which had grown above all at the expense of the ACJB clientele, but was now pushing beyond it.

Rexism became a mass political phenomenon between November 1935 and the elections of May 1936. So rapid a conquest of a vast public cannot be explained simply in terms of the charisma of a single individual, as interpretations which exaggerate the role of Degrelle's personality tend to suggest. It is true that Rexism's propaganda was full of emotive appeals, including the building up of Léon Degrelle's attractions as a person and an orator. The 'Leader' could inspire descriptions such as this one in the liberal daily *La Dernière Heure* of 30 May 1936:

Large brown eyes filled with gentleness and audacity, hands — or rather fists — of extraordinary vigour. A magnificent voice, of muted depth in ordinary conversation, but thunderous in speeches. And what radiant youth! He is so handsome that you are unaware of everything else. He is far more courteous than Mr Goebbels. He has feeling. He can hardly hold back from talking to you about small children or his aged mother. [9]

The term 'Rex-appeal' was coined in poor taste to stress Degrelle's impact on women (who, in any case, had no vote). In like manner one can point to the theatrical staging of meetings. But these elements are not sufficient to explain Rex's success. Whatever the 'shape' of the propaganda, it always delivered a political message. And whatever its interclass pretensions, the propaganda was always directed at a specific public, rendered particularly receptive by the situation. In this sense, another liberal paper, *L'Etoile Belge*, was extremely accurate when it wrote on 6 March 1936:

> That such a jumping-jack can bring out thousands of listeners and be acclaimed by them as a saviour is an eloquent symptom of the state of disarray of part of public opinion, which loses all sense of reality when listening to such claptrappers. [10]

The public which responded to Rexist propaganda in the first half of 1936 had not yet emerged from the economic crisis materially, and even less morally. As the economist F. Baudhuin noted:

> Although the economic recovery was clearly visible, it had not yet been of help to everybody. Two-thirds of the unemployed were still without jobs, and industrial and commercial recovery was only occurring gradually. It is an understandable human reaction that the discontent of the laggards should have eclipsed the satisfaction of those benefiting from the new government policy — especially if one notes that the latter were not necessarily the same as those who had suffered in the crisis. [11]

If one turns to the social composition of Rex, the 'laggards' formed a particularly numerous category, alongside those who had been directly hit by the crisis. The evidence for this is multiple, ranging from the geographical distribution of votes to the proposals for laws presented to parliament after the 1936 elections by the Rexist parliamentary group. An analysis of the social composition of an adequately large sample of Rexist candidates in 1936 gives the following results: 31.7 per cent shopkeepers or artisans; 22.7 per cent teachers, employees, officials; 14.1 per cent industrialists (although no important names were included); 11.5 per cent free professions. Rexist ideology also contained considerable nostalgia for pre-industrial society: 11 per cent of the candidates in 1936 were 'farmers' (*agriculteurs*). The results in the predominantly agricultural province of Luxemburg point to the presence of a peasant base: in this province, Degrelle's native one, Rex got 29 per cent of the votes in 1936 (more than the socialists and liberals) and could still raise 12 per cent of the votes in 1939.

The electoral platform of the Rexists in February 1936 still made much of fear of the crisis continuing: 'The Van Zeeland experiment is going to end in defeat, unemployment is increasing apace, devaluation is bleeding the country, we are moving towards a condition of generalized pauperism and ever more extensive proletarization'. [12] As a remedy, Rex proposed, among other things,

> war on unemployment by the creation of new industries, regulation of hiring of foreign workers, an end to employment of married women through a family wage, the building of 75,000 workers' houses, a partial return by the people to the soil.

But it is arguable that these aspects of Rexist propaganda made little impact. The dominant theme, deliberately chosen as such by the Rexists themselves, was the denunciation of political-financial scandals. At a certain point, the symbol used by the party was a broom to sweep away political immorality, the key word (or insult) was *pourri* ('rotten'), the attacks on opponents were extremely virulent. The best known of Léon Degrelle's pamphlets after the Courtrai incident was about the president of the conservative wing of the Catholic party, which began: 'I accuse M. Segers. I accuse the minister Segers of taking on multiple directorships, of being a bankster, a pillager of savings, and a coward'. [13]

Although the bank failures during the crisis had only

affected 'second-magnitude stars' (to use F. Baudhuin's phrase), they had still left their mark; and the scandals denounced by Rex usually went back to the worst period of the crisis. Behind the torrent of insults and insinuations, the facts were quite banal: attempts by politicians with business links to save a bank from bankruptcy, donations by financial institutions to politicians for electoral campaigns, turning confidential information about balance sheets to personal benefit, and so on. Two incidents, including that of the ex-minister Segers, led before the elections to lawsuits for defamation against Degrelle; in both cases the sentences included comments which were far from flattering for the 'victims' of the muck-raking campaign.

On 24 May 1936 Rex got 271,000 votes and twenty-one seats (out of 202). Degrelle was not a candidate. The Flemish nationalists got 168,000 votes and sixteen seats. The period between May 1936 and April 1937 marked the apogee of fascist movements in Belgium; significantly, the two dates correspond to elections.

Rex was above all a movement of opinion, although it also derived some support from its strength as an organization. But J.-M. Etienne's estimate of 16,000 active members in the movement between the two elections seems too high, if one bears in mind that in October 1936 no more than 5000 took part in the so-called 'march on Brussels', an initiative announced well in advance and publicly confirmed by the Rexist press after it had been banned by the government. In reality, Rex's strength did not lie in its ability to marshal, in military style, a mass following on seditious terrain, but in the relationship it established from the time of the campaign of the 1936 elections with a whole sector of public opinion. This relationship held for about one year. The Rexist French-language newspaper, Le Pays Réel, which first appeared on 3 May 1936, was selling about 100,000 copies in October 1936 and stayed more or less at this level until April 1937. In January 1937 Degrelle was still able to attract 12-15,000 to the Brussels Sports Palace for six evenings in a row — a significant achievement, given that the public had to pay for entry.

But before it began to lose a substantial number of its

supporters, the Rexist movement already found itself increasingly isolated. In October 1936 it signed an agreement with VNV which, on balance, turned out to be a bad bargain, as Rex risked losing the support it had gained among the French-speaking minority in Flanders, which was violently and justifiably opposed to the regional nationalist movement; moreover, support for the unitary state was extremely widespread at that time at Brussels and in Wallonia. The exact terms of the agreement were only made public on 10 April 1937; Rex pledged itself to support 'the transformation of the unitary Belgian state into a federal state'. [14]

Time also did not work in favour of Degrelle. As the months went by, the critical moment which Belgian society had passed through could be seen to belong ever more to the past, while no new problems arose of such gravity as to justify in the eyes of vast sectors of public opinion extreme and radical solutions. 'Among the general conditions of fascism, one needs to include the existence of a given "climate", a special atmosphere of excitement and frenzy,' Angelo Tasca has written. [15] No such atmosphere existed in Belgium between October 1936 and April 1937, except perhaps among Rex's own public. Hence Rex found itself in the contradictory position of a movement which proclaimed the need for order, while itself acting as one of the main causes of disorder. Such a situation certainly did not increase sympathy for Léon Degrelle's movement in conservative circles; and a clearly defined conservative anti-fascism emerged in autumn 1936.

One final point: as time passed, those needs which Rex claimed it wished to meet through its radical solutions began to be picked up in different manner at other points of the political spectrum. Thus, in February 1937, Spaak and De Man declared themselves supporters of a 'national socialism', which was to promote 'the values of order, authority and responsibility' within the democratic framework, and which stressed solidarity between social classes. [16] De Man was to offer support for collaboration after the defeat of 1940. Nevertheless, this 1937 'national socialism' cannot be considered as a masked form of fascism; it is rather to be located among those general ideas, widespread in government circles

at the time (voiced even by Leopold III), which never got
further than projects, about reinforcing the executive and
placing professional organizations on an official state footing.

Because of its organizational weakness, the Rexist movement was particularly vulnerable to defeat. Hence the consequences of Degrelle's electoral failure in April 1937 were the
more catastrophic. The defeat was above all due to the circumstances, rather than loss of votes, which was slight. But
Degrelle himself had sought the encounter and was personally
responsible for encouraging exaggerated illusions about the
further possibilities of the Rexist movement. Indeed, the
'Leader' had declared on various occasions that he felt himself near the seizure of power. This is how he expressed
himself shortly before the 'march on Brussels' in a 'Letter to
Frenchmen':

> Frenchmen! We were young, poor, unknown to everybody
> when we began. Now, thirty years old, we are going to be
> the masters!
> In life, everything is too easy, everything succeeds too
> quickly. One lacks the time even to fight, to suffer ....
> When one wants to triumph, one triumphs!
> Always!
> Without fail! [17]

The optimism exuding from such empty rhetoric had nothing
to do with the real relationship of forces. It could have rung
less hollow if the traditionally thick network of organizations
of which Belgian society consisted had been on the verge of
collapse. But this was not the situation. The middle classes,
which had no strong organizations of their own and which
had provided an easy audience for Rexist propaganda, were
in no way representative.

In March 1937 Degrelle decided to provoke a by-election
at Brussels, as Spaak had done in 1935, and put himself
forward as candidate. He only had the support of the Flemish
nationalists, with 5.9 per cent of the vote in 1936. His
opponents seized the opportunity, putting forward a single
candidate, the Prime Minister Paul Van Zeeland, supported in
practice by the traditional parties as well as the Communist
Party. The Rexist movement was more isolated than in May

1936. Anti-fascism, whose essential focal point till then had been in the working-class organizations, now characterized a far broader front. The press — in contrast to a year earlier — almost without exception adopted clear anti-Rexist positions. Even the Church — imprudently provoked by Degrelle — intervened with a solemn condemnation of Rex by the cardinal primate Van Roey (9 April 1937). The elections took place on 11 April: Van Zeeland received 75.8 per cent of the votes; there were 5 per cent spoiled votes, and Degrelle got 19 per cent (69,242 votes). On 24 May 1936 the combined votes of Rex and VNV in the same constituency had amounted to 63,721.

After 11 April Rex's isolation grew worse. VNV took the initiative of first suspending the agreement between the two movements (June 1937), and then annulling it (September). Meanwhile the supporters and even the organizers of Rex began to defect. The threat of fascism disappeared from the horizon of Belgian domestic politics. In October 1938, when local elections were held, Rex got about 6 per cent of the vote in communes with over 10,000 inhabitants and constituency towns. In the 1939 elections VNV rose from its 7.1 per cent of 1936 to 8.2 per cent, while Rex fell from 11.4 per cent to 4.4 per cent.

As a force capable of playing an independent role in the party struggle, fascism had made a brief but intense appearance on the Belgian political scene. The various fascist movements in Belgium were based on their own local (or national) following, as we have tried to show. Until 1939 the behaviour of Rex and especially VNV was not such that they could be accused of being agents of foreign powers. But Rex was certainly supported financially by the Italian fascist regime between August 1936 and May 1937, while the nazis gave important financial help to Rex for the first time in September 1936, as well as making regular contributions to the VNV press.

With the war and the nazi occupation, the Légion Nationale, after initial confusion, joined the ranks of the Resistance. Verdinaso, whose leader Van Severen had been killed by French troops in May 1940, also provided some members of the Resistance, while others finished in the ranks of

VNV. During the occupation, some specifically collaborationist groups developed, of which by far the most important was a Flemish one, De Vlag; but Rex and VNV also turned to collaboration, in differing manner and with varying fortune. The nazis did not allow the creation of a collaborationist government in Belgium, but insisted on the appointment to major administrative posts of members of VNV and, to a lesser extent, of Rex. During the war VNV rose to over 50,000 members and was even able to gain a degree of mass support for collaboration in Flanders. Rex's growth potential, on the other hand, remained extremely limited; its unpopularity during the occupation is reflected clearly in the small number of copies sold of its newspaper *Pays Réel* — a mere 7000 daily in 1943, compared to the 230,000 daily of the more moderate collaborationist paper *Le Soir*.

Even during the war VNV had its own specific role and cannot be considered simply as an example of continuing loyalty to an original fascist vocation. Flemish collaboration, which had an important precedent in the so-called 'activism' of the first world war, was based in no small measure on (illusory) 'nationalist' motivations, which were in fact merely regional. There was no such ambiguity about Rex: forced on to the margins of political life already before the war, Léon Degrelle's movement became even more unpopular through its role during the occupation.

Fascism in Belgium, as in other countries, had developed in close association with nationalism in its early phase, but was to be identified with the betrayal of the nation by the end. This was not a particularly original trait in the history of Belgian fascisms. Two other, more specific characteristics offer a fit conclusion to this essay. First, it has often been noted that fascism has never gained power unaided, through its own forces. After achieving a certain importance, a fascist movement, in order to make real progress on the path to power, needs to find broad support within the ruling class. In Belgium, although fascism achieved considerable importance, ultimately it never really acted as a temptation for the ruling class taken as a whole. This explains why the Rexist movement's presence on the political scene was so brief. On the other hand — and this is the second point — fascism is only one of various authoritarian tendencies to which socially conservative forces may turn at critical moments. Other possibilities of authoritarian developments may continue to exist even when the fascist path has become impossible. During the *question royale*, which began immediately after the war, it was possible to see how, for a whole sector of the Belgian ruling class, the defeat of fascism had not sufficed to suppress all authoritarian temptations.

References

1 J.-M. Etienne, *Le Mouvement Rexiste jusqu'en 1940*, Paris, 1968, 95-6; J. Denis, *Principes Rexistes*, Brussels, 1936, 14.
2 'Dietschland Hou Zee! Kester 1934-1935', Aalst, 1935, in A.W. Willemsen, *Het Vlaams-Nationalisme de Geschiedenis van de Jaren 1914-1940*, Utrecht, 1969, 373.
3 Etienne, op. cit., 80.
4 D. Kieft, *Belgium's Return to Neutrality*, Oxford, 1972, 186.
5 A.W. Willemsen, 'Geschiedenis van de Vlaamse Beweging', *Encyclopedie van de Vlaamse Beweging*, Tielt Utrecht, 1973, I, 32.
6 L. Degrelle, 'L'Action Catholique des jeunes', *XXe Siècle*, 6 November 1929.
7 L. Degrelle, 'Ce que nous voulons. Ce que nous faisons. Ce que nous ferons', *Rex*, 15 January 1933, 5.
8 G. Hoyois, *Aux origines de l'Action Catholique, Monseigneur Picard*, Brussels, 1960, 160-1.
9 R. Grabiner, 'La Montée du Rexisme: étude de la presse bruxelloise non rexiste', *Res Publica*, 11(4), 1969, 744-5.
10 ibid.
11 F. Baudhuin, *Histoire économique de la Belgique 1914-1939*, vol. 1: *Grandeurs et misères d'un quart de siècle*, Brussels, 1946, 359.
12 L. Degrelle, 'Rex luttera seul aux Elections Prochaines', *Rex*, 28 February 1936.
13 L. Degrelle, *Kessel-Loo*, 1936, 32 pp.
14 French text in R. Pfeiffer and J. Ladrière, *L'Aventure rexiste*, Brussels, 1966, 114-16.
15 A. Tasca, *Nascita e avvento del fascismo*, Florence, 1950, 533.
16 R. De Becker, 'Pour bâtir une Belgique nouvelle. H. Spaak définit le socialisme national', *L'indépendance Belge*, 9 February 1937.
17 L. Degrelle, *Je Suis Partout*, 24 October 1936.

14
FRANCE

◆

G.Warner

One of the main problems confronting the historian of French fascism is to decide whether or not it even existed. As Klaus-Jürgen Müller has observed, there are two diametrically opposed views on the subject.

> While one school of historians, whose leading spokesman is René Rémond, believes that the leagues and similar phenomena were nothing more than updated forms of a traditional, Bonapartist-authoritarian nationalism with at most an occasional tinge of fascism, the authors of the hitherto solitary comprehensive study of the fascist phenomenon in France, Plumyène and Lasierra, take the view that it was definitely a matter of positive, very varied forms of fascism. [1]

Contemporary political debate offers little help. On the right, few movements openly admitted to being fascist. Indeed, most specifically denied it. On the left, the position was reversed. Then, as now, left-wing groups and parties were only too willing to denounce any opponent as fascist. In the circumstances, the historian has no choice but to impose his own criteria, however imperfect these may be.

European fascism was the product of particular circumstances and expressed itself in characteristic ways. Circumstantially, it was a right-wing reaction to three interrelated developments: the dislocation brought about by the first world war; the threat of communist revolution; and the impact of the world economic depression of the 1930s. Its characteristics have been described many times. Juan Linz's summary is one of the most comprehensive:

> We define fascism [he writes] as a hypernationalist, often pan-nationalist, anti-parliamentary, anti-liberal, anti-communist, populist and therefore anti-proletarian, partly anti-capitalist and anti-bourgeois, anti-clerical, or at least non-clerical, movement, with the aim of national social integration through a single party and corporative representation not always equally emphasised; with a distinctive style and rhetoric, it relied on activist cadres ready for violent action combined with electoral participation to gain power with totalitarian goals by a combination of legal and violent tactics .... The appeal based on emotion, myth, idealism and action on the basis of a vitalistic philosophy is initially directed at those least integrated into the class structure — youth, students, demobilised officers — to constitute a self-appointed elite and later to all those disadvantageously affected by social change and political and economic crisis against the political system. [2]

It follows from this that fascism was a revolutionary creed. In normal circumstances, traditional élites would have found it far too risky and adventurous, not to say brash and uncouth. It was only when circumstances were abnormal, when the normal barriers to radical change were not functioning adequately, that they were tempted to turn to fascism as a saviour.

Such a situation certainly did not exist in France at the end of the first world war. The comparison with Italy is instructive. Although France experienced its own version of the *biennio rosso* in 1919-20, when more than thirty-eight million working days were lost through strikes, the industrial disorders never spilled over into the countryside and the traditional conservative political forces were able to hold together and indeed to triumph in the elections to the Chamber of Deputies in November 1919. Moreover, the peace settlement satisfied far more of France's aspirations than it did those of Italy, thereby depriving virulent nationalism of the fascist type of a particularly fertile seed-bed.

It was only after the victory of the left in the Chamber elections of 1924 that France's first authentic fascist movement emerged. Le Faisceau was established on 11 November 1925. Its founder, Georges Valois, was a defector from the royalist Action Française, an organization which he had come to regard as insufficiently militant and too socially exclusive.* Le Faisceau, with its call for the replacement of the existing political, economic and social order by a corporativist dictatorship, enjoyed a brief vogue, attaining a membership of perhaps 25,000 in mid-1929.** It never succeeded, however, in making large inroads upon the traditional right, nor, despite strenuous efforts, in gaining more than a modicum of working-class support. Indeed, the main effect of its campaign to woo the workers was to frighten off many of the movement's wealthy backers. Finally, the accession to power of Raymond Poincaré's right-wing government of national union in July 1926 deprived Le Faisceau of its principal scapegoats: the weak, inflationary governments of the Cartel des Gauches. Valois had himself observed that 'there is no revolution which is not based upon a monetary and financial crisis.' Poincaré's stabilization of the franc brought the crisis which had given Le Faisceau the slenderest of chances to

* There is a lively debate as to whether the Action Française was itself a fascist movement. One of the leading authorities on fascism, Ernst Nolte, argues that it was. Indeed, his book, *Three Faces of Fascism*, deals with the Action Française alongside Italian fascism and German national socialism. I tend, however, to share the view of Juan Linz, who writes that, while there are a number of similarities between the Action Française and other fascist movements,

> it is ... distinct, by the central place given initially to royalism .... This combined with the anti-democratic social élitism, the original identification with Catholicism, the support among traditional sectors of society, particularly the nobility, distinguishes it from the basically more plebeian and generally more secular fascist movements. [3]

** As a measure of comparison, the membership of the French Communist Party at this time is put at around 55,000.

make such a revolution to an end, and the movement soon
faded into oblivion.

The world economic depression of the 1930s hit France
later than most countries, but it also lasted longer. The index
of industrial production (1925-9 = 100) tells the story:

1929	112.0
1930	109.8
1931	96.2
1932	82.7
1933	94.0
1934	87.4
1935	85.6

The fall-back after 1933 was almost unique to France, and unemployment, although never on the same scale as in Britain or
Germany, did not reach its peak until 1936. The slump helped
to foster political extremism in other European countries. It
was hardly surprising that it should do the same in France.

This was all the more likely in view of the fact that
France's political institutions also seemed to be passing
through a period of crisis. The right had governed between
1926 and 1932, but the Chamber elections in the spring of
the latter year returned a left-wing majority of radicals and
socialists. Unfortunately, it did not prove to be a stable one
and no less than six governments succeeded one another in
the brief period between the elections and February 1934.
This was partly due to the eruption in 1933 of an unsavoury
politico-financial scandal − the Stavisky affair − which
involved members of the ruling Radical Party and seemed to
point to the corruption of the whole regime.

The immediate outcome of these developments was an
explosion of mob violence in Paris on 6 February 1934, in
which fifteen people were killed and nearly 1500 injured,
and which led to the resignation of the Prime Minister,
Edouard Daladier, and his replacement by a former President
of the republic, Gaston Doumergue, at the head of a right-
wing government. Apart from the violence, the parallel
between 1934 and 1926, when Poincaré replaced Herriot,
was very close. The longer-term consequences, however,
were very different. Instead of appeasement and stability,

the events of 6 February 1934 gave rise to the most acute political polarization and turmoil which France had experienced since the Dreyfus affair at the turn of the century.

On the left, the riots of 6 February 1934 were seen as a fascist plot to overthrow the republic and eventually led to the rallying of all left-wing forces, including the Communist Party which had been in self-imposed political isolation since the 1928 shift in the Comintern line, to form the Popular Front, a coalition which was to win the next elections to the Chamber of Deputies in the spring of 1936. But this consolidation of the left in response to a perceived fascist threat simultaneously alarmed the right and thereby fostered the growth of that very same threat it was designed to prevent. All this took place against the backdrop of continuing economic depression, which the orthodox deflationary policies of successive right-wing governments between 1934 and 1936 were quite unable to cure.

Recent research has not substantiated the charge that the riots of 6 February 1934 were a plot — fascist or otherwise — to overthrow the republic. What prompted it in the first place was the fact that the riots were master-minded and in large part carried out by a number of right-wing paramilitary organizations known as the leagues. Only one of these movements, Marcel Bucard's Francistes, openly proclaimed that it was fascist. Bucard had had an audience with Mussolini, was to represent France at the international fascist congress in Montreux in December 1934, and drew over half a million lire in subsidies from the Italian embassy in Paris between May 1934 and April 1940. But Bucard's movement was tiny. According to the parliamentary committee of inquiry into the events of 6 February 1934, it had only twelve to fifteen hundred members, and it was never a significant political force.

Apart from the Action Française, the major leagues involved on 6 February 1934 were the Jeunesses Patriotes, the Solidarité Française and the Croix de Feu. Klaus-Jürgen Müller has shown that, during its early years at any rate, the Jeunesses Patriotes, which was founded by the right-wing Paris deputy, Pierre Taittinger, in 1924, was more a pressure group working for the consolidation of the traditional right than an authentic fascist movement, although its paramilitary organization did lend it a certain fascist air. There are no reliable membership figures for 1934. The Solidarité Française is even more of an enigma. Founded in 1933 by the talcum-powder tycoon and political crank, François Coty, its organization was also paramilitary and its programme racialist, authoritarian and corporativist. Coty himself claimed to be a Bonapartist — whatever that might mean in the context of France in the mid-1930s — but he was ailing and the man actually in charge of the movement, Jean Renaud, denied any such affiliation. Once again, there is no reliable information concerning membership.

The most important of the leagues, however, was undoubtedly the Croix de Feu. Originally founded in 1927 as an apolitical organization for ex-servicemen who had been cited at least once for gallantry on the field of battle, it had become an overt supporter of the right in the Chamber elections of 1932. This was due to the influence of Lieutenant-Colonel François de la Rocque, who, after distinguished service in Morocco with Marshal Lyautey, on the western front, on Marshal Foch's staff and in Poland, retired from the army in 1929 and joined the Croix de Feu, becoming its leader two years later. De la Rocque also presided over the expansion of the movement in 1932 and 1933 by creating affiliated organizations of relatives and sympathizers who did not have to be ex-servicemen at all. Soon after the riots of 6 February 1934, he claimed that the total strength of the Croix de Feu and its affiliated organizations stood at 50,000, of whom 12,000 were to be found in the Paris area.

Although it played a relatively unheroic role on 6 February 1934 — de la Rocque deliberately kept his men away from the fighting — it was the Croix de Feu which captured the headlines in the months that followed and increasingly came to symbolize the fascist threat in left-wing eyes. How and why is clear from the following account of the movement's activities in mid-1935, written by Alexander Werth, the brilliant Paris correspondent of the *Manchester Guardian*:

Giant rallies and mobilization exercises began to be held in various parts of France and the behaviour of the Croix de

Feu became rather alarming .... [De la Rocque] swore
that the Croix de Feu had been 'on their guard' during the
cabinet crisis [of May-June 1935] and that there would
have been some fun (*il y aurait eu du sport*) if ... Daladier
had been included in the new government .... Becoming
bolder and bolder, the Colonel proclaimed that 'he did not
care a hang for legality', and that the Croix de Feu would
'take command' at the appropriate moment. The most
impressive rally ... took place at Algiers, complete with
thirty aeroplanes belonging to the Croix de Feu organization; and there were also many other rallies mostly held
on the estate of some wealthy patron, without warning
and with 'lightning speed' .... On several occasions the
roads leading to these 'secret rallies' were policed by Croix
de Feu men. [4]

On 16 November 1935, there was a bloody fracas in Limoges
between supporters of the Croix de Feu and the Popular
Front. It was all too reminiscent of the street fighting which
had preceded both Mussolini's and Hitler's rise to power.

According to one scholarly estimate, the membership of
the Croix de Feu and its affiliated organizations stood at
around 450,000 on the eve of the 1936 elections, which
was roughly twice that of the Socialist and Communist
parties combined. The phenomenal success of the movement
was undoubtedly due, in large part, to the fact that it was the
number one target of the Popular Front. After the 1936
elections, right-wingers often complained that the Croix de
Feu had helped the Popular Front to power by its actions,
but it was equally true that the Croix de Feu would never
have become the force it was without the constant attacks
launched upon it by the Popular Front.

But was the movement fascist? The rallies, the paramilitary
exercises and the open contempt for parliamentary and
democratic procedures were all redolent of fascism. In so far
as it had one, the Croix de Feu's programme also clearly
owed much to the same source. Five points stand out from a
statement of principles published in the movement's newspaper, *Le Flambeau*, on 19 October 1935: (1) the elimination of foreign influences upon the economy and the

establishment of an autarkic system based upon France and her colonial empire; (2) the reorganization of professional associations and the enactment of a corporative labour law; (3) the reinforcement of the executive at the expense of the legislature; (4) rearmament; and (5) anti-communism.

One genuine fascist, however, would have taken Colonel de la Rocque's repeated denials that his movement had any connection with fascism at their face value. This was Signor Landini, the press attaché at the Italian embassy in Paris and one of the main contacts between the Italian government and French extremist groups. In August 1935, one of the younger and more militant members of the Croix de Feu told Landini that he did not think the movement could seize power before the beginning of 1937.

> I observed that it was dangerous to wait until 1937 [Landini reported to Rome]. It reminded me of the sign outside some cheap barber's shops: 'A free shave — tomorrow'. During the intervening period, and without clearly defined aims before them, the troops will stagnate and go soft.

The Croix de Feu militant replied that the French were patient and that 'the troops' had faith in de la Rocque. Landini remained sceptical, however, commenting that, 'for the most part, they [i.e. the Croix de Feu] are only too glad to postpone action until the Greek Kalends and pretend that they are heroes in the meantime.' [5] (It is perhaps significant in this context that there is no evidence of any Italian subsidy to the Croix de Feu.)

The distinctly unfascist caution of the Croix de Feu was shown after the Limoges incident in November 1935 when the movement's spokesman in the Chamber of Deputies announced that it was prepared to dissolve its paramilitary organizations if the left did likewise. This foreshadowed the Croix de Feu's readiness to transform itself into a conventional political party, a step which was eventually forced upon it by the Popular Front government's dissolution of all the leagues on 18 June 1936. Despite his earlier bombast, Colonel de la Rocque had already made it clear that there could be no question of opposing the new government by force:

The country would not understand why the Croix de Feu movement should launch itself upon actions opposed to the will apparently expressed in the recent elections. It would condemn an adventure that would be fatal to the hopes with which it surrounds us: the re-establishment of morality and the reconciliation of patriots of good will. [6]

In other words, if the Croix de Feu for a time embodied some of the ideals and adopted some of the methods which are generally accepted as fascist, there can be little doubt that, by the summer of 1936, its leader was no longer interested in playing the part of a Mussolini or a Hitler, if indeed he ever had been.

After the dissolution of the leagues, the Croix de Feu turned itself into the Parti Social Français (PSF) and continued to increase its membership in its new guise. At the same time, it also continued to move further and further away from fascism. Far from working to overthrow the regime, it set itself the task of replacing one of the regime's characteristic expressions, the Radical Party, as the authentic spokesman of the middle classes. The successes of the Daladier government of 1938-9 prevented this, but it is probable that, if the elections to the Chamber of Deputies had taken place in the normal way in the spring of 1940, the PSF would have done quite well. This would only have shown, however, the extent to which the movement had become completely integrated into the traditional French parliamentary system.

With the mellowing of the Croix de Feu, the fascist torch passed into other hands. On 28 June 1936, at the so-called 'rendez-vous of Saint-Denis', Jacques Doriot founded the Parti Populaire Français (PPF). Doriot was an ex-communist who had broken with his erstwhile comrades soon after the riots of 6 February 1934 when he had had the temerity to advocate a united front with the socialists before this became the official party line. Ironically, the party's adoption of the new policy coincided with his own expulsion, which left Doriot something of a rebel without a cause. His machine in the Paris suburb of Saint-Denis just managed to secure his re-election to the Chamber of Deputies in 1936, and the PPF was designed to put him back on the political map.

Although, as the movement's historian, Dieter Wolf, has reminded us, Doriot himself never openly admitted that he was a fascist until after the French defeat of 1940, some of his lieutenants were less coy, and the PPF's programme, with its condemnation of the liberal-democratic parliamentary system, its ferocious anti-communism, its criticism of social conservatism and its call for an authoritarian and corporativist state, leaves little doubt as to the nature of the movement. The PPF grew rapidly during the early months of the Popular Front government, although Wolf believes that the active membership never exceeded 50-60,000. It was thus much smaller than the PSF. It differed from the latter also in terms of social composition. While the PSF was overwhelmingly a middle-class movement, the PPF had considerable working-class support, thanks no doubt to Doriot's former left-wing connections. Indeed, Wolf estimates that no less than 57 per cent of the delegates to the party's first congress in November 1936 came from a working-class background.

In the spring of 1937, Doriot attempted to enlarge his sphere of influence by calling for the establishment of an umbrella organization, the Front de la Liberté, which would comprise all the country's anti-communist forces. The principal objective of this move was undoubtedly to enable Doriot to get his hands on the manpower and resources of the PSF and when the latter's leadership rejected his proposal in June, it marked the beginning of the PPF's decline, a process which was hastened by the dislocation of the Popular Front. The PPF suffered a further severe setback at the turn of the year 1938-9, when several of its leading members resigned. Their motives were mixed. Pierre Pucheu, a young technocrat who later became Minister of the Interior under the Vichy regime, subsequently wrote that he left the party when he found out it was being subsidized from abroad.* Anti-capitalists resented the support the movement was getting from big business, while nationalists resented Doriot's

---

* There is evidence in Ciano's diary of Italian subsidies to the PPF. The Germans, however, do not appear to have supplied any money.

appeasement-minded attitude at the time of Munich. The PPF did not again become a force to be reckoned with until the German occupation.

While the PPF was largely an urban phenomenon, Henri Dorgères' Défense Paysanne was, as its name implies, a rural movement. Founded in 1929, it gained support during the depression when the French peasantry was subjected to a classic example of a 'scissors crisis', with wholesale farm prices falling by 44 per cent between 1929 and 1935 while retail prices fell by only 25 per cent during the same period. The movement may have enjoyed a membership of some 200,000 in 1937-8. Dorgères was an open admirer of Mussolini and his movement was undoubtedly fascist, especially its youth branch, the Jeunesses Paysannes, with their green shirts and other paramilitary trimmings. The social base of the Défense Paysanne — small landholders and, in the case of the Jeunesses Paysannes, landless labourers — was, however, too restricted to enable it to play a significant political role, especially as it never succeeded in forming close and permanent links with any of the urban fascist movements.

Despite their varying attitudes to republican legality, all the groups and parties discussed so far were legally constituted and operated mainly within the framework of the law. This was not true of the clandestine Comité Secret d'Action Révolutionnaire (CSAR), better known under a title invented by its enemies as the Cagoule, or 'Hood'. Founded in 1936 by a consultant naval engineer and company director, Eugène Deloncle, it consisted mainly of dissident members of the Action Française and the Croix de Feu who felt that their former organizations were not doing enough to combat the communist threat. The CSAR was run on strictly military lines. Like the French army, its high command was divided into four bureaux: overall direction, intelligence, operations and logistics. The basic unit was the cell, which contained between ten and twenty men. Larger units were the unity, the battalion, the regiment, the brigade and the division. Deloncle claimed that he could raise 12,000 men in Paris alone, but this figure is almost certainly an exaggeration and I have seen no reliable estimates of the organization's total membership. Some of the provincial branches enjoyed considerable autonomy, as well as such picturesque designations as 'The Children of the Auvergne' and 'The Knights of the Sword'. The CSAR bore all the marks of a secret society. Cell members knew only their immediate superiors and knew nothing about other cells. Each recruit had to swear a solemn oath of allegiance and serve a probationary period during which he was under constant observation. Discipline was rigid and disloyalty was punishable by death after a court martial. There are, moreover, cases on record of *cagoulards* who were executed in this way. The CSAR planned a seizure of power down to the last detail and accumulated a considerable amount of weaponry to carry it out.

A leading member of the organization told the head of the Italian secret service in August 1937: 'We agree entirely with your Duce in considering that fascism is a norm of political life, not only Italian but European .... The fascist regime must be copied and applied in France. That, in essence, is our programme.' [7] It is doubtful, of course, whether Mussolini really wanted a fascist regime in France. It would have deprived him of one of the more convenient scapegoats for Italy's frustration. In any case, he must have realized that, in spite of its armament, the prospects of a small movement like the CSAR holding on to power even if it succeeded in seizing it in the first place were extremely small. It was, however, extremely useful for sowing confusion in the ranks of the French body politic and for performing certain services on behalf of the Italian authorities. It was members of the CSAR, for example, who brutally murdered two anti-fascist émigrés, the Rosselli brothers, in June 1937.

It would be an interesting, but also irrelevant, story to tell how the French authorities got on to the track of the CSAR. It suffices to say that the socialist Minister of the Interior, Marx Dormoy, who paid for his zeal with his life in 1941 when he was murdered by former members of the organization, disclosed the existence of the conspiracy in November 1937. It was June 1939, however, before seventy-one of the CSAR's members were finally brought to trial. When war broke out in September, the government rashly agreed to amnesty them if they enlisted in the armed forces. Naturally, most of them did so, and were thereby enabled to continue their activities after the collapse of 1940.

There was a curious, symbiotic relationship between French fascism in the 1930s and the Popular Front. As the latter grew in strength, so too did the former; and when the Popular Front broke up, French fascism lost its role in the eyes of many of its supporters. An important part was played in all this by none other than Edouard Daladier, the arch-enemy of the leagues on 6 February 1934, whose government, which was formed in April 1938, marked the effective end of the Popular Front. Taking advantage of the national solidarity created by the Munich crisis, Daladier took plenary powers and used them to enable his new Finance Minister, Paul Reynaud, to launch an attack on the forty-hour week, one of the corner-stones of the Popular Front's reform programme. The trade union movement called a general strike for 30 November 1938, but this was a failure and the change went through. Combined with Reynaud's other measures, the modifications in the forty-hour week produced a remarkable economic recovery, for there is no doubt that its rigid application had largely undone the effects of the Popular Front's reflationary policies, thus causing continued stagnation. Between October 1938 and June 1939, industrial production in France rose by no less than 20 per cent.

In July 1939, as the international situation grew more threatening, the Daladier government postponed the elections scheduled for 1940 by two years. After the conclusion of the Nazi-Soviet pact in August and the outbreak of war in September, it gave further proof of its authoritarian temper by banning the Communist Party and setting up France's first concentration camps to house communists and other opponents of the war effort. Such measures have led some to describe Daladier's government as 'proto-fascist', but a much closer parallel, and one squarely within the French tradition, was Clemenceau's Jacobin-style dictatorship of 1917-18.

Just as Clemenceau enjoyed the support of French conservatives, so did Daladier. There was no need for fascism as long as the existing system could thwart the communists, keep the workers in their place and lead to a profitable economic recovery. Indeed, French fascism never succeeded, throughout the interwar period, in making the decisive breakthrough of attracting the large-scale support of existing élites, notably those of big business. The case of François de Wendel, the powerful iron and steel baron, is instructive in this context. While de Wendel was perfectly prepared to look favourably upon the leagues as auxiliaries in the fight against the left, he strenuously resisted any attempt on their part to replace the traditional conservative parties, especially the Fédération Républicaine, to which he remained deeply committed. Nor is there much evidence to support the assertion of some historians that fascism was more successful in attracting support from the 'modernizing' sectors of French industry. The biographer of the energy magnate and technocrat, Ernest Mercier, who is usually seen as a key figure in this politico-industrial linkage, points out that, although Mercier did join the Croix de Feu in 1933, he played no significant part in the organization and was indeed asked to resign from it in 1936 when the Popular Front used his association with the movement to smear it as a tool of capitalism. While industrialists and bankers undoubtedly did support fascist movements, they did so in an eclectic fashion and without any conviction, except on the part of a few individuals, that they represented the wave of the future.

Only a major catastrophe could bring fascism to power in France. This occurred when the country was defeated and occupied by the Germans in the summer of 1940. To describe Marshal Pétain's Vichy regime as fascism in power may seem at best something of an exaggeration and at worst the Communist Party line, but although Pétain was no Hitler or Mussolini and although his so-called 'national revolution' derived much of its inspiration from authentic French traditions going back well beyond 1922, there were undoubtedly strong elements of fascism in what Vichy said and did. Indeed, there was much talk of the need to 'align' the French political, economic and social system with those of the victorious Axis powers, albeit with certain modifications appropriate to France's particular circumstances. To use terminology from the opposite end of the political spectrum, Vichy hoped that the European new order created by the

Axis victory would be 'polycentric': there would be 'different roads to fascism'.

But the basic unity was still there. On the political side, as Roger Bourderon has pointed out, the new regime

> took up the criticisms and applied the remedies formulated before the war by the fascist and fascistic movements in France and by all the fascist-type parties abroad. The dissolution of political parties, trade unions and municipal councils that were judged undesirable ... the suppression of departmental and district councils, the prorogation *sine die* of the houses of parliament followed by the abolition of their committees, the purging of the civil service, the first steps towards the establishment of an authoritarian hierarchical system to replace the representative system, the considerable extension of the powers of the prefects, the laws of 12 October 1940 on departmental administrative committees, of 16 November on municipal delegations, and of 24 January 1941 setting up the National Council: after one year of power, the *Etat français** had reached the same point as Mussolini's regime in 1930 in the destruction of the previous political system ... and the restructuring of a new one. [8]

On the economic side, the Vichy government borrowed some ideas from Mussolini's corporativist state. Organizing committees to run industry were set up as early as August 1940. In November all trade unions and employers' associations were abolished and in October 1941 a 'labour charter' was introduced which laid down that each industry should be run by 'mixed social committees' consisting of both employers and employees. Strikes and lock-outs were declared illegal. Agriculture was reorganized on corporativist lines in December 1940. But all this legislation, allegedly designed to soften the excesses of capitalism and abolish the class war, was really so much window dressing. Real control of the economy rested in the hands of the government and it preferred to act through the employers, frequently appointing to the industrial organizing committees members of the

---

* The official title of the Vichy regime.

very employers' associations it had supposedly abolished. Anti-capitalist in theory, pro-capitalist in practice: in this respect, as in so many others, the Vichy regime displayed fascist characteristics.

The government even went in for nazi-style racialism. In October 1940 the first anti-Jewish statute was enacted. It excluded Jews, who were defined on the same basis as in the Nuremberg decrees, from the civil service and from a number of other professions. The scope of this legislation was extended in June 1941, and although racial persecution never reached the heights it attained in Germany or German-occupied territory in eastern Europe, it existed and was justified in similar terms.

By the end of 1941, the 'national revolution' was a transparent failure. This was not only because of its inherent dishonesty, but also because the premise upon which it was based — French partnership in an Axis new order in Europe — was becoming increasingly invalid. In the first place, it was clear that Germany and Italy were not interested in partnership with France, but only in exploiting her. Secondly, after the entry of the Soviet Union and the United States into the war, the prospect of an Axis victory grew steadily more remote. From the positive task of building a new France, the Vichy government gradually turned to the negative one of preserving what already existed. From the point of view of this essay, the most interesting aspect of events during the last two years of the Vichy regime is the growing conflict between the government on the one hand and those who may be called the 'hard-core fascists', who refused to admit either the possibility or the consequences of an Axis defeat, on the other.

These 'hard-core fascists' were based in Paris. It should be remembered that, under the terms of the Franco-German armistice of June 1940, France was divided into an occupied and unoccupied zone. Paris, which was in the occupied zone, remained the capital of the country, even though the French government was located at Vichy in the unoccupied zone. In theory, the French government's writ ran equally across both zones, but in practice German influence was more powerful in the occupied zone. The difference survived, albeit in an attenu-

ated form, even after the Germans moved into the unoccupied zone in November 1942, following the allied invasion of
North Africa. Throughout the war, the German military
commander in France, the German embassy and the SS had
their headquarters in Paris. It was only natural, therefore,
that the ultra-collaborationist groups should establish their
headquarters in Paris too.

One important group was led by Marcel Déat, who had left
the socialist party in 1933 to form a new party which became
known as the 'neo-socialists'. Increasingly a believer in the
totalitarian management of the economy and a leading
appeaser — he wrote the famous 'Must we die for Danzig?'
article in his newspaper, *L'Oeuvre*, in April 1939 — Déat
emerged as a fully-fledged fascist after the French collapse of
1940. Failing to obtain the Vichy government's support for
the establishment of an official single party, he began to
attack the regime for its alleged lack of enthusiasm for
collaboration with Germany as early as the autumn of that
year. In February 1941, in Paris, he founded the Rassemblement National Populaire (RNP), an unofficial substitute for
the party he had failed to form the previous summer. At its
peak, in 1942, the RNP probably had a membership of
between 20,000 and 30,000. Local studies have shown that
the party was mainly urban in character, with strong representation of shopkeepers and workers.

Déat's great rival was Jacques Doriot of the PPF. While
Déat condemned Marshal Pétain and the 'national revolution'
from an early date, Doriot was, in his own words, 'one of the
Marshal's men'. It was not until the end of 1941 that he too
began to adopt an attitude of hostility towards Vichy. Like
the RNP, the PPF probably had between 20,000 and 30,000
members in 1942, but their background was rather different.
Although it enjoyed a broader geographical base than its
rival, Bertram Gordon writes that

the PPF did not make quite the inroads that the RNP
did among the French proletariat, nor did it attract as
many teachers and others from the professional strata.
Instead the PPF was much more the party of the artisan
class. [9]

Even more interesting is the fact that, as Gordon points out, over 40 per cent of the delegates at its 1942 congress had no prior political affiliation, leading him to comment that 'many, if not most, of these party militants were quite young, anti-establishment but also anti-communist, and lured by the charismatic personality of Doriot.'

Various minor collaborationist groups and parties tended to gravitate around either the RNP or the PPF, but it proved impossible to unite these two formations. Although both sides sought doctrinal reasons for their disagreement, it was probably due more to the differing backgrounds and personalities of their two leaders. About the only thing they did manage to agree upon was the establishment, in July 1941, of the Légion des Volontaires Français contre le Bolchevisme which was to fight alongside the Germans on the eastern front.

In addition to their quarrel with the Vichy government's policies, Déat and Doriot had a personal grievance against Pierre Laval, who was its effective head during the last two years of the regime and whom they had helped to return to power in April 1942. Despite their support, Laval refused to reward either Déat or Doriot with a post in the government and this, not unnaturally, gave rise to considerable bad feeling. Doriot's supporters, in particular, began to suggest that their leader might prove more successful in dealing with the Germans than Laval himself. Laval was greatly alarmed by this talk, for he suspected that the SS, which had recently expanded its activities in France, was backing Doriot. In December 1942, Laval asked the Germans for permission to dissolve the PPF and combine it with Déat's RNP in a new single party under his leadership. The Germans refused. This decision was in line with their traditional policy. Apart from a few SS fanatics, no one in the German government seriously considered replacing Laval by Doriot, but to keep the threat of a rival government in Paris hanging over it was a highly effective way of making Vichy toe the line.

By the summer of 1943, however, when the French resistance was becoming a serious threat, when the middle and lower ranks of the French police and administration were ever more actively sabotaging German interests and when there was a constant flow of rumours to the effect that Marshal Pétain was about to dismiss Laval, the Germans began to take the view that some of the 'hard-core fascists' should join the Vichy government to stiffen its backbone. Laval did his best to block any such proposal, but a clumsy attempt by Pétain to get rid of him in November 1943 led to a German ultimatum ordering the Marshal 'to entrust ... M. Laval with the task of the immediate reconstruction of the French cabinet in a way which is acceptable to the German government and which will guarantee collaboration'. [10] In particular, the Germans insisted upon the appointment of Déat and, as head of the police, the ex-member of the CSAR and leader of the Milice, Joseph Darnand.

The Milice was formed in the old unoccupied zone in January 1943. This paramilitary organization was originally supported by Laval, who hoped to use it as a counter to the Paris-based collaborationist groups, but he soon discovered that Darnand was just as much a threat to his position as Déat and Doriot. In the summer of 1943, the Germans began to supply the Milice with arms, a process which increased rapidly after the appointment of Darnand as secretary-general for the maintenance of order on 1 January 1944. The Milice had perhaps 30,000 members at its peak. According to German sources, a third of these were to be found in the department of Bouches-du-Rhône, which included Marseilles. 'A city known for its high proportion of toughs and marginal elements,' writes Gordon, 'Marseilles provided fertile ground for fascist movements in occupied France.' [11] (Marseilles was also a stronghold of Doriot's PPF.) A study of membership in another department, the Loire, indicates that it was very youthful, with 38.6 per cent of members under the age of 23 in 1943 and a further 25.4 per cent between the ages of 23 and 33.

Both Roger Bourderon and Bertram Gordon argue that the appointment of the 'hard-core fascists' to the Vichy government and, in particular, the growth of the influence of the Milice and its increasingly brutal civil war with the resistance movement in the first half of 1944 mark the final and inevitable stage in the regime's transformation into what Gordon calls 'a thoroughgoing fascist state'. [12] Fortunately for France, this phase did not last for long. The Allies invaded north-western France in June 1944 and the south in August. By the beginning of September, the Germans had more or less completely withdrawn from the country and the 'hard-core fascists' had gone with them. So too, against their will, had Pétain and Laval. They refused to co-operate any further with their captors, but Déat, Darnand, Doriot and others had no such scruples. Déat and Darnand joined the 'French governmental committee for the defence of national interests', a kind of fascist government-in-exile, while Doriot, unable even at this stage to resolve his differences with Déat, presided over a rival 'French liberation committee'. By this time, however, German support had switched to Doriot and it was only a matter of time before the other French collaborationists were forced to acknowledge his authority. Ironically, on the very day that he set out to receive their 'surrender' (22 February 1945), his car was strafed by an aircraft — accounts differ as to whether it was allied or German — and the PPF leader was killed.

Although fascism in any form would never have come to power in France without her defeat by Germany in 1940, it would be wrong to argue from this that it never enjoyed popular support. The 'hard-core fascists', of course, were never popular. Even those who joined their organizations did not always do so out of genuine political conviction. Local studies of the RNP, for example, show that women in parti-cular tended to join it for some non-political motive, such as the desire to obtain the release of a friend or relative from a German prison camp, or even to have a better social life among the grim realities of occupation. The Vichy regime, on the other hand, was almost certainly supported by a majority of the French people in its early days, not only because it seemed a good idea to back what then looked like the winner in the European contest between fascism and democracy, but also because there had been a genuine reaction against the regime held responsible for the defeat: namely, the Third Republic. Vichy's initial popularity was gradually dissipated, however, as the true consequences of Germany's victory and its own 'national revolution' came to be appreciated. At the time of the liberation in 1944, the regime was even more thoroughly execrated than its predecessor in 1940.

If one were asked to sum up the essence of French fascism, one could do no better than quote the 21-point programme of Joseph Darnand's Milice. It is set out in the form of a diptych, with one side recording what the movement was against and the other side what it was for: a kind of catalogue of vices and virtues. It reads as follows:

1	Against the forgetting of crimes	For the punishment of the guilty
2	Against scepticism	For faith
3	Against apathy	For enthusiasm
4	Against bourgeois selfishness	For human solidarity
5	Against individualism	For the community spirit
6	Against futile freedom	For the real freedoms
7	Against equality	For rank
8	Against influence	For merit
9	Against routine	For the spirit of initiative
10	Against tradition	For worth
11	Against democracy	For authority
12	Against anarchy	For discipline
13	Against demagogy	For truth
14	Against the tutelage of money	For the primacy of work
15	Against the trust	For the profession
16	Against international capitalism	For French corporativism
17	Against the proletarian condition	For social justice
18	Against Gaullist dissidence	For French unity
19	Against bolshevism	For nationalism
20	Against the Jewish leprosy	For French purity
21	Against freemasonry	For Christian civilization

The woolly-mindedness, the barbaric sentiments, the contra-dictions and, above all, the yawning gap between aspiration and achievement express the tragedy of French, and perhaps of all, fascism.

References

1   K.-J. Müller, 'Die französische Rechte und der Faschismus in Frankreich 1924-1932', in Dirk Stegmann *et al.* (eds), *Industrielle Gesellschaft und politisches System*, Bonn, 1978, 413.

2   J. Linz, 'Some notes toward a comparative study of fascism in sociological historical perspective', in Walter Laqueur (ed.), *Fascism: A Reader's Guide*, Harmondsworth, 1979, 25-6.

3   ibid., 67.

4   A. Werth, *The Destiny of France*, London, 1937, 158-9.

5   Italian Collection, St Antony's College, Oxford.

6   Cited by P. Machefer, 'Les Croix de Feu (1927-1936)', *L'Information Historique*, 34 (1), janvier-février 1972, 32.

7   J.R. Tournoux, *L'Histoire secrète*, Paris, 1962, 89.

8   R. Bourderon, 'Le Régime de Vichy était-il fasciste?', *Revue d'Histoire de la Deuxième Guerre Mondiale*, (91), juillet 1973, 38-9.

9   B.M. Gordon, *Collaborationism in France during the Second World War*, Ithaca, New York, 1980, 146, 151.

10 Cited by G. Warner, *Pierre Laval and the Eclipse of France*, London, 1968, 384.

11 Gordon, op. cit., 187.

12 ibid., 290.

15
SPAIN

✦

Paul Preston

In the summer of 1936, the Spanish army rose against the Second Republic. The officers concerned were convinced that they were acting to save their country from proletarian disorder inspired by foreign agents. In fact, they were protecting the reactionary landed oligarchy from sweeping reform of Spain's antiquated economic structures. The political instability which so alarmed them was partly the product of working-class desperation in the face of intransigent oligarchical resistance to change. More immediately, it was the fruit of a deliberate destabilization programme sponsored by the landowners and industrialists most threatened by reform. Before the army assumed their defence, their interests had been guarded by a number of rightist political organizations. For the largest of them, the clerical authoritarian Confederación Española de Derechas Autónomas, military intervention signalled the failure of its Trojan-horse tactic of blocking reform within the limits of republic legality. For the others, the troglodytic Carlists of the Comunión Tradicionalista, the radical monarchists of Renovación Española and the blueshirted fascists of Falange Española, the rising was the fruition of their 'catastrophist' commitment to the violent overthrow of the republic.

With a few notable exceptions, the rank and file and the leaders of both legalist and 'catastrophist' organizations

rallied readily behind the army, providing the cannon fodder
of the rebel war effort and the political service class of the
rebel zone. This was formalized in April 1937 by the so-
called Unificación when prewar rightist groups were sub-
sumed into Falange Española Tradicionalista y de las Juntas
de Ofensiva Nacional Sindicalista. The fact that this strange
amalgam took its title and its tone from the Falange met with
little resistance from the other groups which, hitherto, had
regarded the Falange as a rowdy street-fighting rabble to be
patronized and used. The reasons for such humility were
various. A recognition of the important political and economic issues at stake in the war inhibited manifestations of
ruffled pride which might have disrupted the unity necessary
for victory. Moreover, the aid given to the rebels by Hitler
and Mussolini was helping to build an enthusiastic belief that
the future world order would be a fascist one. In any case,
this did no violence to rightist consciences since, even before
the war, a mimetic sympathy for fascism was a common
feature of all Spanish right-wing organizations.

It is not surprising, given the fulsome praise heaped on the
German and Italian regimes and the proliferation of militarized youth sections, that the left in Spain indiscriminately
regarded these organizations as fascist. It is even less note-
worthy that the Franco war effort, backed by the Axis
powers and with its Falangist façade, was seen by contemporaries, Spanish and foreign, as a fascist enterprise. The subsequent exaggerations of nazism and the assiduous efforts of
Franco to dissociate himself from the Axis after 1943 did
much to undermine this unqualified identification of Francoism with fascism. Indeed, in the last twenty years, scholars
have dwelt on the fact that Francoism was not Hitlerism and
have been influenced by the very unfascist development of
Spain since 1957. These deliberations have resulted in an
increasingly widespread consensus that Francoism was *never*
really fascism but rather some variant of limited, semi-
pluralist authoritarianism. Some authors have gone further
still, postulating, explicitly or implicitly, the view that the
meaningful study of fascism in Spain should be limited to
the Falange Española.

This approach is both understandable and unfortunate. It

starts from the ostensibly laudable premise that contempt for the more reprehensible features of the Franco dictatorship should not permit the unscientific application to it of the term fascist merely as a means of political abuse. Moreover, while debate rages as to the fascist content of organizations like Renovación Española, the Comunión Tradicionalista and the CEDA, the fascist nature of the style, ideology and myths of the Falange are unquestionable. Accordingly, the narrow identification of Spanish fascism with Falange Española obviates the need for examination of the fascist features of other rightist groups and of the Franco regime itself. It is unfortunate because it renders Spanish fascism insignificant and uninteresting except for a period of about twelve months. Before the spring of 1936, the Falange Española was a diminutive organization of students and taxi-drivers. After April 1937, it was emasculated into a bureaucratic and patronage-dispensing machine in the service of Franco. As the Caudillo, in an uncharacteristic outburst of directness and levity, once explained to one of his ambassadors, 'the Falange is the claque which accompanies me on my journeys through Spain.'

This is not the only reason for suspicion of the exclusivist definition of fascism in Spain. Awareness that fascism can be a term of abuse as well as of political definition cuts both ways. An eagerness to exonerate the Franco regime from the taint of fascism can go with a readiness to forget that, after coming to power through a civil war which claimed hundreds of thousands of lives and forced hundreds of thousands more into exile, the dictatorship executed at least a quarter of a million people, maintained concentration camps and labour battalions and sent troops to fight for Hitler on the Russian front. Under any circumstances, the confident exclusion of both prewar Spanish rightists other than the Falange and the Franco regime from a discussion of fascism could be justified only if fascism is taken to be synonymous with nazism at its most extreme. Such a view, since it leads logically to the suggestion that Mussolini's Italy was not really fascist, is so rigid as to be useless.

It is a basic assumption of this chapter that the one movement and the one regime which must be considered generi-

cally fascist are those of Mussolini. That is not to say that the
search for Spanish fascism will be inflexibly restricted to the
quest for similarities with Italy. After all, for all their
common features, most fascist movements, except those
created in the wake of German occupation, were responses to
national crises and drew on national traditions. Thus, if
nazism and fascism, with all their differences, can be
accepted as the German and Italian fascist responses to crises
of German and Italian society, then a case can be made for
the rightist groups which backed the rebels in the civil war at
least to be considered potentially as the Spanish fascist response to a crisis of Spanish society.

This is not to forget significant differences. Unlike
Germany and Italy, Spain did not participate in the first
world war. In consequence, there simply did not exist masses
of veterans to swell the ranks of paramilitary organizations.
On the other hand, the war brought massive social and economic dislocation to an already conflictive Spain. The subsequent revolutionary ferment in the industrial north and the
rural south deeply traumatized Spain's ruling classes. In many
respects, the Spanish crisis of 1917-23 is analogous to the
Italian crisis of 1917-22. That crisis was merely anaesthetized
by the dictatorship of General Primo de Rivera. It re-emerged
with greater intensity in the conditions of the economic
depression of the 1930s. The belief gained currency in Spain,
as it had done earlier in Italy and Germany, that the existing
political order could no longer adequately guarantee the
economic interests of the middle and upper classes. It was
then that the search began for some extraordinary means of
defending those interests.

It is often pointed out that Spain did not suffer the same
crisis of national identity as that undergone by Italy and
Germany as a result of the inadequacies of their unification
processes and of their respective disappointments in the
aftermath of the Great War. On the other hand, the shock of
defeat in the Spanish-American War and the loss of the last
remnants of empire had far-reaching effects. The Regener-
ationist movement which grew up in the wake of the disaster
was to have a profound influence on the thinking of the
Spanish right well into the Franco years. Nostalgía for empire

was common to all rightist groups in the 1930s but was fiercest in the Falange where it was openly claimed that imperial conquest was a means of diverting the class struggle. The main legacy of Regenerationism was the belief that defeat in 1898 was the fault of a political system marked by corruption and incompetence. A better future was associated with a patriotic cleansing of politics and reform imposed from above. Ultimately, this was to breed an anti-parliamentary authoritarianism. Early hopes were pinned on the great conservative politician, Antonio Maura. After his withdrawal from political life, his followers, including José Calvo Sotelo and Antonio Goicoechea, switched their allegiance to General Primo de Rivera and were later prominent in Renovación Española. Another line from Regenerationism to the Falange, and particularly the imperialist emphasis, passed from the philosopher José Ortega y Gasset, via his manic vulgarizer, Ernesto Giménez Caballero, to the son of the dictator.

A further important difference between Spain, on the one hand, and Italy and Germany, on the other, resides in the fact that Franco was not defeated in an external war and maintained his dictatorship for thirty years after 1945. Since neither nazism nor fascism survived, it would be a counterfactual absurdity to speculate that either might have evolved as did the Franco regime. Yet there is an equally unhistorical assumption involved in the comparisons of Franco with Hitler and Mussolini on the basis of the chronological totality of all three regimes. The fact that the Franco regime, in response to changing international realities, evolved away from its overtly pro-Axis positions after 1943 is implicitly taken by some commentators retrospectively to absolve Franco from a fascist past that diminished in importance the longer he lived beyond it. *Mutatis mutandis*, like should be compared with like.

Areas of coincidence arguably outweigh the differences at least between Italy and Spain. This is true not only of the Franco and Mussolini regimes. There are comparisons also to be made between pre-1922 Italian fascism and the various Spanish rightist groups before 1936. It is not simply a question of the ritual trappings associated with fascism, although Roman salutes, strutting, chanting, rallies and paramilitary formations were common enough in Spain before 1936 as they were to be under Franco. There are more interesting comparisons to be made, particularly in the light of the greater differences between fascism and nazism. The Unificación of 1937 and the emasculation and bureaucratization of the radical Falange had their parallel in the fusion of fascists, nationalists and monarchists in 1923. There are fascinating similarities between the social support, ideological objectives and crucial importance to their respective causes of the agrarian fascists and the agrarian CEDA. Equally, there are valid comparisons to be made between Renovación Española and the Italian Nationalist Association, both in their relationships to the more radical, populist Falange and fascist party and in the disproportionate role that their theorists were later to play in each of the dictatorships.

Nevertheless, the most striking resemblances are to be found between the two regimes. Here again, the liturgical paraphernalia, the militarized rallies in honour of the leadership principle, although they existed in both regimes and were significant, are not the really important similarities. No more so are the ideological coincidences, the glorification of peasant life, the rhetorical quest for the 'new man'. Far more crucial are the similarities based on political, social and economic realities. The areas in which some commentators have seen Mussolini falling short of 'full-scale fascism', that is to say, of a notional approximation to nazism, are precisely where his regime coincides with that of Franco. Just as the existence of political and economic pressure groups created a narrowly restricted pluralism under Mussolini, so too did the Franco regime experience a constant jockeying for power and influence between economic interest groups and between Falangists, Catholics, monarchists, the Opus Dei and other political factions. Needless to say, the relation of forces was far from identical in both countries. Nevertheless, although differing in detail and emphasis, compromise with the Church, the harnessing of party radicalism and the subordination of fascist and Falangist syndicates to business interests all point to the survival of the pre-crisis establishment forces in each case. The rapidity with which fascists and Falangists were to bewail the failure of their 'revolution' is a clear symptom of the extent to which both regimes, beyond their rhetoric and their professed intentions before gaining power, found their central functions in the protection and fostering of the existing economic order.

Having widened the scrutiny of fascism in Spain beyond the narrow confines of Falange Española, the enquiry should not be limited to the accumulation of similarities between Italy and Spain. Each national fascism must be permitted its individual characteristics. These derived in part from the country's particular traditions of patriotic and conservative rhetoric. More fundamentally, however, the essential character of a given fascist movement and subsequent regime arose out of the special nature of the crisis that it was their function to resolve. Inevitably, the existence of Soviet communism gave all fascisms a common focus of fear and enmity, just as the vicissitudes of the international economy gave rise to other points of coincidence. Every bit as important as those influences, however, were the national circumstances of social and economic crisis which led to traditional conservative forces being deemed no longer adequate to defend oligarchical interests within bourgeois democracy. The chronological moment at which that happened and the extent to which the threat that they faced came from real or perceived revolution or simply from the achievements of reformist socialism at a time of economic contraction varied from one country to another. Accordingly, any account of a national fascism must be informed by an awareness of the nature and development of the corresponding capitalism to which it was linked.

Until the 1950s, capitalism in Spain was predominantly agrarian. Spanish agriculture is immensely variegated in terms of climate, crops and land-holding systems. There have long existed areas of commercially successful small and medium farming operations, especially in northern regions which also experienced industrialization, Asturias, Catalonia and the Basque country. However, throughout the nineteenth century and for the first half of the twentieth, the dominant sectors in terms of political influence were, broadly speaking, the large landowners. In the main, the great latifundia estates are concentrated in the central and southern regions of New

Castile, Extremadura and Andalusia, although there are also substantial latifundios to be found scattered in Old Castile and particularly in Salamanca. The political monopoly of the landed oligarchy was periodically challenged by the industrial and mercantile classes with virtually no success. Indeed, it was only in the second decade of the Franco dictatorship that industrialists and bankers overtook landowners as the hegemonic economic élite. Until well after the civil war then, the urban haute bourgeoisie was obliged to play the role of junior partner in a working coalition with the great latifundistas. Despite sporadic industrialization and a steady growth in the national importance of the political representatives of the northern industrialists, power remained squarely in the hands of the landowners.

There was never any strong possibility in Spain that industrialization and political modernization would coincide. In the first half of the nineteenth century, the progressive impulses, both political and economic, of the Spanish bourgeoisie were irrevocably diverted. The removal of feudal restrictions on land transactions combined with royal financial problems in the 1830s to liberate huge tracts of aristocratic, ecclesiastical and common lands. This not only diminished any impetus towards industrialization but also created intense social hatreds in the south. The newly released land was bought up by the more efficient among existing landlords and by members of the commercial and mercantile bourgeoisie attracted by its cheapness and social prestige. The latifundia system was consolidated and the new landlords were keen for a return on their investment. The departure of the more easy-going clerics and nobles of an earlier age together with the enclosing of common lands removed most of the social palliatives which kept the poverty-stricken south from upheaval. Thus, the strengthening of the landed oligarchy coincided with an explosive social situation which exacerbated its reactionary tendencies. At the same time, the syphoning into the land of the capital of the merchants of the great sea ports and of Madrid bankers correspondingly weakened their interest in modernization.

Continued investment in land and widespread intermarriage between the urban bourgeoisie and the landed oligarchy debilitated those forces committed to reform. The feebleness of the Spanish bourgeoisie as a potentially revolutionary class was underlined in the period from 1868 to 1874, which culminated in the chaos of the First Republic. In many respects, 1873-4 was Spain's 1848-9. Having plucked up the courage to challenge the old order, the bourgeoisie was frightened out of its reforming ambitions by the spectre of proletarian disorder. Reform was abandoned in return for social peace. The subsequent relation of forces between the landed oligarchy, the urban bourgeoisie and the remainder of the population was perfectly represented by the political system of the 1876 monarchical restoration. Two political parties, the Conservative and the Liberal, represented the interests of two sections of the landed oligarchy, respectively the wine and olive growers of the south and the wheat growers of the centre. It was virtually impossible for any political aspirations to find legal expression outside these two great oligarchical parties. A system of electoral falsification resting on the social power of local landlords ensured that the narrow interests represented by the system were never seriously threatened. External disturbances by the unrepresented majority were dealt with by the forces of order, the Civil Guard and, at moments of greater tension, the army.

Challenges to the system did arise, however, and they were linked to the painfully slow but inexorable progress of industrialization and to the brutal social injustices intrinsic to the latifundia economy. The arrival of anarchism in the 1860s had given a sense of hope and purpose to hitherto sporadic rural uprisings. Now the growth of coal, steel and textile industries in the north saw the emergence of a militant industrial proletariat. Surprisingly, when the inevitable explosion came, it was precipitated not by the rural or the urban working class but by the industrial bourgeoisie. Nevertheless, once the crisis started, proletarian ambitions came into play with the result that the basic polarization of Spanish political life became starker than ever.

The geometric symmetry of the restoration system, with political power concentrated in the hands of those who also enjoyed the monopoly of economic power, was shattered by the coming of the first world war. Not only were political passions aroused by the debate on intervention, accentuating growing divisions within the Liberal and Conservative parties, but massive social upheaval came in the wake of war. The fact that Spain was a non-belligerent put her in the economically privileged position of being able to supply both the Entente and the Central Powers with agricultural and industrial products. Coalmine-owners from Asturias, Basque steel barons and shipbuilders, Catalan textile magnates all experienced a wild boom which constituted the first dramatic take-off for Spanish industry. The balance of power within the economic élite shifted somewhat. Agrarian interests remained pre-eminent but industrialists were no longer prepared to tolerate their subordinate political position. Their dissatisfaction came to a head in June 1916 when the Liberal Minister of Finance, Santiago Alba, attempted to impose a tax on the notorious war profits of northern industry. Although the move was blocked, it precipitated a bid by the industrial bourgeoisie to carry through political modernization.

The reforming zeal of industrialists enriched by the war coincided with a desperate need for change from a proletariat impoverished by the war. Boom industries attracted rural labour to towns where the worst conditions of early capitalism prevailed. At the same time, massive exports created shortages, rocketing inflation and dropping living standards. The socialist Unión General de Trabajadores and the anarcho-syndicalist Confederación Nacional del Trabajo were drawn together in the hope that a joint general strike might bring about free elections and then reform. While industrialists and workers pushed for change, middle-rank army officers were protesting at low wages, antiquated promotion structures and political corruption. Since military complaints were couched in the language of 1898 Regenerationism, the officers were acclaimed as the figureheads of a great national reform movement. Had the movement been successful in establishing a political system capable of permitting social adjustment, the civil war would not have been necessary. As things turned out, the great crisis of 1917 merely consolidated the power of the entrenched landed oligarchy.

Despite a rhetorical coincidence of their calls for reform,

the ultimate interests of workers, industrialists and officers were contradictory and the system survived by skilfully exploiting these differences. The Prime Minister, the Conservative Eduardo Dato, conceded the officers' demands. He then provoked a strike of socialist railway workers, forcing the UGT to act before the CNT was ready. Now at peace with the system, the army was happy to defend it in August 1917 by crushing the striking socialists with considerable bloodshed. Alarmed by the prospect of militant workers in the streets, the industrialists dropped their own demands for political reform and, lured by promises of economic modernization, joined in a national coalition government in 1918 with both Liberals and Conservatives. Yet again the industrial bourgeoisie had abandoned its political aspirations and allied with the landed oligarchy out of fear of the lower classes. Short-lived though it was to be, the coalition symbolized the slightly improved position of industrialists in a reactionary alliance still dominated by the landed interest.

By 1917, Spain was divided more starkly even than before into two mutually hostile social groups, with landowners and industrialists on one side and workers and landless labourers on the other. Only one numerous social group was not definitively aligned within this broad cleavage − the small-holding peasantry. This class was to assume enormous importance when the landed oligarchy was forced to seek more modern forms of defence in the 1930s. In the meanwhile, however, the existing order survived in part because of the organizational naïvety of the left and even more because of its own ready recourse to armed repression. The defeat of the urban socialists in 1917 did not mark the end of the assault on the system. Between 1918 and 1921, the so-called *trienio bolchevique*, the anarchist day-labourers of the south took part in a series of risings. Eventually put down by a combination of the Civil Guard and the army, the strikes and land seizures of these years intensified the social hatreds of the rural south, destroying the last vestiges of paternalism which had mitigated the daily brutality of the day-labourers' lives.

At the same time, urban anarchists were also coming into conflict with the system. Having failed to invest their war

profits in modern plant and rationalization, northern industrialists were badly hit by the postwar resurgence of foreign
competition. The Catalans in particular tried to ride the
recession with wage-cuts and lay-offs. They countered the
consequent strikes with lock-outs and hired gunmen. The
anarchists retaliated in kind and, from 1919 to 1921, the
streets of Barcelona witnessed a terrorist spiral of provo-
cations and reprisals. Restoration politics were no longer
an adequate mechanism for defending the economic interests
of the ruling classes. At this point, a *coup d'état* was carried
out by General Primo de Rivera.

Ostensibly, Primo came to power to put an end to disorder
and to prevent an embarrassing report by a parliamentary
commission causing discomfort to the King. However, as
Captain-General of Barcelona and intimate of the Catalan
textile barons, Primo was fully aware of the anarchist threat
to them. Moreover, as a large landowner from the south, he
also had experience of the peasant risings of 1918-21. He was
thus the ideal pretorian defender of the coalition of industrialists and landowners which had been consolidated during
the great crisis of 1917. Initially, his dictatorship had two
great advantages — a general revulsion against the chaos of
the previous six years and an upturn in the European economy. He outlawed the anarchist movement and made a deal
with the UGT whereby it was given a monopoly of trade
union affairs. A massive public works programme, which
involved a significant modernizing of Spanish capitalism and
the building of a communications infrastructure that would
bear fruit only thirty years later, gave the impression that
liberty was being substituted by prosperity.

Although the Primo de Rivera dictatorship was regarded
in later years as a golden age by the Spanish middle classes
and became a central myth of the reactionary right, its short-
term effect was to discredit the idea of authoritarianism in
Spain. This fleeting phenomenon was born partly of Primo's
failure to use the economic breathing space to construct a
lasting political replacement for the decrepit constitutional
monarchy, but more immediately it sprang from his alienation of the powerful interests which had originally
supported him. A genial eccentric with a Falstaffian approach

to political life, he governed by a form of personal improvisation which ensured that he bore the blame for his regime's failures. Although by 1930 there was hardly a section of Spanish society that he had not offended, his most crucial errors led to the estrangement of industrialists, landowners and the army. Attempts to standardize promotion machinery outraged army officers. The Catalan bourgeoisie was antagonized by an offensive against regionalist aspirations. Northern industrialists were even more enraged by the collapse of the peseta in 1928, which they attributed to his inflationary public spending. Perhaps most importantly, the support of Primo's fellow landowners was lost when, as part of the projected corporative syndicate programme, efforts were made to introduce arbitration committees for wages and working conditions into rural areas. At the end of January 1930, Primo resigned.

There was no question of a return to the pre-1923 political system. Apart from the fact that it had fallen into disrepute by the time that Primo seized power, significant changes had taken place in the attitudes of its personnel. Among the senior politicians, death, old age and, above all, resentment of the King's cavalier abandonment of the constitution had all taken their toll. Of the younger men, some had opted for the republican movement, partly out of pique, partly out of a conviction that the political future lay in that direction. Others, especially those Conservatives who admired Maura's authoritarian side, had thrown themselves wholeheartedly into the service of the dictator. For them, there could be no going back and they were to form the general staff of the extreme right in the Second Republic and were to provide much of the ideological content of the Franco regime.

In desperation, therefore, Alfonso XIII turned to another general, Dámaso Berenguer. His mild dictatorship floundered in search of a formula for a return to constitutional monarchy but was undermined by republican plots, working-class agitation and military sedition. When he held municipal elections on 12 April 1931, socialists and republicans swept the board in the main towns while monarchists won only in the rural areas where the social domination of the local bosses, or *caciques*, remained intact. Faced by the questionable loyalty of both army and Civil Guard, the King took the advice of his counsellors to depart gracefully before he was thrown out by force. The attitude of the military reflected the hope of a significant section of the upper classes that by sacrificing the King it would be possible to contain the desires for change of both the progressive bourgeoisie and the left.

The coming of the republic did belatedly fulfil the aspirations of the industrialists of 1917. If anything, it went beyond them since the previous thirteen years had intensified the reactionary tendencies of the industrial bourgeoisie. On the other hand, far from satisfying the left, as it might perhaps have done in 1917, the coming of a republic could only signify the first step towards sweeping reform of the existing balance of social and economic power. The blocking of change in 1917 and the consequent division of the country into two antagonistic social blocks had taken their toll. Now the failure of Primo's dictatorship found the upper classes temporarily bereft of political formations capable of defending them from the adjustment of social and political privilege implicit in the coming of the republic. The elections of April and June 1931 saw political power pass to the socialists and their urban middle-class allies, the republican lawyers and intellectuals. They intended to use this suddenly acquired share of state power to create a modern Spain by destroying the reactionary influence of the Church and the army but, above all, by far-reaching agrarian reform. This was intended not only to improve the immediate conditions of the wretched *braceros* but also to create a prosperous peasantry as a future market for Spanish industry.

In this sense, the republic was potentially the agent of the bourgeois revolution that Spain's bankers, merchants and industrialists had been historically incapable of realizing. Yet the new regime could not count on their unequivocal support. This was partly because of the close ties between industry and land which had been intensified during the revolutionary upheavals of 1917-23. It was also a reflection of the immediate conditions of the Second Republic. The combination of a context of world depression and substantial increase in the size and influence of trade unions was hardly likely to encourage adventurism among industrialists. There was some sympathy for the republic among the more progressive industrialists and this was, to a limited extent, reflected in the pro-republican stance of the Basque and Catalan bourgeoisies during the civil war and in the anti-industrial economic policy of the Franco regime in the 1940s. In the main, however, most industrialists and bankers were in agreement with the view of the rightist press that the republic was a dangerous, revolutionary regime. This was confirmed both by the legal activities of industrial employers' pressure groups which were disruptive and subversive and by the fact that Basque industrialists were almost as prominent as landowners in the financing of both Renovación Española and the Falange.

Thus the mildly reforming ambitions of the republic were to face the unremitting hostility of both partners in Spain's reactionary coalition. To use the terminology of Otto Bauer, the people's republic in Spain was born of a transitional state of class equilibrium resting on a foundation of capitalist property relations. That is to say, the economic power of industrialists and landowners remained undiminished by the transition from monarchy to republic. On the other hand, they had lost their monopoly of political power. As a result of the relatively honest elections of 1931, the working classes and the urban petty bourgeoisie were now in a position to fulfil their minimal social and political aspirations.

Within months of the foundation of the new regime, the republican-socialist coalition government had introduced reforms which fundamentally challenged the pre-1931 social and economic structure. The intention behind this initial social legislation had been to alleviate the misery of the southern day-labourers. However, the inefficient latifundia system depended for its economic survival on the existence of a reserve army of *braceros* paid starvation wages. The introduction of the eight-hour day where previously men had worked from sun-up to sun-down and of arbitration committees to regulate wages and working conditions infuriated the latifundistas. With the depression forcing down agricultural prices, the consequent wage increases, minimal though they were, signified a potentially significant redistribution of wealth. Traditional means of keeping wages down, the introduction of cheap outside labour and the rural lock-out, were rendered difficult by the decrees of municipal boundaries and obligatory cultivation. With *braceros* flooding into the UGT's Landworkers' Federation and UGT leader Francisco Largo Caballero as Minister of Labour, the southern landowners felt as besieged as did those of the Po valley when faced with the ambitious advances of the Feder-terra after the first world war.

Although Catalan textile manufacturers and light indus-trialists benefited from the increase in the peasantry's dis-posable income, heavy industrialists in the Basque country and mine-owners from Asturias were as badly hit as the latifundistas by the depression and by the increase in trade union power and confidence. They rapidly began to seek new ways of defending economic interests which had never before been subject to legal threats such as those posed by the republic. The methods adopted to combat the problems posed by the establishment of a functioning mass democracy took two forms, one legal, the other violent. Despite the ostensible differences between them, especially in terms of day-to-day tactics, their overall strategies were complemen-tary and their long-term objectives virtually identical. The legal defence of oligarchical interests involved the mobiliz-ation of a mass rightist movement to match the numerical strength of the left. The so-called 'catastrophists' were committed to the outright destruction of the parliamentary regime.

Given the bitterness of class conflict in Spain, there was never much possibility of any significant section of the working classes being mobilized by rightist groups. All efforts made in that direction during the Second Republic were failures. The one substantial social group that was susceptible to right-wing manipulation consisted of the rural lower-middle classes. Efforts to mobilize smallholders against the rising power of the urban and rural working class had already achieved considerable success. The Confederación Nacional Católico-Agraria, financed by big landowners, had half a million members before the Primo de Rivera dictatorship seemed to render it superfluous. Its influence was, however, inherited by Acción Nacional, a mass Catholic political organization founded within a week of the fall of the monarchy and devoted to resistance against any change in the religious, social or economic order. Under the dynamic leadership of a young monarchist, José María Gil Robles, Acción Popular, as it became in 1932, undertook blanket propaganda campaigns to convince the conservative smallholders that the republic's attempts to break the social power of the Church constituted outright religious persecution and that projected agrarian reform was directed at them as much as at the big landowners.

Vast sums of money were spent convincing these poor but proud farmers that the republic would proletarianize them. When Acción Popular absorbed similar rightist organizations in early 1933 and became the CEDA, it could count its support in the millions. That support was consistently presented with the most virulently anti-republican propaganda as part of a process whereby it was being groomed to fight the left for what Gil Robles called 'possession of the street'. Mass rallies were staged at which the audiences were pushed to rabid hostility to the parliamentary regime. In 1937, and also in his memoirs, Gil Robles claimed that the reserves of anti-republican belligerence thus created made possible Franco's civil war victory. Despite the intensity of its anti-republicanism, the CEDA remained within the bounds of legality. However, an open admiration for both Italian fascism and German nazism indicated the fragility of legalism. Hitler and Mussolini were admired for fulfilling the tasks that the CEDA had set itself, the destruction of socialism and communism, the abolition of liberal parliamentarism and the establishment of the corporative state.

Gil Robles's short-term aim was to block the reforming ambitions of the republic. Before his considerable electoral success in 1933, this was done by a skilful programme of parliamentary filibustering. Afterwards, when he had sufficient strength to control the policies of a series of Radical and Radical-CEDA ministries, it took the form of the sweeping abolition of the republic's social legislation. Gil Robles's aim before the 1933 elections had been the legal establishment of the corporative state as a permanent defence against the left. When his victory was insufficient, he switched to the more sinuous tactic of gradually breaking up the Radical Party by means of a series of well-orchestrated cabinet crises in the hope that he would eventually be called upon to form a government. At the same time, the savage reversal of working-class living standards was a second string to his bow. If a left-wing rising could be provoked, a corporative state could be imposed in the aftermath of its suppression. In the event, the insurrection of October 1934 was put down with such difficulty that hopes for a rapid introduction of the corporative state were dropped in favour of a return to the slower legalist tactic. Gil Robles's hopes were finally dashed in late 1935 when a miscalculated cabinet crisis led not to his becoming prime minister but to the calling of elections.

The relative success of Gil Robles in reasserting the pre-1931 social order created the left-wing unity which was to be the foundation of the Popular Front's electoral victory in February 1936. The Asturian insurrection of October 1934 had already indicated the impossibility of a peaceful imposition of a corporative state. The Popular Front elections signified the definitive failure of the CEDA's efforts to use democracy against itself. Henceforth, the landed and industrial oligarchies sought a less hazardous and permanent form of protection. They began to switch their financial support to the 'catastrophist' right. At the same time, the uniformed masses of the CEDA's radical youth movement began to flood into the Falange and, to a lesser extent, the Carlist movement.

The end of illusions about the legal establishment of corporativism gave a welcome lease of life to the ailing Falange. It made little difference to the other 'catastrophist' organizations, Renovación Española and the Carlist Comunión Tradicionalista, except to confirm what they had long predicted. The Carlists in particular were little affected by day-to-day developments in republican politics. Maniac-ally anti-modern and devoted to the establishment of a theocratic monarchy, their commitment to the violent destruction of the laic republic was unswerving. Locked in their Navarrese strongholds, they tended to stand aloof from the rest of the right, although they did make two significant contributions to it. The more obvious was the provision of their fanatical militia, the Requeté, to the right-wing cause in the civil war. The less obvious one was to provide a body of indigenous reactionary doctrine which permitted other rightists to defend fashionable authoritarian and fascist notions as authentically Spanish.

Gil Robles's defeat did not affect Renovación Española financially, after all, its aristocratic and industrialist members were the paymasters of other groups. What it did do was to provide the context for the military rising to which the main activities of Renovación Española were directed. Like Gil Robles and José Antonio Primo de Rivera, its leaders had been members of the Unión Monárquica Nacional, founded in 1930 to make good the demise of the oligarchical parties of the restoration period. Young members of the monarchical political élite, they believed that the monarchy failed because it was tainted with liberal constitutionalism. Accordingly, they sought new means of defending upper-class interests. Devotees of General Primo de Rivera, their ideal was a corporative state under a military monarchy although they were receptive to other solutions to the problem of the rise of the left-wing masses. Sporting a radical youth movement and even belonging to Acción Popular until late 1932, the authoritarian monarchists were repelled by populist politics and inclined towards incisive and élitist schemes to deal with the leftist threat. Renovación Española was thus conceived of as a front organization to spread the idea of the legitimacy of a military rising against the republic, to inject a spirit of rebellion into the army and to provide a cover for fundraising, arms purchases and conspiracy. That the defence of the social order had priority over the preservation of the monarchy was made clear by the group's plans for the future which were a remarkably prophetic blueprint for the Franco regime. Intensely sympathetic to Italian fascism, Eduardo Aunós and José Calvo Sotelo had travelled widely in search of models for the defence of the existing order and had returned enthusiastic advocates of the corporative regimentation of labour and the economy.

It was not surprising that members of the Renovación Española group should be happy to subsidize the Falange.

Having no mass base themselves, the monarchists saw the Falange as potential cannon fodder for street fighting with the left and as an instrument of political destabilization to provide justification for a military rising. In addition, the presence of the dictator's son, José Antonio, at the head of the Falange was a useful guarantee to industrialists and particularly to landowners. The sort of reassurance that the aristocratic young Primo de Rivera provided to southern landlords was duplicated for the Basque haute bourgeoisie by José María de Areilza. In fact, for all its anti-conservative rhetoric, the limits of Falangist radicalism were clear enough. The more outspoken lumpenproletariat elements from the Juntas de Ofensiva Nacional-Sindicalista, with which the Falange merged in early 1934, were quickly brought under control. Moreover, even Jonsista criticisms of the moral and spiritual mediocrity of the bourgeois establishment never extended into attacks on the capitalist system of production. The emptiness of the Falange's revolutionary sloganizing was revealed by its participation in the repression of the left after the October 1934 rising and, most blatantly, by its role in the civil war.

Before 1936, the Falange was unable to develop a significant mass following because its natural constituency, the rural lower-middle classes, had already been recruited by the CEDA. When this became clear, much of the Falange's financial support drained away. Survival was made possible in part by cash from the Italian government, although this should not be taken as an exclusive seal of fascist approval since both the Carlists and Renovación Española were also objects of Mussolini's goodwill. While the Falange was in the doldrums, the main burden of oligarchical effort was directed towards bringing the CEDA masses within the more aggressive orbit of Renovación Española. This was to be done through the device of the so-called Bloque Nacional under the leadership of José Calvo Sotelo. In theory, the Bloque Nacional perfectly anticipated the Francoist Unificación. In practice, both Gil Robles and José Antonio Primo de Rivera stood aside. There was a strong element of personal rivalry at work in this. José Antonio resented the way in which Calvo Sotelo had stolen his ideological baggage in advocating fascist solutions to the Spanish crisis. Aristocratic disdain was revealed in his judgement that Calvo Sotelo could never lead a movement of national salvation because of his inadequate horsemanship. Personal friction also existed between Gil Robles and Calvo Sotelo. However, if formal unity was hindered by personal considerations, the left-wing triumph in February 1936 created a context in which practical unity became an urgent necessity.

The left was now determined to carry out the reforms which had been so successfully thwarted by the CEDA. The obvious challenge to oligarchical interests led to a remarkable closing of ranks on the right. Renovación Española's leadership intensified pressure for military intervention and diverted funds to the Falange for a programme of political destabilization. Attacks on the left by the Falange and members of the Juventud de Acción Popular were used by Gil Robles and Calvo Sotelo as the basis for spine-chilling parliamentary speeches which alleged that Spain was in the grip of anarchy. The middle and upper classes were thereby terrorized into a belief that only the army could save them. The roles of Carlists, Falangists and Renovación Española in the final preparations for the long-awaited catastrophe were almost predictable. More interesting was the behaviour of the CEDA. Having once accepted that legalism had failed, Gil Robles did nothing to stop the flow of his followers to more extreme organizations. He handed over the CEDA's electoral funds to the army conspirators and ordered the party's rank and file to place itself under military orders as soon as the rising began. He praised fascist violence as a patriotic response to the alleged crimes of the left. Much praised for his legalism, Gil Robles did not hesitate to throw his weight behind those who aimed to establish the authoritarian corporative state by violence.

The smooth orchestration of the efforts of both 'catastrophists' and legalists in the spring of 1936 induced many on the left to see the CEDA, Renovación Española, the Carlists and the Falange as regiments in the same army. Throughout the republic, leaders of each rightist group had addressed the meetings of the others and usually been well received. Space was made available in party newspapers for favourable reports on the activities of rivals. All sections of the right shared the same determination to establish a corporative state and to destroy the effective forces of the left. They were all the servants of the landed and heavy industrial oligarchies in so far as they depended on them for financial backing and all their political activities were directed towards the protection of oligarchical interests. There were, of course, differences of opinion and they occasionally led to public polemic. Nevertheless, they rarely went beyond discussions over tactics, and then usually over what seemed to the others to be the excessive legalism of the CEDA. These groups rarely broke unity in parliament, at election times or, most crucially, during the civil war — a stark contrast with the divisions that split the left both in peace and in war. Indeed, it was not uncommon, particularly among the provincial rural bourgeoisie, to belong to more than one, or in some cases all, of these organizations.

Both separately and together, all these groups constituted attempts to resolve a crisis in which the Spanish landed and industrial oligarchies found themselves as a result of left-wing pressure for change. The acuteness of that crisis was partly a consequence of the international situation but it was even more the result of the landed oligarchy's success in holding back change for nearly a century. After the collapse of restoration politics and the ultimate failure of the Primo de Rivera dictatorship, new methods had to be sought to defend oligarchical privilege. It is primarily in this sense that the rightist organizations may be seen variously, and after February 1936 in conjunction, as manifestations of Spanish fascism.

Various differences and similarities between the Italian and Spanish experiences have already been outlined. One crucial difference which underscores similarities in other areas is the fact that the Spanish crisis came to a head fourteen years after Mussolini attained power. The Spanish left had learnt the lesson of Italy, as it had learnt those of Portugal, Germany and Austria. There was no possibility of breaking the left with skirmishing *squadristi* in Spain. The civil war was, in that context, the inevitable culmination of the attempt to impose more or less fascist solutions to the Spanish crisis.

The fact that in the event the defence of the oligarchy led

to all-out war inevitably gave the army an influence in the Franco regime that was not paralleled in Italy. For this reason the rhetoric of anti-oligarchical novelty was rather more subdued under Franco than under Mussolini. Nevertheless, with the rightist groups of the prewar period formally united into a single party, the Franco regime achieved the goals to which they all aspired — the corporative state, the abolition of free trade unions, the destruction of the left-wing press and political parties. Large numbers of working-class cadres were executed and many more put into concentration camps. The social domination of the big landlords was restored intact. Francoist economic policy consistently favoured the landed oligarchy, as was only to be expected. This identification with the traditional oligarchy is one reason why the Franco regime is often assumed not to have been fascist. It is not without irony therefore that the Franco dictatorship, inadvertently fulfilling the modernizing function associated with fascist regimes, was to preside over the eclipse of the landed oligarchy and the final triumph of the industrial oligarchy. The repressive labour relations of the regime led to an accumulation of capital; its rabid anti-communism led to American aid. The combination of the two, in the favourable context of the late 1950s, led to Spain's second, and definitive, industrial take-off. By the 1970s, the industrial élite came to regard the Franco regime as an irksome anachronism and thus were to be found coinciding with the democratic opposition in the quest for change. Reflection on the evolution of the Franco dictatorship and its relation to Spanish capitalism is clearly a dangerous occupation likely to lead to counter-factual speculation about the possible development of fascism and nazism had military defeat not intervened.

16

FASCISM IN CONTEMPORARY EUROPE

◆

Christopher Seton-Watson

In 1946 Alfred Rosenberg, soon after being condemned to death at Nuremberg, declared, 'Within fifteen years we will begin to be talked about again, and within twenty nazism will again be a force.' Undeniably there has been a revival of the extreme right in western Europe over the last thirty-five years. Given the starting point of 1945, it could hardly have been otherwise. It is less clear that there has been a significant revival of fascism. Indiscriminate use of the label 'fascist' in contemporary political controversy adds greatly to the difficulty of defining and identifying the true phenomenon.

It is first of all important to distinguish between what might be called the fascist hard core and the numerous parties and political groupings of the extreme right which have emerged in western Europe over the past thirty-five years.* The hard core is overtly fascist and consists mainly of survivors from the fascist era; it is small and has so far been of negligible political importance. The parties of the extreme right, though not overtly fascist, undeniably contain fascist elements. According to some observers, they are essentially fascist beneath their democratic camouflage; they constitute the mass of the fascist iceberg of which the hard core is the

* The present essay is limited to western Europe for evident reasons. However, Spain and Portugal have been excluded; Spain forms the object of a separate essay.

visible tip. As one of the most articulate of contemporary fascists, Maurice Bardèche, has written in his *Qu'est-ce que le fascisme?*:

> It is a strange phenomenon: the fascist writer, the fascist intellectual, are creatures not to be found; the regime which accepts the fascist label is non-existent .... On the other hand there are fascist groups, and they do not conceal it; there are young fascists, and they proclaim it; there are fascist officers, and men tremble at the discovery; finally there is a fascist spirit, and above all there are thousands of men who are fascist without knowing it. [1]

The preceding essays in this volume have attempted to define European fascism in the interwar years. They show that it was a complex and confusing phenomenon. That is no less true of European fascism today.

The hard core consists of conspiratorial, semi-clandestine extremists, gathering in small groups to indulge their nostalgic memories, occasionally resorting to small-scale violence. They are now past middle age and their efforts to recruit from the postwar generation have so far had limited success. Bardèche describes them in the first postwar years as 'these bands of lost soldiers who recognized each other in the murk of injustice and hatred ... nourishing themselves on duplicated propaganda sheets and singing the songs of Hitler's armies'. [2] They are survivors from the 'heroic' fascist age, who keep their faith alive by refusing to accept the verdict of history. As Giorgio Almirante, the present leader of the Italian neo-fascists, has put it, 'The fortune of arms was never the final judgement on statesmen, their ideals and philosophies.' Colin Jordan, the British National Socialist, expressed the same view, with characteristic aggressiveness, in 1962:

> If the creed was right before its military defeat, it is no less right since that defeat .... Christianity was no less unpopular seventeen years after the death of its founder than is national socialism today. Hitler was right; you can't kill national socialism.

Against such faith no rational arguments can prevail.

The fascist hard core keeps itself alive by continuous intellectual rebellion against the facts of the contemporary world. It rejects *in toto* the Europe of the postwar years, with its 'hypocritical and impotent democratic regimes', its 'propaganda of anti-fascism' and its myth of the heroic anti-fascist resistance. A major aim is the rehabilitation of the fallen fascist regimes, their leaders and their soldiers. Bardèche himself went to prison in 1948 for defending the memory of the 'victims of Nuremberg injustice'. For him, as for his fellow-believers, the accepted facts of Hitler's crimes are merely the fictions of 'atrocity campaigns'; the destruction of Dresden and Hiroshima surpassed anything that Hitler perpetrated, and the atrocities of the Russians rivalled those of the Germans.

These hard-core groups have their international contacts and they speak the same language across the frontiers. From time to time they meet and talk of common action to create a united fascist Europe. It is conceivable that, given another cataclysm on the 1914-18 scale, they could one day become as significant as the small groups of extremists who sowed the seeds of post-1918 fascism within the apparently stable society of pre-1914 Europe. Today their importance lies in the fact that most of their ideas and aspirations are to be found, in a less pathological and uninhibited form, among the parties of the extreme right.

Both Italy and Germany have provided examples of such parties since 1945. The first to appear was Uomo Qualunque (Party of the Common Man), which reached its peak early in 1946. From its right wing was born at the end of that year the Movimento Sociale Italiano (MSI). In Germany the Sozialistische Reichspartei (SRP) was founded in 1949 under ex-Nazi leadership and in 1951 polled 11 per cent of the votes in the *Land* election of Lower Saxony. Next year it was declared 'inimical to the constitution' and banned. Its successor, the Deutsche Reichspartei, merged in November 1964 in a new Nationaldemokratische Partei Deutschlands (NPD) which has survived till today. All these parties proclaimed themselves democratic and denied any intention of seizing power by unconstitutional means. They differed from the fascist hard core in assuming, to a greater or lesser degree, a respectable image, and in trying to adapt themselves to the political realities of the day. Their aim today is to recapture a mass following for the extreme right by exploitation of all discontents and resentments, and by continuous denigration of existing democratic governments and of the parties composing them. In the NPD at least half of the original executive committee were active members of the Nazi Party. The MSI similarly has among its leaders men who remained loyal to Mussolini even in the final phase of the Italian Social Republic of 1944-5, including Almirante himself. The MSI has declared that its policy is 'neither restoration nor renunciation', that it wishes to preserve only those aspects of fascism that are adaptable to contemporary conditions and capable of winning the support of the post-fascist generation. Its problem, like that of the NPD, is how to give sufficient satisfaction to the hard core without either inviting repression by the law, as did the SRP, or alienating the younger voters. Dissension over this question of tactics led in the spring of 1967 to a crisis in the NPD leadership, which ended in the victory of the radical von Thadden over the moderate Thielen. Similar conflicts have occurred within the MSI, and in 1976 a number of moderate leaders broke away to form a new party, Democrazia Nazionale (DN).

In France the pattern of revival of the extreme right has been less simple than in Germany or Italy. The French extreme right has more sources of inspiration than the German or Italian, and some of them have roots deep in the past. Action Française, Bonapartism and the Catholic counter-revolution all have their followers today. On to these national roots were grafted foreign fascist models between 1934 and 1945. The products were so hybrid that it is necessary to speak of French fascisms rather than fascism. The first chance of renewed life for the French extreme right, after the enforced silence that followed the liberation, came with the emergence of de Gaulle's Rassemblement du Peuple Français (RPF). This movement had acquired a membership of a million by 1948 and in 1951 won 120 seats in the National Assembly. Paradoxically, though its leader was the incarnation of resistance to Vichy and Hitler, RPF attracted by its denunciation of the 'system' of the Fourth Republic, its call for a strong state and its quasi-fascist style of organization and propaganda, many survivors of the prewar extreme right and many Vichy supporters. The RPF would have been fascist without de Gaulle, declared Bardèche. By 1953 the RPF had been abandoned by its founder and was close to disintegration. Its successor was Poujade's Union de Défense des Commerçants et Artisans (UDCA), which after polling two and a half million votes in the general election of 1956, went like its predecessor into decline. It was the Algerian crisis of 1954-8 that restored the power of the extreme right.

All its heterogeneous elements, Catholic reactionaries, Bonapartists, survivors of the Cagoule, admirers of the Vichy state, rallied to the defence of Algérie Française and plotted, sometimes in collaboration, more often in rivalry, to overthrow the detested 'system'. Amongst them were a few organizations that were overtly fascist. One, Jeune Nation, was founded in 1950 by the Sidos brothers, sons of a collaborator executed after the liberation. It stood for a popular authoritarian state, both national and social; it was virulently anti-semitic and used the Celtic cross as its emblem, to symbolize its aim 'to unite the very remote past of our people with the hope of a greater future'. [3] In 1954 Biaggi founded a Parti Patriotique Révolutionnaire which found widespread support among students and ex-servicemen, especially in Algiers, and claimed ten thousand members within three years. But the majority of the enemies of the Fourth Republic were not fascist. From the crisis of 1958 one section of the extreme right, the Gaullists, emerged triumphant, to become the establishment of the Fifth Republic. Many non-Gaullists accepted the Gaullist triumph. Others soon turned against de Gaulle, accusing him of betraying the Algerian cause and 'smothering the revolution'. A few plotted to overthrow the Fifth Republic as they had helped to overthrow the Fourth. De Gaulle destroyed them, partly through the trial and imprisonment of their leaders, but, more effectively, by the ballot box. The referendums and parliamentary elections of 1962 obliterated the supporters of Algérie Française, and since then the extreme right has been fragmented and impotent.

All these parties and movements attracted at least temporary fascist support. In most of their programmes and pronouncements traces of fascist ideas and phrases can be found. In a few of them fascists have played a leading role. The German and Italian parties clearly resemble their nazi and fascist predecessors in the rallies they stage, the demagogic oratory in which they indulge, and the undertone of violence implicit in their methods of organization. All contain some of what might be called the 'elements' of fascism. These elements have been identified in the preceding essays of this volume. Between the wars different fascist movements combined them in differing proportions, hence the different characteristics of particular national fascisms. No one element singly can constitute a fascist movement; fascism is the product of a fusion of several. Since 1945 no such fusion has taken place. Nevertheless all the same elements are present in contemporary Europe.

Five may usefully be distinguished: nationalism, racialism, militarism, anti-communism and anti-democracy (often with an anti-capitalist flavour). Nationalism is the basic component of fascism. Where national grievances are deeply felt, where patriotic sentiments have been exasperated or bruised, where irredentist aspirations flourish, there is fertile soil for fascism. It can feed also on imperialist nostalgia and the resentments of decolonization. Irredentism is most powerful in Germany. Ten million refugees from the east settled in western Germany after the war. In Schleswig-Holstein they at one time constituted 40 per cent of the population, in Lower Saxony 30 per cent, in Bavaria 20 per cent. Two-and-a-half million still belong to Landsmannschaften, each representing a different ex-German area, which publish periodicals, organize rallies and keep the old feelings of kinship alive. The Sudeten Germans from prewar Czechoslovakia are among the most active. In its prime, the NPD drew a significantly large proportion of its support from the areas where the refugees are most numerous. It called for a restoration of national dignity and an end to 'one-sided attempts to redeem the past by war crimes tribunals'. It is time, the party declares, to rehabilitate the German soldier and stop 'the glorification of treason' (i.e. of anti-nazism). The NPD appeals also to anti-American feelings by calling for a check to the Americanization of German culture and by pointing to the extravagance and alien ways of the foreign armies stationed on German soil. Germans are urged to stop feeling like 'moral pariahs' and to realize that 'once again we are somebody in the world'.

In Italy the MSI has made the same appeals for rehabilitation of the fascist past and restoration of the nation's dignity, combined with denigration of the resistance. In its early years it thrived on resentment at the harsh peace treaty of 1947 and on accusations against successive democratic governments of 'servility' to the foreigner. Italy also has its refugees from Istria and the eastern Adriatic, and repatriates from ex-Italian Africa: few in total numbers, but receptive to the nationalist appeal. While the fate of Trieste was still unsettled, a favourite theme of the extreme right was denunciation of the 'insidious Slavs' and their protectors in the foreign, especially British, forces of occupation. The MSI for long polled a significantly higher proportion of votes in Trieste than in the rest of Italy. After Trieste returned to Italy in 1954, Italian nationalists turned their attention to South Tyrol, where Austrian nationalists were exploiting the grievances of their compatriots south of the Brenner. Austrian fascists, with German fascist support, fought Italian fascists, and sporadic violence in the form of sabotage, terrorism and assassination persisted as late as 1972, when the Italian government at last conceded sufficient autonomy to pacify the German minority.

Algeria was the clearest example of all. The *colons* and *pieds noirs*, threatened by Muslim Algerian nationalism and in growing fear of a sell-out by democratic governments in Paris, steadily drifted into violence, with nationalist students and schoolboys leading the way. Racial frontiers create tension, fever and hysteria, and extremist movements find in them their natural habitat. And all too often, as happened in France, the nationalist fever spreads inwards from the periphery to the centre and infects the whole body politic.

Racialism in Europe between the wars took mainly the form of anti-semitism. Overt anti-semitism has been rarer since 1945, but it is by no means dead. Many countries have

seen sporadic outbursts of swastika-daubing, attacks on syna-
gogues and desecration of Jewish graves. These are favourite
activities for the bolder spirits of the hard core. There have
also been provocative marches through Jewish districts, in
the East End of London in 1949 and in the Rome 'Ghetto'
in 1962. Sir Oswald Mosley, the Italian neo-fascists, Bardèche
and many others have denied being anti-semitic. Nevertheless
the old spirit often breaks through. Many sections of the
European extreme right, for example, expressed their horror
at the trial and execution of Eichmann, and Poujadists and
leaders of the NPD frequently indulge in euphemistic denunciation of international bankers or the hidden power of
'parasitic, predatory super-capital'.

Contemporary racialism, however, tends to take an anti-
coloured rather than an anti-semitic form. Britain provides
the clearest example in the National Front, founded in 1967,
which enjoyed its first period of significant growth in 1972
with the influx of Ugandan Asians. In Germany the NPD has
delighted in denigrating 'dirty, indisciplined, criminal' foreign
workers (of whom there are a million from southern Europe,
the Middle East and North Africa in West Germany today),
in insisting on priority in employment for Germans and in
warning of the danger of contamination of the German race.
Algerian immigrants have aroused similar reactions in France.
The chairman of NPD, von Thadden, once extolled Ian Smith
as 'the guardian of peace and freedom', and admiration for
South African apartheid is not confined to the fascist hard
core. Xenophobia is a general feature of NPD pronouncements, which call for an end to wasteful spending of public
funds on foreigners, whether in the form of reparations to
Israel or of overseas development aid.

Militarism in the past has often been the precursor of
fascism. The function performed by members of the
Freikorps in Germany in the 1920s, or the Arditi in Italy, or
the veterans of the Croat Guards Regiments of the Habsburg
Army in Yugoslavia, are well known. It has been said of Sir
Oswald Mosley that his approach to politics in the 1920s was
that of the ex-serviceman. There are still many ex-servicemen,
though ageing, in Europe today. In Germany they are loosely
united in the Verband Deutscher Soldaten, in whose activities

heroic commanders from the last war have played an important role. Rehabilitation of the German soldier and welfare of
the ex-serviceman are their main (and legitimate) aims. The
most interesting is Hilfsorganisation auf Gegenseitigheit der
Waffen-SS (HIAG), the veterans' organization of the SS,
which has international connections. It certainly played a
part in August 1977 in assisting the escape of the SS General
Kappler, perpetrator of one of the worst wartime atrocities,
from an Italian military hospital, and in providing him with a
hero's welcome in his Bavarian home town. Two hard-core
organizations, Nation Europa and Jeune Europe, are led by
ex-SS men and make it their business to keep the SS legionaries of all Europe in touch and summon them from time to
time for reunions. In Italy a naval war hero, Prince Valerio
Borghese, who remained faithful to Mussolini to the end,
played a leading part in the neo-fascist movement and even
attempted a *coup d'état*, which ended in farce, in December
1970. The MSI has made deliberate appeals to the spirit and
pride of the crack divisions of the Italian army and to the
veterans (*i ragazzi*) of the western desert and Alamein. The
NPD's equally deliberate appeal has had some success with
serving soldiers of the Bundeswehr. In France veterans of
Indo-China, often active in ex-service associations, played a
key role in the Algerian insurrections of 1958-61.

The psychology of élite or shock troops has much in
common with that of fascism. Arditi, SS, French paratroopers or foreign *légionnaires* share many characteristics:
the cult of the superman, of the hero and death, the mysticism of sacrifice, the sense of being people apart from the
common herd, the abnormal emphasis on *esprit de corps*
and *camaraderie*, the devotion to commanders whose exploits
become legendary, the contempt for the plodding infantry-
man or the office-bound staff officer, for the conscript or the
conventional civilian. All these traits were found in interwar
fascist movements at their most youthful and militant stage.
Contemporary fascists are well aware of this. Colin Jordan
said in 1962, 'The SS man is our model.' [4]

All the leading military rebels of Algeria had served in
Indo-China and been moulded by that traumatic experience.
They returned to France in 1954 with the conviction that

their defeat had been political, not military; that the nation had abandoned them in a distant land and the democratic politicians had stabbed them in the back. Their experience over the next four years in Algeria, where they believed they were fighting the next round of the third world war against the universal enemy, communism, completed their sense of alienation from the parliamentary Fourth Republic, and led them to identify themselves with the cause of Algérie Française, where beat the heart of 'true' France. Fighting in Algeria strengthened their conviction that strong purposeful government was essential to victory, and that war must be total, fought in the minds of civilians as much as on the ground, against the internal as much as the external enemy. Such beliefs drew them into a political position that was close to fascism. When the politicians once again seemed on the point of selling out in 1958, they stood by and watched while the *colons* seized power in Algiers. It was in great part the army that canalized the insurrection into Gaullist channels. But de Gaulle, too, failed to satisfy the extremists. When he showed that he was prepared to compromise with the 'system' and with the old degenerate France, a few officers and élite regiments staged a military insurrection in April 1961. It was the paratroopers and Foreign Legion which provided the force on that occasion; the conscripts of the ordinary regiments remained passive and declined to follow the rebels' lead. The failure of the insurrection drove the irreconcilables of the Organisation Armée Secrete (OAS) into nihilistic terrorism, which made them the heroes of the fascist hard core throughout Europe.

Anti-communism also is a basic component of fascism. All fascists demand, if not the suppression, at least the isolation and harassment of communist parties. Their anti-communism often extends to socialists. On this point the parties of the extreme right share the hard core's views. In Italy they attack the ruling Christian Democratic Party for allying itself with the socialists (and in 1976-9 even with the communists) rather than leaning upon the 'healthy' forces of the right. In Germany the attitude of NPD to the 'grand coalition' of christian democrats and social democrats between 1966 and 1969 was identical.

Anti-communism links up in Germany with irredentism. The NPD's proclaimed goal is to liberate East Germany from communism and roll the iron curtain back. But such sentiments are not confined to Germany. One of the most striking aspects of the extreme right in Europe since 1945 has been the new emphasis on European unity, on 'nationalism within a greater Europe'. The idea of the 'new order' has perhaps been Hitler's most lasting legacy. It is a favourite theme of the hard core. The very names of its publications and organizations show this: *Jeune Europe*, *Europe-Action*, *Nation Europa*, Occident, Ordine Nuovo and Ordre Nouveau, and a very recent arrival, Fédération d'Action Nationale Européenne (FANE).

In 1962 Mosley, von Thadden, Jean Thiriart, the Belgian fascist, and others met at Venice to found a 'National Party of Europe'. In 1978 Almirante was host to a meeting of kindred spirits in Sicily to launch the programme of a European right (Eurodestra) in anticipation of the 1979 elections to the European parliament. The title of Bardèche's periodical was *Défense de l'Occident*. In his words, 'only its [fascism's] mission of the Defence of the West has remained in the memory, and this is still the chief meaning of the fascist idea.' [5] The MSI talks of 'Europe from Brest to Bucharest', the NPD of 'Germany first, then Europe; Germany for the Germans, Europe for the Europeans'. 'Neither Moscow nor Washington' is the ideal of both the hard core and the NPD; a regenerate and truly independent Europe which will constitute a third force in the world. 'History will prove that the idea of a united Europe originated with the Waffen-SS volunteers', declared a high official of HIAG at an SS reunion in Germany in 1965. Not long before Biaggi had declared, 'The paratroopers will create the real Europe.' [6] On the basis of European unity the anti-communists, the racialists, the nationalists and the militarists can find common ground.

The fifth element of fascism, anti-democracy, is the least precise. It can take several forms. In its simplest and commonest it is merely a yearning for strong government and a state above parties and factions, a deep contempt for parliamentary government and a passion for order and discipline.

A second variety may be loosely labelled 'Poujadism'. Its detractors called Poujade's UDCA a 'grocers' party'. Poujade himself, when he founded it in 1953, was a humble stationer from St Céré in south-west France. Starting with a flamboyant refusal to pay his taxes, and skilfully exploiting his personal demagogic talent, he built up a mass movement composed predominantly of small shopkeepers, peasants and artisans. Its greatest strength lay in the economically declining south and south-west (unlike the RPF which appealed primarily to the modern and dynamic sectors of the French economy). Its programme was almost entirely negative; against the supermarkets, against the bankers, against big business, against privilege and élites of all kinds and, in political terms, against parliament and the democratic parties, especially of the left. It was the party of that section of the middle class that earned its living from obsolescent businesses and farms, and felt itself threatened by the pace of modernization. It shared the traditional French radical fear of *les gros*, which included the trade unions and the organized working class. Closely associated with it was a peasant defence movement under Vichyite leadership. In its use of strong-armed thugs and rowdyism at political meetings it imitated its predecessor, the RPF. Middle-aged grocers do not by themselves constitute a fascist movement; they are more concerned with order and stability than with revolution. Nevertheless in times of crisis, especially in times of weak democratic government, they can find common ground with fascists and with other sections of the extreme right with more positive programmes. The Poujadists gladly joined in exploiting the 'scandals' and corruption of the Fourth Republic, and added their voice for strong government, the restoration of national greatness and a halt to decolonization. The anti-semitic and xenophobic note was clearly evident in their pronouncements, and the movement had its contacts with the Algerian *colons*. Some of Poujade's lieutenants (e.g. Ortiz and Lefèvre) played an active part in the insurrection of 1958. The most prominent leader of the extreme right today, Le Pen, started his political career as a Poujadist deputy in 1956.

The other striking example of a Poujadist movement was

Uomo Qualunque, which for a brief moment in 1945-6 captured the support and votes of the small men of Italy, together with the nostalgic and the defeated in the civil war of 1943-5. UQ's main strength lay in the south, the most backward region economically. The MSI has drawn its support from much the same sectors of the population. In Germany, too, NPD has shown that it has Poujadist elements. In its party programme it calls for a struggle against the corrupting aspects of the affluent society. Indeed there is a provincial puritanical side to Poujadism: in France, as in Italy and in Germany, the extreme right protests against the degeneracy and 'public licentiousness' of cosmopolitan Paris or Rome or Bonn. Over half the NPD's supporters are small and medium-sized businessmen and farmers, living often in areas that were old nazi strongholds. It wins votes in small and medium-sized towns rather than in large cities. Like the Poujadists and MSI, it is from the backward regions that it draws its main strength.

The second variation of anti-democracy (also with an anti-capitalist flavour) is corporativism: an even less precise concept than Poujadism, but one that, for all its nebulousness, has had a persistent appeal for fascists and the near-fascist extreme right. The corporatists dream of an 'organic' or 'national-social' state, within which capital and labour, family, profession and local community will be harmoniously integrated in the 'superior interests of the nation'. Such ideas were current in Algiers both before and after the coup of 1958. Bardèche writes of 'socialism' as the ideal, with capital and labour joined in one *fascio*. Mussolini, he declares, died of caesarism, having abandoned the original fascist ideal. Similarly, the MSI corporatists led by Almirante hark back to the 'origins' of 1919, as elaborated in the eighteen points of Mussolini's radical Verona Manifesto of 1944. True corporativism, says Bardèche, will be Europe's third force between capitalism and marxism.

Nationalism, racialism, militarism, anti-communism, anti-democracy: none of these are fascist in origin nor exclusively fascist today. Neither the fascist hard core nor the parties of the extreme right have a monopoly of aspirations to roll back the iron curtain, or build a united Europe, or restore national dignity, or establish strong government, or create an 'organic' state, or secure justice for ex-servicemen, shop-keepers or refugees. The five elements considered above do nevertheless form the bare bones of fascism. What has been lacking in Europe since 1945 has been the breath to give the bare bones life. Fascism between the wars thrived on passions more than on ideas; it threw up charismatic leaders of great power, it recruited massive paramilitary formations and gloried in physical violence, it captured the idealism of youth and persuaded millions in many countries that it had the answer to the world's problems.

Since the second war nothing similar has occurred. Even the constitutional parties of the extreme right have had a very limited appeal. In the French presidential election of 1965 the candidate of the extreme right, Tixier-Vignancour, ex-junior minister under Vichy and legal defender of the OAS rebels, attracted 4.4 per cent of the votes, mostly from the south where the Algerian *pieds noirs* had settled. In the 1974 presidential election, Le Pen, leader of the Front National (founded in 1972), won only 0.75 per cent, and his rival, Royer, champion of the small shopkeepers in the Poujadist tradition, only 3.3. In the parliamentary elections of March 1978 the combined vote of the extreme right (including the Front National and the more moderate Parti des Forces Nouvelles) amounted to only 0.9 per cent. In Germany the NDP reached its peak in April 1968 when it won 9.8 per cent of the votes in the *Land* of Baden-Württemberg. Since then it has declined steadily and has never succeeded in obtaining the minimum of 5 per cent required for representation in the federal parliament. In the federal election of October 1976 its vote fell to 0.6 per cent (exactly the same as the National Front in the British general election of May 1979). Italy is the exception. The MSI has been in decline since 1972, but in the elections of June 1979 it won almost 2 million votes (5.3 per cent) and returned thirty deputies, despite the competition of the breakaway DN, which returned none. It claims a membership of over 200,000, with an affiliated trade union association and active youth and student organizations. Almirante's party has become the model to which Le Pen and von Thadden look with envy.

In France a fascist hard core survives, but few outside its ranks regard it as other than a pathological relic of a previous age. Only in Algeria between 1954 and 1961 has anything that could remotely be called fascism won mass support, and even it met disaster when it failed to move metropolitan France. OAS died with Algérie Française, and since 1962 the *pieds noirs* have mostly reconciled themselves to the Fifth Republic. Jeune Nation was suppressed in May 1958 and its successor, Occident, founded by one of the Sidos brothers, in November 1968. The events of May 1968 brought a certain revival of the extreme right, in reaction against the extreme left, which it challenged in the streets and in the universities. But de Gaulle's successors have been as ruthless with the extreme right as de Gaulle himself. Ordre Nouveau, founded in 1969, was suppressed in 1973. None of these groups attracted more than a few thousand members, though at moments of political tension they were able to stage aggressive demonstrations and draw substantial audiences to their meetings. The fact that the hard core took to terrorism in the 1970s is a measure of its political failure. In 1979-80 FANE achieved notoriety by a series of bombings, and its close links with right-wing Italian terrorism have been revealed. It was dissolved by the French government on 3 September 1980. According to a recent estimate there are about 25,000 neo-fascists in France. They are much fragmented and presumably closely watched.

In Germany the hard core has been even more insignificant and there has been no terrorism of the right. A measure of the failure of the extreme right to achieve its aims has been the continuing stability of German democracy, the successful integration of the refugees, and the lack of effective opposition to the social democrats' *Ostpolitik*, which it prefers to call *Verzichtpolitik*, the policy of surrender.

Italy is the exception. Right-wing terrorism started in December 1969 with the explosion of a bomb in Piazza Fontana in Milan, killing sixteen persons. Shootings and bombings continued over the next five years. The aim of the perpetrators of this so-called 'strategy of tension' was to engender mass fear and to provoke police and government into increasingly repressive measures, in the calculation that this would undermine democracy and create favourable conditions for an authoritarian regime.

The organization mainly responsible for this campaign of terror was Ordine Nuovo, founded in 1956 by a young MSI militant, Pino Rauti. In 1973 it was suppressed and its leaders put on trial; but this did not prevent Rauti from being elected to parliament in 1972 and again in 1976, and becoming a potential rival to Almirante for the leadership of MSI. The ambiguous relations between the MSI and terrorism resemble those between Sinn Féin and the IRA. Almirante repeatedly condemns violence, yet Ordine Nuovo unquestionably recruited, and its successor still recruits, its members from the youth sections of the party. After 1974 right-wing terrorism was overshadowed by that of the extreme left. But in 1978 a new terrorist group was formed, Nuclei Armati Rivoluzionari. It was they who claimed the credit for the bomb which exploded in Bologna station in August 1980, killing over eighty persons.

Yet not even in Italy, and still less in France or Germany, can the extreme right be said to pose a threat comparable to that of the interwar years. How is this to be explained? In the 1950s and 1960s economic growth and affluence seemed to provide the answer. The historical connection between mass unemployment and the rise of fascism has long been recognized. In 1963 Mosley attributed Hitler's success to 'the great unemployment following the great inflation'. A year later he asked himself, 'What are our chances?', and replied, 'None until the crisis.' Some commentators explained the rise of NPD in 1966-8, and the expansion of MSI in 1968-72, by the ending of the German and Italian 'economic miracles'. Yet the present 'crisis' of inflation, recession and high unemployment has not so far strengthened the extreme right. This is doubtless due in part to the greater efficiency of 'welfare' states in dealing with the social consequences of unemployment. But it would seem that economic crisis alone is insufficient to create the conditions for fascism, and that an element of political crisis is necessary.

Three interrelated antidotes to fascism suggest themselves: political stability, strong administration and an effective conservative party. France has enjoyed political stability since

1958, Germany since 1949. In the last months of the Fourth Republic the French administration showed signs of disintegration, but its loyalty and efficiency were rapidly restored after 1958. The efficiency of the German administration has never been in question. In Germany since 1969 the christian democratic parties have moved right in opposition, leaving little ground for the extreme right to occupy. In France since 1958 first the Gaullist parties, and now Chirac's Rassemblement pour la République, have performed the same function.

Italy again is the exception. In one sense Italy has enjoyed greater political stability than either France or Germany, in that one party, the Christian Democratic, has exercised hegemony continuously since 1947. Nor has Italy experienced any equivalent of France's 1958 or 1968, nor of Germany's *Machtwesel* of 1969. But the Italian Christian Democratic Party prides itself on not being a conservative party. Some of its leaders have for brief periods tried to make it so, notably in 1960 and in 1972, by wooing the MSI; but the party remains, in De Gasperi's phrase, 'a party of the centre leaning left'. It therefore leaves a field for exploitation by the extreme right. Furthermore, Italy notoriously lacks an efficient administration. The weakness of the police and intelligence services, and the sympathies (and collusion) of some of their leaders with the extreme right, is not the least cause of the persistence of neo-fascist terrorism today. More generally, some observers fear that the present paralysis of the political system (*immobilismo*) may be generating a loss of faith in democracy comparable to that of 1918-22.

Many authoritative writers on fascism, notably Renzo De Felice, Ernest Nolte and Walter Laqueur, have defined fascism as a phenomenon confined to a single period of history, depending on conditions which will not recur. This perhaps seems less certain today than twenty, or even ten, years ago. One essential condition for a resurgence of fascism must be its conquest of youth. Most of the 'hard-core' survivors of interwar fascism will soon disappear. Will its heritage be taken up by post-fascist generations? It is significant that most of the terrorists of the extreme right (as of the extreme left) are very young. On the fringes of the MSI there are gangs which indulge in violence imitative of the *squadristi* of 1920-2, and give themselves names such as 'knights of war' or 'sons of Odin' or 'Aryan fraternity'. There are similar groups in other European countries. The rituals and mystique of fascism seem to give some of those for whom fascism is history a form of fulfilment and excitement which they do not find elsewhere in contemporary European society.

'Fascism', wrote Bardèche, 'is impossible to define outside periods of crisis .... Where there is no occasion for heroism, it perishes .... It is the party of the nation in wrath: that wrath is indispensable to fascism. It is the very blood that irrigates fascism.' [7] Prolonged economic crisis and an inability of democratic government to deal with it; a heightened fear of communism, external or internal; a sense of national impotence or humiliation; and a charismatic leader: perhaps a combination of these, fortunately improbable, might recreate the conditions for fascist resurgence.

References

1 M. Bardèche, *Qu'est ce que le fascisme?*, Paris, 1961, 12.
2 ibid., 98-9.
3 J. Plumyène and R. Lasierra, *Les Fascismes Français 1923-63*, Paris, 1964, 201.
4 A. Del Boca and M. Giovana, *Fascism Today*, London, 1970, 262.
5 Bardèche, op. cit., 88.
6 Del Boca and Giovana, op. cit., 288.
7 Bardèche, op. cit., 93-4.

CHRONOLOGICAL TABLES

◆

Italy

1919	23 March	Foundation of the first *fascio di combattimento* at Milan.
	12 September	D'Annunzio's occupation of Fiume.
1922	28 October	'March on Rome'.
1923	23 July	Electoral law passed, guaranteeing two-thirds of seats to party with relative majority.
1924	6 April	Elections.
	10 June	Matteotti kidnapped and murdered.
1925	3 January	Mussolini's acceptance of responsibility for all past fascist actions.
	2 October	Palazzo Vidoni pact between the industrialists' association (Confindustria) and the fascist syndicates.
	24 December	Law extending powers of the head of the government, giving him full executive responsibility.
1926	31 January	Decrees given the power of laws.
	3 April	Right to strike abolished; collective contracts reserved to the fascist syndicates.
	25 November	Law for the defence of the state; creation of a special tribunal for political crimes.
1927	15 January	Churchill's visit to Mussolini.
	21 December	Exchange rate fixed at 'quota 90' (L.92.45 to £1).
1929	11 February	Lateran pacts, including the Concordat.
1932	30 October	*Decennale* celebrations.
1933	23 January	Creation of IRI.
1934	14 June	Meeting of Mussolini and Hitler at Venice.
	10 November	Council of Corporations inaugurated at Rome.

1935	5 October	Invasion of Abyssinia.
1936	October	Rome-Berlin 'Axis'.
1938	14 July	Publication of the *Manifesto della Razza*; first anti-semitic measures.
1939	19 January	Creation of the Camera dei Fasci e delle Corporazioni, replacing parliament.
	7 April	Invasion of Albania.
	22 May	Pact of Steel signed.
1940	10 June	Italy enters the second world war.
1943	25 July	Grand Council of Fascism votes Mussolini out of power.
	8 September	Armistice declared; nazis take over the country.
	23 September	Mussolini announces the creation of the fascist social republic (Republic of Salò) over Munich radio.
1945	28 April	Mussolini executed by partisans at Dongo.

Germany

1889	20 April	Hitler born in Braunau in Austria. Educated in Linz. Moves to Vienna.
1918	7-8 November	Bavarian monarchy overthrown.
	9 November	German Kaiser abdicates; Germany becomes a republic.
1919	5 January	Drexler founds 'German Workers' Party' in Munich.
	28 June	Treaty of Versailles signed.
	12 September	Hitler attends his first meeting of the German Workers' Party.
1920	24 February	Hitler — now a leading speaker in the German Workers' Party — reads out its new programme. The party also becomes known as the National Socialist German Workers' Party (NSDAP or Nazis).
	13 March	Kapp *putsch* in Berlin. New right-wing government in Bavaria.
1923	10-11 January	Germany declared to have defaulted on reparations payments. French and Belgian troops occupy the Ruhr. German currency, already badly inflated, collapses completely. Germans answer with passive resistance in the Ruhr.
	26 September	Stresemann, the German Chancellor, announces end of passive resistance. State of emergency declared in Bavaria.
1923	8-9 November	Hitler's first bid for power in the abortive Munich *putsch*. Nazi Party dissolved by order.
1924	1 April	Hitler sentenced to five years' fortress arrest.
	20 December	Hitler released under general amnesty.

1925	27 February	Nazi Party refounded.
1929	7 June	Young plan fixing German reparations payments announced in Paris.
	3 October	Stresemann dies.
1930	14 September	German elections return 107 nazi deputies to Reichstag in Berlin.
1932	10 April	Election of Reich President sees Hitler beaten by Hindenburg but obtaining 13,417,460 votes.
	31 July	General election: 230 nazi deputies elected.
	6 November	New general election; nazis lose votes and fall in numbers to 196 members of Reichstag.
1933	30 January	Hitler appointed Chancellor of Germany.
	28 February	Decree for the Protection of the People and the State, suspending guarantees of individual rights and giving government the power to make arbitrary arrests.
	5 March	General election gives nazis 288 seats and 43.9 per cent of vote.
	23 March	Enabling law giving Hitler the right to govern by decree.
	2 May	Trade unions abolished.
	14 July	Germany a one-party state.
	14 October	Germany leaves the League of Nations.
1934	30 January	German State (i.e. *Länder*) parliaments abolished.
	29-30 June	Purge of the SA. Röhm and others murdered.
1935	16 March	Germany announces compulsory military service.
	15 September	Nuremberg laws discriminating against Jews.
1936	7 March	Hitler occupies demilitarized zone in the Rhineland.
	17 June	Himmler appointed chief of police forces in the Reich.
	September	Hitler proclaims four-year plan.
	October	Rome-Berlin collaboration agreement.
	23 November	German-Japanese anti-comintern agreement signed.
1938	12 March	German invasion of Austria.
	30 September	Munich agreement over partition of Czechoslovakia.
1939	14 March	Germans seize Prague.
	23 August	Nazi-Soviet Pact signed.
	1 September	Germany invades Poland.
1940	10 May	German invasion of France and Low Countries.
	June	Fall of France.
1941	22 June	Germany invades Soviet Russia.
	Summer	Decision to begin mass extermination of Jews.
	11 December	Germany declares war on USA.

1945   30 April   Hitler commits suicide in Berlin.

Austria

1918	12 November	Republic of Austria proclaimed.
1919	10 September	Treaty of St Germain accepted by parliament.
1920	10 October	Klagenfurt plebiscite; southern Carinthia, claimed by Yugoslavia, remains Austrian.
1921	14-16 December	Odenburg (Sopron) plebiscite; capital of Burgenland (transferred to Austria) remains Hungarian.
1927	15 July	Armed clashes in Vienna between police and socialist demonstrators; 89 killed.
1929	7 December	Austrian constitution revised.
1930	18 May	'Korneuburg Oath' of Heimwehr movement.
	September	Starhemberg elected leader of Heimwehr; joins cabinet.
	9 November	Last general election; Social Democrats strongest single party (42 per cent of total vote).
1931	March	Customs union with Germany projected.
	13 September	Heimwehr *putsch* under Pfrimer.
1932	24 April	Last provincial elections; nazi vote increases.
1933	4 March	Parliament suspended by Dollfuss.
	26 May	Austrian Communist Party banned.
	19 June	Austrian NSDAP banned.
	11 September	Dollfuss proclaims authoritarian state.
1934	12 February	Heimwehr and government forces attack socialists; Social Democratic Party, trade unions, etc., banned.
	17 March	'Rome Protocols' on co-operation and consultation between Italy, Hungary and Austria signed.
	25 July	Dollfuss killed in nazi *putsch*, succeeded by Schuschnigg.
1936	20 March	'Rome Protocols' reaffirmed.
	14 May	Starhemberg dropped from Government.
	11 July	'July Agreement' between Austria and Germany.
1938	11-13 March	Schuschnigg resigns under German pressure, succeeded by Seyss-Inquart; *Anschluss* proclaimed.

Hungary

1918	31 October	Democratic revolution. Independence Party, Radicals, and Social Democrats form coalition government under Mihály Károlyi.
1919	21 March	Coalition of Communists and Left Social

		Democrats proclaims 'Hungarian Councils' Republic' — Bela Kun's dictatorship emerges.
	29 May	Nationalist anti-revolutionary government formed in Szeged.
	1 August	Communist-Socialist government resigns. Trade union leaders form government.
	3 August	Rumanian army enters Budapest.
	7 August	Right-wing rising replaces trade unionist government. I. Friedrich Prime Minister.
	19 August	Szeged government resigns and joins forces with I. Friedrich.
	16 November	Rumanian troops evacuate Budapest. Adml Horthy and 'National Army' enter capital of Hungary.
	23 November	K. Huszár forms coalition government.
	5 December	Decree on internments legalizes 'white terror'.
1920	25 January	Elections for national assembly.
	17 February	Two editors of a social democratic daily murdered.
	1 March	Adml Horthy elected Regent by national assembly.
	4 June	Hungarian treaty of peace signed at Trianon Palace, Versailles.
	19 July	Count Paul Teleki nominated Prime Minister.
1921	26 March	Charles IV's first attempt to regain Hungarian throne fails.
	13 April	Count Paul Teleki resigns. Count István Bethlen new Prime Minister.
	20 October	King Charles's second attempt fails.
1922	2 February	Prime Minister Bethlen forms 'united' government party.
	2 March	Secret ballot in rural constituencies abolished.
	May-June	General elections produce big majority for government party.
1923	May	Count Bethlen starts negotiations on international loan.
	2 August	Captain Gömbös leaves government party and forms 'Racialist Party'.
1924	May-July	Hungary under League of Nations financial control obtains stabilization loans. Reconstruction law adopted by parliament.
1926	11 November	Law re-establishes upper house of parliament.
	December	General elections. Racialist Party defeated.
1927	2 April	Italo-Hungarian friendship pact signed in Rome.
1928	6 September	G. Gömbös rejoins government party.
1929	September-October	Strikes and demonstrations of unemployed workers — G. Gömbös Minister of Defence.

1930	15 May	League of Nations control of Hungarian finances terminated.
1931	June-July	General elections. Bethlen victorious.
	14 July	Financial crisis.
	19 August	Regent accepts Count Bethlen's resignation — Count Gyula Károlyi Prime Minister; 'austerity' programme.
1932	1 October	Gyula Gömbös replaces G. Károlyi as Prime Minister.
1933	17 July	Gömbös visits Hitler in Berlin.
1934	17 March	Mussolini, Gömbös and Dollfuss conclude 'Rome Protocols'.
1935	March-April	General elections managed by Gömbös. Bethlen resigns from government party.
1936	23 March	Second Rome Protocol signed.
	6 October	Death of Gömbös in Munich — K. Darányi Prime Minister.
1937	1 July	Law on extension of the powers of the Regent.
1938	5 March	Speech of Darányi in Györ announcing measures against Jews and economic (rearmament) plans.
	13 May	Darányi replaced by B. Imrédy as Prime Minister.
	22 August	Horthy visits Hitler — F. Szálasi condemned to three years in prison.
	2 November	First Vienna award redrafts Hungarian-Slovakian frontier.
1939	13 January	Hungary signs Anti-Comintern Pact.
	12 February	B. Imrédy forced to resign. Count Paul Teleki Prime Minister.
	15 March	Hungarian army occupies the Carpatho-Ukraine.
	11 April	Hungary withdraws from League of Nations.
	5 May	Promulgation of the so-called 'second Jewish law'.
	29 May	General election produces strong national socialist opposition group.
1940	30 August	Second Vienna award allots north-east Transylvania to Hungary.
	20 November	Hungary adheres to the Three-Power Pact.
	12 December	Hungary and Yugoslavia sign friendship treaty.
1941	3 April	Suicide of Count P. Teleki. L. Bárdossy Prime Minister. German troops cross Hungarian territory for attack on Yugoslavia.
	12 April	Hungarian army enters the Bachka (Vojvodina).
	27 June	Hungary declares war on the Soviet Union.
	6 December	Great Britain declares war on Hungary.
	13 December	Hungary at war with the USA.
1942	January	Massacre of civilians in the Bachka by army and gendarmerie units.

	7 March	Bárdossy dismissed by Horthy; Miklós Kállay Prime Minister.
1943	January	Second Hungarian Army destroyed at Voronezh (Soviet Russia).
	September	Secret armistice negotiations between Hungary and Great Britain.
1944	18 March	German army invades and occupies Hungary. Gestapo begins arrest of anti-German politicians.
	22 March	Hitler imposes D. Sztójay as Prime Minister on Horthy.
	May	Mass deportations of Jews begin.
	July	Horthy stops deportations; reorganizes government.
	29 August	Horthy dismisses Sztójay; Gen. Lakatos Prime Minister. All political parties to suspend their activities.
	15 October	Horthy announces armistice with Soviet Russia — German troops move on Budapest.
	16 October	Horthy arrested by Germans. F. Szálasy forms government.
	20 December	Anti-German left-wing coalition government formed in Soviet-occupied Debrecen. Siege of Budapest begins. (Siege ends 11 February 1945.)

Rumania

1919	Corneliu Zelia Codreanu becomes a student at the University of Jassy where he meets the nationalistic demagogue Professor A.J. Cuza.
1920-3	C.Z. Codreanu initiates and takes part in nationalistic student movements in all four Rumanian universities.
1923	C.Z. Codreanu and A.J. Cuza form together a political party, 'The League of the National Christian Defence', which in 1926 wins six seats in the Rumanian parliament.
1927	The foundation of the Legion of the Archangel Michael, which is the political organ of the Iron Guard movement and the first independent political party led by Codreanu.
1932	The Legion wins five seats in parliament. Its first dissolution as a political party.
1937	The Legion, under the name of 'All for the Fatherland', wins sixty seats in parliament representing more than 16 per cent of the electorate.

1938	The Legion is dissolved again and in 1939, the year of martyrdom, more than 1200 Legionaries, including Codreanu, are exterminated.
1940-1	The surviving elements of the Iron Guard under the leadership of Horia Sima join the coalition government headed by General Antonescu. As a result of the abortive *putsch* of January 1941 they are eliminated from the government, and the leadership is decimated.

Poland

1918	Resurrection of independent Polish state.
1920	Russo-Polish War.
1921-6	Parliamentary government.
1926	Pilsudski seizes power.
1935	Pilsudski dies.
1939	German invasion.

Finland

1917	December	Finland declares independence.
1918	January	Socialists attempt to seize power. Civil war follows.
	May	Victory of the Whites, followed by severe repression of the Reds.
	August	Foundation of Finnish Communist Party with programme of renewed revolution.
1919		Establishment of parliamentary republic.
1920		Peace treaty of Tartu with Soviet Russia.
1921-2	Winter	Defeat of final attempt by Finnish activists to invade Soviet Karelia.
1928		Communist-led dock strike. Beginning of economic depression.
1929	Autumn	Lapua movement launched.
1930	March	Attack on communist press at Vaasa, increasing Lapua violence.
	June-July	Formation of Svinhufvud government under Lapua pressure. Diet fails to pass anti-communist laws. Communist deputies arrested. Diet dissolved.
	August	Peasant march on Helsinki.
	October	General election: two-thirds majority to right. Communist Party suppressed.
1931		Svinhufvud elected President of the republic with Lapua support. As return to legality demanded, Lapua plans *coup d'état*.
1932	February	Mäntsälä revolt suppressed. Lapua movement

		transformed into IKL.
1933		General election: IKL wins 14 seats out of 200. IKL modelling itself increasingly on foreign fascist parties.
1936		General election: IKL holds its seats. Victory for Agrarian-Social Democratic alliance.
1938		Legal proceedings against IKL with view to suppression.
1939		High Court refuses to suppress IKL, but at election representation cut to eight.
	November	War with Russia.
1941	January	IKL enters coalition government.
	June	Finland joins attack on Soviet Russia.
1944	September	Armistice with USSR: one condition that fascist organizations be suppressed. IKL dissolved.

Norway

1919-21		Labour Party adheres to Comintern. Major strikes.
1920, 1925		Establishment of strike-breaking and anti-marxist organizations.
1928		Nineteen-day minority Labour government.
1931-3		Agrarian Party in office, with Quisling as Minister of Defence.
1933-7		Successive electoral failures of Quisling's 'National Unity' movement.
1935-40		Labour Party in power, supported by Agrarians: solid majority.
1940	9-15 April	German invasion, enabling Quisling to seize temporary power as self-proclaimed premier.
	25 September	Quisling ministers placed in office provisionally by German authorities.
1942	1 February	Quisling installed as Minister-President under German Reichscommissar.
1945	24 October	Quisling executed for high treason.

Denmark

1914-18		Denmark remains neutral in war.
1920	March-April	Constitutional 'Easter Crisis' consolidates parliamentary democracy.
	July	North Schleswig (South Jutland) returned to Denmark after plebiscite.
1924-40		Social Democrats dominant government party.
1930	November	Danmarks National Socialistiske Arbejder Parti formed. Leader Cay Lembcke.
1932	November	DNSAP takes part in elections in South Jutland.

		Result: 1 per cent of South Jutland votes.
1933	July	Frits Clausen takes over as leader of DNSAP.
1935	October	Elections — DNSAP participates in the whole country. Result: 1 per cent of votes.
1939	April	Elections — DNSAP results: 1.8 per cent of votes.
1940	April	Denmark occupied by Germany.
1940-3		Coalition government of 'the big four' parties, cutting across political colours.
1940	September	Germans hold out hopes to DNSAP of coup 17 Nov.
	November	DNSAP's expected takeover of power fails to happen. Instead, DNSAP demonstrators are scattered and thrashed by the Copenhagen populace.
1941	July	'Free Corps Denmark' is formed (Danes doing military front service for Germans). DNSAP acts as recruiting agency.
1942	March	DNSAP is the subject of the 'petrol allowance scandal', increasing resentment of German favouritism of the party.
	September	'Free Corps Denmark' is home on leave from the East Front as a propaganda exercise, but achieves the opposite of the desired effect.
1943	March	Elections — DNSAP results: 2.1 per cent of votes. Considered a big defeat in view of the party's expectations and the extent of German support.
	August	State of emergency declared as a result of popular resistance and strikes. The Danish government resigns.
1943-5		'Caretaker' executive government.
1943	October	Pogrom against Danish Jews. Most escape to Sweden after prior warning.
		Frits Clausen effectively replaced as leader of DNSAP.
1944	May	Frits Clausen formally resigns from leadership of DNSAP.
	August	Eleventh-hour DNSAP propaganda offensive.
1945	May	Germans in Denmark capitulate.

Great Britain

1896	Oswald Mosley born.
1918-24	Coalition Unionist and Independent MP for Harrow.
1924	Mosley joins the Labour Party.
1925	Great Britain returns to the gold standard.

		Mosley writes *Revolution by Reason*.
1926	December	Mosley returns to parliament as Labour MP for Smethwick.
1927		Mosley elected to the National Executive of the Labour Party.
1929	7 June	Mosley made Chancellor of the Duchy of Lancaster in MacDonald's Labour government.
1930	23 January	Mosley Memorandum sent to MacDonald.
	21 May	Mosley resigns as Chancellor of the Duchy.
1931	February	Mosley forms the New Party.
	30 April	Ashton-under-Lyme by-election.
	24 August	MacDonald forms the National government.
	27 October	New Party wiped out at the general election, Mosley losing at Stoke-on-Trent.
1932	1 October	Mosley forms the British Union of Fascists.
1934	8 January	The *Daily Mail*'s 'Hurrah for the Blackshirts'.
	7 June	Disorders at the Olympia Stadium.
	July	Break with Rothermere.
	28 October	Mosley attacks the Jews at the Albert Hall.
1936	4 October	Battle of Cable Street.
	December	Public Order Act.
1937	6 March	Municipal Elections: BUF win 23 per cent of votes in Bethnal Green North East, 16 per cent in Limehouse, 14 per cent in Shoreditch.
	March	Financial retrenchment; Joyce and Beckett leave BUF to form National Socialist League.
	4 October	March through Bermondsey, South London.
1939	16 July	Peace rally at Earls Court Stadium.
1940	23 May	BUF disbanded; Mosley interned under Regulation 18B.
1980	3 December	Death of Mosley.

Belgium

1922		Foundation of the Légion Nationale.
1930		L. Degrelle editor of Rex publications.
1931		J. Van Severen founds Verdinaso.
1932		Degrelle launches the weekly *Rex*.
1933	February	Alongside *Rex* the political weekly *Vlan* is started.
	October	Foundation of VNV.
1934	March	Merger of *Rex* and *Vlan*.
1935	2 November	Courtrai incident.
	11 November	Mass Rex meeting at the Sports Palace, Brussels.
	20 November	The Church moves away from Rex.
1936	21 February	The Catholic party breaks with Rex.
	3 May	The Rexist daily, *Le Pays Réel*, begins publication.

	8 May	Lawsuit won by P. Segers against Degrelle for defamation.
	24 May	General elections: Rex, 11.4 per cent of votes; VNV, 7.1 per cent.
	8 October	Rex-VNV agreement.
1937	6 January	Degrelle speech broadcast by Turin radio.
	9 February	Interview with P.-H. Spaak on 'national social-ism' published in *L'Indépendance Belge*.
	9 April	Church condemns Rex.
	11 April	By-election at Brussels: P. Van Zeeland, 76 per cent of votes; L. Degrelle, 19 per cent.
	June	VNV first suspends agreement with Rex.
1939	April	General elections: VNV, 8.2 per cent of votes; Rex, 4.4 per cent.
1940	28 May	Surrender of Belgian army.
	9 June	S. De Clercq places the '30,000 members' of VNV 'at the service of the Reich'.
1941	5 January	Degrelle at Liège: 'Hitler has saved Europe, and for this reason Rexists have the courage to shout: Heil Hitler!'.
1944	September	Liberation of Brussels and Antwerp.

France

1918	11 November	Armistice with Germany.
1919	16 November	Elections to the Chamber of Deputies resulting in the victory of the right-wing Bloc National.
1924	11 May	Elections to the Chamber of Deputies resulting in the victory of the left-wing Cartel des Gauches.
1925	11 November	Foundation of Le Faisceau by Georges Valois.
1926	23 July	Raymond Poincaré forms right-wing government.
1928	22-9 April	Elections to the Chamber of Deputies resulting in the victory of the right.
1932	1-8 May	Elections to the Chamber of Deputies resulting in the victory of the left.
1934	6 February	Right-wing riot in Paris; government of Edouard Daladier resigns next day.
	27 July	Signature of 'unity of action' pact between the Socialist and Communist parties marks first major step towards formation of the Popular Front.
1935	14 July	Big Popular Front demonstration in Paris; Croix de Feu counter-demonstration.
1936	26 April-3 May	Elections to the Chamber of Deputies resulting in the victory of the left-wing Popular Front.
	18 June	Popular Front government dissolves leagues.

	28 June	Jacques Doriot founds PPF at 'the rendez-vous of Saint-Denis'.
1938	9 April	Edouard Daladier forms government which marks effective end of the Popular Front.
	30 September	Munich Agreement.
	30 November	Government breaks general strike.
1939	3 September	Outbreak of second world war.
1940	10 May	German attack in the west.
	22 June	Armistice with Germany.
	10 July	National Assembly meeting at Vichy rescinds constitution of the Third Republic and votes full powers to Marshal Pétain.
1941	1 February	Marcel Déat founds RNP.
	4 October	Promulgation of the 'Labour Charter'.
1942	11 November	Germans invade unoccupied zone of France.
1943	30 January	Formation of the Milice.
	4 December	German ultimatum to Marshal Pétain as a result of which Marcel Déat and Joseph Darnand enter the government.
1944	6 June	Allies invade Normandy.
	15 August	Allies invade southern France.
	20 August	Germans forcibly evacuate Vichy government to Belfort.
	26 August	General de Gaulle arrives in Paris.
	7 September	Germans forcibly evacuate Vichy government to Germany.
	9 September	Formation of 'French governmental committee for the defence of national interests', including Déat and Darnand.
1945	6 January	'French liberation committee' formed by Doriot.
	22 February	Death of Doriot.
	7 May	Unconditional surrender of Germany.

Spain

1892	4 December	Birth of Francisco Franco Bahamonde in El Ferrol.
1898		Defeat of Spain by USA. Loss of Cuba, Puerto Rico and Philippines.
1923	13 September	Military coup by General Primo de Rivera.
1930	30 January	Primo replaced by General Berenguer.
1931	14 March	Foundation of *La Conquista del Estado* by Ramiro Ledesma Ramos.
	14 April	Departure of Alfonso XIII and foundation of Second Republic.
	26 April	Foundation of Acción Popular.
	10 October	Foundation of Juntas de Ofensiva Nacional

		Sindicalista by Onésimo Redondo and Ramiro Ledesma Ramos.
	15 December	Foundation of *Acción Española*.
1933	28 February	Acción Popular unites with other rightist groups to form CEDA.
	1 March	*Acción Española* creates political front organization, Renovación Española.
	29 October	José Antonio Primo de Rivera launches Falange Española.
	19 November	José Antonio elected deputy for Cádiz.
1934	11 February	Falange merges with JONS to become FE de las JONS.
	6 October	General strike, rising in Asturias, Catalonia briefly declared independent.
1936	16 February	Popular Front wins elections.
	14 March	FE de las JONS outlawed and its leadership, including José Antonio, arrested.
	18 July	Military uprising. Civil war starts.
	20 November	Execution in Alicante of José Antonio Primo de Rivera.
1937	19 April	Franco unites Falange, Carlists and other rightist groups into FET y de las JONS and suppresses the radical Falangists under Hedilla.
1939	1 April	End of civil war.
1940	13 June	Spain abandons neutrality and adopts non-belligerency.
	14 June	Spain occupies Tangiers.
	17 September	Ramón Serrano Súñer visits Hitler.
	1 October	Ramón Serrano Súñer visits Mussolini.
	19 October	Himmler visits Madrid and inaugurates collaboration of Gestapo in reorganization of Francoist police.
	23 October	Hitler meets Franco at Hendaye.
1941	12 February	Franco meets Mussolini at Bordighera.
	14 February	Discussions between Franco and Pétain at Montpellier.
	25 November	Serrano Súñer visits Berlin and renews Anti-Comintern Pact.
1942	3 September	Serrano Súñer dismissed as Foreign Minister.
1943	3 October	Spain abandons non-belligerency and readopts neutrality.
1944	28 January	Franco refuses to stop wolfram deliveries to Germany.
1945	11 September	Fascist salute no longer obligatory.
	18 September	Spanish withdrawal from Tangiers.
1946	13 December	UNO recommends withdrawal of ambassadors from Madrid.
1947	1 April	Franco's Succession Law defines Spain as a

		kingdom.
1950	4 November	UNO approves possible Spanish membership of international organizations.
1953	27 August	Concordat with Vatican.
	26 September	Pact of Madrid with USA provides for bases in Spain.
1955	8 December	Spain accepted into UNO.
1956	February	Student troubles mark major reverse for Falange.
1957	25 February	Opus Dei technocrats enter government.
1962	March-May	Strike wave in Asturias, Basque country and Catalonia.
1963	20 April	Execution of communist Julián Grimau.
	28 December	Introduction of 1st Development Plan.
1970	3-28 December	Burgos trials of Basque revolutionaries of ETA.
1971	19 October	Arrest of national leadership of clandestine Workers' Commissions.
1973	8 June	Admiral Carrero Blanco made head of government.
	20 December	Carrero Blanco assassinated by ETA.
	29 December	Carlos Arias Navarro made premier and promises reform of system. Workers' Commissions leaders sentenced to 12-20 years jail.
1974	2 March	Execution of anarchist Salvador Puig Antich.
	9 July	Franco falls seriously ill.
1975	21 September	Execution of five ETA and FRAP militants.
	20 November	Death of Franco.
1977	15 June	First democratic elections since 1936.

BIBLIOGRAPHY

✦

General

Allardyce, G. (ed.) *The Place of Fascism in European History* (Englewood Cliffs, 1971).

Carsten, F. *The Rise of Fascism* (London, 1967).

—— 'Critiques of fascism theory from the West German New Left', *International Journal of Politics*, 2:4 (1972-3).

Del Boca, A. and Giovana, M. *Fascism Today* (London, 1970).

Gregor, A.J. (ed.) *Interpretations of Fascism* (Morristown, 1974).

Hayes, P.M. *Fascism* (London, 1973).

Hurst, M. 'What is fascism?', *Historical Journal*, 11 (1968).

'International fascism', *Journal of Contemporary History*, 1:1 (1966).

Kedward, H.R. *Fascism in Western Europe 1900-1945* (Glasgow and London, 1969).

Kitchen, M. *Fascism* (London, 1976).

Kuehnl, R. *Former bürgerliche Herrschaft — Liberalismus — Faschismus* (Reinbeck, 1971).

Lackó, M. 'Le fascisme — Les fascismes en Europe Centrale-Orientale', *XIII International Congress of Historical Sciences* (Moscow, 1970).

Laqueur, W. (ed.) *Fascism: A Reader's Guide* (London, 1979).

Larsen, S.U., Hagtvet, B. and Myklebust, J.P. (eds) *Who Were the Fascists? Social Roots of European Fascism* (Bergen, 1980).

Linz, J.J. and Stepan, A. (eds) *The Breakdown of Democratic Regimes: Europe* (Baltimore, 1976).

Lubasz, H. *Fascism: Three Major Regimes* (New York, 1973).

Nolte, E. *Three Faces of Fascism* (London, 1965).

—— *Theorien über den Faschismus* (Cologne, 1967).

Poulantzas, N. *Fascism and Dictatorship* (London, 1974).

Rogger, H. and Weber, E. (eds) *The European Right* (Berkeley, 1966).

Sauer, W. 'National socialism: totalitarianism or fascism?', *American*

Historical Review, 73 (1967).

'Theories of fascism', *Journal of Contemporary History*, 11:4 (1976).

Turner, H.A. (ed.) *Reappraisals of Fascism* (New York, 1975).

Vajda, M. 'On fascism', *Telos*, 8 (1971).

Weber, E. *Varieties of Fascism* (Princeton, 1964).

Woolf, S.J. (ed.) *The Nature of Fascism* (London, 1968).

Italy

The bibliography on Italian fascism is vast and continues to grow. The earliest analyses were contemporary to the expansion of fascism as a mass movement, before and immediately after the seizure of power. Among the most valuable of these pamphlets are:

Gobetti, P. *Scritti politici* (Turin, 1960).

Salvatorelli, L. *Nazionalfascismo* (Turin, 1923).

Vinciguerra, M. *Il fascismo visto da un solitario* (Florence, 1963).

During the years of the fascist regime and after its fall, writings on fascism tended to concentrate on two main themes — how fascism had come to power, and biographies of Mussolini. The most important contemporary works, still of great value, are:

Gramsci, A. *La costruzione del partito comunista 1923-1926* (Turin, 1971).

'Rossi, A.' (pseudonym of Tasca, A.), *The Rise of Italian Fascism* (London, 1938).

Salvemini, G. *The Origins of Fascism in Italy* (New York and London, 1973).

Since the war, the origins of fascism have been studied exhaustively, by analyses of the political and economic weaknesses of the liberal state, the development of the fascist movement, and regional case studies:

Apih, E. *Italia, fascismo e antifascismo nella Venezia Giulia 1918-1943* (Bari, 1966).

Colarizi, S. *Dopoguerra e fascismo in Puglia (1919-1926)* (Bari, 1971).

Corner, P. *Fascism in Ferrara, 1915-1925* (Oxford, 1974).

Lyttelton, A. 'Fascism, the second wave', *Journal of Contemporary History*, 1:1 (1966).

—— *The Seizure of Power* (London, 1973).

Sechi, S. *Dopoguerra e Fascismo in Sardegna* (Turin, 1971).

Snowden, F. 'On the social origins of agrarian fascism in Italy', *European Journal of Sociology*, 13:2 (1972).

The most important biography of Mussolini (also a history of the party), which has so far reached 1936, is:

De Felice, R. *Mussolini il rivoluzionario, 1883-1920*; *Mussolini il fascista*: I. *La conquista del potere, 1921-1925*; II. *L'organizzazione dello stato fascista, 1925-1929*; *Mussolini il duce*: I. *Gli anni del consenso, 1929-1936* (4 vols, Turin, 1965-74).

For the English reader, a little about Mussolini's personality can be gained in:
Fermi, L. *Mussolini* (Chicago, 1961).
Megaro, G. *Mussolini in the Making* (London, 1938).

Useful general works on Italian fascism are:
Carocci, G. *Italian Fascism* (Harmondsworth, 1973).
Cassels, A. *Fascist Italy* (London, 1969).
Chabod, F. *A History of Italian Fascism* (London, 1963).
Tannenbaum, E.R. *The Fascist Experience: Italian Society and Culture 1922-1945* (New York, 1972).

Detailed factual information can be found in:
Salvatorelli, L. and Mira, G. *Storia d'Italia nel periodo fascista* (Turin, 1966).
Santarelli, E. *Storia del regime fascista* (3 vols, Rome, 1973).

Important contemporary works, respectively from an anti-fascist and fascist point of view, are:
Salvemini, G. *The Fascist Dictatorship in Italy* (London, 1928).
Volpe, G. *Storia del movimento fascista* (Milan, 1939).

Among the more useful works published in recent years on the regime are:
Aquarone, A. *L'organizzazione dello stato totalitario* (Turin, 1965).
—— and Vernassa, M. (eds) *Il regime fascista* (Bologna, 1974).
Cordova, F. (ed.) *Uomini e volti del fascismo* (Rome, 1980).
Diggins, J.P. *Mussolini and Fascism: The View from America* (Princeton, 1972).
Fornari, H. *Mussolini's Gadfly: Roberto Farinacci* (Nashville, 1971).
Lyttelton, A. *Italian Fascisms: From Pareto to Gentile* (London, 1973).
Masella, L. 'Mezzogiorno e fascismo', *Studi Storici*, 20:4 (1979).
Palla, M. *Firenze nel regime fascista (1929-1934)* (Florence, 1978).
Quazza, G. (ed.) *Fascismo e società italiana* (Turin, 1973).
Togliatti, P. *Lezioni sul fascismo* (Rome, 1970).
—— *La Toscana nel regime fascista 1922-1939* (2 vols, Florence, 1971).
Tranfaglia, N. (ed.) *Fascismo e capitalismo* (Milan, 1976).
Ungari, P. *Alfredo Rocco e l'ideologia giuridica del fascismo* (Brescia, 1963).

On the economy, syndicalism and corporativism:
Aquarone, A. 'Italy, the crisis and corporative economy', *Journal of Contemporary History*, 4:4 (1969).
Cassese, S. 'Corporazioni e intervento pubblico nell'economia', *Quaderni Storici* (1968).
Ciocca, P. and Toniolo, G. (eds) *L'economia italiana nel periodo fascista* (Bologna, 1976).

Cordova, F. *Le origini dei sindacati fascisti (1918-1926)* (Bari, 1974).

Corner, P. 'Fascist agrarian policy and the Italian economy in the inter-war years', in Davis, J.A. (ed.) *Gramsci and Italy's Passive Revolution* (London, 1979).

Mori, G. 'Per una storia dell'industria italiana durante il fascismo', *Studi Storici*, 12 (1971).

Passerini, L. 'Work ideology and consensus under Italian fascism', *History Workshop Journal*, 8 (1979).

Salvemini, G. *Under the Axe of Fascism* (London, 1936).

Sapelli, G. 'Per la storia del sindacalismo fascista: tra controllo sociale e conflitto di classe', *Studi Storici*, 19:3 (1978).

Sarti, R. *Fascism and the Industrial Leadership in Italy, 1919-1940* (Berkeley, 1971).

—— 'Mussolini and the Italian industrial leadership in the battle of the Lira, 1925-1927', *Past and Present*, 47 (1969).

On specific aspects:

Binchy, D.A. *Church and State in Fascist Italy* (Oxford, 1970).

Cannistraro, P.V. 'Mussolini's cultural revolution', *Journal of Contemporary History*, 7:3/4 (1972).

—— 'The radio in fascist Italy', *Journal of European Studies* (1972).

Isnenghi, M. *L'educazione dell'Italiano: Il fascismo e l'organizzazione della cultura* (Bologna, 1979).

Ledeen, M.A. *Universal Fascism: The Theory and Practice of the Fascist International, 1928-1936* (New York, 1972).

Webster, R.A. *The Cross and the Fasces: Christian Democracy and Fascism in Italy* (Stanford, 1960).

On foreign policy:

Carocci, G. *La politica estera dell'Italia fascista (1925-1928)* (Bari, 1969).

Cassels, A. *Mussolini's Early Diplomacy* (Princeton, 1970).

Deakin, F.W. *The Brutal Friendship: Mussolini, Hitler and the Fall of Italian Fascism* (London, 1962).

Di Nolfo, E. *Mussolini e la politica estera italiana (1919-1933)* (Padua, 1960).

Mack Smith, D. *Mussolini's Roman Empire* (New York, 1976).

Michaelis, M. *Mussolini and the Jews* (Oxford, 1978).

Salvemini, G. *Prelude to World War II* (London, 1953).

Germany

Allen, W.S. *The Nazi Seizure of Power: The Experience of a Single German Town, 1930-1935* (London, 1966).

Bracher, K.D. *Die Auflösung der Weimarer Republik* (Villingen, 1964).

—— *The German Dictatorship: The Origins, Structure and Effects of National Socialism* (London, 1971).

—— 'The role of Hitler: perspectives and interpretation' in W.

Laqueur (ed.) *Fascism: A Reader's Guide* (London, 1979).
———, Sauer, W. and Schulz, G. *Die Nationalsozialistische Machtergreifung* (Cologne and Opladen, 1960).
Broszat, M. *Der Nationalsozialismus* (Stuttgart, 1961).
——— *Der Staat Hitlers Grundlegung und Entwicklung seiner inneren Verfassung* (Munich, 1969).
Buchheim, H. *Das Dritte Reich* (Munich, 1958).
Bullock, A. *Hitler, a Study in Tyranny* (2nd edn, London, 1962).
Carr, W. *Arms, Autarchy and Aggression: A Study in German Foreign Policy, 1933-1939* (London, 1972).
——— *Hitler, A Study in Personality and Politics* (London, 1978).
——— 'National Socialism — foreign policy and Wehrmacht' in W. Laqueur (ed.) *Fascism: A Reader's Guide* (London, 1979).
Franz-Willing, G. *Die Hitlerbewegung: Der Ursprung, 1919-1922* (Hamburg, 1962).
Funke, M. (ed.) *Hitler, Deutschland und die Mächte, Materialien zur Aussenpolitik des Dritten Reiches* (Düsseldorf, 1977).
Horn, W. *Führerideologie und Parteiorganisation in der NSDAP, 1919-1933* (Düsseldorf, 1972).
Jäckel, E. *Hitlers Weltanschauung: Entwurf einer Herrschaft* (Tübingen, 1969).
Krausnick, H., Buchheim, H., Broszat, M. and Jacobsen, H-A. *Anatomy of the SS State* (New York and London, 1968).
Maser, W. *Die Fruhgeschichte der NSDAP* (Frankfurt-am-Main, 1965).
Mason, T.W. *Arbeiterklasse und Volksgemeinschaft: Dokumente und Materialien zur deutschen Arbeiterpolitik, 1936-1939* (Opladen, 1975).
——— 'The legacy of 1918 for National Socialism' in A. Nicholls and E. Matthias (eds) *German Democracy and the Triumph of Hitler* (London, 1971).
——— 'The primacy of politics — politics and economics in National Socialist Germany' in S.J. Woolf (ed.) *The Nature of Fascism* (London, 1968).
Mommsen, H. 'National Socialism — continuity and change' in W. Laqueur (ed.) *Fascism: A Reader's Guide* (London, 1979).
Mosse, G.L. *The Crisis of German Ideology* (London, 1966).
Neumann, F. *Behemoth: The Structure and Practice of National Socialism* (New York, 1944).
Noakes, J. and Pridham, G. *Documents on Nazism, 1919-1945* (London, 1974).
Nolte, E. *Three Faces of Fascism* (London, 1965).
Nyomarkay, J. *Charisma and Factionalism in the Nazi Party* (Minneapolis, 1967).
Peterson, E.N. *The Limits of Hitler's Power* (Princeton, 1969).
Pulzer, P.G.J. *The Rise of Political Anti-Semitism in Germany and Austria* (New York, 1964).
Schoenbaum, D. *Hitler's Social Revolution: Class and Status in Nazi Germany, 1933-1939* (New York, 1966).

Schweizer, A.A. *Big Business in the Third Reich* (Indiana, 1964).

The Third Reich. Published under the auspices of the International Council for Philosophy and Humanistic Studies and with the assistance of UNESCO (London, 1955).

Tyrrel, A. *Vom 'Trommler' zum 'Führer'. Der Wandel von Hitlers Selbstverständnis zwischen 1919 und 1924 und die Entwicklung der NSDAP* (Munich, 1975).

Zeman, Z.A.B. *Nazi Propaganda* (London, 1964).

For more comprehensive bibliographical information on the history of national socialism the reader is referred to the catalogues issued by the Wiener Library in London and to the bibliographies published in the *Vierteljahrshefte für Zeitgeschichte* in Munich. A valuable survey of the historiography on nazism is: P. Aycoberry, *La Question Nazie* (Paris, 1979, with an English translation published by Methuen, forthcoming).

Austria

Ardelt, Rudolf G. *Zwischen Demokratie und Faschismus* (Vienna, 1972).

Bärnthaler, Irmgard *Die Vaterlandische Front* (Vienna, 1971).

Botz, Gerhard *Gewalt in der Politik* (Munich, 1976).

Carsten, F.L. *Revolution in Central Europe, 1918-1919* (London, 1972).

—— *Fascist Movements in Austria: from Schönerer to Hitler* (London, 1977).

Documents on German Foreign Policy, series C (1933-1937) vol. V (London, 1966).

Fellner, Fritz 'The background of Austrian fascism' in P.F. Sugar (ed.) *Native Fascisms in the Successor States, 1918-1945* (Santa Barbara, 1971).

Gulick, Charles A. *Austria from Habsburg to Hitler* (Berkeley, 1948).

Heimatschutz in Österreich (Vienna, 1935).

Hofmann, J. *Der Pfrimer-Putsch* (Graz, 1965).

Jagschitz, Gerhard *Der Putsch* (Graz, 1976).

Jedlicka, L. 'The Austrian Heimwehr', *Journal of Contemporary History*, 1:1 (1966).

—— 'Zur Vorgeschichte des Korneuburger Eides', *Österreich in Geschichte und Literatur* (April, 1963).

Kerekes, L. 'Die "weisse Allianz" ', *Österreichische Osthefte*, 7:5 (1965).

—— *Abenddämmerung einer Demokratie: Mussolini, Gömbös und die Heimwehr* (Vienna, 1966).

Lochner, L. (ed.) *The Goebbels Diaries* (London, 1948).

Mosse, G.L. 'The genesis of fascism', *Journal of Contemporary History*, 1:1 (1966).

Neubacher, H. *Sonderauftrag Südost 1940-45* (Göttingen, 1956).

Nolte, E. *Three Faces of Fascism* (London, 1965).

Pelinka, Anton *Stand oder Klasse* (Wien, 1972).

Picker, H. *Hitler's Table Talk* (London, 1952).

Pulzer, P.G.J. *The Rise of Political Antisemitism in Germany and Austria* (New York, 1964).

Rape, Ludger *Die österreichischen Heimwehren und die bayerische Rechte* (Wien, 1977).

Schilling, A. *Dr Walter Riehl und die Geschichte des Nationalsozialismus* (Leipzig, 1933).

Seton-Watson, H. 'Fascism, right and left', *Journal of Contemporary History*, 1:1 (1966).

Stadler, K.R. *Austria* (Nations of the Modern World Series) (London, 1971).

—— *The Birth of the Austrian Republic, 1918-1921* (Leiden, 1966).

Starhemberg, E.R. *Between Hitler and Mussolini* (London, 1942).

Sweet, P.R. 'Mussolini and Dollfuss, an episode in fascist diplomacy' in J. Braunthal, *The Tragedy of Austria* (London, 1948).

Wandruszka, W. 'Österreichs politische Struktur' in H. Benedikt, *Geschichte der Republik Österreich* (Vienna, 1954).

Whiteside, Andrew G. *Austrian National Socialism before 1918* (The Hague, 1962).

—— *The Socialism of Fools* (Berkeley, 1975).

Hungary

Barany, G. 'The dragon's teeth: the roots of Hungarian fascism', in P.F. Sugar (ed.) *Native Fascism in the Successor States, 1918-1945* (Santa Barbara, 1971).

Bibó, I. *A Harmadik Út* (The Third Way — Essays in History and Politics), introd. by Z. Szabó (London, 1960).

Darvas, J. *Város az Ingoványon* (The City on the Swamp) (Budapest, 1945).

Deák, I. 'Hungary' in H. Rogger and E. Weber (eds) *The European Right* (Berkeley, 1966).

Horthy, H. *Memoirs* (London, 1965).

Ignotus, P. 'Radical writers in Hungary,' *Journal of Contemporary History* 1:2 (1966).

Kállay, N. *Hungarian Premier* (New York, 1954).

Károlyi, M. *Memoirs* (London, 1956).

Lackó, M. *Arrow Cross Men: National Socialists, 1935-1944* (Budapest, 1969).

—— 'The social roots of Hungarian fascism: the Arrow Cross', in S.U. Larsen, B. Hagtvet and J.P. Myklebust (eds) *Who Were the Fascists? Social Roots of European Fascism* (Bergen, 1980).

Lévai, J. *Black Book on the Martyrdom of Hungarian Jewry*, Zürich (Hungarian edition: Budapest, 1946).

—— *L'Eglise ne s'est pas tuée — Dossier Hongrois, 1940-1945* (Paris, 1966).

Macartney, C.A. *October Fifteenth — A History of Modern Hungary, 1929-1945* (2 vols, 2nd edn, Edinburgh 1961).

—— and Palmer, A.W. *Independent Eastern Europe — A History* (London, 1962).

Nemes, D. *Az Ellenforradalom Története Magyarországon, 1919-1921* (History of the Counter-revolution in Hungary) (Budapest, 1962). An implicit but devastating criticism of this sort of 'simpliste' historiography can be found in T. Pethö's essay 'A király nêlküli királyság és a tenger nélküli tengernagy korszaka' (The epoch of the kingdom without a king and of the admiral without a sea — Characteristic traits of the ruling class of the Horthy epoch), published in the *Magyar Hirek Kincses Kalendáriuma* (Budapest, 1966) pp. 87-98.

Ránki, G. 'The fascist vote in Budapest in 1939', in S.V. Larsen, B. Hagtvet and J.P. Myklebust (eds) *Who Were the Fascists? Social Roots of European Fascism* (Bergen, 1980).

—— 'The problem of fascism in Hungary', in P.F. Sugar (ed.) *Native Fascism in the Successor States, 1918-1945* (Santa Barbara, 1971).

Seton-Watson, H. *Eastern Europe between the Wars* (Cambridge, 1946).

—— *The East European Revolution* (London, 1950).

Sulyok, D. *A Magyar Tragédia* (The Hungarian Tragedy) (Newark, 1954).

Szabó, A. and Pamlényi, E. (eds) *A határban a halál kaszál.... Fejezetek Prónay Pál feljegyzéseiböl* (Death scything nearby .... Chapters from the notes of Pál Prónay). With an intr. study by the editors (Budapest, 1963).

Szinai, M. and Szücs, L. (eds) *The Confidential Papers of Admiral Horthy* (Budapest, 1965). See especially the following documents:

No. 15. Minutes of the first cabinet meeting convened during the Gömbös administration.

No.16. Draft letter of M. Horthy to PM G. Gömbös ... on race protection (1933).

No. 30. Memorandum of Count I. Bethlen *et al.* to M. Horthy on the policy of the Imrédy government.

No. 35. Letter of PM Paul Teleki to M. Horthy on his controversy with the Chief of Staff (1 Sept. 1940) — see also Appendix no. 1.

No. 39a. Farewell letter of PM Teleki to M. Horthy before his suicide (3 April 1941).

No. 40. Letter of M. Horthy to A. Hitler on the suicide of Paul Teleki and the military measures taken ... by Hungary against Jugoslavia (3 April 1941).

No. 52. Memorandum of the MPs of the National Socialist Party, Federation of Hungarian Renewal, to M. Horthy on the policy of the Kállay administration. Signed by B. Imrédy, L. Baky and 31 other MPs (5 May 1943).

No. 62. Rescript of M. Horthy to PM D. Sztójay on the 'mitigation of certain exaggerations' in the 'solution' of the Jewish problem and on the dismissal of L. Baky and L. Endre (early June 1944?).

No. 64. Memorandum of Count I. Bethlen on the necessity of dismissing the Sztójay administration (end of June 1944).

Rumania

Barbu, Z. 'Psycho-historical and sociological perspectives to the Iron Guard, the fascist movement of Rumania', in S.U. Larsen, B. Hagtvet and J.P. Myklebust (eds) *Who Were the Fascists? Social Roots of European Fascism* (Bergen, 1980).

Codreanu, C.Z. *Pentru Legionari* (For the Legionari) (Bucharest, 1936).

Fischer-Galati, S. 'Fascism in Rumania', in P.F. Sugar (ed.) *Native Fascism in the Successor States, 1918-1945* (Santa Barbara, 1971).

Motsa, L. *Cranii de Lemn* (Wooden Skulls) (Sibiu, 1936).

Papanace, C. *Martiri Legionari* (Rome, 1952).

Patrascanu, L. *Sous Trois Dictatures* (Paris, 1946).

Prost, H. *Destin de la Roumanie* (Paris, 1954).

Roberts, H. *Rumania* (New Haven, 1951).

Turkzynski, E. 'The background of Rumanian fascism', in P.F. Sugar (ed.) *Native Fascism in the Successor States, 1918-1945* (Santa Barbara, 1971).

Weber, E. 'The men of the Archangel,' *Journal of Contemporary History*, 1:1 (1966).

—— 'Rumania' in H. Rogger and E. Weber (eds) *The European Right* (Berkeley, 1966).

Poland

No objective analysis of Polish politics between the wars and its social background exists. This is not a topic on which one can truthfully write in present-day Poland, while the exiled writers view the recent past with a romantic nostalgia, and are anxious to avoid mentioning anything which might throw a bad light on the country, as if an entire nation could be judged by the behaviour of its politicians, or as if one could not find plenty of disreputable deeds in every country's history. Anyway, a sociological analysis of this picturesque society and culture – full of extraordinary contrasts and contradictions – remains to be done.

A competent account of the framework of events can be found in:

Roos, Hans *A History of Modern Poland* (London and New York, 1966), where further bibliography is given.

Wereszycki, H. and Wandycz, P.S., essays on Polish fascism in P.F. Sugar (ed.) *Native Fascism in the Successor States, 1918-1945* (Santa Barbara, 1971).

Although it deals only in part with Poland, Hugh Seton-Watson, *Eastern Europe Between the Wars* (Cambridge, 1946) offers the best general account of the interplay between its economy, social structure and politics. An analysis of the causes of anti-semitism, which explains a number of points made in the present article, can be found in S. Andreski

Elements of Comparative Sociology (London, 1964) ch. 21.

Finland

Most of the writings on this subject are in Finnish or Swedish, and they are cited in a review article by J. Kalela, 'Right-wing radicalism in Finland during the interwar period', *Scandinavian Journal of History*, 1 (1976). The principal contributions in English are as follows:

Alapuro, R. 'Mass support for fascism in Finland', in S.U. Larsen, B. Hagtvet and J.P. Myklebust (eds) *Who Were the Fascists? Social Roots of European Fascism* (Bergen, 1980).

—— and Allardt, E. 'The Lapua movement 1930-1932' in J.J. Linz and A. Stepan (eds) *Crises and Breakdowns of Competitive Democratic Regimes: Comparative Studies* (New Haven, 1978).

Rintala, M. *Three Generations: The Extreme Right-Wing in Finnish Politics* (Bloomington, 1962).

—— 'The peoples' patriotic movement', *Journal of Central European Affairs*, XXI, 1961.

—— 'Finland' in H. Rogger and E. Weber (eds) *The European Right* (Berkeley, 1966).

Norway

Information about Norwegian fascism is widely scattered and mainly in the Norwegian language. Reference may however be made to the bibliography and reference notes in:

Derry, T.K. *A History of Modern Norway, 1814-1972* (Oxford, 1973).

'Fascism and National Socialism in the Nordic countries', in S.U. Larsen, B. Hagtvet and J.P. Myklebust (eds) *Who Were the Fascists? Social Roots of European Fascism* (Bergen, 1980).

Denmark

Little has been written on Danish nazism, and almost all of the printed material is in Danish. Unpublished but available from the British Lending Library's Monograph Division is Malene Djursaa's Ph.D. thesis: *Danish Nazism: The Membership of 'Danmarks National Socialistiske Arbejder Parti' 1930-1945*. A Danish translation of this, with English conclusions, is scheduled for publication by Gyldendal, Copenhagen in 1981, with the title *DNSAP – danske nazister 1930-1945* (DNSAP – Danish Nazis 1930-1945). Henning Poulsen's thesis *Besaettelsesmagten og de danske nazister* (The Occupying Power and the Danish Nazis) (Copenhagen, 1970) includes a summary in German.

Written in the preparatory stages of Malene Djursaa's thesis was the article 'Who were the Danish nazis? A methodological report on an ongoing project', in Reinhard Mann (ed.) *Die National-sozialisten – Analysen fascistischer Bewegungen* (Stuttgart, 1980).

Finally S. U. Larsen, B. Hagtvet and J.P. Myklebust (eds) *Who Were the Fascists? Social Roots of European Fascism* (Bergen, 1980), includes an article by Henning Poulsen and Malene Djursaa, 'Social basis of nazism in Denmark'.

Great Britain

Benewick, Robert *Political Violence and Public Order* (London, 1969).

Cross, Colin *The Fascists in Britain* (London, 1961).

Holmes, Colin *Anti-Semitism and British Society, 1876-1939* (London, 1979).

Jacobs, Joe *Out of the Ghetto* (London, 1978).

Lebzelter, Gisela *Political Anti-Semitism in Britain, 1918-1939* (London, 1978).

Lunn, K. and Thurlow, R. (eds) *British Fascism* (London, 1980).

Mandle, W.F. *Anti-Semitism and the British Union of Fascists* (London, 1968).

Mosley, Oswald *The Greater Britain* (London, 1932).

—— *Tomorrow We Live* (London, 1938).

—— *My Life* (London, 1968).

Mullally, F. *Fascism Inside Britain* (London, 1946).

Nicolson, H. *Diaries and Letters, 1930-1939* (London, 1966).

Piratin, Phil *Our Flag Stays Red* (London, 1948).

Skidelsky, Robert *Politicians and the Slump* (London, 1967).

—— *Oswald Mosley* (new edn, London, 1980).

Stevenson, John and Cook, Chris *The Slump* (London, 1977).

Belgium

The present essay has been based mostly on printed sources, especially for Rexism. The following bibliography is limited to a selection of books and articles, for which two criteria have been used: (a) supplementary reading, consisting mainly of works offering different interpretations or dealing with aspects not explored in this essay; (b) works directly related to the analyses put forward in the present essay.

Supplementary reading

Beaufays, J. 'Aspects du nationalisme Belge au lendemain de la grande guerre', *Annales de la Faculté de Droit de Liège*, 16:1-2 (1971).

Degrelle, L. *La Cohue de 1940* (Lausanne, 1949).

De Jonghe, A. *Hitler en het politieke lot van België* (Antwerp, 1972).

Gérard-Libois, J. and Gotovitch, J. *L'an 40: La Belgique occupée* (Brussels, 1971).

Kieft, D. *Belgium's Return to Neutrality* (Oxford, 1972).

Krier, E. 'Rex et l'Allemagne (1933-1940): une documentation', *Cahiers d'Histoire de la Seconde Guerre Mondiale*, 5 (1978).

Laurent, P.H. 'The reversal of Belgian foreign policy, 1936-1937', *The Review of Politics*, 31:3 (1969).

Martin, D. 'De Duitse "Vijfde Kolonne" in België, 1936-1940', *Belgisch Tijdschrift voor Nieuwste Geschiedenis*, 11:1-2 (1980).

Peemans-Poullet, H. 'Le Rexisme et les femmes', *Les Cahiers du GRIF*, 14-15 (1976).

Serruys, J. *Sous la signe de l'Autorité* (Brussels, 1935).

Stengers, J. 'Belgium' in H. Rogger and E. Weber (eds) *The European Right* (Berkeley, 1966).

Willequet, J. 'Les Fascismes belges et la seconde guerre mondiale', *Revue d'Histoire de la Deuxième Guerre Mondiale*, 17:66 (1967).

Works on specific aspects

Bartier, J. 'La Politique intérieure', in H. Pirenne, *Histoire de Belgique*, 4 (Brussels, 1952).

Baudhuin, F. *Histoire économique de la Belgique, 1914-1939* (Brussels, 1946).

Carpinelli, G. 'Per l'interpretazione del fascismo belga: studi recenti sul rexismo', *Il Movimento di Liberazione in Italia*, 109 (1972).

Cobb. R. *A Second Identity: Essays on France and French History* (London, 1969) (pp. 296-306 on Van Severen).

Daye, P. *Trente-deux mois chez les députés* (Brussels, 1942).

Defoort, E. *Charles Maurras en de Action Française in België* (Bruges, 1978).

Devleeshouwer, R. 'L'Opinion publique et les revendications territoriales Belges à la fin de la première guerre mondiale 1918-1919', *Mélanges offerts à G. Jacquemyns* (Brussels, 1968).

Elias, H.J. *25 jaar Vlaamse Beweging, 1914-1939* (Antwerp, 1969).

Etienne, J.-M. *Le Mouvement Rexiste jusqu'en 1940* (Paris, 1968).

Grabiner, R. 'La Montée du rexisme: étude de la presse Bruxelloise non rexiste, octobre 1935 — mai 1936', *Res Publica*, 11:4 (1969).

Hojer, C.-H. *Le Régime parlementaire Belge de 1918 à 1940* (Uppsala, 1946).

Hoyois, G. *Aux origines de l'Action Catholique: Monseigneur Picard* (Brussels, 1960).

Pfeiffer, R. and Ladrière, J. *L'Aventure Rexiste* (Brussels, 1966).

Schoeters, H. 'Les Interventions de crise et les collusions politico-financières en Belgique entre 1930 et 1940', *Revue Belge d'Histoire Contemporaine*, 7:3-4 (1976).

Stengers, J. *Léopold III et le gouvernement: les deux politiques Belges de 1940* (Gembloux, 1980).

Sylvestre, J. *La Dévaluation du franc Belge: mars 1935 — avril 1936* (Paris, 1939).

Vanlandschoot, R. 'Joris Van Severen' and 'Verbond van Dietsche Nationaal-solidaristen', *Encyclopedie van de Vlaamse Beweging*, 2 (Tielt, 1975).

Willemsen, A.W. *Het Vlaams-nationalisme: De geschiedenis van de jaren 1914-1940* (Utrecht, 1969).

France

The following bibliography does not pretend to be exhaustive. It merely lists the published sources which have proved most useful to me in the preparation of my essay.

Allardyce, G. 'The political transition of Jacques Doriot', *Journal of Contemporary History*, 1:1 (1966).

Azéma, J.-P. *De Munich à la libération, 1938-1944* (Paris, 1979).

Edouard Daladier, Chef de gouvernement (Paris, 1977).

La France et les Français en 1938-1939 (Paris, 1978).

Gordon, B. *Collaborationism in France during the Second World War* (Ithaca, 1980).

Le Gouvernement de Vichy, 1940-1942 (Paris, 1972).

Irvine, W.D. *French Conservatism in Crisis: The Republican Federation of France in the 1930s* (Baton Rouge, 1979).

Jeanneney, J.-N. *François de Wendel en République: l'Argent et le Pouvoir, 1914-1940* (Paris, 1976).

Kuisel, R.F. *Ernest Mercier: French Technocrat* (Berkeley, 1967).

Linz, J. 'Some notes towards a comparative study of fascism in sociological historical perspective', in W. Laqueur (ed.) *Fascism: A Reader's Guide* (London, 1979).

Machefer, P. *Ligues et fascismes en France 1919-1939* (Paris, 1974).

Michel, H. *Pétain et le régime de Vichy* (Paris, 1978).

Müller, K.-J. 'Die französische Rechte und der Faschismus in Frankreich 1924-1932', in Stegmann, D. *et al.* (eds) *Industrielle Gesellschaft und politisches System* (Bonn, 1978).

—— 'French fascism and modernisation', *Journal of Contemporary History*, 11:4 (1976).

Ory, P. *Les Collaborateurs 1940-1945* (Paris, 1976).

—— 'Le Dorgérisme: institution et discours d'une colère paysanne (1929-1939)', *Revue d'Histoire Moderne et Contemporaine*, 22:1 (1975).

Paxton, R. *Vichy France* (London, 1972).

Plumyène, J. and Lasierra, R. *Les Fascismes Français, 1922-63* (Paris, 1963).

Rémond, R. *The Right Wing in France from 1815 to De Gaulle*, (2nd edn, Philadelphia, 1969).

Revue d'Histoire de la Deuxième Guerre Mondiale, No. 91 (1973): special number on collaboration. It includes the important article by Bourderon, R. 'Le régime de Vichy était-il fasciste?'

—— No. 97 (1975): special number on aspects of French fascism.

Rossi-Landi, G. *La Drôle de Guerre* (Paris, 1971).

Soucy, R. 'France, veterans' politics between the wars', in S.R. Ward (ed.) *The War Generation* (Port Washington, 1975).

—— 'The nature of fascism in France', *Journal of Contemporary History*, 1:1 (1966).

Sternhell, Z. 'Anatomie d'un mouvement fasciste en France: Le Faisceau de George Valois', *Revue Française de Science Politique*, 26:1 (1976).

Warner, G. 'The Stavisky affair and the riots of February 6th 1934', *History Today* (June 1958).
—— 'The Cagoulard conspiracy', *History Today* (July 1960).
Wolf, D. *Die Doriot Bewegung* (Stuttgart, 1967).

Spain

The Spanish right in the 1930s and the subsequent Franco dictatorship can only be adequately explained in the context of the political and economic development of Spain in the previous hundred years. The best introductions remain Gerald Brenan's beautifully written and deeply felt *The Spanish Labyrinth* (2nd edn, Cambridge, 1950) and two immensely thought-provoking, but solidly reliable, works by Raymond Carr, *Spain, 1808-1939* (Oxford, 1966) and *The Spanish Tragedy* (London, 1977). The crucial role of the army is described in Stanley G. Payne's informative narrative *Politics and the Military in Modern Spain* (Stanford, 1967). The Primo de Rivera dictatorship, an arcadian interlude longingly evoked by most Spanish rightists, is discussed as a pre-fascist experience in Shlomo Ben-Ami's important article, 'The forerunners of Spanish fascism: Unión Patriótica and Unión Monárquica', *European Studies Review*, 9:1 (January 1979), and in the same author's 'The dictatorship of Primo de Rivera: a political reassessment', in *Journal of Contemporary History*, 12:1 (January 1977).

The Carlist movement, touchstone of reactionary attitudes, and its relations with other right-wing groups, especially fascist ones, are analysed with learning and clarity in Martin Blinkhorn's *Carlism and Crisis in Spain, 1931-1939* (Cambridge, 1975). The other radical authoritarian movement, Renovación Española, is presented as the central precursor of Francoism in an article by Paul Preston, 'Alfonsist monarchism and the coming of the Spanish civil war', *Journal of Contemporary History* 7:3-4 (July-October 1972). A similar approach is adopted by the Spanish political scientist, Raúl Morodo, in his *Acción Española: orígenes ideológicos del franquismo* (Madrid, 1980).

The most hotly debated area of the Spanish right remains the authoritarian Catholic CEDA. Its many ambiguities and its flirtation with fascism are admirably captured in its semi-official handbook, José Monge Bernal, *Acción Popular* (Madrid, 1936), and in its leader's fascinating and voluminous memoirs, José María Gil Robles, *No fue posible la paz* (Barcelona, 1968). The most favourable scholarly account is Richard A.H. Robinson's *The Origins of Franco's Spain* (Newton Abbot, 1970) which stresses the CEDA's Christian Social rhetoric. The opposing view is to be found in Paul Preston, *The Coming of the Spanish Civil War* (London, 1978) and in José R. Montero's massive, and intensely critical, *La CEDA: el catolicismo social y político en la II República*, (2 vols, Madrid, 1977).

For obvious reasons, there is less disagreement about the Falange. The standard work is Stanley G. Payne's sweepingly titled *Falange: A*

History of Spanish Fascism (Stanford, 1961). The most stimulating and original approach, with its stress on Falangist imperialism, is Herbert R. Southworth's 'The Falange: an analysis of Spain's fascist heritage' in Paul Preston, (ed.) *Spain in Crisis: Evolution and Decline of the Franco Regime* (Hassocks, 1976). A recent marxist interpretation, Javier Jiménez Campo, *El fascismo en la crisis de la II República española* (Madrid, 1979), amply repays careful reading. There are many works by Falangists which tend to hagiography of the movement's leader, José Antonio Primo de Rivera. One which goes beyond that is Maximiano García Venero, *Falange en la guerra de España: la unificación y Hedilla* (Paris), 1967) which faithfully recounts the version of José Antono's proletarian successor, Manuel Hedilla. It should be read in conjunction with Herbert R. Southworth's mordant commentary, *Antifalange* (Paris, 1967).

The Franco regime is constantly examined for evidence of fascist features. Recent analytical accounts are Paul Preston, *Spain in Crisis* (see above) and Raymond Carr and Juan Pablo Fusi, *Spain: Dictatorship to Democracy* (London, 1979). Max Gallo's *Spain under Franco* (London, 1973) is vivid but not without its inaccuracies. Amando de Miguel, *Sociología del franquismo* (Barcelona, 1975), examines the various pressure groups within the Francoist élite and makes an important contribution to the debate on the nature of the regime. Two stimulating and original interpretations are by Juan J. Linz, 'An authoritarian regime: Spain' in E. Allardt and Y. Littunen, (eds) *Cleavages, Ideologies and Party Systems* (Helsinki, 1964) and by Eduardo Sevilla-Guzmán and Salvador Giner, 'Absolutismo despótico y dominación de clase: el caso de España', *Cuadernos de Ruedo Ibérico*, 43-45 (January-June 1975).

The regime's openly fascist period is not really disputed. Its imperial ambitions, and their author's quest for preferment, are expressed in many works of which the most explicit is José María de Areilza and Fernando María Castiella, *Reivindicaciones de España* (Madrid, 1941). Franco's Russian adventure is described in down-home style by Gerald R. Kleinfeld and Lewis A. Tambs, *Hitler's Spanish Legion* (Carbondale, 1979). The alleged architect of pro-Axis policy, Ramón Serrano Súñer, has defended his record and shifted the burden of nazi sympathies onto Franco in *Entre Hendaya y Gibraltar* (Madrid, 1947) and *Memorias* (Barcelona, 1977). Interesting studies of Francoist attempts to regiment labour and the economy are Miguel A. Aparicio, *El sindicalismo vertical y la formación del Estado franquista* (Barcelona, 1980), and Joan Clavera *et al.*, *Capitalismo español: de la autarquía a la estabilización* (Madrid, 1973).

Easy identification of Franco with fascism is, however, rendered difficult by his cousin's recent publication of his table talk, Francisco Franco Salgado-Araujo, *Mis conversaciones privadas con Franco* (Barcelona, 1976). The stifling mediocrity portrayed therein could not be further removed from the veneer of anti-establishment novelty conventionally assumed to be central to authentic fascism.

Fascism in contemporary Europe

The best source of information in English on the political under-
world of the fascist hard core is the Wiener Library Bulletin. The
two most comprehensive works, covering both hard core and parties
of the extreme right are:

Del Boca, A. and Giovana, M. *Fascism Today* (London, 1970), translated from the Italian edition of 1965, *I figli del sole*.

Milza, P. and Bentelli, M. *Le Fascisme au XXe Siècle* (Paris, 1973).

See also Eisenberg, D. *The Re-Emergence of Fascism* (London, 1967),
informative but uncritical, with few references to sources.

Bardèche, M. *Qu'est ce que le fascisme?* (Paris, 1961) is an illuminating
and beautifully written apologia by a contemporary fascist intellectual.

On fascism and the extreme right in France:

Anderson, M. *Conservative Politics in France* (London, 1974).

Bell, D. 'The extreme right in France', in M. Kolinsky and W.E. Paterson (eds) *Social and Political Movements in Western Europe* (London, 1976).

Brigoulex, B. *L'Extrême Droite en France* (Paris, 1977).

Duprat, F. *Les Mouvements d'extrême droite en France depuis 1944*
(Paris, 1972), informative but partisan account by a leading member
of the extreme right.

Hoffmann, S. *Le Mouvement poujade* (Paris, 1956).

Plumyène, J. and Lasierra, R. *Les Fascismes Français 1923-63* (Paris,
1964).

On Germany:

Montagu, I. *Germany's New Nazis* (London, 1967), which events since
1967 have shown to be unduly alarmist.

Warnecke, S. 'The future of rightist extremism in West Germany', in M.
Kolinsky and W.E. Paterson (eds) *Social and Political Movements in
Western Europe* (London, 1976).

Wiener Library Bulletin, New Series, 4 and 6 (1966-7), two informative
articles on NPD.

On Italy:

Cianflone, G. and Scafoglio, D. *Fascismo sui muri* (Naples, 1976).

Setta, S. *L'uomo qualunque* (Bari, 1975).

La strage di stato: dal golpe di Borghese all'incriminazione di Calabresi
(Rome, 1971).

INDEX

◆